THE VICTORIA HISTORY
OF THE
COUNTIES OF ENGLAND

—

A HISTORY OF
WILTSHIRE

VOLUME I

PART 2

THE VICTORIA HISTORY
OF THE
COUNTIES OF ENGLAND

EDITED BY R. B. PUGH, D.LIT.

THE UNIVERSITY OF LONDON
INSTITUTE OF
HISTORICAL RESEARCH

Oxford University Press, Ely House, 37 Dover Street, London, W1X 4AH

GLASGOW NEW YORK TORONTO MELBOURNE WELLINGTON
CAPE TOWN IBADAN NAIROBI DAR ES SALAAM LUSAKA ADDIS ABABA
DELHI BOMBAY CALCUTTA MADRAS KARACHI LAHORE DACCA
KUALA LUMPUR SINGAPORE HONG KONG TOKYO

ISBN 0 19 722735 X

© *University of London 1973*

*Printed in Great Britain
at the University Press, Oxford
by Vivian Ridler
Printer to the University*

INSCRIBED TO THE

MEMORY OF HER LATE MAJESTY

QUEEN VICTORIA

WHO GRACIOUSLY GAVE THE TITLE TO

AND ACCEPTED THE DEDICATION

OF THIS HISTORY

Battlesbury Camp, Warminster: iron-age hill-fort

A HISTORY OF

WILTSHIRE

EDITED BY ELIZABETH CRITTALL

VOLUME I

PART 2

PUBLISHED FOR

THE INSTITUTE OF HISTORICAL RESEARCH

BY

OXFORD UNIVERSITY PRESS

1973

Distributed by Oxford University Press until 1 January 1976
thereafter by Dawsons of Pall Mall

CONTENTS OF VOLUME ONE, PART TWO

LIST OF PLATES

Thanks are rendered to the following for permission to reproduce material in their possession and for the loan of prints and photographs: the Royal Commission on Historical Monuments (England), the Committee for Aerial Photography of the University of Cambridge, the Ashmolean Museum, Oxford, the Wiltshire Archaeological and Natural History Society, and Mr. G. N. Wright.

LIST OF FIGURES IN THE TEXT

All the figures were drawn by Mrs. Morna Simpson. Where they are based on plans or pictures already published or prepared, the source for Mrs. Simpson's re-drawing is given in the list below. Where no source is given, the drawings are either original or were made from material supplied by the authors. Maps and plans are based upon the Ordnance Survey with the sanction of the Controller of H.M. Stationery Office, Crown Copyright reserved. Thanks are due to the Royal Commission on Historical Monuments (England) for much assistance with the preparation of the figures.

xi

LIST OF FIGURES IN THE TEXT

EDITORIAL NOTE

PART TWO of Volume I is the tenth volume in the Wiltshire series to be published. It has been prepared, like all earlier volumes, under the superintendence of the Wiltshire Victoria County History Committee. That committee, whose origin and constitution are described in the Editorial Note to the *Victoria History of Wiltshire*, Volume VII, has been good enough to continue its generous grants and has made additional ones to meet the particular needs of both parts of Volume I. The University of London has thus been able to continue publication of the *Wiltshire History* and takes pleasure in renewing the expression of its gratitude to the participating authorities in Wiltshire for their friendly co-operation.

The chapters now published were not originally intended to form a separate volume. They were planned to accompany an archaeological gazetteer of the county begun by Mr. L. V. Grinsell in 1949. The preparation of the gazetteer, however, outstripped the writing of the chapters. So as not to withhold from the public the important information it contained for too long a time, it was decided to publish the gazetteer, along with a series of maps and a chapter on the Physique of Wiltshire, as part one of Volume I. That part appeared in 1957. A brief note on the editorial method used in part two in order to link it to part one appears on page xv.

Thanks are rendered to many persons who have helped in the compilation of the volume by offering advice, by lending plans and drawings, or by granting special facilities. Professor Stuart Piggott, C.B.E., F.B.A., kindly agreed to revise his chapters more than once during the period that it took to complete the volume. Particular mention must also be made of the services of Mr. D. J. Bonney of the Salisbury office of the Royal Commission on Historical Monuments (England) who helped in many ways besides writing the final chapter. To the Curator of the Museum of the Wiltshire Archaeological and Natural History Society at Devizes (Mr. F. K. Annable), to the Assistant Curator (Mr. A. M. Burchard), to the Hon. Librarian of that society (Mr. R. E. Sandell), to the Director of the Institute of Archaeology of the University of London (Professor W. F. Grimes, C.B.E., D.Litt.) and to the staff of that Institute the editors are likewise most grateful.

An outline of the structure and aims of the *History* as a whole, as also of its origins and progress, is included in the *General Introduction to the History* (1970).

WILTSHIRE
VICTORIA COUNTY HISTORY
COMMITTEE

As at 1 January 1972

NOTE ON EDITORIAL METHOD
AND ABBREVIATIONS USED

The chapters that follow are based chiefly upon the information contained in part one of this volume, but incorporate later material available up to the end of May 1970. A place-name in capital letters, either alone or combined with a site name, indicates that further information, particularly reference to sources, is to be had under that place in the parish gazetteer in part one (pp. 21–131). The identification of barrows and a few other sites by letters and numbers (e.g. *Bii* Amesbury 24) is taken from the lists of sites in the same volume (pp. 134–279). All places mentioned in the text are in Wiltshire unless otherwise stated. The following list of abbreviations used covers those which occur throughout the volume in an abbreviated form. Other sources cited in the footnotes in abbreviated form, but not included in the list, are generally cited in full on first occurrence.

Acta Arch.	*Acta Archaeologica* (Copenhagen)
Antiq.	*Antiquity*
Ant. Jnl.	*Antiquaries Journal*
Arch.	*Archaeologia*
Arch. Camb.	*Archaeologia Cambrensis*
Arch. Jnl.	*Archaeological Journal*
Arch. Rozh.	*Archeologické Rozhledy* (Prague)
Ausgrab. und Funde	*Ausgraben und Funde* (*Nachrichtenblatt für Vor- und Frühgeschichte*) (Berlin)
Bayerische Vorgeschichtsblätter	*Kommission für Bayerische Landesgeschichte* (Munich)
Ber. R.-G. Komm.	*Bericht Der Römisch-Germanischen Kommission* (Frankfurt)
Ber. Rijks. Oudheid Bodem.	*Berichten van de Rijksdienst voor het Oudheidkundig Bodemonderzoek* (Amersfoort)
Ber. V Internat. Kong. Vor- u. Frühgesch.	*Bericht über den V Internationalen Kongress für Vor- und Frühgeschichte, Hamburg*, 1958
Bull. W.A. & N.H. Soc.	*Bulletin of the Wiltshire Archaeological and Natural History Society*
Bull. Mus. Roy. d'Art et d'Hist.	*Bulletin des Musées Royaux d'Art et d'Histoire* (Brussels)
D.M. Cat.	*Catalogue of Antiquities in the W.A.N.H.S. Museum at Devizes* (Devizes, 1934)
D.M. Cat. Neo. and B.A. Colls. (1964)	*Guide Catalogue of the Neolithic and Bronze Age Collections in Devizes Museum*, compiled by F. K. Annable and D. D. A. Simpson (Devizes, 1964)
E.H.R.	*English Historical Review*
Ec. H.R.	*Economic History Review*
HVS/DKS	Hilversumurnen/Drakensteinuren
Invent. Arch. GB.	*Inventaria Archaeologica* (International Congress of Prehistoric and Protohistoric Sciences), ed. C. F. C. Hawkes
Jnl. R. Soc. Ant. Ireland	*Journal of Royal Society of Antiquaries of Ireland*
Hants Field Club	*Proceedings of the Hampshire Field Club*
Katalog Straubing	*Materialhefte zur Bayerischen Vorgeschichte*, xi (Munich)
M.O.P.B.W.	Ministry of Public Buildings and Works
Medit. Arch.	*Studies in Mediterranean Archaeology* (Gothenburg)
P.N. Wilts (E.P.N.S.)	*The Place Names of Wiltshire* (English Place-Name Society, xvi)
P.P.S.	*Proceedings of the Prehistoric Society*
P.P.S. E.Ang.	*Proceedings of the Prehistoric Society of East Anglia*
Palaeohist.	*Palaeohistoria* (Groningen)
Památky Arch.	*Památky Archeologické* (Prague)
Pitt-Rivers, *Cranborne Chase*	A. H. L.-F. Pitt-Rivers, *Excavations on Cranborne Chase* (1887–98)
Proc. Brit. Acad.	*Proceedings of the British Academy*
Proc. Devon Arch. Explor. Soc.	*Proceedings of Devonshire Archaeological Exploration Society*

NOTE ON EDITORIAL METHOD AND ABBREVIATIONS USED

Proc. Nutrit. Soc.	*Proceedings of the Nutrition Society*
Proc. Soc. Ant. Scot.	*Proceedings of the Society of Antiquaries of Scotland*
R.C.H.M. (Eng.)	Royal Commission on Historical Monuments (England)
Recs. Bucks.	*Records of Buckinghamshire*
Sbornik Narod. *Mus. v Praze*	*Sbornik Narodniho Musea v Praze* (Prague)
Suss. Arch. Colls.	*Sussex Archaeological Collections*
Suss. N. & Q.	*Sussex Notes and Queries*
Univ. Lond. Inst. Arch.	University of London, Institute of Archaeology
W.A.M.	*Wiltshire Archaeological and Natural History Magazine*
W.A.N.H.S.	Wiltshire Archaeological and Natural History Society

THE BEGINNINGS OF HUMAN SETTLEMENT: THE PALAEOLITHIC AND MESOLITHIC PERIODS

TO *c.* 4000 B.C.

THE evidence for the earliest human occupation within the area now covered by Wiltshire is provided by stone (normally flint) tools within the Palaeolithic tradition. Although found in lesser numbers than in some southern English regions, Palaeolithic tools in Wiltshire extend the general distribution of the material of this period from the neighbouring counties of Berkshire, Hampshire, and Dorset, as can be seen from the generalized distribution map of Lower and Middle Palaeolithic finds in Britain published by D. A. Roe.[1]

The so-called 'eoliths' championed by earlier Wiltshire archaeologists need not now be seriously considered as of human manufacture, and the main bulk of the material is archaeologically within the Acheulian group of industries, and in terms of chronology and climate falls almost wholly within the Hoxnian or Great Interglacial period, with the exception of an important site at Fisherton (SALISBURY),[2] belonging to an early stage of the last glacial phase. No evidence of Clactonian or Levalloisian industries has been recognized in Wiltshire.

The Acheulian flint tools or hand-axes are of frankly unknown function, but presumably served as undifferentiated, all-purpose, cutting and grubbing implements. Chronologically the Hoxnian Interglacial phase dates from about 200,000 and 300,000 years ago, and the mean temperature was probably some 3 °F. warmer than today, with January temperatures from 2 °F. to 11 °F. higher than the present. Britain was of course still a part of the north European land mass, sharing with it, in the south at least, a forested landscape with some 17 per cent of species exotic to the latitude today and proper to sub-tropical areas, and among its fauna including the specialized interglacial woodland elephant (*Elephas antiquus*), Merck's rhinoceros, the hippopotamus, probably water buffaloes, and monkeys of the Macaque type. In this environment man was a rare species, inferentially organized in small hunting bands, with a knowledge of fire and highly competent tool-making techniques. In the modern classification, man of the Hoxnian Interglacial is *Homo sapiens*, represented in England by the skull from Swanscombe (Kent) and as a species including the Neanderthaloids; preceded by *Homo erectus* (the Pithecanthropoids), and to be followed during the final (Weichselian) glacial period by the emergence of modern man (*Homo sapiens sapiens*).

Palaeolithic flint tools in Wiltshire are represented by scattered finds except in two areas: the gravels of the river Avon near SALISBURY (especially at Bemerton and Milford Hill), and the site at Knowle Farm (LITTLE BEDWYN). The latter site is of some particular interest: it yielded flake implements of High Lodge type, and the curious surface gloss on many of the artefacts has been the subject of discussion. Furthermore, the

---

[1] *P.P.S.* xxx, pl. xxvii (facing p. 248); *W.A.M.* lxiv. 1–18. A complete schedule of Palaeolithic finds is that of D. A. Roe, *Gaz. Brit. Lower and Middle Palaeolithic Sites* (C.B.A. Res. Rep. viii).

[2] A place-name printed in capital letters indicates that information about the site will be found under the entry for that place in the general gazetteer in *V.C.H. Wilts.* i (1), 21–131.

implements and flint débris are contained in material washed from the neighbouring downland by torrent waters into a shallow coomb, implying occupation of the downs above the valley. Any other traces of Palaeolithic occupation on the hills would have been destroyed by the disastrous effects of the severe climatic conditions which prevailed when, during the Weichsel Glaciation, the ice-sheet moved southwards so that southern England endured periglacial conditions, and the chalk downs of Wiltshire were subjected to intense frost action and weathering. J. G. Evans in a discussion of this phase noted in 1968 that although some open grasslands existed in the valleys, the downs themselves would have been a 'dry, open, and windswept landscape' of tundra type, unsuitable for habitation though possible as seasonal hunting-grounds.[3]

Finds at Fisherton were, as shown above, of a glacial period: only a couple of flint tools are recorded, but they are sufficient to attest the presence of man in a setting very different from that of the warm Hoxnian Interglacial. The one surviving hand-axe is of the *bout coupé* type, characteristic elsewhere of Middle Palaeolithic industries of Mousterian type, and the sole representative in Wiltshire of that phase. The brickearth in which it was found is formed by dust, originating in dry, icy, exposed conditions and later redeposited by glacial melt-water, and the conditions of the glaciations which followed the Hoxnian warm period would be appropriate to such a deposit. An early Weichsel date seems likely, with a fauna including not only mammoth and reindeer, but musk ox, marmot, lemming, and arctic goose. On current chronologies the Weichsel Glaciation began about 70,000 years ago, and with intermittent ameliorations or instadial periods, continued until the beginning of modern climatic conditions about 8000–9000 B.C.[4] The Upper Palaeolithic is not represented in Wiltshire: the nearest site of the period is that on Hengistbury Head (Hants), probably dating from around the 9th millennium B.C.

As shown above, the climatic severity in areas near enough to the southern edge of the permanent ice-sheet to experience periglacial conditions resulted in the breaking-up and weathering of the chalk downs into altered surface deposits. Evans writes 'by the end of the Late Weichselian, periglacial deposits must have mantled a large part if not the total area of the Chalk'. This final phase of severe cold and physical weathering is the equivalent of Zone III (Younger Dryas) in the palaeobotanists' and climatologists' schemes, and thenceforward, with the gradual move towards a temperate climate in what had become post-glacial times, the periglacial deposits covering the Chalk broke down into soils, probably of the 'brown-earth' type, which would have supported forest cover. This natural situation was to be altered by the action of man on the landscape from prehistoric times onwards, and the treeless downs of recent times must be regarded as human artefacts. This point will be referred to again when considering the first agricultural colonization of Wiltshire from the late 4th millennium B.C. For the present, however, the evidence must be examined for post-glacial occupation before that date, in the form of flint or stone implements produced by hunting- and food-gathering societies within the Mesolithic cultures.

On present showing none of the Wiltshire Mesolithic material can be dated before the later 6th millennium B.C., within Zone VIIa, the Atlantic climatic phase, characterized by the dominance of woodland cover of the mixed-oak forest type. The insulation of Britain from the Continent, with the formation of the English Channel in more or less its present form, had taken place at the beginning of Atlantic times, around 6000 B.C. There are two settlement sites in Wiltshire, at Downton in the south and at Cherhill in

[3] *W.A.M.* lxiii. 12–26.
[4] Unless otherwise stated, all radiocarbon dates, such as these, are quoted in their 'conventional' uncalibrated form.

the north, the latter with a C14 date of 5280±140 B.C., and for the rest, there are isolated or small groups of finds of characteristic microlithic blades and other material from a dozen or so sites.[5] Radiocarbon dates for broadly comparable industries in southern Britain range from c. 4500 to c. 4000 B.C., and it is therefore likely that Mesolithic hunting bands settled in, and hunted over, the area now Wiltshire throughout the 5th millennium B.C., if not until a later date. The separation of Britain from continental Europe resulted in the development of distinctive insular cultures, combining features from the continental Maglemosian, Sauveterrian, and Tardenoisian traditions of flint-working.

The Downton site[6] lies on a gravel terrace of the river Avon at 140 ft. O.D., in an area occupied also in Late Neolithic and Early Bronze-Age times. The Mesolithic settlement was marked by an artificial irregular hollow, dug into the gravel, probably for obtaining flint nodules for working, a hearth indicating 'a small fire of short duration', and a number of stake-holes denoting shelters or lightly built huts framed by uprights and oblique poles, averaging some 4 in. in diameter. It is impossible to interpret the stake-holes so as to vizualize the coherent plans of structures, but in one part of the site they were associated with small shallow cooking-pits and a spread of charcoal. The flint industry has features of Maglemosian derivation and is comparable in most respects with those from other south English sites, from Dorset to Sussex, but with fewer microlithic forms, and with heavy transverse arrowheads indicating a comparatively late date. In view of this fact and of the presence among the charcoal of buckthorn, a species not recorded in British palaeobotanical records before Zone VIIa, and one which flourishes in cultivated contexts, the excavator suggests that the Downton settlement could have been contemporary with the earliest agriculturalists in that region.

In a valley near the south bank of the brook running west from Cherhill, on a late glacial deposit of drift from the Lower Chalk, a Mesolithic site was identified and excavated in 1967.[7] A characteristic flint industry with affinities to that of Peacock's Farm (Cambs.) was scattered over a wide area, and various non-local stones had been brought to the site. Animal bones included wild ox and beaver, and a C14 date of 5280±140 B.C. (BM–447) was obtained. The site was abandoned because of flooding, which had caused the formation of a layer of tufa over the Mesolithic occupation, and at a later period with the onset of drier conditions a Neolithic settlement was established on the same site. Tufa formation has been noticed as a phenomenon of the wetter climate of the Atlantic (Zone VIIa) phase in association with Mesolithic industries; at Blashenwell (Dors.) tufa and microliths were dated to c. 4490 B.C., and a flint flake of Mesolithic type from tufa at Box belongs here.

The presence in the Cherhill site of non-local stones, such as Portland and other cherts, coloured flints, sandstones, and limestones, is consonant with other evidence for the distribution of raw materials by human agencies over large areas of south Britain in Mesolithic times.[8] The mobility of hunting- and gathering-communities of Mesolithic type would facilitate such interchange of material, and the contacts between the eastern and western areas of southern England, established in the 5th millennium B.C., may not be unrelated to those perceptible in Neolithic contexts in the third. Quartzite pebble 'mace-heads' with hour-glass perforation, known from eight or so Wiltshire finds, may have a Mesolithic origin, and the source of the pebbles may be the Bunter Beds of Devon or Somerset or the Thames Valley.[9]

[5] Mapped on Map I and listed in gen. gaz. in *V.C.H. Wilts.* i (1). A more up-to-date statement is in *W.A.M.* lxiv. 18–20.
[6] *P.P.S.* xxv. 209–32.
[7] *W.A.M.* lxiii. 107.
[8] *P.P.S.* xv. 193; W. F. Rankine, *Mesolithic of Southern Eng.* (Surrey Arch. Soc. Res. Papers, iv), 54.
[9] Rankine, op. cit. 58.

THE FIRST AGRICULTURAL COMMUNITIES: THE NEOLITHIC PERIOD

c. 3000–*c.* 1500 B.C.

CLIMATE AND ENVIRONMENT

As shown above, the climatic severity of the last glacial period had, up to the 9th millennium B.C., weathered and broken the surface of the south English Chalk to a degree that resulted first in periglacial deposits forming over the chalk rock throughout the whole area, and subsequently the breaking-down of these, in more favourable climatic conditions, into soils probably of 'brown-earth' type. While the Chalk today would hardly support forest cover of the normal mixed-oak type, the soils resulting from the superficial periglacial deposits would allow the roots of large trees to penetrate with ease, and the natural post-glacial conditions of the downland are, therefore, likely to have been woodland. It is in these areas of Wiltshire that there is the heaviest incidence of prehistoric population, and the recent conditions of open grass-covered downland have been brought about by subsequent alteration of the original conditions by the destruction of soils by weathering and solution, partly natural but largely the result of man's activity in the landscape since the end of the 4th millennium B.C. J. G. Evans has remarked that 'with the onset of Neolithic clearance and agriculture accelerated erosion of the deposits on the slopes would have been brought about by such processes as the removal of arboreal vegetation and a resulting instability of the soil'.[1] Increased cultivation up to Roman times led to the formation of large deposits of plough-wash in the valleys.

After the withdrawal of the ice-sheets climate changed and with it the botanical climax, that is the optimum plant cover within the limitations of altitude, soil, humidity, and temperature. By the Atlantic (Zone VIIa) phase higher temperatures than the modern average obtained in north-western Europe, with average mean temperatures in July 2 °F. above the present figures, and there was relatively high precipitation as on the Atlantic coast-lands today. Within the phase there is evidence of wet conditions, leading for instance to the formation of tufa deposits such as that at Cherhill, where the underlying Mesolithic occupation is dated to *c.* 5280 B.C. Just before 3000 B.C. there seems to be evidence, at least on the Continent, of a short cold spell, followed by a rapid improvement in the climate with drier and more 'continental' conditions.[2] Fenland conditions were drying out in Somerset by the time the Neolithic bog causeways were built, with radiocarbon dates ranging between *c.* 2890 and 2115 B.C., and the

[1] *W.A.M.* lxiii. 24.
[2] 'World Climate 8000–0 B.C.', *Proc. Internat. Sympos.* *Imperial Coll. London, 1966* (pub. R. Meteorolog. Soc. 1967), ed. J. S. Sawyer, 99.

dry phase then continued there until the return of wetter conditions necessitating the construction of a new series of fen causeways dated between *c.* 900 and *c.* 450 B.C. Comparable dry conditions during the Sub-Boreal climatic phase (Zone VIIb) are demonstrated in Wiltshire by the filling of the open and abandoned Y and Z holes at Stonehenge by wind-blown soil, implying both atmospheric dryness and the likelihood of extensive areas of arable in the vicinity: there is a radiocarbon date for these holes (1240±105 B.C.; I-2445) coincident with that for evidence for dry climatic conditions under a barrow at Poole in Dorset (1260±50 B.C.; GrN-1684).[3] In terms of climate, therefore, virtually all the 3rd millennium, and much of the 2nd, coincide with the optimum conditions of the Sub-Boreal period, and the worsened climate of the Sub-Atlantic does not show itself until around 1000 B.C. or even later.

FOREST CLEARANCE

It can hardly be coincidence that the first appearance of stone-using agricultural communities, contrasting in their subsistence-economy of mixed farming with the hunting and gathering mode of life of their precursors, should in Britain, as in much of north-western Europe, be dated around 3000 B.C. Certain phenomena, notably the decrease in elm population and the coincident appearance of weeds such as plantain, perceptible in the pollen-diagrams around this date, have been interpreted as everywhere indicating the influence of man upon the landscape, clearing woodlands and creating agricultural or pastoral clearances. It is possible, however, that such phenomena could also have resulted from natural causes following unstable environmental conditions for plant growth: such as a sudden cold or perhaps a dry spell at the end of the 4th millennium.[4] But in many instances forest clearance can be equated with the first agricultural activities in a region at this time. It has also been pointed out that the possibility cannot be dismissed of such human activities among Mesolithic hunters, on analogy with the former practice among North American Indians of burning forests in the autumn and spring to facilitate hunting, encourage game, and improve the growth of grass for natural grazing.[5]

Wiltshire has contributed important evidence for the beginnings of Neolithic forest clearance and land-use, particularly as a result of recent research on molluscan assemblages reflecting contemporary environments from Neolithic sites in the north of the county. At Windmill Hill and Knap Hill mollusca from the old land-surface under the Neolithic earthworks denote an environment of scrub and grassland, but with more woodland than the broadly contemporary environments represented by the old land-surfaces under the Neolithic long barrows of the early 3rd millennium B.C. at Avebury: *B i* AVEBURY 22 (West Kennet), 47 (Horslip), and 68 (South Street).[6] At the last site the mollusca indicate a shaded, open woodland environment, followed by intermittent activity leading to clearance and more open conditions. That this was in fact Neolithic agriculture is demonstrated by the presence of the furrows of a light plough visible in the chalk surface beneath the barrow and discussed in more detail below (fig. 1).[7]

THE HUMAN POPULATION

The physical type of modern man responsible for Mesolithic culture in south Britain is unknown, but at least the initial phases of Neolithic culture must have been

[3] *P.P.S.* xix. 129.
[4] *Vegetatio*, xv. 292–6.
[5] *Domestication and Exploitation of Plants and Animals*, ed. P. H. Ucko and G. W. Dimbleby, 113.
[6] References given thus are to the tables of barrows in *V.C.H. Wilts.* i (1), 134–226.
[7] *W.A.M.* lxi. 91; *Antiq.* xli. 289–301.

due to the immigration of new population groups, however small. The eventual sum of this population over a period of a thousand years is represented by the skeletal remains from the long barrows and chambered tombs discussed below and appears to be broadly in line with the main Neolithic stocks of continental Europe. Older discussions of detail must be dismissed as invalid and there is need of new assessments on a statistical basis using numerical or non-metrical systems of multivariate analysis.[8] L. H. Wells, summing up the evidence from the West Kennet chambered tomb, notes that the long-headed Neolithic assemblage there shows considerable variation between robust and gracile individuals and considers their cranial features to be north European rather than Mediterranean in affinities.[9] The incidence of caries and tooth-loss, indicative of dental health and largely conditioned by diet, is greater in British Neolithic populations (4 per cent carious teeth, 16 per cent tooth-loss) than in those of the Single-Grave burials of Beaker and allied affinities from *c.* 2000 B.C. onwards (2 per cent caries, 4 per cent tooth-loss), though after this the curve of deterioration rises steeply throughout British prehistory.[10] The change here could of course as well be due to new populations as to diet variations.

Demographic problems in prehistory are of more than ordinary complexity, but cannot be entirely shirked. R. J. C. Atkinson has boldly faced the question of the likely population figures for the builders of long barrows and chambered tombs, which has considerable bearing on 3rd-millennium Wiltshire. He stresses two points at the outset: first the thousand-year period of time over which the archaeological evidence for Neolithic cultures must be spread, and then the likelihood on reasonable ethnographical analogy that ancient populations were of sizes surprisingly small in modern terms.[11] The problem of the early population in Wiltshire may in fact be approached by using the figures for recent hunting groups, such as the Caribou Eskimos, which approximate to 13 persons per 100 square miles and compare well with the figure, arrived at by other means for the Mesolithic population of England and Wales, of not more than some 7,000 people. Such a figure would indicate a Mesolithic population of Wiltshire of not more than 175, or for the 120 square miles of Salisbury Plain of 15 or so persons—a single hunting band. Using the figures of long-barrow burials with appropriate allowances, Atkinson showed that with a crude death-rate of 40 per 1,000 the population responsible for and buried in all the British long barrows by the end of the Neolithic period need not have been more than 140 and could have been as low as 70. Even if the likely Mesolithic population of Salisbury Plain is multiplied by 10, the total is only 150; by 100, 1,500, which is about the same number of persons to the square mile as in Sutherland at the beginning of the 20th century. Abercromby drew attention to the very small initial number of colonists needed to produce and maintain quite large populations over a few centuries,[12] and Atkinson gave a reasoned estimate that a family (of the nominal 5 members), growing 10 acres of grain, could clear $\frac{1}{3}$ square mile of forest in a century. On this figure 30 families (150 persons) would have cleared 100 square miles in a thousand years—a considerable proportion of Salisbury Plain. It is clear, then, that given a millenial span and the likelihood of an exponential population increase over this time, the initial Neolithic colonization of Wiltshire, as elsewhere in Britain, could have been tiny by modern standards.

[8] Cf. *Man*, N.S. ii. 551–68.

[9] Stuart Piggott, *West Kennet Long Barrow* (H.M.S.O. 1962), 79–89.

[10] *Proc. Nutrit. Soc.* xviii. 59.

[11] *Studies in Ancient Europe, Essays Presented to Stuart Piggott*, ed. J. M. Coles and D. D. A. Simpson, 83–93.

[12] John Abercromby, *Bronze Age Pottery*, i. 68.

NEOLITHIC

FOOD RESOURCES

The natural food resources available to the first Neolithic settlers in Wiltshire, and to prehistoric man thereafter, have been discussed more than once.[13] The main source of meat would have been the large mammals such as wild cattle, red deer, pig, and probably some horses. Brown bear is attested from a Late Neolithic context at Ratfyn (AMESBURY). Less is known about the consumption of birds and fish, though chub bones were found in a Late Neolithic pit at Woodlands (DURRINGTON). The prehistoric flora of Wiltshire was reviewed in 1964[14] and there is evidence for the consumption of crab-apples at Windmill Hill, perhaps deliberately split and dried as in Neolithic Switzerland.

So far as the appearance of the first domesticated animals in Britain is concerned, the complex problems of the nature of the first association of man and animals in mutual symbiosis do not arise,[15] for Britain takes its place with the rest of north-western Europe as an area of secondary agricultural colonization by societies already with a long tradition of domestic animals and cultivated plants behind them. The possibility of local cross-breeding between wild and domestic cattle or pigs cannot, however, be ruled out, or of deliberate domestication of wild stock. So far as Neolithic Wiltshire is concerned there are the usual animal domesticates brought in from outside, and ultimately from the Continent: cattle, pigs, sheep and goats, and dogs. While Mesolithic dog-training seems in fact to have occurred, the Windmill Hill dogs at least are of breeds characteristic of Neolithic central and north Europe.[16] The Windmill Hill site is the only one of the earlier Neolithic with a sufficiently large series of bones to show the proportion of animals favoured for food. There are very few wild animals or birds; among the domestic stock, cattle predominate, followed by sheep and goats, and pigs in approximately equal proportions, although the Late Neolithic series shows an increase in pigs. These proportions may be compared with those of the animal population at the Late Neolithic settlement between Durrington Walls and Woodhenge, with pigs at 61 per cent, cattle 35 per cent, and sheep and goats 3·5 per cent. The increase in pig-keeping in later Neolithic cultures has been noticed in Europe, where however areas with a 'pig-breeding tradition' of long standing have been isolated.[17]

The cultivation of cereal crops, forming an essential part of the mixed farming tradition which, beginning in Neolithic times, persisted throughout prehistory and history, could be achieved in Britain (as with all Europe) only by the initial importation of grain from its Near Eastern homeland.[18] The grain impressions in pottery from Windmill Hill provide the most abundant evidence of the proportions of the mixed wheat and barley crops, with a ratio of 91·6 per cent wheat to 8·4 per cent barley. By the early 2nd millennium, among the Single-Grave–Beaker cultures in Britain, the ratio had changed to one around 20 per cent wheat to 80 per cent barley, proportions to be maintained throughout the millennium. Cereals do not necessarily mean bread, as flour (attested by the numerous Neolithic saucer- and saddle-querns) can be used for various forms of porridge and gruel, and both wheat and barley can yield fermented drinks. The increase in dental decay from the early 2nd millennium B.C. onwards has been noticed, and dietetic changes (such as one from gruel to bread or wheat to barley) cannot be ruled out as contributory factors to the eventual situation. In addition to

[13] Stuart Piggott, *Neolithic Cultures of Brit. Isles*, 10–13.
[14] *W.A.M.* lix. 58–67.   [15] Cf. *Antiq.* xliii. 31–41.
[16] Isobel F. Smith, *Windmill Hill and Avebury. Excavations by Alex. Keiller, 1925–39*, 147.

[17] Ibid.; *Ant. Jnl.* xxxiv. 135; *Anc. Europe*, ed. Coles and Simpson, 71.
[18] *P.P.S.* xviii. 194–233.

wheat and barley, flax (*Linum usitatissimum*) was cultivated, presumably for the nutritive oily seeds rather than thread, since linen fabrics are not known in contemporary contexts.

AGRICULTURE

Wiltshire has recently provided the earliest archaeological evidence for the use of the traction-plough in Britain, though not in north-west Europe. Under the South Street long barrow (*B i* AVEBURY 68) the molluscan evidence showed a shaded environment that is open woodland, followed by Neolithic agriculture indicated by plough-furrows in the chalk surface. These are the narrow scratches, which are made with a light plough of 'ard' type, and show cross-ploughing at right angles with individual furrows up to 46 ft. long. Similar evidence of cross-ploughing has been recovered in Britain in the 2nd millennium B.C. in Cornwall and on numerous sites in north Europe and south Scandinavia at this date or earlier, but the radiocarbon dates from South Street show that the ploughing there must be before *c.* 2800 B.C.[19] and must, therefore, rank among the earliest evidence in Europe. At South Street there appear to have been two cultivation phases followed by fallow, and early in the 2nd millennium B.C. there was further ploughing, with renewed forest clearance, round the barrow in the same criss-cross technique (fig. 1).[20]

The plough employed (and throughout prehistory) would be a light implement of 'ard' type[21] and its traction would demand a pair of oxen. Such draught-animals imply a knowledge of castration, known in Neolithic Europe by the 5th millennium B.C. With paired ox-traction might also go paired draught for wheeled or other vehicles.[22] Wheeled carts or wagons are known at the end of the 3rd millennium B.C. in the Netherlands and south Scandinavia, but the fen trackways in Somerset, contemporary with the South Street ploughing, seem certainly not to have been used for wheeled transport, though the sledge or travois is not excluded.[23] Experiments with cattle smaller than those of Neolithic type show that a pair working at 2 m.p.h. could plough a field 70 yds. square (about an acre) in an 8 to 9 hour working-day.[24] Here, as throughout so much of prehistory, the basic agrarian problems have already been solved by Neolithic communities.

MATERIAL CULTURE

In terms of a broad grouping made some years ago the earlier Neolithic in Wiltshire was defined as a part of the Windmill Hill culture.[25] It is now perhaps preferable to think rather in terms of Early, Middle, and Late phases within a generalized Neolithic period, within which certain pottery styles and other distinctive features manifested themselves as chronological or regional variants. Such a classification is made possible by the evidence of stratigraphy and, above all, of radiocarbon dating. For over a generation a phase of culture has been recognized by archaeologists, which could be called Neolithic, and which was earlier than that represented by Single-Grave burials with Beaker pottery: an intrusive culture associated with the beginnings of copper and bronze metallurgy, the inception of which in Britain can now be dated from *c.* 1900 to 1800 B.C. Radiocarbon dating similarly places the beginning of the Neolithic phase to *c.* 3400 B.C. (Lambourn long barrow, Berks.), *c.* 3300 (Hembury causewayed camp,

---

[19] *Antiq.* xliii. 144.

[20] The stake-holes of a light fence ran across the Neolithic ploughed area under the barrow: *W.A.M.* lxi. 91; *Antiq.* xli. 289.

[21] P. V. Glob, *Ard og Plov*; H. C. Bowen, *Ancient Fields*, 7.   [22] *P.P.S.* xxxiv. 306.

[23] Ibid. 251.   [24] *W.A.M.* lxii. 25.

[25] Piggott, *Neolithic Cultures Brit. Isles.*

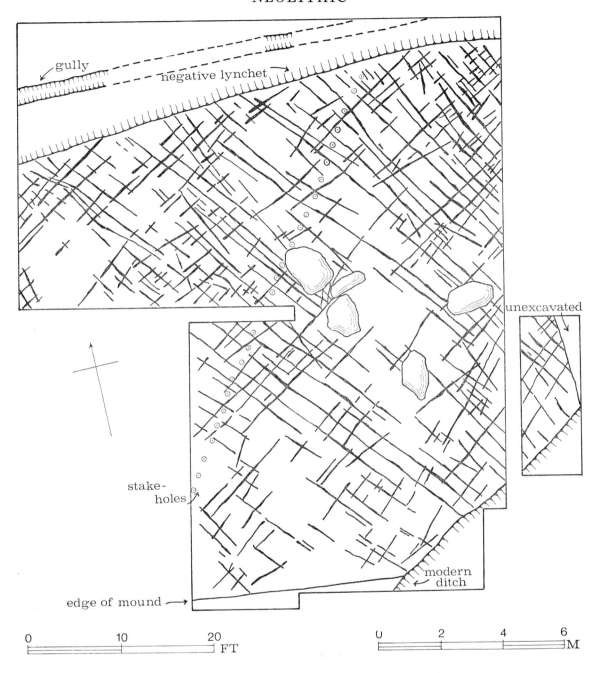

gully

negative lynchet

unexcavated

stake-
holes

modern
ditch

edge of mound →

0   10   20
⊨⊨⊨⊨⊨⊨⊨⊨⊨⊨ FT

0   2   4   6
⊨⊨⊨⊨⊨⊨⊨⊨⊨⊨ M

SOUTH STREET LONG BARROW: PLOUGH MARKS

FIG. 1

Devon), or *c.* 3200 (Fussell's Lodge and Horslip long barrows, both in Wilts.). It can also be seen that the cultural traditions, especially in pottery styles, begun in the earlier Neolithic, do not come to an end with the advent of the Beaker cultures in Britain, but continue in parallel with them until *c.* 1500 B.C.

Such a view has largely been created through the recognition that the diverse pottery styles of Neolithic Britain do not represent separate entities or cultures but are products of a continuous stylistic evolution within this country (figs. 11, 12).[26] When combined with the absolute chronology provided by C14 dating the following sequence

[26] Smith, *Windmill Hill and Avebury, passim.*

presents itself. An Early Neolithic phase is represented in Wiltshire from *c.* 3000 B.C., as it is in the south-west (dates quoted above), the south-east (Shippea Hill, Cambs. *c.* 2990), or the north-east (Willerby long barrow Yorks. E.R., *c.* 3000 B.C.). This phase is represented by several long barrows and by the pre-enclosure phase at Windmill Hill, and also by Windmill Hill II, the primary use of the earthwork enclosure. The pottery styles are simple, ornament is scarce or very restrained, and generically the wares are closely related to the Hembury–Maiden Castle group (fig. 11 a, b, c, e). Direct links with the south-west are provided by rare vessels made of the gabbroic clay of the Lizard Head region found at Windmill Hill and Robin Hood's Ball: such pottery has a distribution eastwards from Cornwall and the Wiltshire sites mark its furthest extension (fig. 2).[27] Its presence in Windmill Hill II associates it with a C14 date of 2570±150 B.C. and further links with the south-west are provided by stone axes imported from Cornish sources. A terminal date for the Early Neolithic around 2600 B.C. seems reasonable.

Stratigraphy and C14 dates show that already by the end of the early phase a new decorated pottery style ornamented with cord impressions, the Ebbsfleet style, has developed (figs. 11 d, 12 a)[28] and this, with a continuance of plain wares, goes on to *c.* 2000 B.C. and the first beakers to form a Middle Neolithic. In the middle period at Windmill Hill and Robin Hood's Ball pottery with a grit derived from fossil shell and oolite from the Jurassic outcrops constitutes 30 per cent and 17 per cent respectively, pointing to connexions with new areas. These connexions are also implied by the imported stone axes from North Welsh (Craig Lwyd) or Lake District (Great Langdale) centres of production. Into this picture of the Wiltshire Middle Neolithic fit the Severn-Cotswold chambered tombs on the northern edge of the county associated with Ebbsfleet pottery in Gloucestershire and in the remarkable outlier of Capel Garmon in North Wales, hinting once again at the connexions implicit in the Craig Lwyd axes.[29]

The decorative motifs and the emphasis of profile, which begins in the Ebbsfleet pottery style, become more pronounced in the subsequent developments of Mortlake and Fengate wares, characteristic of the Late Neolithic and in Windmill Hill III with a C14 date of 1550±150 B.C. (fig. 12 b, c, d). The heavy-rimmed forms with abundant ornament made by impressing cords, the ends of small bones, or finger-nails into the clay, give rise to the cinerary urns of the 2nd millennium B.C., a type already current in the Late Neolithic, and contemporary with beakers.[30] To the Late Neolithic phase also belongs the Rinyo-Clacton pottery style, wholly distinctive and of unknown origins, partly contemporary with beakers, and at the Durrington Walls ceremonial monument with dates of 1680±110 B.C. and 1610±120 B.C. (BM–286, 285) (fig. 12 e, f). Craig Lwyd axes continue to be used in the late phase, as do others from Cornish sources, and a variety of attractive stones were made into mace-heads with tubular shaft-holes, a technique of hafting probably derived from the shaft-hole battle-axes of the Beaker cultures.[31] One such mace-head from the cremation cemetery of Stonehenge I cannot be earlier than *c.* 2180 B.C., the date of the bank and ditch of that phase into which the burials in the cemetery are inserted, and another (from Wales) is of the Prescelly spotted dolerite used in Stonehenge II, *c.* 1620 B.C.

Within this general framework can now appropriately be placed the remaining aspects of Neolithic material culture in Wiltshire. The acquisition of the stone axes from sources among the igneous rocks of west Britain, plentifully scattered as surface finds throughout the county with a marked concentration of all types in the Avebury region, has

[27] *Antiq.* xliii. 145.
[28] Smith, op. cit.; *Antiq.* xliii. 144.
[29] *Megalithic Enquiries in W. of Britain*, ed. T. G. E. Powell and others, 161; cf. *P.P.S.* i. 125.
[30] Smith, *Windmill Hill and Avebury*, 82; *Palaeohist.* xii. 469; *P.P.S.* xxii. 122.
[31] *Anc. Europe*, ed. Coles and Simpson, 145.

already been touched upon.[32] Such 'trade' is well attested among other Neolithic communities and its circumstances can be illuminated by parallels drawn from recent ethnography.[33] Less can be said about axe-blades made of mined flint: in Wiltshire the Easton Down flint-mines date from *c.* 2530 B.C. and the Durrington mines seem to be Late Neolithic, as do the Grimes Graves (Norf.) galleried shafts, but C14 dates imply Early Neolithic flint-mining in Sussex. The source of the polished flint axes in Early and Middle Neolithic contexts at Windmill Hill might then lie outside the county. The flint industry of these phases as a whole is based on flakes sharply differentiated in type and means of production from any Mesolithic tradition, and is equally distinct from the Late Neolithic industries, as in Windmill Hill III or the West Kennet Avenue site. One curious feature is related to what seems to be a change in archery techniques. The standard arrowhead in the Early and Middle Neolithic is leaf-shaped, and, while the type continues into the Late Neolithic, there appears at that point a wide range of forms of transverse or oblique arrowheads in the *petit tranchet* tradition, which themselves seem soon to be supplanted by the barbed-and-tanged types of the Beaker culture. *Petit tranchet* arrowheads have a Mesolithic ancestry in north-west Europe, though used in such widely separated regions as Egypt and Mesopotamia for fowling and hunting small game.[34] Their sudden appearance in Late Neolithic Britain appears to be mainly in the context of the Rinyo-Clacton pottery style, and may represent the development of a new method of obtaining small game, wild-fowl, or even fish which demanded this form of projectile point.

There remain for mention a few characteristic bone and antler types, notably the 'combs' probably used (on Eskimo analogies) in preparing skins, and a Middle, if not an Early, Neolithic type with counterparts as far north-east as Yorkshire; small chalk carvings, including cups, and at Windmill Hill a phallus, probably figurines, and a decorated pendant, all within the Middle Neolithic phase.

OUTSIDE RELATIONSHIPS

This is not the place to discuss the very complex problems concerned with the origins of the initial British Neolithic cultures in terms of those on the European mainland. It has already been shown how in Wiltshire, a central region of southern England, an eastern and a western strain appears to be present from the beginning. From the west within the Early Neolithic come the characteristic pottery, made of gabbroic clay from the Lizard (fig. 2), and the greenstone axes from Cornish sources. Probably from the Middle Neolithic at the latest occur indications of the less remote westerly contacts implied by pottery, some from the Jurassic regions, the chambered tombs of Severn-Cotswold type, and the stone axes from North Wales and the Lake District. On the other hand the counterparts of the Wiltshire long barrow with chambers made of perishable materials lie to the east of the county and have C14 dates at the very beginning of the 3rd millennium B.C. As shown above, the source of the flint axes found at Windmill Hill may also lie to the east in the Sussex flint-mines which have recently been dated to the Early Neolithic. Long barrows and flint axes look then like easterly components in the Wiltshire Neolithic; the causewayed camps and the 'antler combs' might also be so regarded.

This duality within the county is representative of southern Britain as a whole and it is consequently imagined that the original colonists came from various points of the

[32] *P.P.S.* xxviii. 209–66; Smith, op. cit.
[33] *Ec. H. R.* 2nd ser. xviii. 1–28; Creighton Gabel, *Anal. Prehist. Econ. Patterns,* 38.
[34] *Arch. Jnl.* xci. 38; *Antiq.* ix. 210–15; J. G. D. Clark, *Prehist. Europe: The Economic Basis,* 36.

European coast from the Atlantic to the North Sea. This resulted in the formation of indigenous cultures of mixed ancestry, owing features to all north European Neolithic cultures from the Chassey culture (or cultures) of France to the Funnel-Beaker culture of the north European plain. The central geographical position of Wiltshire would make it an area peculiarly susceptible to an amalgam of such traditions, and the archaeological evidence implies that this was in fact the case.

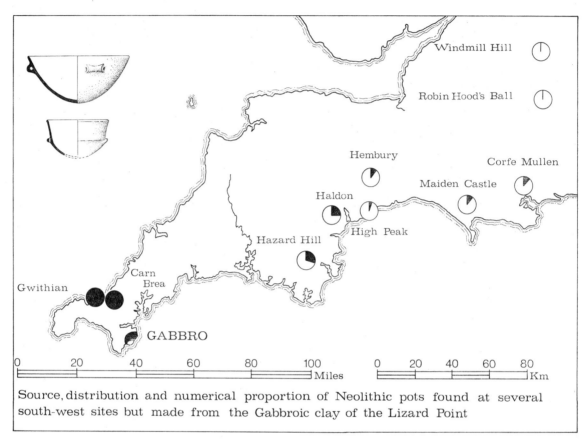

Source, distribution and numerical proportion of Neolithic pots found at several south-west sites but made from the Gabbroic clay of the Lizard Point

Fig. 2

Once introduced, insular traditions established themselves which were to be the foundation of centuries of subsequent development. The pottery styles of the full Bronze Age of the 2nd millennium B.C. have their main roots in the Middle and Late Neolithic, and the ceremonial monuments peculiar to Britain have similar origins. At the beginning of the 2nd millennium a new cultural component is added, that of the makers of beaker pottery and Single-Grave burials, with a demonstrable origin in the Low Countries and the Rhineland, and from this point Britain develops along lines unshared by the Continent.

THE FIELD MONUMENTS

The field monuments of Neolithic Wiltshire are numerous and often striking, and many represent the earliest man-made structures still forming a visible part of the landscape. They are described below and fall into recognizable groups. The erosion and solution of the chalk surface since the 3rd millennium B.C. has probably led to the disappearance of most settlement sites,[35] but the few remaining traces range from Early

[35] *Antiq.* xxxi. 228–31.

to Late Neolithic. The earthwork enclosures of the causewayed-camp class seem to have been constructed in Early to Middle Neolithic times, but continued to be frequented, for whatever purpose, down to the end of the period. Flint-mines in Wiltshire are, however, Middle to Late Neolithic. Burial mounds without stone chambers, of the long-barrow type, seem mainly to fall into the Early Neolithic phase, but their construction also continued into the Middle Neolithic, whereas the chambered tombs, known only in the north of the county, are probably mainly not earlier than the middle phase. The West Kennet chambered tomb affords striking evidence of their continued use into Late Neolithic and Beaker times. Some miscellaneous burials under round barrows are presumably also Late Neolithic and owe their form to contacts with Single-Grave burial traditions in the early 2nd millennium B.C. The remarkable group of ceremonial monuments, including those of Avebury and Stonehenge, are on present showing not earlier than Late Neolithic, although henge monuments as a class go back to Middle Neolithic times. Stonehenge, in its three main phases of construction, spans a period from *c.* 2000 to 1500 B.C. or later, and presents unique problems. The excavations of the 1960s at Silbury Hill have shown that that monument too belongs to the Late Neolithic, with a C14 date of *c.* 2100 B.C. In the ensuing sections these various types of structure are discussed under the appropriate heads with details of important excavated sites.

CAUSEWAYED CAMPS

An important class of Neolithic field monument, first recognized as such as a result of the excavation of the site on Windmill Hill (AVEBURY) in the 1920s, is that of the causewayed camps (fig. 3). These bank-and-ditch structures, 'camps' in the 19th-century archaeological usage of the term for ancient earthwork enclosures, received their distinctive name from the fact that the ditches, instead of being continuous, had been dug in a series of discontinuous segments interrupted by 'causeways' of undisturbed soil. Ditches so dug were seen to be invariably associated with pottery of Neolithic types, and, when beaker sherds characteristic of the earliest metal-using cultures occurred in excavated contexts, they appeared only in the final phase of occupation. With increasing knowledge of the developmental styles of Neolithic pottery it was seen, too, that, when present, Late Neolithic pottery appeared in similarly secondary positions, and that the primary construction of causewayed camps was attributable to the makers of Early and Middle Neolithic wares. Some fifteen or so of these enclosures have been recognized, from Devonshire to east Sussex and northwards to the Thames and the Chilterns, and five lie in Wiltshire.

As will be shown, subdivisions can be made within the general class, but as a group on present showing Hembury in Devon, Maiden Castle in Dorset, and Robin Hood's Ball (FIGHELDEAN) belong to the Early Neolithic; a larger proportion, including Windmill Hill and, for instance, Abingdon (Berks.), Staines (Mdx.), and Whitehawk (Suss.) belong to the Middle Neolithic. Radiocarbon dates have been determined for four sites only: Hembury, 3236±150 B.C.; Hambledon (Dors.), 2790±90 B.C.; Knap Hill, 2760±115 B.C., and Windmill Hill, Phase II, 2570±150 B.C. Coombe Hill (Suss.) has Neolithic pottery in the Ebbsfleet style in primary contexts, and the type-site of Ebbsfleet (Kent) itself has a date of 2710±150 B.C. A general date in the first half of the 3rd millennium B.C., therefore, seems probable for the majority of sites.

The Wiltshire examples (fig. 3) demonstrate forcibly the need for subdivisions within the general class, with the contrast between the three concentric rings of ditches on the gently rounded summit of Windmill Hill, and the single, incomplete, circuit on the precipitous spur of Knap Hill (ALTON). This has been remarked upon more than once[36] and the problem is of wider application. Hembury and Abingdon both have ditches cutting off promontories of land, and in some respects could be thought to resemble Knap Hill; Hambledon and Rybury (ALL CANNINGS) have outworks beyond the main enclosure; Whitesheet (KILMINGTON) shares the feature of a single enclosing ditch with Barkhale (Suss.). Windmill Hill, on the other hand, is the largest example of the group with roughly circular concentric ditches, and Robin Hood's Ball is another, smaller, site. The Trundle and Whitehawk sites in Sussex, and the Staines site in Middlesex are broadly similar to both. It is these multi-ditched enclosures which form the most distinctive sub-group, and they are further linked by evidence for what appears to be common non-utilitarian functions. The unifying factor within the whole causewayed-camp group is in fact no more than the interrupted ditch-digging, a technique virtually unknown in other broadly contemporary British Neolithic structures, where long lengths of ditch were required, as in the cursus monuments (such as that near Stonehenge), or the elongated long barrows of the bank-barrow class in Dorset. Somewhat similar causewayed ditches are found at this time in certain ceremonial sites within the henge-monument class, such as the first phase of Stonehenge, and some of the Dorchester (Oxon.) circles. On the Continent it has long been recognized that causewayed ditches, which might be partially comparable, appear in the Michelsberg culture of the Rhineland at the turn of the 4th and 3rd millennia B.C., and in northern France, although their date may be, like the concentric ditched enclosures in western France, as at Les Matignons in Charente, rather later.

Differentiation of type may perhaps be related to differentiation of function. Although when first identified as a class the causewayed camps were taken to be the enclosing ditches of normal settlements or villages, the evidence from Windmill Hill in particular placed formidable difficulties in the way of this straightforward interpretation, and those difficulties were accentuated by the similar results from other sites. The whole question was discussed in the mid 1960s in detail in the instance of Windmill Hill itself.[37] It could be demonstrated there that all three ditches must have been open at once, for sherds of the same pots were found scattered in the filling of two or more, and at varying levels in the accumulated material. Furthermore, the sherds with flints, animal bones and tools, burnt stones, and the débris from hearths and fires, were concentrated into heaps, which had been deliberately covered with rubble, in many cases obtained by pushing back part of the bank. Such a phenomenon was also detectable at Robin Hood's Ball and Whitesheet, as also in other causewayed camps outside the county. Even when allowance is made for the surface weathering and solution, which would have removed up to 20 inches or so of the chalk surface on Windmill Hill over the past 5,000 years, the lack of normal occupation features, such as pits and major postholes in the inner area, demands an explanation.

Dr. Isobel Smith, in estimating the problem of function of the Windmill Hill enclosures (and, by analogy, other sites showing similar features), stresses the curious character of the ditch fillings and the fact that at the time when the Late Neolithic and Beaker material was deposited, all ditches were deeply filled, and indeed the middle and inner ditches must have been practically invisible. She notes, too, the long continuity of tradition shown by the appearance of successive ceramic styles within the

---

[36] e.g. *W.A.M.* lix. 12; lx. 21.
[37] Smith, *Windmill Hill and Avebury*, 17 sqq.; *Palaeohist.* xii. 469.

British Neolithic series, and a comparison might be made here with the contents of the filling of the burial chambers in the West Kennet tomb discussed below. The animal bones may best be interpreted as the remains of meals, deliberately covered before they could be disturbed or gnawed by dogs, but the evidence does not in fact support the theory once advanced that there had been regular autumn killing, nor that cattle had been pole-axed. The stone and bone tools suggest flint-knapping and skin-working on the site, and seasonal occupation in spring and autumn seems probable. The wide range of contacts implied by imported pottery and stones must mean that a more than purely local gathering took place, and Windmill Hill may well have been a 'centre or rallying-point for the population of a fairly wide area'. Abundant ethnographic parallels could be used to support the thesis of such regional centres of ceremonial and social significance, and the periodic 'fairs' in the early Irish world may well show the same idea in a later, Celtic, context. Such an explanation would accord with the long continuity of regard implied by the internally developing pottery styles from Early to Middle Neolithic, and their continuance in the Late Neolithic side by side with the intrusive types of Rinyo-Clacton and the Beaker tradition. Such continuity of regard existed not only in the instance of the West Kennet chambered tomb just mentioned but in the successive timber and stone monuments at the Sanctuary and probably Avebury itself, and may have lasted for the best part of a millennium.

If Windmill Hill (and other similar sites) are seen as in some sense ceremonial rather than utilitarian in concept and function, the question arises as to the possible relationship of causewayed camps to henge monuments. That such a connexion might exist has been hinted at by more than one archaeologist. They stress the roughly circular plans of many causewayed camps; the similarity of the ditch-digging in certain monuments of henge type associated with Late Neolithic cremation cemeteries, as at Stonehenge I (see p. 326) or the Dorchester (Oxon.) sites,[38] and the fact that the henge monuments, like the causewayed camps, are an insular phenomenon peculiar to prehistoric Britain. The chronology provided by C14 dating shows that henge monuments such as Arminghall (Norf.), dated to 2490±150 B.C., or Barford (Warws.) to 2416±64 B.C., imply that such structures go back to the middle 3rd millennium B.C., while later dates (Stonehenge I, 2180±105 B.C.; Durrington Walls, 1680±110 and 1610±120 B.C.) show a continuance of the tradition into Late Neolithic and Beaker times. In other words they are broadly contemporary with the main period of the use and construction of Windmill Hill. It can hardly be maintained that the whole henge-monument class originated in the causewayed camps. The henges are extremely widespread in the British Isles, and the dozen or so relevant causewayed camps are restricted to a limited area of southern England. More may indeed await detection from the air or on the ground, yet despite numerous new discoveries of henges, and indeed of contemporary cursus monuments, all over Britain in recent years, the area of distribution of causewayed camps has remained hardly altered. If a connexion between causewayed camps and henge monuments is to be accepted, it would presumably be seen as a purely local development within the causewayed-camp area of a modified form of enclosure with interrupted ditches. Such a modified form, it would have to be assumed, was required for some set of ceremonial practices akin to those which there and elsewhere were also bringing into being the single-entranced henge monuments of classic type and their subsequent variants.

Little can be said of the enclosures with causewayed ditches which do not have the peculiar features just described. There has been less excavation in such sites, and it has

[38] R. J. C. Atkinson and others, *Excav. at Dorchester, Oxon.* (First Rep. Dept. of Antiq. Ashmolean Mus. Oxford, 1915).

been suggested that Knap Hill may have been unfinished. Details of five sites are given below.

Knap Hill (ALTON) (fig. 3)

This site was first recognized as Neolithic as a result of excavations in 1908–9, and further excavations were carried out in 1961.[39] The hill is a steep-sided spur overlooking the Vale of Pewsey, rising to a height of 857 ft. The enclosure consists of a single line of ditch with 5 causeways and marked gaps corresponding to these in the banks. The circuit is incomplete on the steepest slope on the SW. and obscure on the SE., but the total area involved measures some 500 ft. by 350 ft.

The ditch varied in depth, in the cuttings excavated, from 6 ft. to 4 ft. There appeared to be no evidence of deliberate filling by pushing back the bank. Pottery broadly comparable with that from Phase II of Windmill Hill occurred in the lower levels, with a proportion of shell-gritted wares, worked flints, and animal bones. In the upper levels were sherds of late beakers, and flint scrapers of characteristic Early Bronze-Age type. C14 dates of 2760±115 B.C. for the primary levels, and 1840±130 B.C. for the Beaker phase, were obtained (BM–205, 203).

Robin Hood's Ball (FIGHELDEAN) (fig. 3)

This causewayed camp lies at a height of some 450 ft., 2½ miles NE. of Shrewton, and consists of two irregular concentric rings of earthwork with causewayed ditches about 100 ft. apart, the outer enclosing an area some 650 ft. by 550 ft. Small-scale excavations were carried out in 1956.[40]

The outer ditch was shallower (4 ft.) than the inner (7½ ft.) and the filling of both suggested that in places the banks had been deliberately pushed back in the manner first noted at Windmill Hill (see below). The site had been occupied before the construction of the earthwork, but there was no evidence that the area had been cultivated. The pottery throughout was comparable with that from Windmill Hill, Phases I and II, with a high proportion of sherds containing shell grit from Jurassic sources, and 1·3 per cent gabbroic clay from the Lizard in Cornwall. Animal bones and a few flint implements were present but no pottery of the Ebbsfleet or Late Neolithic styles.

Rybury (ALL CANNINGS) (fig. 3)

In 1930 Cecil Curwen interpreted the earthworks of Rybury as a causewayed camp overlaid by a later earthwork, with another causewayed ditch forming a half-circle outwork to the SE.[41] The site is much mutilated by chalk-digging, and Mrs. M. E. Cunnington shortly afterwards dismissed the apparently Neolithic features as the result of this then recent activity.[42] Thereafter the site was disregarded, but recent trial excavations and a find of Neolithic pottery have confirmed Curwen's original interpretation.[43]

There appear to have been two concentric oval ditches, enclosing an area some 600 ft. by 500 ft. on a knoll above the 700 ft. contour, with 8 segments of ditch visible on the NW., overlaid by a later single bank and ditch, presumed Early Iron Age. The outwork is on another smaller knoll, and is an arc with a chord of about 250 ft. with 7 segments of ditch.

[39] W.A.M. xxvii. 42–65; lx. 1–23.
[40] Ibid. lix. 1–27.
[41] Antiq. iv. 38–40.
[42] W.A.M. xlvi. 199 n.
[43] Ibid. lix. 185; lx. 127.

Whitesheet Hill (KILMINGTON) (fig. 3)

This site, although recorded by Colt Hoare, was not recognized as a Neolithic earthwork until recent recognition by air photography and field observation. Trial excavations in 1951 confirmed its character.[44] The earthwork lies on a slightly rounded

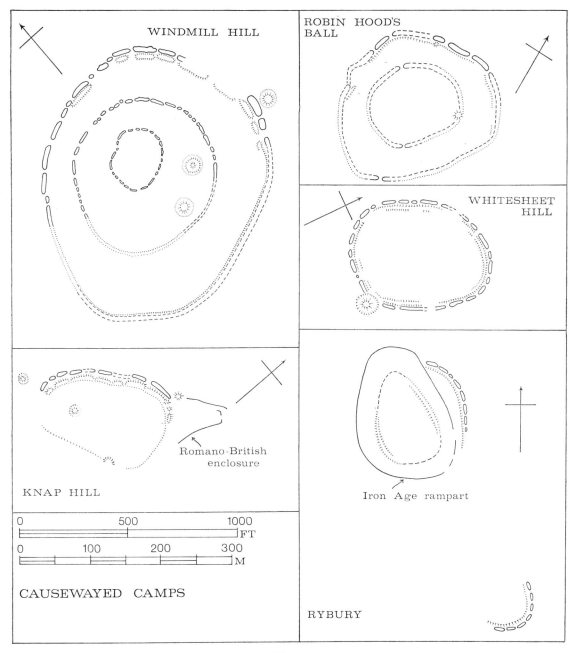

FIG. 3

hill-top NW. of the well-known Iron Age hill-fort on Whitesheet Hill, and consists of a single line of causewayed ditch with traces of an internal bank in places. Breaks in this bank occur opposite some, but not all, the visible ditch causeways. The area enclosed is egg-shaped, measuring some 650 ft. by 425 ft.

A section cut on the N. revealed a 'semi-causeway' or partial bridge across the ditch, similar to those at Windmill Hill, and invisible on the surface. A few sherds of

[44] Ibid. liv. 404-10.

Neolithic pottery of Early–Middle Windmill Hill type (including some with Jurassic grit), flint flakes, and a scraper, were found scattered in the primary silt. An almost complete skull of an ox was found against the side of the flat-bottomed ditch, covered by chalk rubble pushed down from the bank. A second cutting on the S. revealed a very shallow flat-bottomed ditch but no finds.

A remarkable feature of the earthwork is that on the SE. the line of the ditch is partially overlaid by a large round barrow with a conspicuous polygonal ditch (*B ii* KILMINGTON 4). Hoare dug into the barrow and reported that it 'had contained a skeleton and had been investigated before', and it is presumably of the Early Bronze Age.

Windmill Hill (AVEBURY) (fig. 3)

This site was first identified as Neolithic in 1923. It was extensively excavated in 1925–9 by Alexander Keiller, and small-scale control excavations were made in 1957–8. The whole material has been published in full.[45] The hill with its 3 concentric earthworks rises to 640 ft., a mile NW. of the ceremonial monument of Avebury (see p. 324).

The excavations revealed the following sequence of prehistoric activity on the site:

Phase I. A Neolithic settlement represented by pits and post-holes mainly concentrated in a restricted area on the E. side of the circuit of the *Inner Ditch*; similar pits, holes, and a hearth under the *Outer Bank* in the areas excavated in 1957–8; and probably a small enclosure, known as the *Square Earthwork*, beyond the *Outer Ditch* on the SE. The pottery shows this occupation to be Early Neolithic, and there is evidence of agricultural activity. The C14 date is 2950±150 B.C. (BM–73).

Phase II is marked by the digging of the 3 roughly concentric, interrupted, or causewayed ditches and the subsequent deposition in them of a remarkable quantity of potsherds, flint, stone, bone, and antler implements, animal bones, and a few human and animal burials. Apparently in connexion with these deposits not only was natural weathering-silt allowed to accumulate in the ditches, but the chalk rubble banks were partially pushed back over the deposits in the ditches. The C14 date for the lower levels in the *Middle* and *Outer Ditches* is 2570±150 B.C. (BM–74).

Phase III. At a time when the *Inner* and *Middle Ditches* were filled almost to the top, and there was a great depth of accumulation in the *Outer Ditch*, continued interest in the site is denoted by numerous sherds and flint implements of Late Neolithic and Beaker types, and animal bones and charcoal, which gave a C14 date of 1540±150 B.C. (BM–75).

The evidence shows that whatever the precise nature of the site and its function or functions in the societies responsible for first occupying the hill-top and at one stage digging the earthworks, it retained a significance for at least a thousand years and probably for over fifteen hundred.

With the likely removal of some 20 in. of the chalk surface by natural weathering processes since the early 3rd millennium B.C., as noted earlier, the lack of coherent post structures in Phase I is not unexpected. The *Square Earthwork*, roughly 30 ft. across, may have been a palisaded ritual or mortuary enclosure with analogies for its square plan in the ditched enclosure of Site I at Dorchester (Oxon.)[46] and, in general, in the long mortuary enclosure on Normanton Down (see p. 316).

The triple enclosing ditches constitute the largest Neolithic earthwork of this type in Britain, the *Outer Ditch* being some 1,200 ft. in diameter and enclosing about

---

[45] See above, n. 16.   [46] Atkinson, *Excav. at Dorchester, Oxon.* (First Rep.), 5.

21 acres. The *Middle Ditch* has a mean diameter of about 660 ft. and the *Inner* 280 ft. The average depths are, *Outer Ditch* 7 ft., *Middle* 4 ft. 6 in., and *Inner* 3 ft. The 'causeways', or gaps between the ditch segments, vary in width from 1 ft. to 25 ft. and none of those excavated showed post-holes or other evidence of gateways. As shown, the inner banks derived from the ditch-digging appear to have been wholly or partially pushed back into the ditches in Neolithic times, and remains of the *Outer Bank* (up to 3 ft. 6 in. high) alone exist as visible features.

The stratified material in the ditches shows evolving pottery styles in which that from Phase I is differentiated from the Phase II material, in which not only modifications and developments marking the emergence of Middle Neolithic styles appear, but pottery differentiated in style and fabric. A very few sherds (0·2 per cent) are made of the gabbroic clay from the Lizard region in Cornwall, and in common with others from Robin Hood's Ball, Maiden Castle (Dors.), and a few other sites, must denote contacts with the west. Other sherds have shell and other grits indicating imports from the Jurassic zone in the Frome–Bath region some 20 miles to the south-west. In Phase II is seen the first appearance of the Ebbsfleet style of pottery, continuing into Phase III, where it is accompanied by Late Neolithic wares of the Mortlake, Fengate, and Rinyo-Clacton styles, as well as beakers and collared-urn sherds. Imported stone axes begin to appear in Phase II, but are mainly concentrated in Phase III. Characteristic Late Neolithic flint types also appear in the latest phase.

Throughout the occupation of the site there is evidence for 'the metropolitan character of the Avebury region', which culminated in Late Neolithic times with the construction of the Avebury ceremonial monuments at a time when the Windmill Hill enclosures were still resorted to by peoples of varying cultural traditions.

SETTLEMENTS

At the time of their first recognition the causewayed camps, described in the preceding section, were assumed to be normal ditch-enclosed settlements of Neolithic date. It can now be seen that features present in many of them preclude this straightforward interpretation, and that it is better to regard the concentric-ditched enclosures at least (as at Windmill Hill) as having in some sense a ceremonial significance. The identification of other settlements is rendered difficult by several factors, the first being the lack of surface features so as to make recognition on the ground possible. In addition, the surface weathering and solution of the Chalk, on which most Neolithic occupation might be expected to lie, would since the 3rd millennium B.C. have resulted in the obliteration of all structural features that did not penetrate the subsoil to a depth of more than 2 ft., and so eliminate the survival of a variety of possible post- or stake-supported structures. The exceptions which have survived in favoured conditions serve only to emphasize this situation, and in general the presence of settlements has been inferred from sites containing Neolithic pits, presumed to be for the storage of grain or other commodities,[47] or where the old ground surface has been preserved under slightly later barrows.

Early or Middle Neolithic sites include Windmill Hill, Phase I, with a C14 date of *c.* 2950 B.C., and with pits under the *Outer Bank* and in the *Inner Ditch* area; on Waden Hill and Hackpen Hill, Avebury, the former with a pit.[48] An Early–Middle Neolithic settlement of some kind existed at Durrington Walls, where a pottery scatter preserved under the bank of the henge monument has C14 dates of 2620±40, 2630±70 B.C.[49]

---

[47] *P.P.S.* xxx. 352–81.   [48] *W.A.M.* lvi. 167.   [49] *Antiq.* xlii. 20.

Under the barrows *B ii* Avebury 55, Bishop's Cannings 81, and West Overton 6*b* the pottery scatter on the old surface denoting a pre-barrow occupation included Early–Middle Neolithic pottery, in the second instance with 5 pits.[50] On Easton Down (Winterslow) remains of a rectilinear structure at least 17 ft. long and marked by the remains of bedding-trenches and stake-holes, was associated with pottery in the earlier Neolithic tradition, distinct from the Late Neolithic and Beaker pottery and features of the rest of the site. The site excavated at Cherhill in 1967 (see p. 283) had, cut into the tufa layer, which had formed over the earlier occupation, a Neolithic settlement of two phases.[51] Phase I consisted of a continuous, very irregular, linear excavation running east-west for over 100 ft., containing pottery of Early–Middle Neolithic affinities, animal bones and quern fragments, in primary contexts, with Late Neolithic and Beaker secondary.

The second Neolithic phase at Cherhill, with Late Neolithic (Mortlake) pottery and a C14 date of 2765 ± 90 b.c. (BM–493), comprised 2 ditches, one at least causewayed, cutting into the Phase I feature after it had been deliberately filled. At Winterbourne 4 pits, one surrounded by stake-holes, at Old Sarum 3,[52] and at West Overton one[53] contained Late Neolithic wares in the Peterborough–Mortlake styles. In the same general area as the Mesolithic settlement at Downton irregular hollows and a post-hole were associated with Middle–Late Neolithic pottery of Ebbsfleet–Mortlake types.[54]

A curious occupation site was excavated on the line of the West Kennet Avenue at Avebury, in the region of the stone pairs Nos. 28–32. Two pits and ten smaller holes were found, containing dark soil, charcoal, and artefacts; five of the holes had a thick lining of clay. Late Neolithic pottery, predominantly Peterborough but with some Rinyo-Clacton, and a characteristic contemporary flint industry, stone axe and Niedermendig lava fragments, were found in the pits and holes, and as an extensive surface scatter.[55]

A group of pits containing Late Neolithic pottery, exclusively of the Rinyo-Clacton type, occurs in the general region of Woodhenge, preceding in date that of the site itself, at Woodlands, and at Ratfyn.[56] The curious nature of the contents of these pits was commented on by J. F. S. Stone who suggested a possible ritual function, and quoted the West Kennet Avenue site as a parallel.[57] The Woodhenge holes at least appear to form part of an extensive Late Neolithic settlement covering a large area, including that on which the Woodhenge henge monument was subsequently built and associated with the larger henge-monument complex of Durrington Walls, both discussed below. Part of the settlement site, adjacent to the southern edge of the bank of Durrington Walls, was excavated in 1952.[58] A discontinuous linear hollow, reminiscent of that in the first Neolithic phase at Cherhill, was found. It had been refilled in antiquity and was devoid of finds. Over and along this refilled hollow an irregular double line of post-holes ran for at least 70 ft. A considerable amount of occupation material of Late Neolithic type, with Rinyo-Clacton pottery predominating, came from this area, which resembled one side of a long house of continental Linear-Pottery type, but no corresponding line of posts could be found on the south. The ground here rises steeply, however, and surface weathering might have removed features corresponding to those preserved, which were covered by hill-wash and lay in the hollow formed between the higher

50 *W.A.M.* lx. 24; *P.P.S.* xxxii. 122–55.
51 *W.A.M.* lxiii. 107.
52 Ibid. lvii. 179.
53 Ibid. lix. 82.
54 Ibid. lviii. 116.
55 Dr. Smith in *Windmill Hill and Avebury*, p. 212, writes: 'Whatever the significance of the general scatter of material, the whole ... cannot be interpreted as adjuncts of normal habitation. It is difficult to evade the conclusion that this site has a direct connexion with the Avenue.'
56 *P.P.S.* xxx. 379–80.
57 *W.A.M.* lii. 287–306.
58 *Ant. Jnl.* xxxiv. 155–7.

ground and the tail of the henge bank. Radiocarbon dates for the Rinyo-Clacton and Beaker material in Durrington Walls itself are 1680±110 and 1610±120 B.C. (BM–286, 285).

Excavations in 1966 immediately east of this area revealed a curious subrectangular setting of irregular holes, 54 ft. by 30 ft., apparently not post-holes, containing Late Neolithic pottery of Rinyo-Clacton type.[59]

FLINT MINES

The need for good flint for axe-heads was met in England, as elsewhere in Neolithic Europe, by mining in the flint-bearing chalk deposits for superior material from deep seams, rather than utilizing derived nodules or inferior flint from surface deposits. Flint axe-factories were accordingly set up with mines to supply the raw materials. In Sussex recent radiocarbon dates for six sites average c. 2960 B.C., and so place the mining activity in the Early Neolithic; the Easton Down mines, described below, have a date of c. 2530 B.C., and the Grimes Graves (Norf.) mines are around 2000 B.C. The need for flint axes in areas remote from these sites on occasion led to the exploitation of the mines by members of Neolithic and Beaker communities with varied cultural traditions, and at the main mining centre known within Wiltshire, that at Easton Down (WINTERSLOW), just such a mixture of cultural elements can be seen. It is, however, convenient to describe the working-floors and mines at this stage, for the C14 date of 2530±150 B.C. (BM–190) shows that work began on the site at least in Middle Neolithic times.

The area over which the remains of mine-shafts and dumps are visible extends to 40 acres and at least 90 shafts can be identified. Of those excavated the most significant are Pits B. 1 and B. 49, both of which reach the required 'floorstone' flint, at 10 ft. and 8 ft. below the solid chalk surface respectively. In B. 1 there was slight undercutting at the base of the 10 ft. diameter shaft, and in B. 49 shallow galleries up to 4 ft. deep had been driven out radially at floorstone level. In this shaft, too, a trial pit had been sunk in the floor, but without striking flint (except a worthless tabular seam), although it reached to 16 ft. below ground-surface. The mining had been carried out by the usual method of using Red Deer antler levers, or 'picks', and the ox scapulae used as shovels include those of the wild *Bos primigenius*.

Around, and sometimes over, the filled-up shafts of the mines were working floors, the débris upon which showed clearly that the end-product aimed at was the chipped and polished axe. Indeed one finished specimen of such an axe was found still lying in floor B. 7. Here, as in other working-floors at Easton Down and elsewhere, pseudo-palaeolithic forms occurred as intermediate stages in the manufacture of axes from the parent nodules, and there was a proportion of used flakes etc. among the waste. One floor (B. 3) showed the progress of axe manufacture as a systematized operation, one half of the accumulation consisting solely of large flakes and the other of unfinished axes and smaller chippings.

One working floor (B. 7), overlying a filled-in mine shaft, had at its base three sherds apparently of Neolithic ware and identical with those from the rectangular house-site referred to above (see p. 300). On the whole, however, the material from the shafts and floors cannot be precisely assigned to any phase of Neolithic or Beaker activity. The *tranchet* axe from floor B. 1, and possibly some heavy waisted scraper forms, which may be small adzes, might belong to the Late Neolithic cultures, and the single polished axe

[59] Ibid. xlvii. 166–84.

is again of a type which occurs in Late Neolithic contexts in northern England. As has been said, however, this continuance of tradition is only to be expected, and is further illustrated by mixture of pottery styles in the adjacent settlement site, where, in addition to Beaker pottery, vessels exhibiting the characteristics of both Middle and Late Neolithic wares have occurred.

A group of abortive flint-mines, yielding antler picks and a broken *petit tranchet* derivative arrowhead of Late Neolithic type, were found at DURRINGTON.[60]

A remarkable series of axes made of jade, and often of large size and exquisite finish, is known from the British Isles, where some 70 examples have been recorded. There are two marked southern concentrations, one in East Anglia and the other in southern Wessex. Three axes come from Wiltshire: one from BROAD TOWN, one from 'a barrow near Stonehenge', and one from WINTERSLOW. The only associated find in Britain is a fragment from the Cairnholy I chambered tomb in Scotland, where its position leaves it uncertain whether it belongs to the primary use of the tomb, or to its later use in late Neolithic–Beaker times. For a worn fragment the first alternative may be the more plausible, and at all events the axes as a whole can hardly be later than the 3rd millenium B.C. Closely comparable axes are known in Europe from the Loire to the Elbe, but the source or sources for the jade of the entire British and continental series is still obscure.[61]

BURIAL MONUMENTS: LONG BARROWS AND CHAMBERED TOMBS

With few exceptions noted below the burials of Neolithic Wiltshire, from the later 4th until at least the first half of the 3rd millennium B.C. and probably throughout it, are under elongated mounds of earth or rubble which may form conspicuous field monuments. This is also true of the rest of southern and eastern England. It was almost entirely upon the Wiltshire evidence that the priority of long barrows over round barrows was established a century ago by John Thurnam:[62] long barrows, he observed, contained no metal objects 'and, so far as we know, they are of the Stone period'; round barrows frequently yielded bronze objects in primary contexts and were, therefore, of 'the Bronze period' or later. All subsequent work has confirmed the soundness of Thurnam's diagnosis, and it can now be seen that in Wessex and Sussex or in north-east England long barrows are the products of Early or Middle Neolithic peoples, who in Wessex were also the constructors of the causewayed camps. Radiocarbon dates show that excavated examples range from the middle 4th to the middle 3rd millennium B.C., the extreme permissible dates being *c.* 3570–*c.* 2570 B.C., comparable with those for Windmill Hill Phases I–II which are 3100 and 2420 B.C.

Thurnam perceived that long barrows in southern England could be subdivided into two types, which he named respectively 'unchambered long barrows' and 'chambered long barrows', the latter containing various forms of stone-built burial chambers, the former without such structures. In the wider geographical field, and in the perspective of a century's archaeology, it is possible, while accepting the validity of this classification, to see the 'chambered long barrows' as members of a larger class of funerary monument distributed widely in western and northern Britain and in Ireland. They may here be conveniently grouped as chambered tombs, in which the burial chambers are covered by mounds or cairns of varying form but basically either circular or elongated.

[60] *W.A.M.* liv. 381–8.   [61] *P.P.S.* xxix. 133–72; xxxi. 25–33.   [62] *Arch.* xlii. 161–243.

In the still wider range of western and northern Europe, chambered tombs have an extensive distribution from Iberia to Scandinavia, with those of the British Isles forming a group with marked insular characteristics. In southern Britain those tombs under long cairns, i.e. Thurnam's 'chambered long barrows', form a regional group centred on the Bristol Channel, and can be classed as the Severn–Cotswold tombs. In Wiltshire there are a dozen such tombs in the north of the county, three on the Oolite being integral members of the main Severn–Cotswold group, and the others outliers on the Chalk in the Avebury–Marlborough region. So far as a meaningful nomenclature of the two classes of long barrow is concerned, the chambered tombs may be so defined, but Thurnam's 'unchambered' class poses problems. Modern excavations have now repeatedly shown that barrows of this type cover, in almost all instances, timber settings or structures, which in some cases at least can be best interpreted as roofed mortuary houses, thus rendering 'unchambered' an inapposite term. 'Wooden chambered' would be equally unsatisfactory, as it begs the question of the evidence for such chambers, the interpretation of which is not always unambiguous, and fails to allow for barrows in which a timber-built mortuary house was certainly not present. Paul Ashbee, facing this problem in 1969, decided on 'earthen long barrows',[63] but perhaps the simplest and most logical course, having isolated chambered tombs as a category, would be to call the remainder 'long barrows' without qualification. This provides a parallel to the 'round barrow', which is an accepted archaeological term for a circular burial mound, not a stone cairn, and covering burials burnt or unburnt, and contained within any form of grave or structure. Here, then, the funerary monuments of the Neolithic in Wiltshire will be divided into long barrows, chambered tombs of Severn–Cotswold type, and a few burials which can be assigned to the Neolithic but not of either of the foregoing classes.

LONG BARROWS

The total number of barrows in Britain, which conform to this classification, is about 260, the English distribution falling into two main areas, a southern and a northern. In the southern area the westernmost barrows lie in Dorset, and none west of a line drawn from Bridport inland to Chippenham; in the Avebury region they slightly overlap with the outliers of the Severn–Cotswold chambered tombs; and in the east they are found in Hampshire and along the Sussex Downs as far as Eastbourne. Within this roughly triangular area, and including outliers in Kent, the Chilterns, and East Anglia, the Wiltshire long barrows constitute about 57 per cent of the total number, and indeed about 35 per cent of the total long barrows in both southern and northern areas. In part one of this volume 109 certain, probable, or possible long barrows and chambered tombs are listed.[64] Ashbee accepts 65 long barrows in the sense used here. Six of these have been completely excavated within recent years, and earlier excavation records, all very imperfect and some virtually useless, exist for about 35 more barrows.

The Wiltshire long barrows (fig. 4) are almost exclusively sited on the chalk uplands: *B i* SHERRINGTON 1 is on the flood-plain of the river Wylye. As Ashbee has shown, they fall into two main groups in south Wiltshire, Salisbury Plain West, around the headwaters of the Wylye and its tributaries, and Salisbury Plain East, around those of the Avon and confluent streams in the Stonehenge region. A third group is that of the north Wiltshire Chalk where for the purposes of distribution long barrows and chambered tombs may be taken together, either round the headwaters of the Kennet or on the

---

[63] Paul Ashbee, *Earthen Long Barrow in Brit.*   [64] *V.C.H. Wilts.* i (1), pp. 137-46.

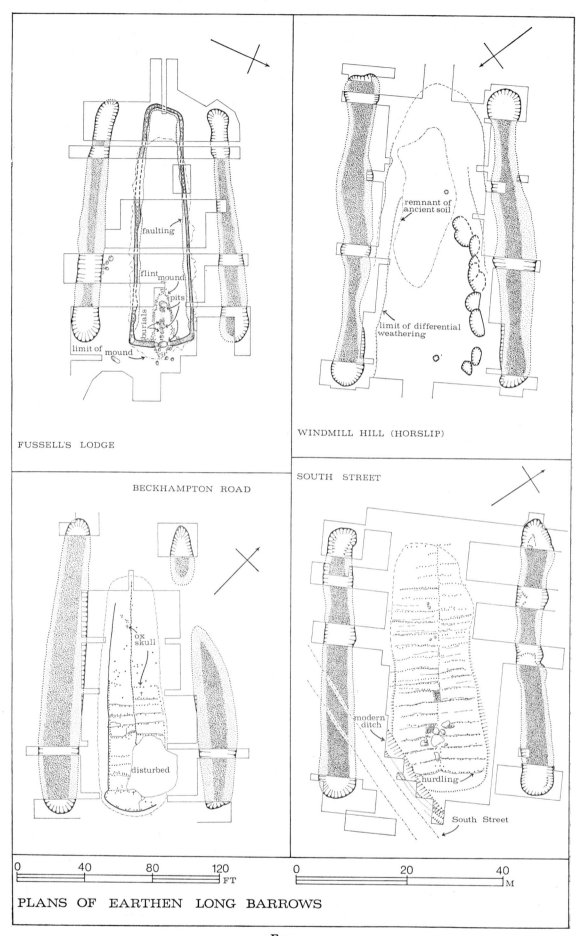

FUSSELL'S LODGE

WINDMILL HILL (HORSLIP)

BECKHAMPTON ROAD

SOUTH STREET

PLANS OF EARTHEN LONG BARROWS

FIG. 4

304

southern escarpment overlooking the Vale of Pewsey. Grouping round water supplies can be seen elsewhere among the southern long barrows, as those round the head-waters of the river Allen in Dorset, or the springs of Rockbourne Down in Hampshire. It is difficult to be sure whether grouping can be associated with other contemporary sites; there are four long barrows near the causewayed camp on Robin Hood's Ball, but the ceremonial monument of Stonehenge I can hardly be regarded as a focus, unless the barrows are as late as *c.* 2000 B.C. In north Wiltshire the concentration seems to be rather around Avebury than Windmill Hill.

The range of size among long barrows is considerable, and subdivisions of type can be made on surface appearance quite apart from the separation of the enormously elongated 'bank barrows' of southern Dorset, over 500 ft. in length. Among the remainder, some 57 per cent measure between 200 ft. and 100 ft. long; 18 per cent between 100 ft. and 65 ft.; 14 per cent between 250 ft. and 200 ft.; and smaller proportions between 400 ft. and 250 ft. It is difficult to see any consistency in the distribution of Wiltshire long barrows by size, although there is a high proportion of medium or small barrows in the Stonehenge region. Exceptionally large barrows include *B i* Milton Lilbourne 7 (315 ft.), Amesbury 42 (265 ft.), Winterbourne Stoke 1 (240 ft.), and Tilshead 2 (390 ft.) in the south; in the Avebury region *B i* Bishop's Cannings 92 measures 230 ft.; but *B i* Avebury 22, the West Kennet long barrow, 340 ft. long, contains a chambered tomb, as almost certainly does *B i* East Kennet 1 (344 ft.). It may be noteworthy that the two remarkably similar and apparently non-sepulchral barrows of *B i* Avebury 68 and Bishop's Cannings 76 are identical in length (138 ft.).

Two main types of long barrow can be detected, although not invariably by surface indications alone. First there are those in which the barrow is approximately rectangular, with parallel sides, and secondly there are those with sides slightly converging to give a trapezoid plan as is well seen at Fussell's Lodge, *B i* Clarendon Park 4a. The material of the mound was derived from flanking quarry-ditches conterminous with the mound or occasionally continuing round one end. The orientation is normally roughly east–west, 80 per cent of the British long barrows being within 45° of this, although exceptional north–south monuments appear, and in normal orientation the higher part, and the burial, if there is one, are at the easterly end of the mound, occupying only a small part of the total: at Fussell's Lodge it was ⅛ of the length of the trapezoid enclosure.

When considering the details of structure and burial rite revealed by excavation, it must be remembered that in Wiltshire only six barrows have been examined by modern techniques, and only one of these excavations has been fully published; outside Wiltshire another ten or so long barrows have been similarly examined. These excavations have shown that great diversity of internal structure and arrangement exists, and the inferences to be drawn from less precise observations in earlier reports underlines this view, so that extrapolation and generalization become dangerous. Details of the six Wiltshire barrows referred to are given below (see p. 309) and at this point it may be convenient to discuss the features revealed in these, with evidence taken from old excavations where that seems relevant (fig. 4).

Mound Construction

Many of the observations in the earlier excavations of William Cunnington, Hoare, and Thurnam indicate, if they indicate structural details at all, that the barrow was built over an old soil, showing as a thick dark layer (*B i* Tilshead 2, 4, Warminster 14,

KNOOK 5, SHERRINGTON 1), or that the lower part of the mound consisted of heaps of dark soil, which may represent turf and top-soil derived from the first operations on the flanking ditches (*B i* BRATTON 1, TILSHEAD 2, 5, HEYTESBURY 4). In some barrows an axial cairn of stones was recognized, as again in HEYTESBURY 4 and also in HEYTESBURY 1 (Bowl's Barrow), where one stone was a massive block of spotted dolerite, one of the constituent rocks of the 'Blue Stones' used in the second phase monument at Stonehenge.[65] Certain chronological difficulties are raised by the C14 date of Stonehenge II, 1620 ± 110 B.C. (I–2384), if this is to be thought of as implying an equivalently late date for Bowl's Barrow. Axial cairns have been recorded behind the chambered tomb at West Kennet (*B i* AVEBURY 22) and also at Wayland's Smithy in Berkshire,[66] where it was suggested that the sarsens used resulted from field clearance during agricultural activity. Such activity might also have yielded the flints forming cairns such as that over the burials at Fussell's Lodge. Modern excavations have tended to be rescue operations when mounds have been largely or completely removed by ploughing, and details of construction have often hardly been preserved above ground-level. Two barrows showing internal hurdle-work surviving in plan, and to some extent in section, are described below (see p. 310). The Horslip (Windmill Hill) long barrow (*B i* AVEBURY 47) not only retained no mound but no perceptible trace of structures save for two small pits and an irregular line of infilled quarry-pits, perhaps comparable with those briefly reported from the first phase of *B i* WOODFORD 2.

Timber Enclosures

The Fussell's Lodge barrow was found to cover a continuous bedding-trench for massive timber uprights, trapezoid in plan, 135 ft. long, 20 ft. wide at the south-west, and double this width at the north-east, where it was broken by an entrance (fig. 4). The timbers employed were up to 3 ft. in diameter at the north-east end and of large scantling throughout, and they presumably held a revetment containing the mound of the barrow when first built. In *B i* WOODFORD 2 the brief interim report assigns a rectangular timber setting, 36 ft. by 12 ft., to a constructional phase earlier than an irregularly trapezoidal setting, 16 ft. long by 16 ft. at its wider end, and the setting of a timber façade is similarly reported under *B ii* KINGSTON DEVERILL 1 (formerly taken for a round barrow).

Two enigmatic and remarkably similar barrows, *B i* BISHOP'S CANNINGS 76 (Beckhampton Road) and AVEBURY 68 (South Street), have been shown to contain no trace of burials nor of any provision to house them, but both are structurally divided by an axial line of stakes holding hurdling. From this line, offsets at right angles enclose a series of bays throughout the length of the mound, in many instances differentiated by the varying character of the barrow material from bay to bay (fig. 4).

The trapezoid bedding-trench at Fussell's Lodge has a good parallel in a Yorkshire E. Riding long barrow on Willerby Wold, as re-excavation has recently shown,[67] and dates of 3010 ± 150 B.C. (BM–189) and 2950 ± 150 B.C. (BM–188) show it to be broadly contemporary with the Wiltshire barrow. No comment can be made on the Woodford and Kingston Deverill barrows pending fuller publication, but the hurdling at Bishop's Cannings and Avebury has partial parallels in the Giants' Hills, Skendleby, long barrow in Lincolnshire—again a link in structural details between the northern and southern groups. Recent excavation of a Severn–Cotswold chambered tomb at Ascott-under-Wychwood (Oxon.) has revealed a very complex structural history

[65] *W.A.M.* xlii. 431.   [66] *Antiq.* xxix. 126–33.   [67] *P.P.S.* xxix. 173–205.

embodying a line of axial stakes as well as stone-built bays, the whole combining features of long barrows of the type under discussion with those of the Severn–Cotswold chambered tombs. But in all discussion of features dependent on complete and skilful excavation it must be remembered that only 15 or so long barrows have been adequately excavated in Britain, and no Severn–Cotswold tombs other than Wayland's Smithy and Ascott. The question of the relationships between the long barrows and the Severn–Cotswold chambered tombs under long cairns is bound up with that of the significance of the trapezoid plan, and both are discussed below from the standpoint of Wiltshire.

Wooden Mortuary Houses

As shown above, the original term 'unchambered long barrows' was called in question when it was realized from new excavation evidence from the Wayland's Smithy long barrow in Berkshire that wooden burial chambers of an unsuspected kind could exist in such monuments. Recent views advanced in the discussion over the past five years must be examined since Fussell's Lodge and other Wiltshire long barrows are involved. In 1962–3 excavation showed that Wayland's Smithy (an outlier of the Avebury group of long barrows and chambered tombs, and situated only 14 miles north-east of Windmill Hill) was of two periods, the earlier monument being a small long barrow and the later a chambered tomb of Severn–Cotswold type, with a C14 date of 2820±130 B.C. immediately antecedent to its construction. In the Wayland's Smithy I monument the burials (of not less than 15 persons) lay on a sarsen pavement 16 ft. by 5 ft., axial to the mound and between two large **D**-shaped post-holes 5 ft. across. These and other features could only be interpreted as a timber mortuary house with a ridge-roof supported on a pair of massive uprights, and in the interim excavation report it was suggested that features in the Fussell's Lodge and Willerby Wold (Yorks. E.R.) long barrows could be similarly understood.[68] At Fussell's Lodge Ashbee,[69] influenced by the Wayland's Smithy evidence, took the three axial pits at the north-east end of the barrow, beneath the disarticulated skeletons and a spread of flints, to represent the sockets of three large posts approximately 20 ft. apart. These, he surmised, supported a ridge-roofed mortuary house not less than 40 ft. long, originally housing the burials and covered by a flint cairn. The cairn itself was surrounded by the trapezoid enclosure containing the chalk rubble mound of the barrow. Certain difficulties in this interpretation have been pointed out by D. D. A. Simpson.[70] These do not, however, seem to invalidate the interpretation in general terms, and on the whole it seems reasonable to accept it. Ashbee has further suggested that, in a dozen instances in old and inadequately recorded Wiltshire long-barrow excavations, features are described which might well have belonged to analogous structures.[71]

In considering these excavations it must be recalled that Cunnington, Hoare, and Thurnam were not looking for structural features, particularly those of vanished timber buildings, but for bones, pottery, and flint artefacts. The dispersed burial areas, which we know to exist in long barrows, were not necessarily explored to their limits, and artificial holes in the Chalk ('cists') if encountered, were thought of as isolated and inexplicable phenomena. With these reservations the circumstances are, however, often highly suggestive. In *B i* BOYTON 1 the burials of eight individuals were found between two 'oval cists or pits . . . about four feet long and two and a half deep', 7 ft. apart; the whole was covered with a ridged cairn of stones 20 ft. long and 10 ft. wide. At *B i*

[68] *Antiq.* xxxix. 131. This suggestion was enlarged upon in *Palaeohist.* xii. 381.
[69] *Arch.* c. 1 sqq.
[70] *Antiq.* xlii. 142–4.
[71] Ibid. xliii. 43.

WINTERBOURNE STOKE 53 there was a scorched paving and 'two deep cists' full of charcoal under a cairn, and at *B i* HEDDINGTON 3 a single skeleton lay between two axial holes 2 ft. in diameter, 15 ft. apart. In six other instances single 'cists' alone were noticed, in association not only with the burials but often with pavements as well. The 'semi-circular cist' at the west end of the pavement, 15 ft. by 6 ft., underlying the burials in *B i* KNOOK 2, and the 'oval cist' by the admittedly incompletely examined burial pavement in *B i* TILSHEAD 2, may be compared with the big **D**-shaped holes at Wayland's Smithy, each holding a half tree-trunk, and the oval holes at Fussell's Lodge. At the end of the burial pavement in *B i* WARMINSTER 1 was an upright sarsen 5 ft. high, and two obliquely pitched sarsens formed one end of the Wayland's Smithy chamber. A burial chamber of pitched stone slabs terminating in a single upright stone in Cairn B on Great Ayton Moor, in north-east Yorkshire, may be interpreted as a stone version of the ridge-roofed wooden structures under discussion.[72] The mortuary house in the Leubingen barrow, in Saxo-Thuringia, of mid-2nd-millennium date but of analogous construction to the Neolithic ridge-roofed chambers, shows that a single massive post may be all that is necessary.[73] On the whole the cumulative weight of evidence from Wiltshire and elsewhere supports the original thesis that the ridge-roofed mortuary house is a feature recurrent in several, though by no means all, long barrows in Britain, and with at least partial parallels, as will be shown, on the Continent.

The Burials

Apart from four Wiltshire instances of apparent single burials, which may well be due to imperfect excavation, the normal practice recorded is that of collective or multiple burial. At Fussell's Lodge between 53 and 57 individuals were represented by the remains found. When the site was first excavated the number was estimated at many fewer and this has suggested to Ashbee that even fairly high recorded totals, such as 18 in *B i* NORTON BAVANT 13, or 14 in HEYTESBURY 1, are likely to be below the true number. Atkinson, however, has somewhat discounted this in his estimates of Neolithic population.[74] At Fussell's Lodge consideration of anomalous circumstances in the burial deposit, such as the lack of small bones, suggested 'that burial initially took place elsewhere, and when the bones were partially or completely clear of soft tissue attachments major regions were removed for barrow burial'. The same factors implied a similar sequence at Wayland's Smithy. In such circumstances the collection and storage of burials could have taken place over a longer period of time than that of the likely half-century during which a timber mortuary house in a barrow would have survived for recurrent use as an ossuary in the manner of the stone-built chambers of a Severn–Cotswold tomb. That, as the Wiltshire evidence from West Kennet indicates, could have been of the order of a thousand years. The imperfectly recorded conditions of the burials in early Wiltshire excavations are consonant with such a view. Disarticulated skeletons were noted in *B i* HEYTESBURY 1, 4, FITTLETON 5, and elsewhere; in NORTON BAVANT 13 the remains of eighteen individuals were piled into a space, 8 ft. by 3 ft., and at *B i* TILSHEAD 7 eight skeletons were in a heap 4 ft. in diameter and 18 in. high. In HEYTESBURY 1 it was further noted that the skulls had been separately placed to one side, as at Fussell's Lodge. Sporadic charring or scorching of the bones was noted here, and in *B i* BRATTON 1, TILSHEAD 1, and WINTERBOURNE STOKE 53. Not quite conclusive evidence of trepanning was noted in two instances at Fussell's Lodge.

---

[72] Scarborough and District Arch. Soc. *Res. Rep.* vii. 127. [74] *Anc. Europe*, ed. Coles and Simpson, 83–93.
[73] Stuart Piggott, *Anc. Europe*, 127.

Associated Finds

As elsewhere with long-barrow burials, grave-goods in the sense of those familiar from 2nd-millennium Bronze-Age graves are virtually non-existent in the Wiltshire sites. Scattered sherds were recovered at *B i* GRAFTON 5 and AVEBURY 68, in both cases of Early Neolithic type. A large part of a probably Middle Neolithic shell-gritted pot came from *B i* NORTON BAVANT 13, and at Fussell's Lodge were sherds representing a minimum of seven vessels, two virtually complete pots being with the burials. The pottery is stylistically Middle Neolithic though dated to the end of the 4th millennium B.C. A flint leaf-arrowhead was found in *B i* MILTON LILBOURNE 7 near the burials. The ditch siltings, where excavated, show the same basic stratification as those of the causewayed camps, with Late Neolithic and Beaker pottery in the upper levels only. Secondary Beaker or other Early Bronze-Age burials also occur in the mounds of long barrows as at *B i* WILSFORD (S.) 34 and FIGHELDEAN 31.

Animal bones have been found in several instances; red deer antlers in *B i* KNOOK 2 and an alleged complete goose skeleton in AMESBURY 14. Ox bones and skulls are, however, the most frequent, and in the cenotaph-barrow of *B i* BISHOP'S CANNINGS 76 three skulls were placed widely spaced down the axial fence-line. At Fussell's Lodge a skull, foot-bones and caudal vertebrate in association with the mortuary house area suggested a hide-burial, and Thurnam commented on the preponderance of skulls and feet-bones in his excavations, adding 'the appearance of the foot-bones as well as those of the neck, clearly proved that the entire members, head and feet, had been cut off while held together by the tendons, ligaments, hoofs, and probably the skin'. This may be compared with the widespread practice of hide-burial in the South Russian Pit-Grave and Catacomb cultures, from the 3rd millennium B.C. and sporadically elsewhere in prehistoric and early historic Europe,[75] without in any way arguing cultural contacts; a Wiltshire hide-burial of the Beaker period in the round barrow of *B ii* BISHOP'S CANNINGS 81 has been recorded.[76] At Fussell's Lodge the shattered ox-skull was found centrally at the front of the presumed ridge-roofed mortuary house and it is tempting to suggest that it and the outspread hide had originally graced the crest of the gabled roof at the entrance, in the manner of the bulls' heads shown in certain central European Neolithic house-models.[77]

Discussion of the place of the Wiltshire long barrows in the wider field of the British Neolithic cultures is reserved until the county's chambered tombs have been described (see p. 311). Details of the six long barrows excavated to modern standards are given below.

B i AVEBURY 47 (fig. 4)

This barrow, known as the Horslip or Windmill Hill long barrow, lies only 800 yds. SW. of the Windmill Hill causewayed camp. It was excavated in 1959 and the mound, 185 ft. long, was found to have been virtually destroyed by ploughing. It was flanked by almost parallel quarry-ditches and lay SE.–NW. No trace of internal structures or of burials survived, but there were 2 small unrelated axial holes and a line of interconnected quarry-pits on the inner side of the SW. ditch. The ditch stratification was similar to that in the Windmill Hill ditches, with Late Neolithic and Beaker pottery in the upper levels of the silt. There were many fragments of imported stones of

[75] *Antiq.* xxxvi. 110–18.
[76] *Excavs. Ann. Rep. 1965* (M.O.P.B.W. 1966), 7.
[77] E. and J. Neustupný, *Czechoslovakia before the Slavs*, 56.

Jurassic–Mendips derivation, and a C14 date of 3240±150 B.C. (BM–180) was obtained, thus showing the barrow to be contemporary with Windmill Hill Phase I.[78]

B i AVEBURY 68 (fig. 4)

This, the South Street long barrow, was inaccurately recorded by Stukeley as having a peristalith and had been considered a probable chambered tomb. Excavation, however, in 1966–7 showed it to be a rubble mound 138 ft. long and 55 ft. wide, lying ESE.–WNW., with nearly parallel quarry-ditches, and covering an axial line of stakes and hurdling with offsets making at least 40 roughly rectangular bays. There was a core of small sarsens, with some larger blocks at the eastern end, but no burials nor provision for them: the structure very closely resembles the Beckhampton Road long barrow, less than two miles away. Early Neolithic sherds occurred in the mound, and Late Neolithic and Beaker pottery high in the ditch silt. The barrow had been built on a cross-ploughed land surface, and subsequent ploughing had taken place in Beaker times. C14 dates of 2810±130, 2750±135 and 2670±140 B.C. (BM–356–358) were obtained.[79]

B i BISHOP'S CANNINGS 76 (fig. 4)

The Beckhampton Road long barrow, less than two miles S. of South Street, was excavated in 1964. The mound, SE.–NW., was 138 ft. long and 36 ft. wide at the wider E. end. The flanking quarry-ditch on the SW. was continuous, that on the NE. in two irregular segments. There had been a round barrow built on the E. end, and there was considerable recent disturbance, but no trace of primary burials nor provision for them was found. Like South Street there was an axial line of stakes and hurdling with offsets probably making an original 20 bays, the outer ends closed by further hurdling, giving the barrow a more or less trapezoid plan. Three ox-skulls had been placed on the axis and Early and Middle Neolithic sherds were found in the mound.[80]

B i CLARENDON PARK 4a (fig. 4)

The Fussell's Lodge long barrow was excavated in 1957. The mound was 160 ft. by 80 ft., lying NE.–SW. between slightly converging quarry-ditches. A trapezoid bedding-trench had held massive timber uprights and was 135 ft. long, 40 ft. wide at the NE., and 20 ft. at the SW.; 4 post-holes formed a 'porch' or fore-building at the NE. end. The disarticulated skeletons of between 53 and 57 persons lay on the axial line within the trapezoid enclosure at its broader end, with 3 pits and a cairn of flints apparently indicating a collapsed ridge-roofed timber mortuary house about 40 ft. by 10 ft. Two skulls showed possible traces of trephining. Pottery of Middle Neolithic type was associated with the burials and in other primary contexts, and Beaker and Bronze-Age pottery was in the upper silt of the ditches. An ox-skull was at the entrance to the trapezoid enclosure, and foot-bones and caudal vertebrae over the burials suggested a hide-burial. A C14 date of 3230±150 B.C. (BM–134) was obtained.[81]

B ii KINGSTON DEVERILL 1

This, originally thought to be a round barrow and listed in the gazetteer as such,[82] was excavated in 1964 and found to be a small long barrow, 60 ft. by 30 ft., with flank-

[78] *Antiq.* xxxiv. 297–9; *W.A.M.* lvii. 392.
[79] *Antiq.* xli. 289–91; xlii. 139–42.
[80] *Ibid.* xlii. 138–9.
[81] *Arch.* c. 1 sqq.
[82] *V.C.H.* i (1), p. 179.

ing quarry-ditches containing Neolithic pottery, animal bones, and antlers. Post-holes, many recut, of a timber façade and a mortuary house were found, but any burials had been removed by ploughing.[83]

B i WOODFORD 2

A small long barrow, 67 ft. by 45 ft., lying approximately N.–S. excavated in 1963. Four phases of Neolithic activity were determined; Phase I comprised 6 large pits probably for open-cast flint working, which were filled in and levelled before the barrow was built; Phase II consisted of a rectangular timber building 36 ft. by 12 ft.; Phase III was an irregularly trapezoid structure 16 ft. long by 16 ft. at its wider end; Phase IV comprised a rectangular flint cairn with weathered human bones covered by a mound of chalk derived from flanking ditches.[84]

CHAMBERED TOMBS

Within the county boundary are two groups of chambered tombs beneath long cairns, both architecturally recognizable as members of the Severn–Cotswold group. In the north-west are three sites (*B i* CHIPPENHAM 1, LUCKINGTON 1, and NETTLETON 1) situated on the Oolite, which are on the edge of the main area of Cotswold concentration and form an integral part of that group. Around the headwaters of the Kennet, on the Chalk of the Avebury region, however, is a compact group of barrows which form a detached colony of the main series with their closest relative, geographically and structurally, in Wayland's Smithy on the Berkshire Downs to the north.[85]

The three Cotswold-fringe tombs are all of the same type, representing that variant of plan (probably a late and local development) in which several burial chambers are placed laterally in the long cairn. At *B i* NETTLETON 1 (Lugbury) (fig. 5) a massive 'false portal' links the Wiltshire tombs to such well-known sites in the Cotswolds as Belas Knap (Glos.). That feature is also present at LUCKINGTON 1 (fig. 5) and another appears to have existed at CHIPPENHAM 1 (Lanhill). There is an imperfect record of skeletons from Lugbury, and at Luckington the disordered bones from a wrecked chamber included the metatarsal bone of a foot showing a marked inward bending. Such bending has been interpreted as possibly being caused by the pressure of a sandal-strap, a condition also seen in another Cotswold tomb at Nympsfield (Glos.) and in a chambered tomb in the Channel Islands. Scraps of shell-gritted Neolithic pottery were also found at Luckington.

The Lanhill chambered tomb (*B i* CHIPPENHAM 1) has suffered successive depredations since first recorded by John Aubrey and is now largely destroyed (fig. 5).[86] It appears, however, to have had an original length of about 185 ft., probably trapezoid, and some 75 ft. wide at the wider end. It lay E.–W. and was constructed of oolite rubble with dry-walled revetments, assumed at the sides and extant at the east end, where the incurving walls of a 'forecourt' were traced in 1963, converging on a probable 'false entrance' of three stones. There appear to have been two lateral burial chambers on the north side, the north-western one alone surviving, and one at least on the south side. The north-east chamber, excavated in 1936, contained 1 articulated and 8 disarticulated burials but no other finds: the southern, excavated in 1909, contained 11 or 12 disarticulated skeletons and fragmentary Middle Neolithic pottery. In the excavations

[83] A preliminary note only has been published: *W.A.M.* lx. 132.

[84] A preliminary note only has been published: *W.A.M.* lix. 185.

[85] *Megalithic Enquiries*, ed. Powell and others, 13–104, 292–5.

[86] *P.P.S.* xxxii. 73–85.

of the forecourt in 1963 Late Neolithic sherds were found and a piece of a sarsen saucer-quern. More recent excavations in *B i* LUCKINGTON 1 have not been published, except for a plan.[87]

The Avebury group of chambered tombs shows that the Severn–Cotswold architectural traditions, best represented in an area of oolite and allied rocks admirably suited to the construction of such monuments, was equally well adapted to the less tractable material of sarsen. There is however evidence from West Kennet (*B i* AVE-BURY 22) and Adam's Grave (ALTON 14) that some stones from the Great Oolite and Forest Marble deposits were actually imported from the Frome and Calne regions for use in dry-stone walling. Fragments of such rocks were, however, being brought to north Wiltshire in other Neolithic contexts, as at Windmill Hill and in long barrows *B i* AVEBURY 47, 68, BISHOP'S CANNINGS 38, 44, 65, some of which certainly do not cover chambered tombs.[88] The long stretches of fine dry-stone walling in the Cotswold tombs should probably be regarded as a local abnormality made possible by the peculiar nature of the available material, for in the combination of standing stones and dry-walling panels the tombs of the Avebury region repeat architectural modes widely employed in western and northern Britain. The covering mound, above and behind the burial chamber, contained at West Kennet an elongated core of sarsen boulders covered by rubble from the flanking ditches, like those that surrounded the unchambered barrows. There are cases (e.g. *B i* PRESHUTE 1, on Manton Down) where a true cairn appears to have been constructed.

The West Kennet chambered tomb is by far the most impressive of the Avebury group and the excavations of 1955–6 have shown it to be a very remarkable monument (fig. 5).[89] The mound itself, some 340 ft. long, is formed of an axial core of sarsen boulders covered by chalk rubble from two flanking ditches: sherds of Windmill Hill pottery were found on the old turf-line beneath the boulders. At the eastern end the five burial chambers are arranged in two pairs and one terminal chamber opening from an axial passage. The whole structure is built of massive sarsens, with capstones supported on corbelling and panels of fine dry-stone walling from the Frome and Calne regions. The passage opens upon a semi-circular forecourt, beyond which on each side upright sarsens and dry-stone panels form a straight façade to the eastern end of the mound. The peristalith recorded by Aubrey has now vanished and no trace was found in excavation. The tomb had been ceremonially blocked, presumably after the final funerals, by filling the semi-circular forecourt with sarsen boulders and setting up three flat stones, the centre one of enormous size, in line with the façade. In the forecourt immediately behind the centre blocking-stone two further stones were set up continuing the line of the passage in the manner of a false entrance.

The terminal (western) chamber had been dug out by Thurnam but the remaining four were intact. Skeletons representing a total of some 30 individuals were found on the floors of the chambers, mostly in various stages of disarticulation, accompanied by scattered sherds of Early Neolithic pottery and, in the south-east chamber, a bowl of Middle Neolithic style with shell grits. An articulated skeleton in the north-east chamber had a leaf-shaped flint arrowhead in the region of the throat. Early Neolithic pottery was also found in stone-holes of the structure.

After the final burials had been laid on the floors, the chambers and passage had been deliberately filled in successive stages with chalk rubble up to the roof. The stratification included several layers of dirty ash-laden rubble, and a large quantity of sherds,

[87] *Megalithic Enquiries*, ed. Powell and others, fig. 20.
[88] Smith, *Windmill Hill and Avebury*, 117.
[89] Piggott, *West Kennet Long Barrow* (H.M.S.O. 1962).

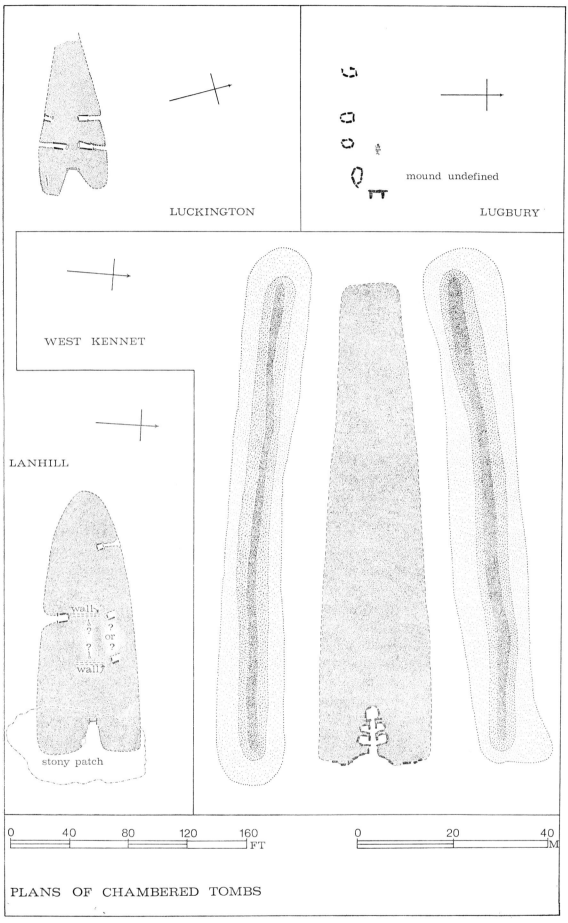

LUCKINGTON

LUGBURY

mound undefined

WEST KENNET

LANHILL

wall
? or ?
wall

stony patch

0   40   80   120   160
FT

0   20   40
M

PLANS OF CHAMBERED TOMBS

FIG. 5

animal bones, bone and flint tools, and beads including perforated shells. In the north-east chamber a mass of cremated bones representing two persons lay immediately above the primary burials. The pottery comprised large quantities of Late Neolithic wares, including the Ebbsfleet, Mortlake, and other styles, Rinyo-Clacton sherds of types closely similar to those of south-east England, and Beaker pottery including All-over-cord sherds. In the uppermost filling of the north-west chamber an almost complete early-type beaker had been inserted inverted beneath a corbel. Beaker sherds also occurred in the lowest layer of filling in the north-east chamber. In Thurnam's excavations in the last century sherds of Peterborough ware and late beakers were found in the western chamber in similar filling, but no late beaker sherds were found in the 1955–6 excavations.

The Manton long barrow (*B i* PRESHUTE 1), excavated in 1955, consisted of a single burial chamber set in the south-east end of a short broad mound. The mound, measuring 45 ft. in length and 35 ft. in width, was totally destroyed by the owner in the 1950s. It appears to have been about 4 ft. high, and to have consisted chiefly of sarsen boulders up to 15 in. in diameter with a capping of soil. At the time of its destruction it was covered with bushes and infested by rabbits.

The chamber was a single rectangular cell measuring 9 ft. by 6 ft., walled by single upright sarsen slabs on one side and at the back, and by two such slabs on the remaining side, with a single large capstone. It appears to have been intact in the 17th century, but had been in ruins at least since the 1860s. The original contents had been robbed.

Excavation revealed the stone-holes of an irregular façade across the south-east end of the mound, continued as a peristalith right round the margin. The centre portion of the façade was recessed to a depth of some 8 ft. to form a shallow forecourt into which the chamber opened. This forecourt was blocked by a setting of 3 stone-holes in line, askew to the line of the façade. The centre hole still contained a large stone, 9 ft. in height, which had fallen inwards over a pit containing an ox-skull. The two flanking holes were joined by a shallow ditch (a bedding-trench for smaller stones) which curved inwards round the inner margin of the pit. A small quantity of pottery recovered from primary positions in the stone-holes included Middle and Late Neolithic wares.

The remaining chambered tombs in the Avebury region provide practically no information except for a few architectural features, summarized elsewhere.[90] Peristaliths appear to have existed at *B i* ALTON 14 and WINTERBOURNE MONKTON 17*a*, while at the destroyed Old Chapel site (*B i* PRESHUTE 10*c*) and the Devil's Den (*B i* PRESHUTE 3*a*) some sort of a curved façade seems, from Stukeley's drawings, to have flanked the chamber entrance in a manner comparable with West Kennet. At Old Chapel (now destroyed) the chamber seems to have been rectangular, perhaps similar to that surviving at Manton Down, while the existing stone structure at the Devil's Den may either represent (as is usually thought) a 'false portal' in the Lugbury–Belas-Knap manner, or it may be the remains of another rectangular chamber. A similar explanation has recently been put forward for the analogous surviving stones at Kits Coty House (Kent). The excavations in the Temple Bottom chamber (*B i* OGBOURNE ST. ANDREW 19) did not elucidate its precise plan, but inhumations and cremations appear to have been found, together with a bone chisel-ended tool (comparable with two from West Kennet) and a stone pounder.

If the Wiltshire long barrows and chambered tombs present complex problems, they are problems common to such tombs throughout the areas of their distribution in

[90] *Megalithic Enquiries*, ed. Powell and others, 292–5.

Britain, and the Wiltshire monuments, although with individual characteristics, have features which can be paralleled elsewhere. Other cenotaph long barrows are known, such as Thickthorn in Dorset; the subdivision by hurdling has partial parallels in the Giants' Hills, Skendleby, barrow in Lincolnshire, or in stone versions in the Severn–Cotswold tombs. Fussell's Lodge contains features, such as trapezoid enclosure and mortuary house, which can be compared with several other British long barrows.

It can be seen that the Wiltshire long barrows, like those on the Chalk of Wessex and Sussex, are the products of communities which also made and used causewayed camps, and are chronologically contemporary with those sites over the first half of the 3rd millennium B.C. Their distribution, however, stopping on the west along a line from Bridport (Dors.) to Chippenham, as shown above, precludes their assignation to the same branch of Early Neolithic known from such sites as Hembury and Hazard Hill (Devon), and as far west as Carn Brea (Cornw.). Furthermore their distribution pattern, overlapping in the Avebury region, virtually complements that of the Severn–Cotswold chambered tombs set in stone-built mounds of similar plan. If it is accepted that the British Early Neolithic cultures contained at least two basic elements, with broadly eastern and western continental antecedents, this distribution suggests affiliations with the easterly component.

It is very hard to decide whether long barrows and the Severn–Cotswold chambered tombs were the burial-places of all the members of a community or only of part of it. This cardinal demographic problem has been touched upon in an earlier section. Atkinson has argued that the long-barrow evidence might favour the former, the chambered tombs the latter alternative. Whatever the answer, it is clear that we are dealing with small population groups in a social situation in which organized communal labour in tomb-building could be mustered when needed. Ashbee, commenting on the massive timbers required at Fussell's Lodge, has made the point that shifting tree-trunks weighing up to $2\frac{1}{2}$ tons demands labour commensurate with building megalithic monuments.

The trapezoid or elongated rectangular plans of the long barrows and the ridge-roofed mortuary houses have both been used to support a connexion with similar structures in the Funnel Beaker (TRB)[91] and other cultures of the north European plain, and despite recent criticism, already noted, the thesis cannot easily be dismissed. It now seems beyond dispute that the similar planning of the Severn–Cotswold tombs is derived from long barrows with timber structures and that the 'Pornic–Notgrove' type of tomb chamber, with lateral transepts, represents a separate architectural element relating, as the name implies, the Severn estuary to the west French coastal areas. The Wiltshire chambered tombs such as West Kennet would then be monuments representing a fusion of traditions in ritual and funerary architecture brought about along the western edge of the long barrow distribution-area. No date can be given to West Kennet in the lack of suitable primary material for radiocarbon assay, but at Wayland's Smithy the similar chambered tomb, forming Phase II on the site, overlay a small long barrow with mortuary house and was constructed about 2800 B.C. The date of West Kennet should be the same or rather earlier: pottery of Early Neolithic type was primary there, but at Wayland's Smithy such pottery belonged to the Phase I barrow, the chambered tomb being associated with shell-gritted wares appropriate to the Middle Neolithic. It is even possible that the huge mound of West Kennet contains an earlier long barrow, a possibility not foreseen during the 1955 excavations before the Wayland's Smithy evidence was known.

[91] TRB standing for *Trichter-Rand-Becher.*

OTHER BARROW-BURIALS

Three burials should be mentioned here, which have claims to be regarded as Neolithic, although under round barrows of a type usually associated with the Bronze Age. At Dilton (*B ia* WESTBURY 7) 7 or 8 disarticulated skeletons were found beneath a barrow the material of which had been dug from a series of quarry-pits around its circumference in a manner recalling the ditches of causewayed camps; such collective burial under a round mound is also known from Cambridgeshire and Yorkshire. A less easily paralleled burial is that at *B ia* MERE 13*d*, with a cremation and a round-based shouldered bowl of a type which, while precise analogies are wanting, should come within the Windmill Hill group.

The excavation in 1961 of *B ii* AMESBURY 71, a round barrow on Earl's Farm Down, showed it to be a burial monument of several periods (fig. 17).[92] Phase I consisted of a small ring-ditch, 22 ft. in diameter, containing an irregular **C**-shaped setting of 17 stakes, irregularly spaced 3–4 ft. apart, within which had been an inhumation burial on the old surface. The surface had been disturbed and the whole site covered with a subsequent barrow in Phase II, with an unaccompanied inhumation-burial in a deep grave-pit and a C14 date of 2010±110 B.C. (NPL–77). This barrow represents a Single-Grave burial of the general type associated in Britain with the Beaker and allied cultures in the early 2nd millennium B.C. and Phase I is likely to be a Late Neolithic burial. But even here there are presumably early Single-Grave traditions, as in W. Glasbergen's Type 3 post-circles in the Netherlands.[93]

LONG MORTUARY ENCLOSURES

A single example of a rare type of Neolithic funerary monument existed on Normanton Down until its surface features were destroyed by ploughing in the 1950s. It was excavated in 1959 (fig. 6).[94] It was found to be an oblong enclosure with rounded ends, lying ESE.–WNW., with a small causewayed ditch and internal bank, 124 ft. by 68 ft. overall. A wider causeway formed an entrance at the western end, within which a pair of bedding-trenches had each held three timber uprights with longitudinal wood bracing. No other internal features were found, but such features could have been destroyed by natural weathering of the Chalk and subsequent deep ploughing. Antler picks occurred in the primary ditch silt, and a sherd of Late Neolithic (Mortlake) pottery in the upper level. The timber structure might be analogous to Corded-Ware mortuary houses in Thuringia.[95]

Similar enclosures are known in Oxfordshire at Dorchester and North Stoke on the Thames gravels, and another formed part of the primary features in the Wor Barrow long barrow in Dorset: at Dorchester Middle–Late Neolithic (Ebbsfleet) pottery was in a secondary context in the ditch, and the site was earlier than a cursus monument of a type discussed in a later section.[96] It has been thought likely that such enclosures were related to funerary practices associated with long-barrow burials, including the exposure of corpses.

[92] *P.P.S.* xxxiii. 336–66.
[93] *Palaeohist.* iii. 19–42.
[94] *P.P.S.* xxvii. 160–73.

[95] G. Behm-Blancke, *Alt-Thuringen*, i. 63.
[96] *Arch. News Letter*, Nov.–Dec. 1951, 56; Atkinson and others, *Excav. at Dorchester, Oxon.* (First Rep.).

CEREMONIAL MONUMENTS

One of the most arresting and remarkable features of the later Neolithic cultures in Britain is the widespread construction of what may best be termed ceremonial monuments, which appear on occasion to be grouped in cult centres. These monuments, not directly sepulchral though often associated with burials, may be circular or linear earthwork constructions, sometimes of great size, and settings of standing stones, wooden posts, or non-utilitarian pits, all of which may reasonably be regarded as serving ritual or religious functions associated with communal ceremonial activities. Wiltshire has two of the most extraordinary cult centres in the country, at Stonehenge and Avebury, as well as other monuments in the ceremonial class of outstanding interest. In general, the British sites of this type have virtually no counterparts in contemporary cultures on the European Continent. They must, therefore, be regarded as the products of indigenous traditions, developed under social conditions which permitted and encouraged the employment of manpower on a relatively large scale under the direction of centralized authority and the training and maintenance of skilled craftsmen dedicated to this end.

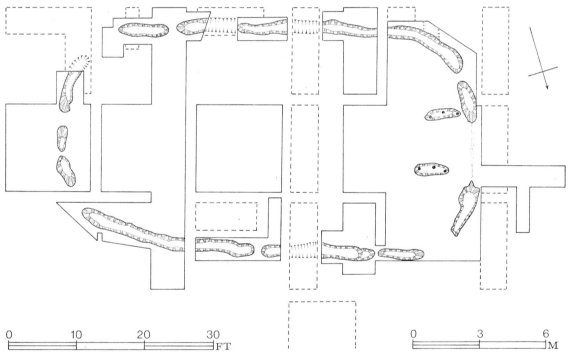

0   10   20   30 FT   0   3   6 M

NORMANTON DOWN: LONG MORTUARY ENCLOSURE

FIG. 6

That organization and authority can be inferred, but in the non-literate context of prehistoric religion and ritual practice its nature can only be guessed at in the vaguest terms, and the nature of the beliefs, which prompted the activity of which the monuments are the tangible memorial, must remain unknown. A concern with astronomical and calendrical observations is not unlikely, though the evidence cannot be used without caution: it is discussed briefly in a later section, but it may be said here that because modern mathematicians can demonstrate that a site could have been used for certain defined purposes it does not follow that it was so used by its builders. An ethnological parallel for the British situation, which may well be a valid one, is the construction of large and elaborate ceremonial centres consisting of circular and linear earthworks among the North American Plains Indians in the early centuries A.D.: those of the Adena and Hopewell cultures in the Ohio region present remarkably apt parallels to the Wiltshire situation in the early 2nd millennium B.C., including elaborate and richly furnished round-barrow burials in association with the earthwork enclosures.[97] Ritual timber circles were, as is known from John White's drawings, used by the Virginian Indians in the 16th century.[98] In view of the affiliations of much of Amer-indian religion, it may even not be wholly fantastic to remember the circular shaman's hut with its attendant settings of posts and post-images in recent Siberia.[99]

Individual ceremonial monuments in Wiltshire are described briefly at the end of this section; full descriptions are now available of Stonehenge[1] and of Avebury[2] and need not be repeated here. The main concern is to outline the classification of the various types of monument, to set them in a chronological framework, and to consider briefly some problems of interpretation.

Henge Monuments

The major group of structures are those which have become called henge monu-ments, a jocular back-formation from 'Stonehenge' which has come to be accepted. In their essentials these monuments consist of a circular area enclosed with a ditch and a normally external bank, with one entrance (Class I) as at Stonehenge I and Wood-henge, or two (Class II) as at Durrington Walls, or exceptionally as at Avebury, four (fig. 7); Marden is quite anomalous.[3] Such structures are widely spread in Britain, from Cornwall to the Orkneys, and the inner area may contain no trace of structures, as at Gorsey Bigbury in Somerset or King Arthur's Round Table in Westmorland. The Wiltshire monuments, however, all have internal features which are of three kinds, ritual pits with associated cremation burials, timber settings, and stone settings. The first kind occurs in the first phase of Stonehenge and at Dorchester (Oxon.). Timber settings exist at Woodhenge, within Durrington Walls, and at Marden, with a more or less comparable site at Arminghall in Norfolk; the stone settings at Avebury have many counterparts, as at the Stripple Stones in Cornwall, Arbour Low in Derbyshire, or Cairn-papple and the Ring of Brogar in Scotland. Stonehenge has an exceptional series of building phases subsequent to the first monument, and more than one phase is possible but unproved at Avebury and at Durrington Walls. The timber settings at Woodhenge and at the Sanctuary (Avebury) unditched site, described below, have been interpreted as roofed structures, but free-standing posts are perhaps equally possible here and at Durrington Walls and Marden.

As shown above, there may be some connexion in tradition and basic structure between henge monuments and the concentric-ditched causewayed camps, and C14 dates from Arminghall and Barford (Warws.) may suggest that the former were already being built in Middle Neolithic times around the middle of the 3rd millennium B.C. Finds of pottery and other artefacts in henge monuments are normally so rare as to suggest that the sites were kept ritually clean, but the evidence from Stonehenge I and Avebury imply a Late Neolithic date for both monuments, confirmed by the C14 date of 2180±105 B.C. (I–2328) from the Stonehenge site. At Woodhenge and the nearby Durrington Walls the very large amount of occupation debris seems best accounted for by supposing Woodhenge, and the southern part of Durrington Walls, to have been

[97] J. G. D. Clark and Stuart Piggott, *Prehistoric Societies*, 180; *Archaeology of E. United States*, ed. J. B. Griffin, 83.
[98] Cf. *Arch. Jnl.* xcvi, p. 195, fig. 1.
[99] *Studies in Siberian Shamanism*, ed. H. N. Michael, 84, fig. 8.

[1] R. J. C. Atkinson, *Stonehenge* (Pelican edn. 1960).
[2] Smith, *Windmill Hill and Avebury*, 175–254.
[3] For Marden see BEECHINGSTOKE in *V.C.H. Wilts.* i (1).

constructed over a slightly earlier settlement of some size, and dates of 1680±110 B.C. and 1610±120 B.C. (BM–236, 285) from this material at Durrington Walls, which included Late Neolithic (Rinyo-Clacton) and Beaker pottery, must be virtually those of the monuments themselves. With Middle Neolithic origins, therefore, the henges seem as a whole to be phenomena that developed in Late Neolithic times and were in part contemporary with the Beaker cultures later to be described.

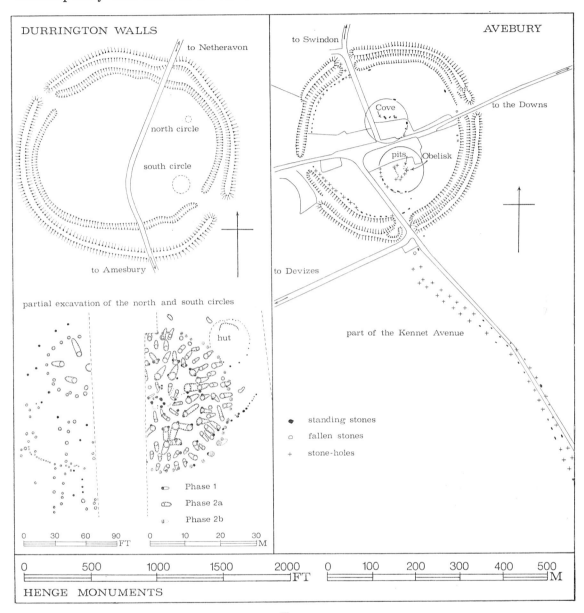

FIG. 7

Timber Circles

A unique setting of timber and stone uprights was excavated at the Sanctuary site, which forms the termination of the West Kennet Avenue of standing stones at Avebury. Here there was no enclosing ditch, and the complex stone and post rings are almost certainly of different constructional phases, the timber elements of which have been interpreted as a succession of roofed structures. While the alternative of free-standing posts cannot wholly be excluded, the interpretation of the relatively large amount of pottery, flints, etc., on the site as successive votive offerings deposited under cover may support the former interpretation. This material may go back to Middle Neolithic times

319

but is predominantly Late Neolithic, and a Beaker burial of the penultimate phase would, on Dutch analogies, have a likely date of *c.* 1650 B.C., contemporary with Wood-henge and Durrington Walls. At Durrington Walls two free-standing multiple timber circles were found within the huge henge monument and more may exist unexcavated elsewhere within the circuit. The excavations of 1969 at Marden revealed an analogous situation and in both instances roofed structures may be represented.

Stone Circles

The Durrington Walls situation suggests comparison with the free-standing Inner Circles at Avebury, which appear to be broadly contemporary with the main henge monument in construction. Other simple stone circles exist in the county, as at Winter-bourne Bassett, and are presumably broadly within the first half of the 2nd millennium B.C. Such free-standing stone circles have a wide distribution in Britain.[4]

Cursus Monuments and Avenues

Two linear forms of ceremonial monuments may be taken together, the cursus, and the avenues bounded by earthworks or rows of standing stones (figs. 8, 9). The first group consists of very elongated rectangular enclosures of bank-and-ditch construction such as the Stonehenge Cursus, 1¾ mile long and 330 ft. wide, first recognized by Stukeley and named a *cursus* from his belief that chariot-racing took place along its length. Cursus monuments are now known to have a wide distribution from Dorset to Perthshire, and often occur in proximity to henges as components of ceremonial centres. The Stonehenge Cursus has its eastern termination just short of a long barrow lying at right angles to its line, and the Dorset Cursus can be shown to be later than one long barrow and almost certainly than a second. At Dorchester (Oxon.) a cursus is later than a long mortuary enclosure and a small henge monument comparable with Stonehenge I, while at Thornborough (Yorks. N.R.) a cursus is overlaid by a large Class II henge. In general, then, these monuments seem to be Late Neolithic in date.

Ceremonial avenues occur in Wiltshire at Stonehenge and Avebury. The Stonehenge Avenue was added to the re-aligned entrances of the henge monument of Stonehenge I in Phase II, and is defined by parallel banks and ditches 70 ft. apart running straight for 1,800 ft. on the axis of Stonehenge II/III, thence curving across the ridge to the river Avon. Even though considerable land must have been cleared of forest for agricultural purposes by the 17th century B.C., it cannot be assumed that Stonehenge stood in open country at that time, and the Avenue could well have marked a clearance through woodland. At Avebury the West Kennet Avenue is defined by pairs of standing stones and is some 50 ft. wide, running in an irregularly curving course for 1½ mile south-east of the Great Circle to the Sanctuary post and stone circles. Its construction is tied to the main phase of building on the site in the Late Neolithic–Beaker phase, contemporary with Stonehenge II, for which there is a C14 date of 1620±110 B.C. (I–2334), and with Windmill Hill III (1550±150 B.C. BM–75). The bank-and-ditch construction of the Stonehenge Avenue is unique, but partial parallels to the Avebury Avenue can be found at Stanton Drew (Som.) and in the double alignments of standing stones associated with simple stone circles in Wales and on Dartmoor. In the Netherlands Barrow 75 in the Noordse Veld at Zeijen shows a miniature version, 150 ft. long, of an avenue of double-post-rows leading up to the timber circles of the barrow itself, the whole probably not earlier than the 13th–14th century B.C.[5]

---

[4] Atkinson and others, *Excav. at Dorchester, Oxon.* (First Rep.), fig. 29, for generalized map.
[5] S. de Laet, *The Low Countries*, 119.

Silbury Hill

The radiocarbon date obtained from primary material under the innermost core of Silbury Hill, 2145±95 B.C. (I–4136), shows that this enormous circular mound, 550 ft. in diameter and 130 ft. high, belongs to the Late Neolithic and is strictly contemporary with Stonehenge I. It therefore takes its place as an element in the Avebury ceremonial centre and one may perhaps compare the situation with that of Knowlton in Dorset, where an exceptionally large circular mound, 125 ft. in diameter, adjoins the henge monuments. Further discussion of Silbury Hill must await the full result of the excavations of the 1960s.

Stonehenge

The Stonehenge sequence is set out at the end of this section, but the structures of Phases II and III are extraordinary and without parallels and demand comment here (fig. 8). Following the more or less traditional henge monument of Stonehenge I (Bank, Ditch, Aubrey Holes, cremation-cemetery, and Heel Stone) there comes the unfinished monument of Stonehenge II, composed of stones (bluestones) brought from the Prescelly Mountains in Pembrokeshire. Such a transportation of stones to build a ceremonial monument is unique, as was the plan of the double circle with elaborate entrance on an axis differing by 5° from Stonehenge I but coincident with the subsequent Stonehenge III. This Phase II circle was never completed but when partially erected was dismantled. The C14 date of 1620±110 B.C. (I–2384) for Stonehenge II is consonant with the finds of Beaker pottery on the site and with the known use of Prescelly stone for battle-axes in Late Beaker contexts. Such a date for the bluestone block in the long barrow of Bowl's Barrow (see p. 306) would, however, be quite at variance with the date of such barrows in the Early and Middle Neolithic which all other evidence implies. It remains, therefore, an unresolved problem.

Stonehenge III, in its three sub-phases, raises an entirely new set of problems. The use of dressed and tooled stones; the architectural concepts embodied in the lintels to trilithons and peristyle; the skeuomorphs of carpentry techniques; the engineering problems involved in the transport, dressing, and erection of the sarsen blocks; the social implications of the organization of skilled craftsmen and heavy labour forces— all these factors, unique to the monument, have led many archaeologists to look to centres of higher civilization outside Britain for the motivating force behind this extraordinary display of authoritarianism and technical expertise in the 2nd millennium B.C.

The question is bound up with that of the status of the 'Wessex culture' of the 2nd millennium B.C., discussed in a later section, with which the Phase III structures of Stonehenge have been inferentially associated. In both instances Mycenaean Greece has been invoked to explain the exotic or unparalleled features at Stonehenge and in the rich barrow-burials, but that arresting and perhaps romantic thesis of thirty years ago[6] may fail to stand up to a reassessment of the evidence in modern terms. The question is discussed at greater length below, but for Stonehenge III the following points must be made. In the first place the well known dagger carving on Stone 53, originally claimed as representing not a British but a Mycenaean type, can hardly be used with any degree of confidence as conclusive evidence, especially with the very imperfect knowledge existing of the details of dagger-hafts in Britain in the 2nd millennium B.C. The second point arises from a consideration of radiocarbon dating.

[6] *P.P.S.* iv. 95.

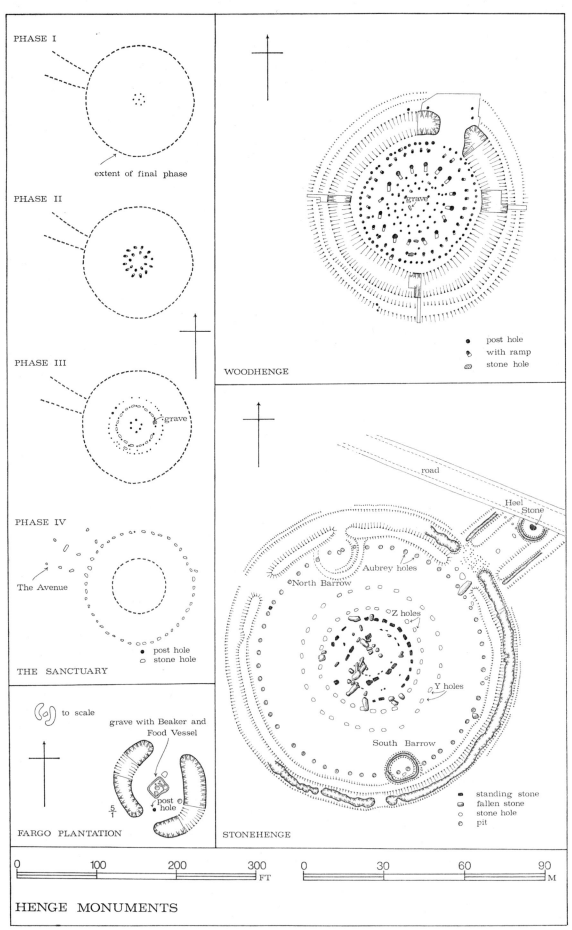

PHASE I

extent of final phase

PHASE II

PHASE III

grave

PHASE IV

The Avenue

● post hole
○ stone hole

THE SANCTUARY

(◦) to scale

grave with Beaker and
Food Vessel

post
hole

5
1

FARGO PLANTATION

WOODHENGE

● post hole
◐ with ramp
▨ stone hole

road

Heel
Stone

Aubrey holes

North Barrow

Z holes

Y holes

South Barrow

■ standing stone
▢ fallen stone
○ stone hole
◉ pit

STONEHENGE

0   100   200   300
FT

0   30   60   90
M

HENGE MONUMENTS

FIG. 8

322

Here there are at the outset difficulties at Stonehenge itself. An antler from the ramp of Stone 56, dug at the Stonehenge III a/b transition, gave a C14 date of 1720±150 B.C. (BM-46). This is in conflict, not only with the Stonehenge II date of *c.* 1620 referred to above, but more seriously, with that of 1240±105 B.C. (I-2445) from an antler in Hole Y 30 of Stonehenge II b, a situation that could only be resolved by assuming that the Stone 56 antler was derived from a Stonehenge II 'horizon'. If such an explanation be accepted, the relationship of C14 dates to the solar calendar years as normally employed in historical dating must be considered, for comparisons between Wiltshire and Greece in the 2nd millennium B.C. must be in terms of radiocarbon dates as compared with dates derived from historical extrapolation from the chronology of Egypt. It is now becoming apparent that, back at least to 4000 B.C., C14 dates diverge from 'true' solar years in an irregular but increasing degree, and on the curve currently available the 'corrected' Stonehenge dates would read approximately Stonehenge I 2940±105 B.C.; Stonehenge II 2080±110 B.C.; Stonehenge III b (Y 30 date) 1500± 105 B.C. Such readings would in fact give Stonehenge III, the elaborate dressed stone structure, an historical date which would still permit correlation with Mycenaean Greece in the Early Helladic I–II periods, even if, as will be shown, the same calibration would suggest that the Wessex culture was in being before 2000 B.C. on the historical time-scale. If this is indeed the case, the evidence of the barrow-burials cannot be used to support a Mycenaean connexion for Stonehenge III as has been the tendency in the past.

Mathematics and Astronomy in Ceremonial Monuments

In the 1960s several writers reverted to earlier theories, themselves discredited when formulated,[7] that Stonehenge, and indeed other henge monuments and stone circles, were designed by men of advanced mathematical and astronomical knowledge and that the purpose of the monuments was at least partly to aid mathematical and astronomical calculations.[8] The mathematics underlying the recent exposition of these theories are indeed beyond the capacity of the average archaeologist, but the mathematicians have mistaken some of the archaeological evidence and have disregarded the historical probabilities. G. S. Hawkins argued that the 56 Aubrey Holes were an eclipse-predictor but ignored their nature and conflated the evidence of more than one period. Fred Hoyle, using the same evidence as Hawkins, suggested a different astronomical use. Each has done no more than show how Stonehenge could be used for astronomical purposes, which is by no means the same as showing that it was constructed for such purposes. It is indeed true that the axis of Phases II and III is aligned upon the midsummer sunrise, but it must be remembered that in southern England at least, such monuments as these probably stood in country relatively densely wooded where the horizon was not a more or less clear straight line.

Alexander Thom has suggested that stone circles and timber settings such as Woodhenge were all, however off-circular, laid out by precise and often complicated geometrical processes, involving, among other things, a standard unit of measurement (2·72 ft.), undeviatingly adhered to from Cornwall to Orkney, and a knowledge of Pythagorean triangles. He also suggests that accurate sightings of celestial phenomena,

[7] Foremost amongst those suggesting an astronomical use was Sir Norman Lockyer: *Stonehenge . . . Astronomically Considered.*

[8] G. S. Hawkins and J. B. White, *Stonehenge Decoded*; Fred Hoyle, 'Speculations on Stonehenge', *Antiq.* xl. 262–76; Alexander Thom, 'Megaliths and Mathematics',

Antiq. xl. 121–8; discussion by R. J. C. Atkinson, 'Moonshine on Stonehenge', *Antiq.* xl. 212–16; Jacquetta Hawkes, 'God in the Machine', *Antiq.* xli. 174–80; review by A. H. A. Hogg, *Arch. Camb.* cxvii. 207–10; Euan MacKie, *Current Archaeology*, xi. 279–83.

especially of stars, were intentional functions of such monuments. It is to be noted, however, that in the instance of Woodhenge Thom would not accept the excavators' plan, but used one made from the modern reconstructed layout of concrete posts, the precise relationship of which to the original posts is unknown. A follower of Thom has taken his Woodhenge alignment and assigned it to the rising of Betelgeuse in 2500 B.C. (Thom preferred Capella in *c.* 1800) and thence concluded that the plan and orientation of the chancel of Canterbury Cathedral were determined by a pre-existing monument of Woodhenge type.[9]

All these theorists seem to forget that it is most improbable that the non-literate farming communities of 3rd- and early 2nd-millennium Britain could have possessed a knowledge of advanced mathematics beyond the standard reached by the civilized societies of antiquity. To maintain their theses Hoyle had to postulate an abnormal gene-pool of mathematically gifted persons in the Wiltshire of the age, Thom a 'headquarters from which standard rods were sent out' to maintain consistently the unit of 2·72 ft. all over Britain. To build Stonehenge III did indeed require skilled craftsmanship and powers of organizing labour of a high order, but since many early civilizations with no more than rudimentary mathematics achieved greater architectural feats, there is no need to suppose that Neolithic Wiltshire was peopled by mute inglorious Newtons. 'The mathematical requirements', it has been said, 'for even the most developed economic structures of antiquity can be satisfied with elementary household arithmetic which no mathematician would call mathematics.'[10]

THE MONUMENTS

Ceremonial Complex, AVEBURY

The henge monument and ancillary sites at AVEBURY (fig. 7) have been described in several publications.[11] Here attention will be concentrated on the building sequence so far as one can be worked out. The complex of ceremonial monuments consists of four main elements: the Henge or Great Circle, the West Kennet Avenue, the Sanctuary, and the problematical Beckhampton Avenue. Throughout the stones used are local sarsen, and, while certainly selected with an eye to specific shapes, are not worked.

The Great Circle

The Circle, containing much of the village of Avebury, consists first of a huge *Bank* with internal *Ditch*, roughly circular, with four original entrances. It encloses some 28 acres, an area rather less than that of Durrington Walls and considerably less than that of Marden. The Middle and Late Neolithic pottery and *petit tranchet* derivative arrowheads on the old surface under the Bank imply that the Circle was constructed in Late Neolithic times. Contemporary with the Bank and Ditch and following the inner edge of the latter is the *Outer Circle* of standing stones, probably originally 98 in number. Contrasting broad and narrow stones occur but not in regular relationships.

Within the circuit are two free-standing stone circles. The *North Inner Circle* probably originally consisted of 27 stones in a circle, 320 ft. in diameter, with a probable inner circle of 12 stones, 140 ft. in diameter. Centrally there was originally a setting of three stones (the 'Cove'). The *South Inner Circle*, originally of 39 stones with a diameter of 340 ft., had a central stone, now destroyed (the 'Obelisk'), and an eccentric

[9] L. B. Borst, 'Meg. Plan underlying Cant. Cath.', *Science*, clxiii, no. 3867, 567–9.

[10] O. Neugebauer, *Exact Sciences in Antiquity*, 71–2.

[11] For detailed account see Isobel Smith, *Windmill Hill and Avebury*, 175–254; for short account see D. D. A. Simpson in Pevsner, *Wilts.* (Buildings of Eng.), 87 sqq.

Stonehenge, Amesbury: sarsen trilithon

WEST KENNET CHAMBERED TOMB, AVEBURY

stone (D) within its circuit. It also contained an *Inner Setting* of small stones arranged in a rectilinear plan. The presence of Lower Chalk packing blocks obtained from the lowest level of the Ditch makes the Inner Setting and Ditch contemporary. The stone-hole (D) contained weathered Beaker sherds and should thus be later and is probably contemporary with the Beaker sherds late in the sequence of the Ditch silting.

Other stones, or stone-holes, within the Outer Circle include the *Ring Stone*, a naturally perforated sarsen formerly S. of the South Inner Circle, and stone-hole (A) at the N. The Lower Chalk packing in the socket of the *Ring Stone* makes it contemporary with the digging of the Ditch; stone-hole (A) is earlier than the Outer Circle.

There is no evidence that the monument is not basically of one period, although probably with successive structural phases following closely on one another. It is probably of the early 2nd millennium B.C. within the mixed context of Late Neolithic and Beaker cultures described below.

The West Kennet Avenue

The Avenue consisted of a double line of standing stones some 49 ft. apart in pairs wherein a broad stone faces a narrow one. There were probably originally 100 such pairs, running SE. from the southern entrance of the Great Circle in an irregularly curved course for $1\frac{1}{2}$ mile, ending in the stone and wood circles of the Sanctuary on Overton Hill. The northern third of the Avenue was excavated in 1934–5 and 1939. Graves with Beaker inhumations were found against two stones (25b and 29a) and one with a bowl of Rinyo-Clacton affiliations against Stone 22b. The beakers are both early in the British sequence (see p. 341). The Late Neolithic occupation site on the line of the Avenue has already been described (see p. 300).

The Sanctuary

The complex of stones and post circles on Overton Hill, the 'antiquarian' title of which was recorded by Stukeley, was excavated in 1930 when the stones had been long destroyed.[12] It was reinterpreted in terms of successive roofed structures ten years later[13] and discussed in the context of the whole Avebury complex by Isobel Smith (fig. 7).[14]

Whether or not the roofing interpretation is accepted, the constructional sequence still seems fairly valid: support for the idea of covered buildings is given by the presence of abundant finds of pottery, bone, and flint, suggesting offerings in a ritual or mortuary building. The sequence would start with Phase I, the circular hut of the F Ring of post-holes. No pottery came from these holes but the phase is presumably contemporary with the Ebbsfleet and sandy Middle Neolithic sherds on the site. The Phase II building (D and E Rings) would follow quickly in construction and be contemporary with the Rinyo-Clacton and All-over-cord Beaker pottery and, at Avebury itself, with the Great Circle and part at least of the West Kennet Avenue. Phase III involves both posts and stones in the B, C, and G Rings and is dated by an inhumation burial with a beaker broadly of 'Barbed-Wire' type against one of the stones; such beakers in the Netherlands have dates of 1670 ± 65 B.C. (GrN-352) and 1645 ± 85 B.C. (GrN-1977). This phase would be contemporary with the Late Beaker sherds in the filling of the Ditch at Avebury, with Durrington Walls, with the Food-Vessel burials in *B ii* AMESBURY 71, and with some graves of the Wessex culture (see p. 354). Phase IV, the

---

[12] *W.A.M.* xlv. 300 sqq.　　[13] *Arch. Jnl.* xcvi. 193–222.　　[14] Smith, *Windmill Hill and Avebury*, 244.

stones of the A Ring at the Sanctuary, would be later, perhaps contemporary with the collared-urn fragments in the Avebury Ditch, and Windmill Hill III, *c.* 1540 B.C. An alternative possibility is to modify the sequence so as to make the two stone circles subsequent to all the timber features.

The Beckhampton Avenue

The existence of an avenue comparable with that of West Kennet, but running from the west entrance of the Great Circle, has often been called in doubt since Stukeley's claim that evidence was sufficient on the point. The case was restated in 1965 in detail[15] and recent unpublished finds of buried stones on the presumed line add further support. This line would incorporate the pair of standing stones (the Longstones, the Devil's Coits, or Adam and Eve) to the W. of Avebury; one of these had an inhumation burial at its base with an early (European type) beaker.[16]

Silbury Hill, AVEBURY

Excavations in 1968 showed that the building of the mound was apparently a continuous process, divided into four stages. Silbury I lay at the centre and was a conical mound of complex layered construction, about 120 ft. in diameter and 16 ft. high, composed of turf, soil, and gravel dug out from the surrounding slopes and from the valley to the E. and N. of the site. It contained a core of piled turves and soil reveted by a ring of stakes.

This innermost mound had been in turn covered by the chalk mound of Silbury II, dug out from a large ditch with an inner diameter of about 350 ft. Before the excavation of this ditch was completed, it was evidently decided to build an even bigger mound. The ditch already excavated was carefully filled up and covered over by the enlarged mound of Silbury III, built of chalk rubble obtained from the ditch which is still visible round the base of the hill. It seems likely that the third mound was constructed originally, to secure structural stability, in the form of a stepped cone, and that the steps were later filled in, after the original material had consolidated, to give the present smooth profile. The chalk rubble used in this final phase (Silbury IV) may have been derived from the westwards extension of the ditch of Silbury III.

That ditch appears to be about 20 ft. deep and is filled with alluvial silt, probably as the result of intermittent flooding from very early times. Little, if any, of this silt seems to have been eroded from the slopes of the mound, which is substantially still in its original form.

The turf stack in the centre of the primary mound preserved considerable prehistoric vegetation and insect life, and gave a C14 date of 2145±95 B.C. (I–4136).[17]

Stonehenge, AMESBURY

There are two up-to-date and detailed accounts of Stonehenge.[18] The constructional sequence is complex, and in every stage the monument has unique features unparalleled elsewhere (fig. 8).

Phase I consists of the bank and its external ditch, 320 ft. in diameter crest-to-crest, the ditch being of 'causewayed' construction and having a single entrance, 35 ft. wide,

[15] Smith, *Windmill Hill and Avebury*, 216.
[16] *W.A.M.* xxxviii. 1–11.
[17] *Bull. W.A. & N.H. Soc.* v. 1; *Antiq.* xliii. 216.
[18] Atkinson, *Stonehenge* (Pelican edn. 1960); D. D. A. Simpson, in Pevsner, *Wilts.* (Buildings of Eng.), 439–45.

on the NE. Within and contemporary is the accurate circle of 56 *Aubrey Holes*, 288 ft. in diameter, and consisting of pits from $2\frac{1}{2}$ ft. to 6 ft. in diameter and from 2 ft. to $3\frac{1}{2}$ ft. deep, refilled and sometimes partially re-excavated and filled again in antiquity. A cremation-cemetery of at least 55 burials lies over the E. and SE. of the perimeter, some of the burials having been inserted immediately after the digging of the ditch and others in its silt or in the filling of the Aubrey Holes. Symmetrical with the layout of Phase I is the upright unworked sarsen, the *Heel Stone*, 4 post-holes, and stone-holes D and E, all outside the entrance; they are earlier than the Phase II layout and so assigned to

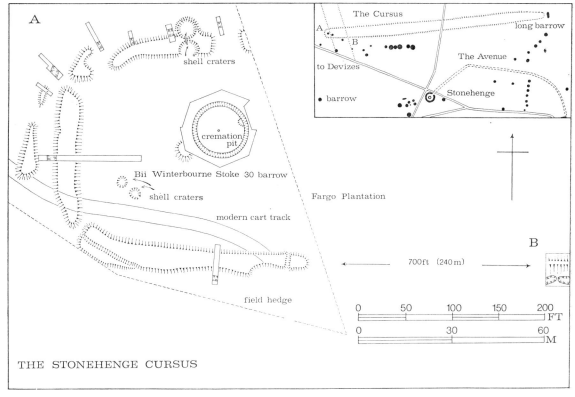

THE STONEHENGE CURSUS

FIG. 9

Phase I. The bank, ditch, Aubrey Holes, and cremation-cemetery together constitute an aberrant but recognizable version of a Class I henge monument, with good parallels at Dorchester (Oxon.). Rinyo-Clacton pottery was primary in the ditch silt, and Beaker secondary, while Late Neolithic bone pins and a stone mace-head were associated with some of the cremations. A C14 date for the construction of the bank and ditch is 2180 ± 105 B.C. (I-2328).

Phase II is marked by the transport to Stonehenge of the bluestones from a restricted area of south-west Wales and mainly the Prescelly Mountains, and by the abortive setting-up of these, as unworked blocks into unfinished double circles having mean diameters of 86 ft. and 74 ft. in the middle of Stonehenge I. An elaborate entrance was aligned on the same axis of what was to be the Phase III monument. The entrance through the bank and ditch of Phase I was adjusted by filling in part of the ditch to become symmetrical with the new plan, which probably shared the Phase III centre, rather than that, $3\frac{1}{2}$ ft. away, of the Aubrey Holes of Phase I. The double circle was not completed, although stones were set up in such sockets as had been dug. Also within this phase a small circular ditch was dug round the Heel Stone, the 4 posts and Stones

D and E dismantled, and an avenue demarcated, leading NE. from the entrance. The avenue consisted of a pair of parallel banks and ditches, 70 ft. apart at the entrance, running on the axial line straight for 1,800 ft.; turning E. through 50° and running for another 2,000 ft. to the King Barrow Ridge; thence making down the slope towards the river Avon, varying in width between 84 ft. and 113 ft. and having a total length of 1¾ mile.

A radiocarbon date for the unfinished double circle is 1620±110 B.C. (I–2384), which would be in agreement with Late Beaker dates elsewhere or the Food-Vessel burials in *B ii* AMESBURY 71. The use of Prescelly stone for shaft-hole battle-axes of early types would also be consonant, but it remains difficult to account for the massive bluestone block in the long barrow of Bowl's Barrow.

Phase IIIa begins with the change of plan which necessitated the cessation of building the bluestone double circle, the dismantling of such stones as had been erected, and the making good of their sockets. There followed a complete rebuilding of the monument on a new and grandiose plan with dressed sarsens of great size brought from the Avebury region, and employing lintels held with mortice-and-tenon joints. The plan was that of a *Peristyle* of 30 lintelled uprights some 14½ ft. high in a circle, 98 ft. in diameter, enclosing a *Horseshoe* of 5 trilithons or lintelled pairs of stones up to 22 ft. high. To this phase presumptively belong the 4 sarsen *Station Stones*, on diameters intersecting on the Phase III centre, which, as has been said, appears to be also that of Phase II. The dagger, axes, and other carvings on the sarsen uprights are also presumably of Phase IIIa, but could be later; the axes are types current in the early–mid 2nd millennium B.C. (see p. 346) and the 'Mycenaean' character of the dagger can hardly be maintained today. There is a C14 date, unfortunately conflicting with the others from the site, from an antler in the ramp of Stone 56, which should be on the boundary of Phases IIIa and b, of 1710±150 B.C. (BM–46): it has been suggested that it could be a fragment derived from an earlier phase.

Phase IIIb involved the selection, dressing to shape, and erecting of certain bluestones in what was probably an oval setting with a symmetrical plan incorporating two small trilithons, the 'tongue' and 'groove' bluestone pair, and the *Altar Stone*, itself dressed. There would have remained some 60 bluestones from the estimated original total. It has been presumed that the *Y and Z Holes* were dug in two concentric and rather irregular circles, 180 ft. and 128 ft. in diameter, outside the sarsen peristyle, to accommodate them. They were, however, never so used, but allowed to fill naturally with an aeolian deposit deriving from exposed soil under dry conditions (see p. 285). An antler from Y 30 gave a C14 date of 1240±105 B.C. (I–2445).

Phase IIIc, the final constructional period, was marked by the dismantling of the oval bluestone setting of Stonehenge IIIb, and the rearrangement of its stones and those not placed in the Y and Z holes, into the present settings of a circle and a horseshoe echoing the sarsen plan. The two lintels from the IIIb oval setting were utilized as uprights in the circle, and the dressed bluestones were re-erected in the horseshoe, giving a diameter of 78 ft. for the bluestone circle and a horseshoe 40 ft. by 36 ft. Apart from subsequent ruin this is the monument seen today.

Woodhenge, DURRINGTON

The site, later known as Woodhenge, had been for long regarded as a large disk-barrow until air observation and photography in 1925 showed it to contain concentric circles of pits or holes. It was excavated in 1926–8 and was found to be a single-entranced henge monument of Class I, 250 ft. in diameter crest-to-crest of the encircling bank.[19] The name was invented during the excavations as a joke, but has since become a part of archaeological nomenclature (fig. 8).

The internal quarry-ditch is separated from the bank by a marked berm, and has at least one partial causeway resulting from gang-work. It is flat-bottomed and shallow in proportion to its width. At one point on the E. a crouched inhumation was found in a grave cut in the bottom of the ditch before silting had begun. The single entrance is to the NE., at a bearing of 26° from the centre.

Within the area enclosed by the ditch are six slightly oval settings of post-holes, the maximum dimensions of the outer ring being 142 ft. by 132 ft. The post-holes vary in size, increasing from the outer ring inwards to the third (C Ring), where the holes have ramps and average 5 ft. 8 in. deep and 5 ft. in diameter, and decreasing in size again in the inner three rings. A burial of an infant with its skull cleft in two was found within the innermost ring, off centre to the W., and a cremation in hole C14. A few holes on the entrance causeway and under the bank are earlier than the henge monument and have been considered as Neolithic storage-pits.[20]

The post-hole settings raise the problem, also posed at the Sanctuary at Avebury and Durrington Walls, whether they represent a series of free-standing wooden uprights or a timber building. There is no direct evidence to suggest that the six rings are not contemporary one with another, and a reconstruction has been made involving an open-centred structure with a ridge-roof carried on the huge posts of the C Ring.[21] Alternative interpretations in terms of free-standing posts, in settings of one or more constructional periods, are, however, possible.

The finds from the site include pottery of Early–Middle Neolithic, and Late Neolithic Rinyo-Clacton types, as well as beaker sherds. The beaker sherds were found on the top of the secondary silt but the others came from primary locations such as the rapid silting of the ditch, the old turf line beneath the bank, and in the post-holes. From primary locations also came two ritual chalk axes, flint scrapers, serrated flakes, and *petit tranchet* derivative arrowheads. The monument, in fact, appears to have been built over part of an extensive Late Neolithic settlement, other parts of which lie across the main road near the Durrington Walls monument and within the henge itself.

While Woodhenge as a whole falls within the henge class, there are no precise parallels to the timber settings from known sites in Britain. Durrington Walls and the Sanctuary offer, however, partial counterparts, as presumably would Marden, and a relationship between Woodhenge and the sarsen structures at Stonehenge has been urged in view of the carpentry techniques seen at the Stonehenge site (see p. 328).

Durrington Walls, DURRINGTON

Lying near Woodhenge to the N., the earthworks of Durrington Walls represent a huge Class II henge monument with double entrances and internal ditch, enclosing an area some 1,720 ft. by 1,470 ft., larger than Avebury but less than the Marden Henge (see p. 330). Rescue excavations in advance of roadworks were made in 1966–7 (fig. 7).[22]

On the S. the bank of the earthwork overlay an Early–Middle Neolithic settlement with radiocarbon dates 2620±40 and 2630±70 B.C. The monument itself has Rinyo-Clacton and Beaker wares in primary contexts, and dates of 1680±110 and 1610±120 B.C. (BM–286, 285).

[19] Maud E. Cunnington, *Woodhenge* (Devizes, 1929). [21] *Arch. Jnl.* xcvi. 193.
[20] *P.P.S.* xxx. 352. [22] *Ant. Jnl.* xlvii. 166–84; *Antiq.* xlii. 20–6.

The bank is separated from the ditch by a wide berm, and the ditch is up to 20 ft. deep on the S. Pottery, flints, bone, and antlers lay in the primary silt and on the ditch bottom, where a pile of 57 deer-antlers were found near the south entrance. Within the enclosure adjacent to that entrance, but not on its axis, was a complex series of concentric post-holes divisible into three phases. In Phase 1 four post circles, 7·5, 25, 50, and 75 ft. in diameter respectively, have a common centre; to Phase 2a are assigned a series of five large holes with ramps for massive posts, with approximate diameters of 35, 50, 75, 100, and 120 ft. Phase 2b consists of a single circle of small posts, with a pair of larger posts forming an entrance on the SE., 127 ft. in diameter, and enclosing the nine circles of Phases 1 and 2a. To Phase 1 is also assigned a straight line of posts, 150 ft. long, running NE.–SW. on the SE. of the settings. To the NE. there was a scatter of domestic debris and a stake-hole setting.

Further N. within the main henge enclosure were other post settings, eroded by surface weathering and solution. Some almost vanished post-holes may constitute two concentric circles of 62 ft. and 90 ft. in diameter, later replaced by a more tangible structure of four massive ramped post-holes in a square 21 ft. across. An outer post ring, 48 ft. in diameter, is approached by a double post-row or 'avenue' from the S., itself crossed by a curved line of posts.

Rinyo-Clacton and late Beaker pottery was associated with the timber structures, as with the bank and ditch, and all should be approximately contemporary, that is around the middle of the 17th century B.C. The interpretation of the timber settings, as roofed buildings or free-standing circles with or without lintels, separately or in combination, is uncertain, but roofed structures seem plausible.

The Marden Earthworks, BEECHINGSTOKE

These earthworks constitute a very large irregularly planned ditch with external bank forming an arc against a stream and containing an area of some 50 acres, with entrances to the NE. and SW. A recent magnetometer survey made within the area, suggested comparison with the timber circles at Durrington Walls, and trial excavations in 1969 near the NE. entrance revealed post-holes of a circular timber monument immediately within the entrance causeway across the ditch. Late Neolithic pottery of Rinyo-Clacton type was found in the ditch and post-holes, and the monument is evidently contemporary with Durrington Walls and the largest henge monument in Britain. Its position on the low-lying Greensand of the Pewsey Vale is very unusual.

Fargo Plantation, AMESBURY

A remarkable monument in Fargo Plantation, excavated by Stone in 1938, seems to represent a miniature version of a Class II henge monument (fig. 8). An oval ditch with external bank and two opposed entrances enclosed an area only 30 ft. in diameter, containing a central grave, in which were a fractional burial with a late beaker, a cremation with a food vessel (see p. 354), and an unaccompanied cremation, all apparently contemporary. The ditch silting contained an unaccompanied cremation in the upper part, a sherd of Late Neolithic Mortlake ware, and a piece of Stonehenge rhyolite.[23]

Stone Circles

Within the general heading of ceremonial monuments may be considered the few stone circles in the county not already described in connexion with the major monuments.

[23] *W.A.M.* xlviii. 357–70.

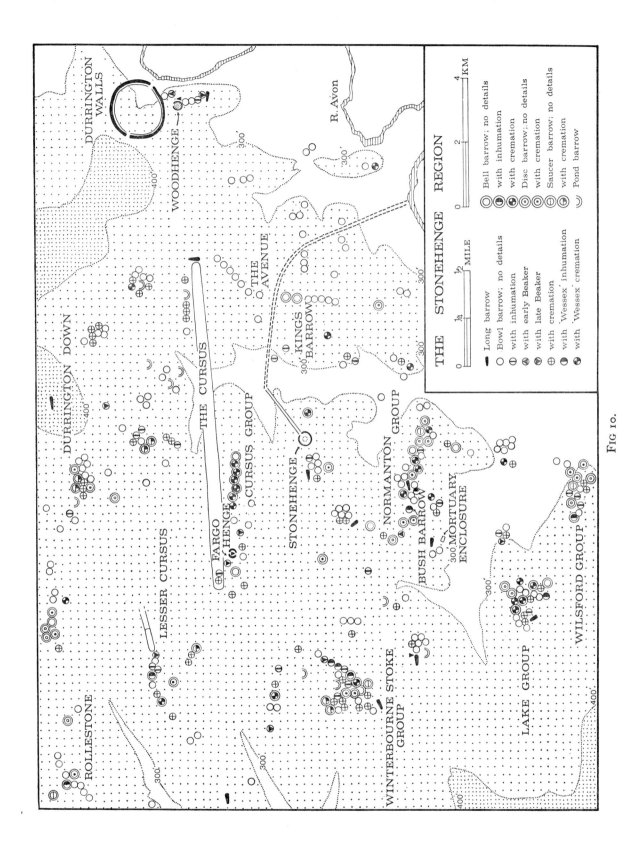

THE STONEHENGE REGION

0	¼	½	MILE

0	2	4	KM

◣▬ Long barrow
○ Bowl barrow; no details
⊕ with inhumation
◐ with early Beaker
◑ with late Beaker
⊕ with cremation
◕ with 'Wessex' inhumation
◉ with 'Wessex' cremation

◎ Bell barrow; no details
◉ with inhumation
◉ with cremation
◉ Disc barrow; no details
◉ with cremation
◉ Saucer barrow; no details
⊕ with cremation
) Pond barrow

ROLLESTONE
DURRINGTON DOWN
LESSER CURSUS
THE CURSUS
CURSUS GROUP
FARGO HENGE
STONEHENGE
WINTERBOURNE STOKE GROUP
NORMANTON GROUP
BUSH BARROW
MORTUARY ENCLOSURE
LAKE GROUP
WILSFORD GROUP
THE AVENUE
KINGS BARROW
WOODHENGE
DURRINGTON WALLS
R. Avon

FIG 10.

331

That in WINTERBOURNE BASSETT appears to have consisted of two concentric circles of stones, 234 ft. and 148 ft. in diameter respectively, with a single standing stone in the centre. Not more than half-a-dozen stones are now visible, but an additional ten were identified by probing in the 19th century. A probable stone circle at Day House Farm, Coate, in CHISELDON, is now represented by nine recumbent sarsen stones in an approximate circle some 200 ft. in diameter.

South of Avebury two sites have been claimed as stone circles, and of these Falkner's Circle (AVEBURY) now represented by a single stone, seems to have been 120 ft. in diameter, but the so-called Langdean Circle (EAST KENNET) appears to be the retaining sarsen kerb of a round barrow 30 ft. across. Another site, nearly a mile south of Silbury Hill in AVEBURY, has been confused by the moving of stones, but the earlier accounts suggest that it was oval or elliptical in plan.

Some record exists of two destroyed sites. Near Place Farm (TISBURY) Hoare records 'a circular work with a vallum set round with stones, and a large stone placed erect in the centre'. At the foot of the stone, which was 12 ft. high, an inhumation burial was found. The second site is that at Broome (SWINDON) where Aubrey recorded a standing stone 10 ft. high, with smaller stones forming an alignment.

The Cursus, AMESBURY

The monument known since Stukeley's original description of it as the *Cursus* lies ½ mile north of Stonehenge, and is a very long earthwork enclosure, 3,030 yds. long (nearly 1¾ mile), and varying from 110 yds. to 145 yds. across, delimited by a low bank with external ditch (fig. 9). It is on gently undulating ground and crosses a shallow valley, with each end visible from the other, and its axis is approximately E. and W.

The eastern end stops just short of a long barrow (*B i* AMESBURY 42), lying at right angles to the line of the Cursus, which has a slightly rounded end, now almost obliterated by cultivation, but recorded by Stukeley and Hoare; the western end is similar. Hoare and Stukeley recorded two gaps in the banks and ditches opposite one another some 1,800 ft. from the E. end, and there may have been others now obliterated (as these are) by cultivation. Within the western end of the monument are two round barrows, *B ii* AMESBURY 56 and *B ii* WINTERBOURNE STOKE 30, the former containing a primary inhumation with a bronze riveted knife-dagger and the latter an unaccompanied cremation.[24]

Excavations in the southern bank and ditch near the western end were made in 1947,[25] and in the western end itself in 1959.[26] The ditch was found to be 5–6 ft. wide on the S. side and only 2½ ft. deep, but was up to 6 ft. 9 in. deep at the W. end. The scanty finds from both excavations comprise flint flakes from the primary ditch silt, and a fragment of Cosheston Sandstone on the outer edge of the southern ditch.

The Lesser Cursus, WINTERBOURNE STOKE

To the NW. of Stonehenge lies an earthwork enclosure, oblong in shape with a total length of 1,350 ft., bluntly rounded at the W. end and open at the E., with a width varying from 155 ft. to 190 ft., and with a transverse ditch across it 660 ft. from the W. end. The N. ditch is approximately aligned on what appears to be a small long barrow, 150 ft. long (fig. 10).

In plan the monument resembles both the long mortuary enclosures and cursus monuments in general. It is unexcavated, but it is likely that it is of Late Neolithic date, and of ceremonial purpose.

[24] *W.A.M.* lviii. 370–82.   [25] *Arch. Jnl.* civ. 7–19.   [26] *W.A.M.* lviii. 370–82.

THE LATER NEOLITHIC: SINGLE-GRAVES AND THE FIRST METALLURGY

c. 2000–*c.* 1500 B.C.

CULTURES AND CHRONOLOGY

IT has already been noted that from a date around 2000 B.C., in Wiltshire as elsewhere in Britain, a phase of great cultural complexity is entered. In it indigenous and immigrant traditions meet and form various combinations, and the important technological innovation of working in gold, copper, and later bronze is introduced to otherwise stone-using communities in the British Isles.

The background is provided by the continuance of earlier cultural traditions implicit in the developing pottery styles which had evolved in Middle Neolithic times from those associated with the initial Neolithic settlement of southern England. The Mortlake pottery style (fig. 12 b) had appeared by the late 3rd millennium B.C. (2340±150 B.C. BM–97) in Pit 12 at Grimes Graves (Norf.) and continued, with its later Fengate derivative, well into the 2nd millennium (Windmill Hill III, *c.* 1540 B.C.). These wares do not appear in primary grave contexts, but may be secondary to chambered tombs, as at West Kennet, or they may be associated with ceremonial monuments. An additional Late Neolithic component with origins outside the Windmill Hill–Mortlake–Fengate series is represented by a complex which seems to be associated with Rinyo-Clacton pottery (fig. 12 e, f). Within it are included distinctive arrowheads of the *petit tranchet* derivative series and other flint types such as polished-edge knives, specialized bone pins, shaft-hole stone mace-heads, and cremation burial in cemeteries.[1] So far as Wiltshire and probably Wessex as a whole are concerned, it is likely that this cultural complex was introduced from north of the Thames Valley around the 17th century B.C., and was perhaps connected with other north-south movements among the immigrant Beaker cultures discussed below.

The most important component in the cultural amalgam of the early 2nd millennium B.C. is, however, that associated with the makers of pottery within the Bell-Beaker tradition. It is certain that in this instance we are dealing with a wholly immigrant and intrusive culture, representing actual colonization at more than one point of the British seaboard from Aberdeenshire to the Channel coast, and with continental origins which can be fairly well pin-pointed to certain areas including the Low Countries and the Middle Rhine. The individuality of the British Beaker cultures is marked from the outset by a complex of traits without indigenous antecedents in the preceding Neolithic cultures. These traits included completely novel pottery types, new or characteristically modified types in flint and stone, the replacement of the collective burial rite by Single-Grave inhumation burials, frequently under a circular mound or barrow, and with material equipment appropriate to the individual, the beginnings of copper (and soon tin-bronze) metallurgy, and gold-working; finally

---

[1] *Anc. Europe*, ed. Coles and Simpson, 145–72.

333

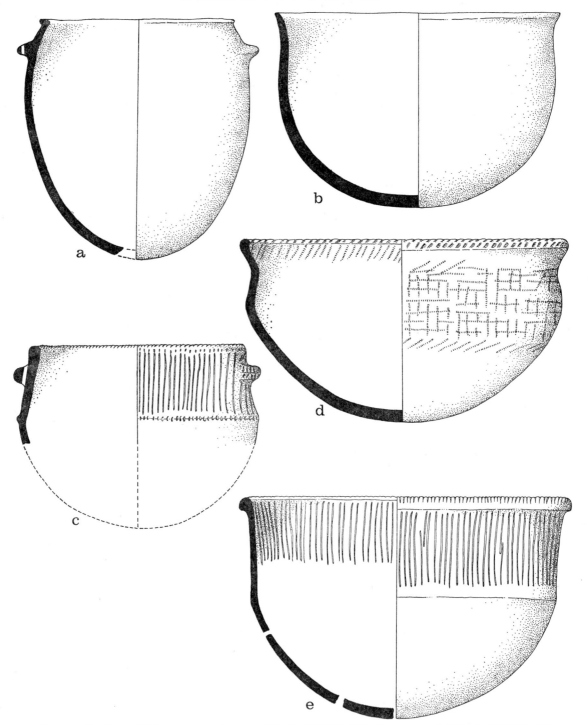

FIG. 11. Early neolithic pottery, a, b, c, e (Windmill Hill). Ebbsfleet ware, d (Windmill Hill). (¼)

there was a change in the human physical type represented in the new-style burials. The chronological and cultural framework for this phase of British prehistory can best be constructed from the evidence of the characteristic beakers themselves, of which some 2,000 are known from the British Isles. From Wiltshire there are between 65 and 70 vessels and numerous sherds, finds as elsewhere being mainly from graves.

The assemblage and interpretation of this large, and therefore potentially reliable, mass of pottery and its associated objects in modern terms has been undertaken by D. L. Clarke and two preliminary studies of his results are available.[2] On the basis of

[2] *P.P.S.* xxviii. 371–82; *Palaeohist.* xii. 179.

these a provisional assessment may be made of the Wiltshire material pending his definitive publication. Clarke distinguishes seven typological groups of beakers in Britain, whose characteristic features link them with sufficient precision to prototypes on the European Continent to interpret them as the result of manufacture by immigrant groups whose origins lie in separately identifiable locations across the Channel and North Sea. After the initial colonization a not unnaturally complex process of inter-action and insular development can be observed within Britain, crystallizing into recognizably northern and southern traditions. The European origin and dispersal of the Bell-Beaker cultures is at present the subject of considerable discussion. The view favoured by many that these cultures originated in the Iberian peninsula, were trans-mitted thence to central Europe, were mixed there with the already established Corded-Ware–Single-Grave cultures, and spread later westward and northward by a process of 'reflux' is now disputed. In its place a central European origin begins to be favoured, though such an origin cannot be confidently demonstrated. So far as Britain is concerned, this vexed problem need hardly be discussed here. Our immigrant cultures are products of the mixed tradition incorporating Corded-Ware elements as established in various west European areas and so, if the 'reflux' theory is accepted, products of a secondary diaspora.[3] More C14 dates would go far to answer this crucial question, but for the present these dates, which come mainly from the Netherlands, at least show that the earliest immigrant cultures in Britain should date from soon after 2000 B.C.; further continental and British dates demonstrate the continuance of the Beaker tradition at least to the 16th or even 15th century B.C. both here and in certain regions abroad, notably the Netherlands.

In Wiltshire three out of Clarke's seven immigrant groups are well represented as evidence of primary colonization, and in addition the insular development of these ceramic styles in terms of a southern tradition of techniques can be traced. Moreover, there is evidence pointing to a secondary intrusion into the county from the north by communities making beakers which represent, occasionally, the British immigrant traditions proper to east Scotland and north England. More often, insular develop-ments of types occurring normally in areas north of the Thames are represented. While the pottery styles provide the main determinant here, confirmatory evidence is afforded by other elements of material culture, notably the metal or stone equipment associated with specific beaker types in men's graves. Consideration of this non-ceramic evidence leads to the recognition of a class of graves representing insular developments in funerary ritual, in which inhumation burials under barrows are not accompanied by pottery but by other characteristic objects. Other inhumation graves are also recog-nized in which pottery in the Beaker tradition is replaced by the so-called food vessels, a ceramic type ultimately derived from the Late Neolithic Fengate style of ware and forming a wholly insular development parallel with beakers.

In all these instances the evidence is virtually confined to burials, and the peculiar nature of such evidence is touched upon again later. The first appearance of a type of pottery as a piece of grave furniture in a given community does not necessarily mean that it had not already been in use within that community for non-sepulchral purposes. This could probably be shown more forcibly if settlement sites of the earlier 2nd millennium B.C. were not so sparse. The situation becomes particularly clear when, with the adoption of the rite of cremation in place of inhumation, a type of pot known as the cinerary urn (also of Late Neolithic Fengate ware derivation) appears as a container

---

[3] For some discussion of the 'reflux' theory see E. Sangmeister, 'La Civilisation du Vase Campaniforme', *Actes du premier Colloque Atlantique*.

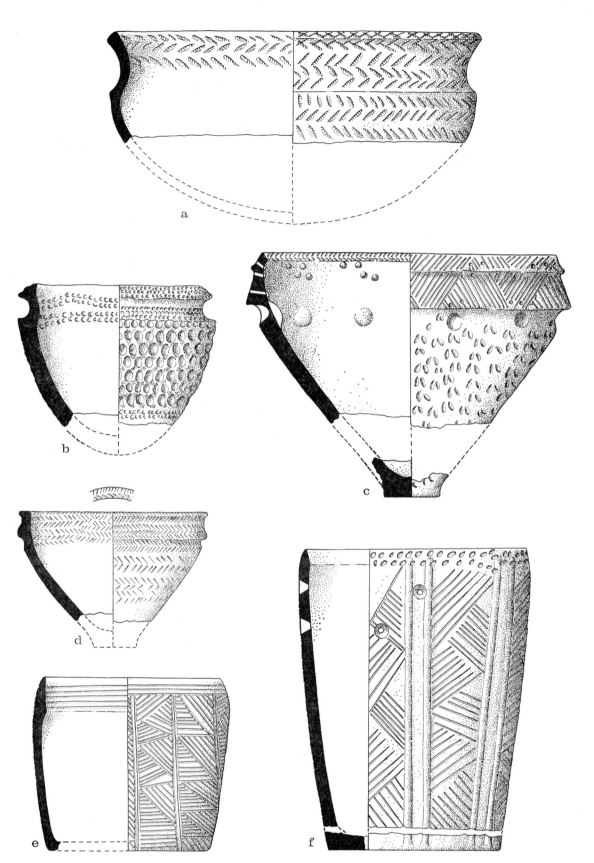

FIG. 12. Later neolithic pottery: a, Ebbsfleet ware, b, Mortlake ware, c, d, Fengate ware (all West Kennet chambered tomb); e, Rinyo-Clacton ware (Durrington Walls), f, Rinyo-Clacton ware (*B ii* Wilsford (S.) 51). ($\frac{1}{3}$)

for the burnt bones. This, as is shown by non-funerary finds, is a ceramic type going back to the Late, if not the Middle Neolithic. A Wiltshire site, *B ii* WEST OVERTON 6*b*, demonstrates the contemporaneity there of cremation burials in cinerary urns with a late Beaker inhumation. The general appearance of such vessels in barrows after the mid 2nd millennium B.C. does not mean that they were first devised as a pottery form at that time, but that the use of a formerly domestic vessel as a funerary container became common at that period.

Late in the phase, probably in the 17th century B.C. on conventional C14 dating schemes, a localized aspect of the Single-Grave cultures of Britain emerges in Wiltshire and adjoining areas of Wessex, concurrently with the later inhumation graves of the Beaker tradition. These graves for both males and females are exceptionally richly furnished. They cover both inhumations and cremations and are frequently under specialized round-barrow forms. For a generation they have been grouped within a Wessex culture of the Early Bronze Age,[4] and present peculiarly difficult problems of interpretation to be discussed later. For the present it is sufficient to recognize this phenomenon of enriched graves as a component, at least in its earlier stages, in the mixture of traditions; indigenous, immigrant, and locally evolving, which make the first half of the 2nd millennium B.C. in Britain a phase confusing and conflicting in its interpretation, but undoubtedly of the greatest importance in the formation of the next stage of development of our insular prehistory.

Hitherto it has been assumed that these graves cover a 500-year span and inevitably archaeological types, or events inferred from them, have been referred to an early or late stage in that period. In fact the observable sequence of grave-types, modifications of funerary ritual, and changes in metal technology enable archaeologists to make a provisional tripartite division of the Wiltshire Beaker graves. That division may serve as a framework within which the enduring Neolithic traditions and other aspects may be fitted. An Early Phase is defined in Britain generally by beakers with particularly close European affinities (Clarke's Group E) (fig. 13 A), and by those, also demonstrably early on the Continent, with an all-over decoration of zones of cord impressions (the AOC Group). Metal objects are very rarely associated and are confined to small gold ornaments and copper awls. No such associations with E or AOC beakers are known from Wiltshire, and the cord-ornamented type is not known from single-graves, although found among the offerings in the chambered tomb of West Kennet, and as sherds at Windmill Hill, the Avebury Sanctuary, and Woodhenge. Both beaker pottery types in the Early Phase suggest an origin around the Rhine Delta, and C14 dates of 2190–2000 for the cord-zoned vessels and *c.* 1950 for the 'European' bell-beakers have been obtained in the Netherlands.[5]

The Middle Phase in Wiltshire is marked by the appearance of beakers, which specifically link Wessex with the Middle Rhine area (the W/MR Group) in their characteristic decorative motifs, and 80 per cent of burials with such beakers in Britain come from within a 60-mile radius of Stonehenge. The associated grave-finds, when present, indicate male burials with archery equipment (arrows and bracers) and a broad-tanged copper knife, and occasionally gold ornaments: there is evidence of the occasional knowledge of bronze with a low tin content. Some of the earliest, unassociated, flat copper axe-blades in Britain possibly belong here. There are no directly informative C14 dates either in Britain or on the Continent for this phase (fig. 13 C, D).

The Late-Phase graves are those representing the insular traditions of beaker development either in the south (Clarke's Groups S1–4) or the north (Groups N2–4) of

[4] *P.P.S.* iv. 52–106.   [5] J. D. Van der Waals, *Prehist. Disc Wheels,* 52.

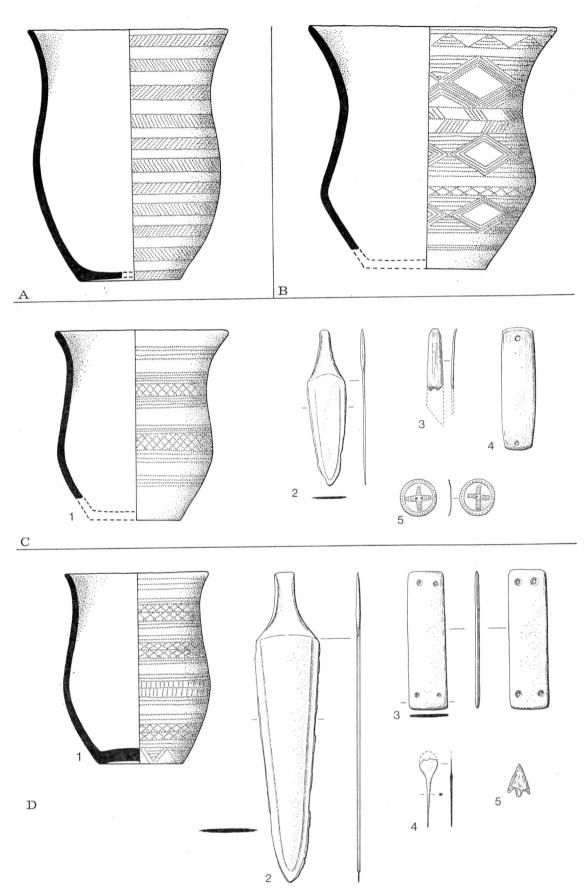

FIG. 13. Early beakers: A, (*B ii* Wilsford (S.) 54); B, (West Kennet chambered tomb). Early beaker grave-groups: C, (*B ii* Mere 6a), 1, beaker, 2, copper knife-dagger, 3, worked bone, 4, stone braces, 5, gold disks; D, (*B ii* Roundway 8), 1, beaker, 2, copper knife-dagger, 3, stone bracer, 4, copper pin, 5, flint arrowhead ($\frac{1}{3}$).

Britain (fig. 14). Where demonstrably male equipment is present, it shows a change in the 'weapon-group' from archers' equipment to a riveted knife (now almost invariably of full tin-alloy bronze) and often a stone shaft-hole battle-axe, or the dagger and battle-axe together or alone with or without a beaker. Here again directly applicable dates are lacking, although derivative beakers in the northern tradition are as early as 1850–1800 in the Cambridge region; at Windmill Hill virtually all the beaker types are congregated in Phase III, c. 1540 B.C. The development of a whole range of derivative types of beaker in both north and south Britain may be held to imply that this late phase lasted longer than its predecessors. The two earlier phases between them may span no more than a century or so, with the last Beaker period lasting three or even four times as long in part of the country at least. In Wiltshire, as in much of the Wessex area, Late Neolithic pottery styles must also have been developing during this Late Phase, and some Fengate pottery seems to show Beaker-derived motifs and techniques.[6] It has already been suggested that a contemporary cultural complex whose distinctive features included cremation-cemeteries (as at Stonehenge I), ceremonial stone mace-heads, and Rinyo-Clacton ware may be of north British origin. If this is so, the appearance of these cultural traits in Wiltshire could be seen in the context of the more or less contemporary appearance of beaker types, themselves with origins north of the Thames, in the Late Phase. The Woodhenge variant of Rinyo-Clacton ware might again be interpreted as containing elements of Beaker derivation, and the whole insular mace-head series could be thought to derive its features of drilled shaft-holes from the similarly hafted stone battle-axes of ultimately continental origin and belonging to the final Beaker phases in Britain.

Finally, as seen earlier, it would be to such a Late Phase in Wiltshire that must be assigned the inhumation burials with food-vessel pottery, certain early cremation-burials in cinerary urns (as in the West Overton barrow), and some, if not many of the enriched burials assigned to the Wessex culture. The last present problems, which will be discussed fully in a subsequent section, but chronologically they must in part be considered as yet another component in the cultural complex which formed in Wiltshire in the two or three centuries before 1500 B.C.

THE BEAKER POPULATION

As with the British Neolithic skeletal material, that attributable to the Beaker culture and its congeners with Single-Grave inhumation burials awaits a full and up-to-date treatment. A short discussion, with particular reference to Yorkshire but of wider application, has been published and is used here.[7] For long it had been realized that the Beaker population of Britain was on the whole taller, more robustly built, and with shorter skulls (brachycephalic) than the Neolithic series, and that in fact the two groups could be thought to present striking contrasts. While this still holds, the sample from Beaker and other Single-Grave burials, in Yorkshire and probably elsewhere, shows considerable variability in skull type, either as a result of a non-homogeneous immigrant population or from subsequent intermarriage. In Wiltshire the 14-year-old boy with a typically 'Neolithic' dolichocephalic skull from the burial at the Sanctuary at Avebury may be compared with the 45–50-year-old man from *B ii* DURRINGTON 67 (near Woodhenge) with a massive brachycephalic skull of typically 'Beaker' type.[8]

[6] Cf. Piggott, *West Kennet Long Barrow* (H.M.S.O. 1962), 38, 77.

[7] *Advancement of Science*, lxiv. 311. Here D. R. Broth-well compared skeletons from Brit. Beaker cultures with skeletal material from the Danish 'Late Neolithic'. The Danish group is in fact later than the Brit. Beaker cultures.

[8] *W.A.M.* xlv. 330; Cunnington, *Woodhenge*, 57.

The average height of the British Beaker male is calculated at just over 5 ft. 8 in. whereas the Neolithic male averages 5 ft. 5¾ in. The evidence for greater dental health in the former group has already been noted (see p. 286), as have the difficulties in making any estimates of population. As with the Neolithic burials in long barrows and chambered tombs, it is not known what proportion of the Beaker population was entitled to the Single-Grave burials, with or without a covering barrow, by which the people are characterized. Moreover, the total excavation of barrows such as *B ii* WILSFORD (S.) 1, with eleven burials, five of infants with beakers, and all off-centre, shows how unreliable figures based on old excavations confined to the centres of barrows may be.[9] Abercromby's figures, already quoted,[10] show how few initial colonists are needed to produce a surprisingly large total of deaths in a few centuries: a colony of 10 persons (5 men, 4 women, and a child) could be expected to lead to 1,735 deaths in the course of 300 years, and still leave a population at the end of that time of 559 people.

THE SINGLE-GRAVE BURIALS

Since knowledge of Beaker settlements in Wiltshire is very slight, it is convenient to consider first the burials which provide the bulk of such knowledge as exists. It is worth while pointing out straight away that 'grave archaeology' presents its own peculiar problems and has limitations even more restrictive than those applicable to other archaeological evidence. What are usually termed 'grave-goods' placed with the dead are themselves of uncertain significance: ethnographical parallels present a bewildering number of possible alternative explanations among which provision for a future life is only one. Whatever the irrecoverable reasons behind the deposition of artefacts in a grave, the selection of such artefacts is not based upon criteria susceptible of inference on rational or utilitarian grounds, but upon religious beliefs unascertainable by archaeological means. In the graves under discussion certain inferences may be made in relation to sex and status: male equipment seems especially distinctive and female graves difficult to detect except through anatomical deductions from the skeleton; burials of children or infants are not uncommon. There is a reasonable supposition that the pots in graves are domestic vessels adapted for funerary use, but whether as receptacles for drink or food for the dead or as personal belongings rendered tabu by the decease of their owner is unknown.

In Wiltshire, as elsewhere in Britain, Beaker or allied Single-Grave burials normally take the form of oval pits containing the crouched body lying on its side. These may be isolated or in small groups with no visible mounds, as on Overton Down,[11] or under large flat sarsens (AVEBURY, WINTERBOURNE MONKTON). In some instances low mounds may have been removed by ploughing. Where barrows exist there seems to be a significant distinction in size between those covering burials of the Early and Middle Phases (E or W/MR beakers), which average about 40 ft. in diameter and about 2 ft. in height, and those of the Late Phase, averaging 85 ft. in diameter and 5 ft. high, with exceptional examples of up to 100 ft. across and a height of 10 ft. or more. In the barrow of *B iv* WINTERSLOW 3 the Beaker burial was subsequently covered by an enlarged mound of the Wessex culture, a bell-barrow of a type discussed at a later stage, and a member of a class of encircled barrows, surrounded by geometrically laid-out circular ditches peculiar to this context. A similar sequence perhaps existed in *B iv* AMESBURY 85, with an inhumation-grave with a bronze riveted dagger appropriate to the Late-Phase burials earlier than a Wessex culture cremation-grave, but they could be contemporary.

[9] *W.A.M.* lviii. 30.   [10] Abercromby, *Bronze Age Pottery*, i. 68.   [11] *W.A.M.* lxii. 16–21.

The comparative rarity of modern excavations leads to a very scanty knowledge of ritual features associated with the Wiltshire burials under discussion. An exceptional burial in Fargo Plantation (AMESBURY) comprised a large grave-pit containing an incomplete inhumation, a Late-Phase beaker, a food vessel, and three contemporary cremations, centrally placed within a miniature double-entrance henge monument with massive ditches, only 20 ft. across internally. Another remarkable and presumably contemporary burial was that of a detached human skull, by which a flaked rod of flint had been set upright, in a large grave under the small barrow *B ii* WINTERSLOW 20. Early-Phase Beaker burials occurred at the foot of standing stones of the Avebury complex, by Stone 29a of the West Kennet Avenue, and one of the Beckhampton Long Stones; a Middle-Phase (W/MR) vessel by Stone 25b of the Avenue and a Late-Phase (BW) beaker at the Sanctuary. Under *B ii* AMESBURY 61 a close-set circle of stakes was associated with Early- or Middle-Phase Beaker pottery and both inhumation and cremation burials.[12] In *B ii* AMESBURY 71[13] an important structural and chronological sequence was established (fig. 17). The primary burial within a ring-ditch and a stake-hole setting has already been mentioned (see p. 316); that was followed by an unaccompanied inhumation burial in a deep grave, covered by a mound incorporating triple stake-settings and a ditch separated from it by a berm in the manner of a bell-barrow. There were two stake-holes in the floor of the grave, with remains of decayed timber, suggesting a small ridge-roofed mortuary house 7 ft. 8 in. long. A C14 date of 2010±110 B.C. (NPL–77) was obtained. A post circle in *B ii* COLLINGBOURNE DUCIS 3a with a cremation burial with trepanned skull-roundel and Rinyo-Clacton and Beaker sherds may belong to the Late Phase.[14] In *B ii* AMESBURY 51 one of the original three inhumations associated with a Late-Phase beaker had a trepanned skull with an exceptionally large roundel excised. This is paralleled in an earlier Beaker context at Crichel Down in Dorset,[15] in the barrow mentioned above (*B ii* COLLINGBOURNE DUCIS 3a), and in an adjacent barrow, *B vi* COLLINGBOURNE KINGSTON 6, in a cremation-grave probably of post-Beaker date. The trepanned inhumation-burial in *B ii* AMESBURY 71 is secondary to the final phase of the barrow and is undated.[16] It has been suggested that the trepanning operation, from which a surprisingly large number of people recovered, may have originated in Late Neolithic France.[17]

In *B ii* AMESBURY 51 remains of a probable mortuary-house structure of wood within the burial pit could be traced. The same feature occurred in *B ii* AMESBURY 71 with an unaccompanied inhumation (fig. 17),[18] and with an Early–Middle-Phase Beaker burial in *B ii* BISHOP'S CANNINGS 81.[19] Such mortuary houses, recoverable only by adequate excavation, are probably to be related to traditions originating in the Corded-Ware component of the Beaker cultures on the Continent. In the filling of the Bishop's Cannings grave were the skull and four legs of an ox, reminiscent of the two ox-skulls from a contemporary grave in *B ii* WINTERBOURNE MONKTON 9. In the first instance there certainly seems to be an example of a ritual hide-burial of a type well known in prehistory.[20]

Material Culture

In the absence of reliable anatomical sexing of skeletons, the distinction between male and female burials can only be made by assuming that graves containing metal or

[12] *Arch. Jnl.* cxiv. 1–9; *W.A.M.* lvi. 238.
[13] *P.P.S.* xxxiii. 336–66.
[14] *W.A.M.* lvi. 143–6.
[15] *P.P.S.* vi. 112–32.
[16] Ibid. xxxiii. 336–66.
[17] *Ausgrab. und Funde*, ix. 238–42.
[18] *P.P.S.* xxxiii. 336–66.
[19] *W.A.M.* lx. 102.
[20] *Antiq.* xxxvi. 110–18.

flint knives (or daggers), archers' equipment, or shaft-hole stone battle-axes are those of men. The contrary assumption, that graves not so furnished are those of women, cannot, however, be made. The bronze awl, which might be thought a woman's sewing tool, from *B ii* WEST OVERTON 6*b* was in a man's grave, and the pair of gold ear-rings from a Beaker burial at Radley (Oxon.) were worn by a young man who was also an archer.[21] Only the graves of males can in fact be distinguished, but among those both graves of 'warriors' (braves or hunters) and of specialist craftsmen can be detected. The 'warriors' ' graves belong, as shown, to both the Middle and Late Phases. The two phases are distinguished here, as elsewhere in Britain and indeed on the Continent, by the composition of what has been termed the 'weapon-group' deposited with the dead. In the earlier graves the group comprises archers' equipment (arrows, bracers) together with a copper knife; in the later it consists of a bronze dagger together with a stone battle-axe or bronze axe-blade.[22]

Archers' Equipment

Three classic graves with Middle-Phase (W/MR) beakers in Wiltshire have the characteristic archers' equipment of a perforated stone wrist-guard and in one instance (Roundway) a single flint barbed-and-tanged arrowhead as a *pars pro toto* symbol of the sheaf of arrows (*B ii* MERE 6*a*, ROUNDWAY 8; *B iv* WINTERSLOW 3) (fig. 13 C, D). With these may be taken *B ii* BISHOP'S CANNINGS 81 (beaker and bracer), *B ii* WILSFORD (S.) 54 (6 arrowheads and Early-Phase beakers), *B ii* MONKTON FARLEIGH 2 (gold disk as at Mere, 4 arrowheads and beaker sherds), and bracer finds such as those in *B ii* LONGBRIDGE DEVERILL 3*b* and at CALNE.

The bracers are of a type known from a dozen finds in southern and eastern England, and are closely related to continental forms in Beaker contexts within the four-holed group classed by Edward Sangmeister as Form 1.[23] The small barbed-and-tanged arrowheads, however, in common with other British finds in Beaker contexts, do not compare with the forms, usually hollow-based, associated with beakers on the Continent. In Bavaria barbed-and-tanged flint arrowheads appear, sometimes with bracers and with tanged or riveted copper or bronze knives, in graves which mark a transition between the latest Beaker and the earliest bronze-using cultures in that region.[24] In the Netherlands such types of equipment rarely appear in Beaker contexts[25] but in later cultures, such as that of the Hilversum urns, as at Vogelenzang in Holland.[26] The C14 date at this site is 1190 ± 70 B.C. (GrN–2997), which is later than would be expected from the dates of 1470 ± 45 and 1500 ± 100 B.C. (GrN–050; 1828) from the Hilversum urn burial at Toterfout, but the culture is definitely post-Beaker, and its Wessex connexions are discussed in a subsequent section. Arrowhead assemblages with cremation burials, as in *B ii* COLLINGBOURNE KINGSTON 19, are also noted at a later stage.

The form of bow used is unknown from direct evidence from Beaker graves, but two British finds of simple stave-bows, both about 5 ft. long, have C14 dates of *c.* 1730 and 1320 B.C., and so would be of the appropriate period, as would comparable finds in the Netherlands.[27] On the other hand the Corded-Ware representation of a bow in the Gölitsch (Halle) cist-grave has been identified as distinctively a composite non-reflex type,[28] and a series of little pendants in south German and other Beaker contexts

[21] *Invent. Arch.* GB. 2.

[22] *Ber. R.-G. Komm.* xl. 1; *Culture and Environment, Essays in Honour of Sir Cyril Fox,* ed. I. Ll. Foster and Leslie Alcock, 53–91.

[23] *Studien aus Alteuropa,* ed. R. von Uslar and K. J. Narr, i. 93.

[24] *Ber. R.-G. Komm.* xl. 16, 18, figs. 4, 5.

[25] e.g. Lunteren, *Palaeohist.* xii. 67, fig. 136, no. 4.

[26] *In Het Voetspoor van A.E. van Giffen* (2nd edn.), ed. W. Glasbergen and W. Groenman-van Waateringe, 85.

[27] *P.P.S.* xxix. 50–98; Gad Rausing, *The Bow,* 43, 52–3.

[28] Rausing, *The Bow,* 38.

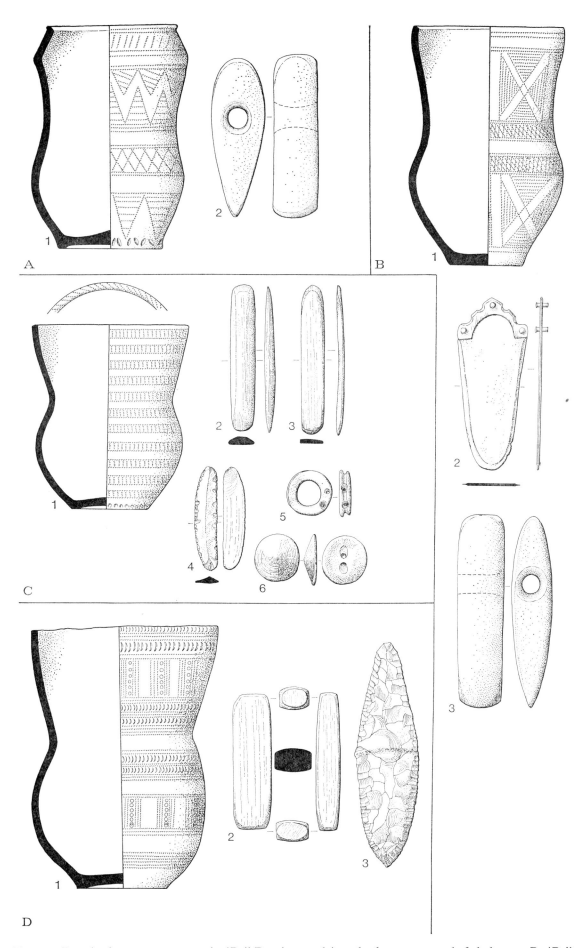

FIG. 14. Late beaker grave-groups: A, (*B ii* Durrington 67), 1, beaker, 2, stone shaft-hole axe; B, (*B ii* East Kennet 1c), 1, beaker, 2, bronze knife-dagger, 3, stone shaft-hole axe; C, (*B ii* Winterbourne Stoke 54), 1, beaker, 2, 3, stone polishers, 4, flint knife, 5, shale ring, 6, shale V-bored buttons; D, (*B ii* Amesbury 54), 1, beaker, 2, stone polisher, 3, flint knife-dagger. ($\frac{1}{3}$).

appear to represent short composite bows with transverse strapping.[29] Such a short bow would be easier to accommodate in a grave than a normal long-bow.

'Occupational' Graves

While archery equipment might be thought to indicate a man's occupation as a hunter or warrior, another group of graves, to which attention has recently been drawn,[30] contain objects which seem to represent more specialized craftsmen's equipment. *B ii* West Overton 6*b* contained the primary burial of a man with a Late-Phase beaker of the southern insular tradition together with a bronze awl, a flint knife and strike-a-light, two stone 'polishers' of distinctive 'sponge-finger biscuit' type, and a spatula-shaped object of antler (fig. 19). This assemblage, with numerous counterparts, partial or complete, in contemporary Beaker and allied graves in Britain, was interpreted as the tool-kit of a leather-worker. Similar bone or antler spatulae were instanced from *B ii* Mere 6*a* and Amesbury 51, and similar stone polishers from *B ii* Winterbourne Stoke 54 (a pair) and a flat grave at Durrington. It is clear that such assemblages should be taken as significant and may indicate a particular manufacturing process. An individual spatula or polisher in a grave, however, can hardly have the same significance. A continental association of bell-beaker, bone spatula-polisher, and a polishing-stone occurred in a grave at Stedten in Saxo-Thuringia.[31]

A similar situation is apparent in another context. J. J. Butler and J. D. Van der Waals have recently published certain Dutch finds in Beaker contexts of small cushion-shaped stone tools, convincingly interpreted as metal-workers' equipment for smoothing and hammering.[32] In Wiltshire *B ii* Upton Lovell 2*a* covered remarkable burials, which belong either to the Late Phase under discussion, or to the Wessex culture, as the stone battle-axe types imply. It is further discussed in a later section (see p. 362), but the nine 'smoothing stones' with the primary male burial clearly belong to the same class as the Dutch metal-workers' tools from Lunteren or Soesterberg and should be interpreted in the same sense.[33] The presence of two analogous stone tools from *B ii* Winterbourne Stoke 8, a Wessex culture inhumation, may indicate another metal-worker's grave, and the beaver's incisor teeth also found could have been engraving tools.[34] The occurrence, however, in each of the Late-Phase Beaker graves of *B ii* Amesbury 54 and Winterbourne Monkton of a single polishing-stone could be no more than a personal whetstone, functionally similar to the perforated examples in the Wessex culture graves of *B ii* Wilsford (S.) 23 (fig. 22 B), *B iv* Milston 3 (or *Bii* 7), or *Bii* Wilsford (S.) 60. In the last instance the stone was accompanied by bone and stone objects that may themselves be polishers.

Copper and Bronze Working

As shown, the Middle-Phase graves are characterized not only by archers' equipment, but also by broad-tanged knives or daggers which on analysis have proved to be of copper. The three graves with archers' equipment already mentioned (*B ii* Mere 6*a*, Roundway 8 (fig. 13 C, D), and *B iv* Winterslow 3) all contain such knives, minor variants of a type widespread in the British Isles, and represented by a dozen or more finds in Britain and about half that number in Ireland. On the Continent this type of

[29] *Ber. G.-R. Komm.* xl. fig. 4, 9 from Straubing, with bracer.
[30] *P.P.S.* xxxii. 122–55.
[31] *Antiq.* xxxix. 220.
[32] *Palaeohist.* xii. 63.
[33] *W.A.M.* lxi. 1–2.
[34] Cf. ethnographic evidence in Piggott, *West Kennet Long Barrow* (H.M.S.O. 1962), 49.

knife is everywhere typical of bell-beaker assemblages, and on occasion very close comparison can be made, down to details such as the 'hollow-grinding' at the edges, a feature which is present in the three Wiltshire examples just noted and in other examples found as far afield as the Netherlands and Sardinia.[35] The beakers at Roundway and Winterslow, and another from a similar grave at Dorchester (Oxon.), belong to the Wessex–Middle Rhine group and the knives are probably imports or close copies of such. The Roundway and Dorchester knives appear to be of central European metal; that from Mere is indeterminate, but the Winterslow knife is made of an Irish sulphide ore.

The tanged knife from a grave in *B ii* SHREWTON 5 *k* represents a variant with a rivet through the tang, known from half a dozen other examples in the British Isles and one in the Netherlands. It is a type found in north England and Scotland with beakers of the Dutch-derived group, and is associated at Shrewton with a vessel of this type. It evidently shows that at least one individual came into Wiltshire from the north, presumably in the Middle Phase, as a beaker in the southern-derived late tradition was secondary to it.

In the Late Phase in Wiltshire, as elsewhere in Britain, there is, almost universally, a change not only in the weapon-group (from archers' equipment to knife and shaft-hole stone axe), but in the type and composition of the knives, now riveted to their hafts at their heel and made of tin-bronze. Exceptions occur, however, as in a barrow on Oakley Down, Dorset (Wimborne St. Giles 9)[36] with four flint arrowheads, a riveted bronze dagger, shale button, and belt-ring,[37] but here, as with the five arrowheads in a cremation-grave in *B ii* COLLINGBOURNE KINGSTON 19, the arrowheads are of a late type discussed later. A typology can be worked out beginning with very small knives and moving into forms with large blades and massive rivets of peculiarly insular types. In Wiltshire such knives occur at *B ii* EAST KENNET 1*c*, with a Late-Phase beaker and stone battle-axe (fig. 14 B), with a battle-axe alone, as probably in *B ii* WILSFORD (S.) 54,[38] or with the inhumation alone, as at *B ii* FIGHELDEAN 16 and *B iv* AMESBURY 85. These knives fall into Group III of a classification made in 1963,[39] while in Group V the knife from *B ii* MILSTON 51 is a rare type, of which three other examples only, from Leicestershire, Derbyshire, and Yorkshire, are known. Here the hilt-plates are fastened together with multiple rivets to form a decorative feature, further enhanced at Milston by pointille ornament, recorded at the time of its discovery but not surviving today.

There are no analyses of the Wiltshire riveted knives, but those made of comparable examples from elsewhere have all shown the metal to be bronze, with a very variable tin content, ranging from 5 per cent to as high as 17·2 per cent. The low values compare well with other Beaker examples known to be early, e.g. the tiny riveted bronze knife in the Dorchester grave-group, found with a tanged copper knife and some early Wessex culture knife-daggers.[40] The figures of over 10 per cent, however, can only be matched in the second of A. M. ApSimon's Wessex culture series, suggesting continuance and overlap of the typologically earlier forms.

The riveted knife or dagger of copper or bronze marks on the Continent the post Beaker phases of what was to become the Early Bronze Age: Ai in the Reinecke scheme. The Late Phase, and part of the Middle Phase also, must, therefore, represent late Beaker traditions persisting in Britain long after their extinction in, for instance, the

[35] *Culture and Environment*, ed. Foster and Alcock, 53–91; *P.P.S.* xxiii. 91–104; *Antiq.* xxxix. 220–2; *Palaeohist.* xii. 41, 141.
[36] As numbered in L. V. Grinsell, *Dors. Barrows* (Dors. N. H. and Arch. Soc. 1959), 144.
[37] *D.M. Cat. Neo. and B.A. Colls.* (1964), nos. 77–85.
[38] Ibid. nos. 143, 145.
[39] *Culture and Environment*, ed. Foster and Alcock, 53–91.
[40] *Archaeometry*, iv. 39.

Rhineland. The little broken tanged object from the Roundway grave (fig. 13 D 4) might help here if it could certainly be interpreted as a small disk-headed pin of the German Early Bronze-Age *Scheibennadel* class, but its square shaft has produced the suggestion that it is a tanged 'Palmella' point, of a type known abundantly in Iberia and occasionally in Brittany. The decorated bronze strip-bracelet from an inhumation grave in *B ii* AMESBURY 41 relates to types found further north in Britain, associated with late beakers or in contemporary contexts, and to Early Bronze-Age continental types.[41]

Bronze knives or daggers were also imitated in flint, as in the Wiltshire Late-Phase Beaker graves of *B ii* AMESBURY 54 (fig. 14 D) and flat graves at DURRINGTON (fig. 14 A) and WEST OVERTON. Such flint daggers are a well known type in late Beaker graves in east and north-east England, and probably owe something of their origin to the tradition of large bifacially flaked points as at Mildenhall (Suff.) in Middle Neolithic contexts. As with comparable continental examples in the Low Countries and north-east Germany,[42] they were a response to a need in areas where metal was difficult to obtain.

Stone Battle-Axes and Belt Equipment

A recent study of shaft-hole stone battle-axes in Britain (some 500 examples) makes it possible to place the Wiltshire material in its rightful setting.[43] A long continuously evolving series can be subdivided into five main stages. Both association and typology show that the stages are chronologically and culturally valid. In Wiltshire, as elsewhere, the earliest axes are of stages I and II, both within the Late Phase, with other forms elaborated in the Wessex culture and later. In *B ii* DURRINGTON 67 (near Woodhenge) and EAST KENNET 1c battle-axes were associated with late insular derivative beakers (fig. 14 A, B); at *B ii* WILSFORD (S.) 54 (a disturbed grave) almost certainly with a flat riveted knife; and in *B ii* BULFORD 27 and in a flat grave at Ratfyn (AMESBURY) simply with an inhumation. Elsewhere in Britain association of these types with late beakers or riveted daggers is consistent. The Durrington axe is made of Tourmaline Granite from the Land's End district, and that from Wilsford of the Prescelly stone used also at Stonehenge, first in Period II (with a C14 date of *c.* 1620 B.C.).

The inception of the battle-axe series, quite suddenly and at a late stage of the Beaker cultures, poses many problems. Ultimately, as with the occurrence of weapons of the same general class with Bell-Beaker cultures elsewhere (e.g. in the Netherlands), the stone battle-axe derives from the Corded-Ware tradition. But the Dutch finds are either in Corded-Ware graves, with the PF beakers, or in those containing zigzag-ornamented beakers. The latter represent the earliest hybrid Bell-Beaker–Corded-Ware forms, with C14 dates of *c.* 2090 and 1930 B.C., and the axes are not typologically related to the British series.[44] The best comparisons here are probably with axes from late Corded-Ware graves between the Elbe and Oder, but these have no certain chronology.[45]

An innovation found in the Late-Phase graves under discussion, unknown in the earlier groups, is the presence of what may be regarded as belt-fastenings of jet or lignite, in the form of a conical button with **V**-perforation and a ring with external groove and two or more **V**-perforations. The types are well known elsewhere in Britain in contemporary graves, especially in Yorkshire, and are best interpreted as

[41] *Culture and Environment*, ed. Foster and Alcock, 53–91; *Invent. Arch.* GB. 20; *P.P.S.* xxx. 426.
[42] *P.P.S. E. Ang.* vi. 340.
[43] *P.P.S.* xxxii. 199–245.
[44] Van der Waals, *Prehist. Disc Wheels*, 35, 52.
[45] *P.P.S.* xxxii. 228.

elements in a loop-and-stud fastening, presumably for a belt, the ring acting as a tightening device for a looped thong engaging the button. Such buttons are a central European, probably Corded-Ware, contribution but the rings are peculiar to Britain. Their ancestry probably lies, however, partly in the tanged bone belt-loops from such Beaker graves as Sittingbourne (Kent), Stanton Harcourt (Oxon.), and Melton (Elloughton, Yorks. E.R.), with a good continental counterpart in a Bell-Beaker grave in Thuringia,[46] and partly in the bone rings probably of similar function associated with early Scottish beakers.[47] Wiltshire finds of ring-and-button fastenings come from *B ii* WINTERBOURNE STOKE 54, and flat graves at DURRINGTON and WINTERBOURNE MONKTON (fig. 14 C). The **V**-bored buttons also appear in the Wessex culture and well into the period of cremation graves, but the rings are not represented, and the belt-fastening takes the form of a bone (exceptionally metal) hook.

Inhumation Burials with Food Vessels and Allied Pottery

There remain for mention certain inhumation burials accompanied by pots of types which do not come within the Beaker series, and in certain instances are representatives of the food-vessel type of pottery. These are frequent with inhumation burials of the earlier 2nd millennium B.C. in northern England and Scotland and represent an insular derivative, with many variants, from Mortlake- or Fengate-ware origins. In Wiltshire such graves hardly form a distinctive class.

The bowl found with a burial against Stone 31 of the Kennet Avenue at Avebury is difficult to parallel in its entirety (fig. 20 a). But as J. F. S. Stone pointed out,[48] its affinities should lie on the one hand with the Rinyo-Clacton series of Late Neolithic wares (see p. 371), and on the other with a small group of bowls, usually handled, found with inhumations in Wessex.[49] Fragments of a vessel from Ashley Hill (LAVERSTOCK AND FORD) seem to represent a beaker related to this group (fig. 20 c), and the vessel from West Runton in Norfolk is relevant in this connexion.[50]

An undecorated handled vessel from *B ii* COLLINGBOURNE DUCIS 16 (fig. 20 b), found with an inhumation of a child and a biconical shale bead, could be regarded as coming approximately within a class of handled vessels of the earlier Bronze Age of Britain, although these are normally decorated and betray affiliations to either beaker or food vessel stocks. The Collingbourne vessel does, however, bear a strong resemblance to the large series of handled pots characteristic of the central European Straubing culture.[51]

In *B ii* FIGHELDEAN 25 an inhumation burial, secondary to that with a late beaker, was accompanied by a food vessel with rounded shoulder and a bevelled rim decorated with a row of impressions along its outer edge. A cremation in an inverted undecorated food vessel was also secondary to the Early–Middle-Phase Beaker burial in *B ii* BISHOP'S CANNINGS 81.[52] In *B ii* AMESBURY 71[53] a barrow covering an unaccompanied inhumation of Beaker type was truncated, and burials by inhumation and cremation, associated with three food vessels, deposited (fig. 20 d, e, f). A hearth of this phase gave a C14 date of 1640±90 B.C. (NPL–75), and the biconical urn and bronze razor previously found in this barrow are probably contemporary (see p. 381). A food vessel accompanied an inhumation in *B ii* SUTTON VENY 4*a* within a wooden coffin.[54]

[46] *Culture and Environment*, ed. Foster, and Alcock, 79.
[47] *Proc. Soc. Ant. Scot.* xc. 229–31.
[48] *P.P.S.* xv. 122.
[49] Ibid. iv. 98.
[50] *Ant. Jnl.* xxix. 81.
[51] Hans-Jurgen Hundt, *Katalog Straubing*, i, pls. 1–6 for variants.
[52] *W.A.M.* lxi. 102.
[53] *P.P.S.* xxxiii. 336–66.
[54] *W.A.M.* lx. 133.

Reference has already been made (see p. 330) to the food vessel found with the late Beaker burial in the henge monument at Fargo (fig. 8). The relation of this and of the fragments from *B ii* WILSFORD (S.) 74 to other representatives of the type in southern England have been discussed elsewhere.[55]

SETTLEMENTS AND ECONOMY

Domestic sites of the period under discussion are extremely scanty in Wiltshire as elsewhere. The natural forces of solution and erosion of the chalk surface over the millennia, already referred to in connexion with the paucity of earlier Neolithic settlements are, it seems, partly responsible. It should be noted, however, that this rarity of settlements attributable to the Bell-Beaker cultures extends to areas in Britain not subject to such erosion, and is true also of the Continent, where Bell-Beaker domestic sites are equally scarce. At one or two Wiltshire sites Beaker material, often mixed with late Neolithic pottery, has been found when total excavation has exposed the old land-surface under later barrows, as in those of the Snail Down (COLLINGBOURNE KINGSTON) group.[56] Under *B ii* AVEBURY 55 was a similar scatter of pottery and flints, and several pits attributable to the late Beaker times, one containing the dismembered bones of an infant. The land mollusca show that the settlement implied was in woodland, cleared by the time of the cremation-burials and the barrow of Wessex culture date.[57]

Adjacent to the flint-mines and axe-factory sites on Easton Down (WINTERSLOW) Stone explored a part of a settlement site which in its earlier phase seems to have contained at least one rectangular house associated with Neolithic pottery (see p. 300 and fig. 15). Within the area of 50 ft. by 60 ft. examined, however, the majority of structures comprised 10 irregularly oval scoopings in the Chalk, up to 10 ft. by 5 ft. overall, surrounded with the small stake-holes of light hurdle-work, and 3 small circular pits similarly enclosed and containing dark ashy material. Sherds of late Beaker pottery, flint implements, and animal bones were found scattered over the area. The animal bones included the complete skeleton of a dog which should be compared with several other instances of ritual animal burials in Neolithic and Early Bronze-Age Europe.[58]

The presence of Beaker pottery in a secondary position in the ditch silt of causewayed camps has already been mentioned. It has also been suggested that the abundant Rinyo-Clacton pottery and occasional Beaker sherds at Woodhenge and Durrington Walls henge monuments belong to a large settlement just preceding these structures.

There has been a long-standing belief that the British Beaker cultures and their successors in the 2nd millennium B.C. were those of pastoralists rather than of settled agriculturalists. 'The Beaker folk seem to have been even more pastoral than their precursors' wrote V. G. Childe, stressing that the absence of settlements 'enhances the impression of pastoral nomadism'.[59] Hans Helbaek, however, working on the evidence of impressions of food seeds in Beaker pottery in Britain, showed that not only was cereal agriculture an important part of the new economy of the early 2nd millennium B.C., but that the Beaker immigrants were responsible for reversing the wheat-barley ratio of the preceding Neolithic. In Beaker and allied contexts the ratio was 83 per cent barley, and barley was maintained as the dominant crop up to and to some degree into the Early Iron Age.[60] As shown above, at the South Street long barrow (*B i* AVEBURY 68)

[55] *W.A.M.* xlviii. 363; *P.P.S.* ix. 27.
[56] *W.A.M.* lvi. 127–48; lvii. 5–9.
[57] Ibid. lx. 24–43.
[58] H. Behrens, *Neol.-Frühmetallzeit. Tierskellet. Alt. Welt.*
[59] V. G. Childe, *Prehist. Communities of Brit. Isles*, 98.
[60] *P.P.S.* xviii. 194–212.

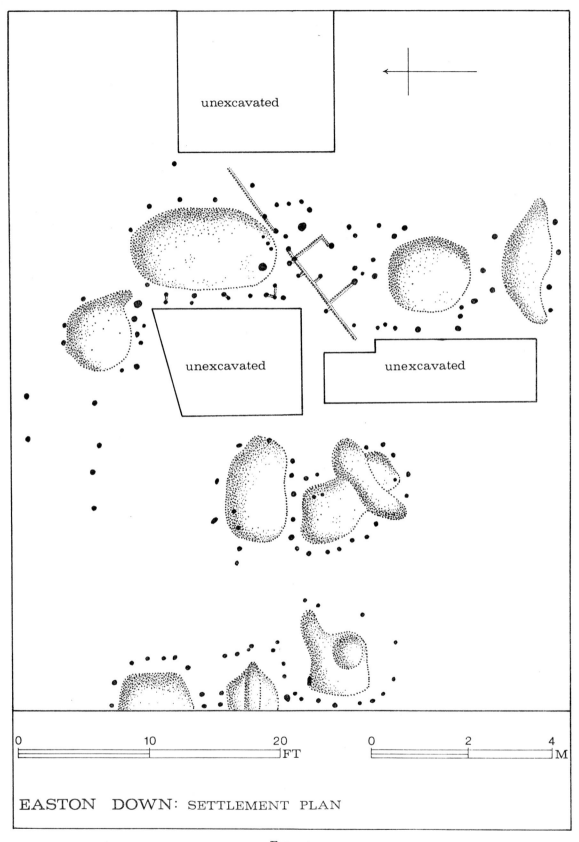

unexcavated

unexcavated

unexcavated

0		10		20		0		2		4

FT

M

EASTON DOWN: SETTLEMENT PLAN

FIG. 15

349

there was, in addition to the ploughing before the building of the monument, evidence of a reversion to fallow, with subsequent clearance of woodland, followed by cross-ploughing which could be directly associated with Beaker pottery. Stock-breeding was, of course, also practised, with some evidence, for instance at Easton Down and in the settlement under *B ii* AVEBURY 55, of a smaller breed of cattle than that characteristic of the Neolithic.[61] On the Continent a palisaded enclosure at Anlo in the Netherlands has been interpreted as a cattle-kraal, and pollen evidence has been used to suggest that the Dutch version of the Corded-Ware cultures was 'responsible for the expansion of grasses and plantain as a result of intensive cattle grazing'.[62] On the other hand a more recent study of the economy of the Corded-Ware cultures as a whole has demonstrated their solid basis in stable mixed farming, with barley the dominant grain in the north European group, and has emphasized the inherent improbability of nomadic pastoralism in the forested landscape of northern Europe.[63] Increased pig-breeding is also noted in Corded-Ware contexts in Little Poland, and may possibly be related to the same phenomenon already noted in the late Neolithic settlement in the Woodhenge–Durrington Walls area. The Corded-Ware component in the immigrant Beaker cultures must have been considerable, if difficult to comprehend in precise terms, and evidence from such a context is relevant to the present enquiry.

The presence of sheep bred for wool as well as flesh and milk is attested by woollen textiles in Beaker and other early 2nd-millennium contexts from several British localities, and these represent the earliest woven fabrics known in these islands. Wiltshire examples of this period belong to the Wessex culture, as in the man's grave in Bush Barrow (*B ii* WILSFORD (S.) 5) and the woman's grave at Manton (*B ii* PRESHUTE 1*a*). At Bush Barrow it was 32 by 28 threads to the inch and at Manton, rather coarser, 22/24 by 28/32 threads.[64] There is no evidence of early linen fabric, although flax-seeds were gathered for their oily nutrient content.[65]

SUMMARY

The survey of the half-millennium *c.* 2000–1500 B.C. is not yet complete, for consideration must be given to the phenomenon, already touched upon, of the appearance at this time of a group of burials with exceptionally rich grave-goods, often in elaborated and formalized types of round barrow (bell, disk, etc.) and with a restricted geographical distribution centred on Wessex and particularly upon Wiltshire. Before turning to this problem it will be as well to summarize the already complicated situation outlined in the foregoing section.

It is necessary in the main to deal with two basic elements, indigenous and immigrant, neither of them unitary. The indigenous traditions may be divided into two, those of southern English (and for the purposes of these chapters Wessex–Wiltshire) origins, and those fairly certainly with origins north of the county, and broadly speaking, of the Thames Valley. In the southern indigenous traditions may be placed first of all the continuity implied in the unbroken development of Neolithic pottery styles from the Middle Neolithic–Ebbsfleet ware through Mortlake into Fengate, and beyond this again, with contributions from immigrant Beaker pottery forms, into cinerary urns. Continuity is again implicit in the persisting 'interest in' if not construction of causewayed camps, chambered tombs, and perhaps to some extent long barrows, though

[61] *W.A.M.* xlv. 368–9; lx. 43.
[62] *Palaeohist.* viii. 59, 83.
[63] *Arch. Rozh.* xxi. 43.
[64] *P.P.S.* xvi. 150.
[65] Ibid. xviii. 194–212.

these do not appear to have been constructed in late Neolithic times. Ceremonial monuments, including some henge monuments, seem to begin in the Middle Neolithic, although they are mainly a feature of the Late Phase.

Northern indigenous traditions in the sense defined above certainly include the development of the food-vessel class of pottery from Mortlake or Fengate pottery traditions, running parallel with the development of cinerary urns but with a much stronger Beaker component. Less certainly, but still probably, it is to northern traditions, that may extend as far as the Orkneys, that should be attributed a vaguely linked complex of culture traits including Rinyo-Clacton pottery, certain flint and bone types, such as *petit tranchet* derivative arrowheads and specialized pin forms, ceremonial shaft-hole stone and antler mace-heads, the cremation rite and the practice of burial in cremation-cemeteries, not infrequently within circular enclosures. Cremation seems certainly an early rite in the north, with a date of *c.* 2270 in Perthshire. These northern traditions seem to have been brought into Wessex in the final phase of the Late Neolithic period.

The immigrant movements, although broadly representing the introduction of the same continental Beaker culture, again fall into southern and northern components. Common to both, however, are the wholly new features of an alien physical type; probably new or modified farming methods with a predominantly barley crop and new breeds of cattle; new types of pottery and new techniques for its manufacture and new types of arrowhead; a radical change of burial-rite from collective to individual Single-Grave inhumations, usually under a round barrow; and finally the first introduction of copper, followed soon by bronze metallurgy, and the working of gold. As a part of the southern immigrant Beaker tradition the appearance of pottery denoting the earliest colonists shows Wiltshire to have formed a part of the country affected by the entrance phase of Beaker immigration in the Early Period. In the subsequent Middle Phase explicit contacts between Wiltshire–Wessex and the Middle Rhine region are perceptible, with the decisive appearance of the first copper and gold working. In the Late Phase, not only is seen the development of southern Beaker traditions, now themselves of a century or so's standing, but also the appearance of elements from the northern insular Beaker tradition. The second of these probably includes the use of tin-bronze and of distinctively British riveted knives or daggers and their copies in flint. In this context it seems likely that the northern indigenous Neolithic traditions just referred to were also spread south of the Thames, and that some makers of food vessels also moved southward.

It appears to have been a highly complicated situation in Wessex, however simplified a picture is attempted, and all evolving within a period which can hardly span more than four centuries or so. The emergence of the Wessex culture, now to be discussed, adds perhaps the most controversial and difficult factor in the whole affair. Is it really a 'culture' in the full archaeological sense? How much does it owe to the intricate background just sketched, and how much is new? If anything is new, from what source or sources does it derive? Is it necessary to assume a new immigrant people in however small numbers, or can the situation be better explained in terms of 'trade' and similar contacts? What is its relation to the final monument of Stonehenge, and of both to possible long-term connexions with the Aegean area? What is the absolute chronology of the phase? It may be impossible to answer any of these questions, but they are among those which must now be posed.

THE WESSEX CULTURE OF THE EARLY BRONZE AGE

THE PROBLEMS

THE final cultural component in Wiltshire prehistory between *c.* 2000–1500 B.C. is what has been known as the Wessex culture of the south English Early Bronze Age. It has been agreed to consider the period as a single complex phase, using a technological model based on non-ferrous metallurgy. Viewed as a chronological unit, however, the half-millennium seems to comprise stone-using traditions of 'Late Neolithic' type, co-existing with the introduction of copper (and gold) working, very soon followed by the development and use of tin-bronze which marks, in the technological classification of prehistory, the beginning of 'the Early Bronze Age'. A group of graves occurs in Wessex, however, containing bronze (very exceptionally copper) objects; no beakers or other types characteristic of the Beaker cultures; burials by inhumation or cremation, often under barrows of specialized types; novel forms of miniature pottery vessels; and above all ornaments of gold, amber, and the vitreous paste, faience. These, as will have been seen, can be shown to overlap with Late-Phase Beaker graves, but they present distinctive characteristics which have led them to be considered as representatives of a separate tradition peculiar to Wessex at the time. About 70 per cent of such graves lie in Wiltshire, so it is a problem concentrated on the county, and its problems can be appreciated only by a brief survey of the past thirty years' thought.

The Wessex culture was first defined and claimed as an entity by the present writer in 1938 after an analysis of some 100 inhumation and cremation graves linked by recurrent characteristics of grave-goods.[1] It was thought chronologically to follow 'immediately upon the Beaker period . . . forming a final phase of the Early Bronze Age', and was not only marked by considerable evidence of contacts or trade with central Europe and Brittany, but its inception was thought to be the result of colonization from the latter region.[2] Furthermore, it was hinted, trade relations might be seen stretching still further afield, and linking Wessex to the Mycenaean world of the mid 2nd millennium B.C. The absolute dates for the duration of the culture, following current European chronology, were given as *c.* 1800–1500 B.C. The thesis was further advanced in 1954 when Nicholas Thomas made a detailed study of six Wiltshire grave-groups[3] and further comments were added by him in 1966[4] as the result of the publication of the new and revised catalogue of the Devizes Museum collections.[5]

The general thesis was widely accepted, and in the post-war years several studies contributed to a fuller understanding of its problems. Miss N. K. Sandars in 1950 pointed out that the new knife-dagger types characteristic of both the Wessex culture and of the Breton tumulus-graves had common origins in central European types, notably the Oder–Elbe group,[6] and in 1954 A. M. ApSimon made a re-examination of the British daggers in question. He showed convincingly that these could be classified

---

[1] *P.P.S.* iv. 52–106.
[2] 'Its origin lies in the ethnic movement from N. France': ibid.
[3] *W.A.M.* lv. 311–26.
[4] Ibid. lxi. 1.
[5] *D.M. Cat. Neo. and B.A. Colls.* (1964).
[6] Univ. Lond. Inst. Arch. *Ann. Rep.* vi. 44.

into an 'Early' Group, found in 14 graves (6 in Wiltshire), and a 'Late' Group found in 36 graves (9 in Wiltshire) and so divided the culture into a Wessex I (Bush Barrow) and a Wessex II (Camerton–Snowshill) phase.[7] He played down the contribution of Brittany in favour of central Europe, and, partly on the evidence of the apparent Mycenaean contacts, gave approximate dates of *c.* 1550–1375 B.C.[8] An important re-examination of ApSimon's second group of daggers was made by Mrs. E. V. W. Proudfoot.[9] Further comment on both Aegean and central European connexions was made by J. M. de Navarro,[10] and two studies of the amber spacer-beads found in Wessex and in both central European and Mycenaean contexts were made by Rolf Hachmann[11] and Miss Sandars.[12] J. F. S. Stone and L. C. Thomas, in a detailed examination of the faience beads, found the spectrographic analyses unilluminating as to origins, but regarded the beads, though not known in Mycenaean contexts, as somehow connected with the general pattern of Aegean trade with Britain.[13] The discovery of the Stonehenge carvings with one showing a weapon having features 'characteristic of early Mycenaean daggers'[14] seemed indirectly to support the similar relationships of the Wessex culture graves, and this was further strengthened by the discovery in 1953–4, in Grave Iota of the B Grave-Circle at Mycenae, of a set of bone shaft-mounts closely resembling those from the Wessex culture grave under Bush Barrow (*B ii* WILSFORD (S.) 5) (fig. 21 A 1).[15]

By the 1960s the Wessex culture was generally thought of by British archaeologists as a local enrichment of communities with mixed antecedents of indigenous Late Neolithic and Beaker traditions, strongly influenced by central European metal-working traditions, and with Mycenaean elements 'somewhat imprecisely represented' but at least implicit in the amber evidence and the Grave Iota mounts.[16] J. G. D. Clark, however, in a paper representative of current reactions to certain archaeological assumptions, raised the question of the whole status of the Wessex culture. He disputed the classing of these rich burials as though they constituted a culture, preferring to regard them as pointers to economic and social change, and seeing no reason to attribute their presence to immigration. C. F. C. Hawkes in a rejoinder, however, felt that archaeologists were still no nearer disproof of an invasion of Wessex.[17]

Finally, a problem of a totally new order presented itself in the 1960s with the demonstration that radiocarbon 'years' do not have the one-to-one equivalence with calendar years that for practical convenience is normally assumed, but diverge from 'true' dates in an irregular but increasing degree as time recedes. When comparing one radiocarbon date with another, this is immaterial, since one is comparing like with like, but when comparing a C14 date in north-west European prehistory with one obtained by historical computation in the Aegean, the former must be corrected in terms of the divergence curve to find its 'historical' equivalent: when such corrections are made on the evidence currently available, the conclusion is reached that much of the duration of the Wessex culture, however conceived as a social unit, precedes the emergence of Mycenaean civilization. This situation is to be discussed later, but in the meantime radiocarbon dates will be quoted in the normal manner, and similarly, in the ensuing summary of the evidence, the term 'Wessex culture' will continue to be employed without prejudice to its social and economic implications, until these themselves come under discussion.

[7] Camerton in Som. and Snowshill in Glos.
[8] Univ. Lond. Inst. Arch. *Ann. Rep.* x. 37.
[9] *P.P.S.* xxix. 406–11, 419–21.
[10] J. M. de Navarro, *Early Cultures in NW. Europe*, 77.
[11] *Bayerische Vorgeschichtsblätter*, xxii. 1–36.
[12] *Antiq.* xxxiii. 292–5.

[13] *P.P.S.* xxii. 37–84.
[14] Ibid. xviii. 236–7.
[15] Piggott, *Anc. Europe*, 134, 164.
[16] *Sbornik Narod. Mus. v Praze*, A, xx. 121.
[17] For Clark's objections see *Antiq.* xl. 182–5, and for rejoinder by Hawkes, see ibid. 297.

BURIAL RITES

In the Wiltshire burials with grave-goods typical of the Wessex culture as conceived in 1938, some 19 are by inhumation and 48 by cremation, and all are under round barrows of various types. The rite of Single-Grave inhumation under a barrow is, as shown, characteristic of the immigrant Beaker cultures, their insular descendants, and of the related graves containing food vessels or equipment, such as riveted bronze daggers, other than pottery. Such 'dagger-graves', which include those with blades of Wessex culture types discussed below, are presumptively male since, as stated above (see pp. 341–2), female graves are difficult to identify with certainty. It therefore follows that ApSimon's division is one of 'dagger-graves' only, and so cannot necessarily be extended to divide the total Wessex culture into two equivalent phases, a point returned to later. His small early group of daggers come from two inhumation and three cremation graves; his late group entirely from cremations.

Another assumption, and acknowledged as such, which has been used in an attempt to subdivide the graves into chronological phases, is the priority of inhumation over cremation as a rite in 2nd-millennium Britain. While broadly speaking cremation burial does succeed inhumation burial completely around the middle of the 2nd millennium, the situation is more complicated in detail. The cremation rite was certainly practised among British Late Neolithic communities, especially in the north, where the pre-Beaker cremation-cemetery at Cairnpapple, West Lothian, may be instanced, or the cremation dated to *c*. 2270 B.C. at Pitnacree in Perthshire.[18] This date is supported by the cremation-cemetery at Stonehenge, where some of the burials are broadly contemporary with the digging of the ditch of Stonehenge I, namely *c*. 2180 B.C. At Fargo Plantation cremations were contemporary with a beaker and a food vessel, and in *B ii* WEST OVERTON 6*b*, four cremations, two in cinerary urns, were contemporary with an inhumation burial with a Late-Phase beaker (see p. 337 and figs. 18, 19). In the third phase of *B ii* AMESBURY 71 cremations with food vessels were dated to *c*. 1640 B.C. (see p. 347 and fig. 20 d, e, f). On rite alone cremation-graves cannot necessarily be placed as later than inhumations, but can be dated only by the associated grave-goods, and West Overton shows that cremations in certain types of cinerary urn can be as early as any. A highly distinctive bead in the same context links the burials to the Wessex culture, as will be shown. On the other hand the arrangement of some Wiltshire barrows in linear cemeteries, as at Winterbourne Stoke Cross-roads and near the Lesser Cursus, shows a sequence beginning with Late-Phase Beaker inhumations and continuing through other inhumation burials to end with cremation. This suggests a priority of inhumation over cremation at least in these specific barrow-groups. That a change in burial rite can take place without outside stimulus or newcomers can be demonstrated from historical situations, such as the repeated alternation between cremation and inhumation in early Athens.[19]

All known barrow-burials with beakers are covered by simple bowl-shaped mounds, but in Wessex and sporadically elsewhere there are a number of barrows with a precisely circular lay-out emphasized by encircling ditches and banks. Such encircled barrows have been divided into four classes: bell-barrows, large mounds with a ditch at a set distance from the base; disk-barrows with a very small central mound within a geometrically circular bank and ditch of considerable diameter; saucer-barrows, low mounds completely covering the enclosed area; and pond-barrows, whose areas,

---

[18] *Proc. Soc. Ant. Scot.* lxxxii. 68; *P.P.S.* xxxi. 34–57.   [19] *Antiq.* xxxiv. 178.

accurately circular, are embanked and hollowed. Cremation cemeteries, as on Easton Down, are occasionally found. All barrow types frequently occur in groups or cemeteries, and the Wiltshire figures are approximately 125–130 bell-barrows, about 100 disk-barrows, 45 saucer-barrows, and 30 pond-barrows. Grave-goods characteristic of the Wessex culture are found in the first two types, 13 from bell-barrows and 8 from

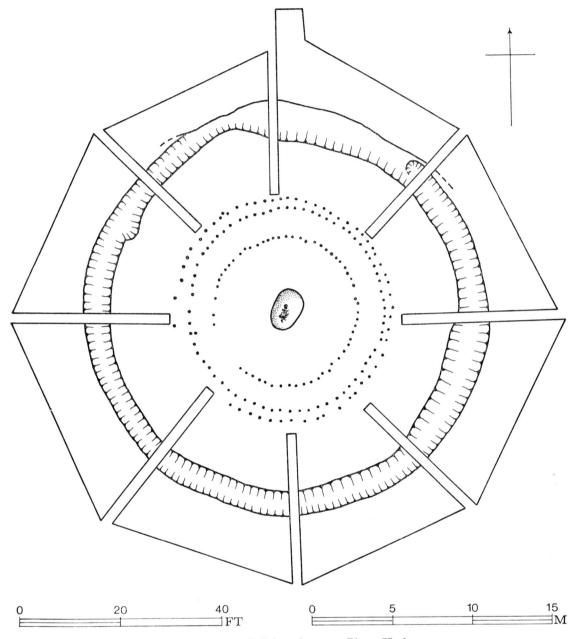

0   20   40 FT   0   5   10   15 M

FIG. 16. Barrow *B ii* Amesbury 71, Phase II plan.

disk-barrows, which are peculiar in having no dagger-graves. The burial rite is divided into 15 inhumations from bowl-barrows and 3 from bell-barrows, and 29 cremations from bowl-, 8 from bell-, and 10 from disk-barrows.

The origin of these encircled barrows must be sought within Britain. Their partial counterparts in the Low Countries, for instance, are there regarded as likely to derive from British prototypes in circumstances discussed later. In some sense they may be formalized versions of the embanked circle theme inherent in henge monuments, and they may also not be unconnected, especially in the disk and pond varieties, with the tradition of the enclosed cremation cemeteries of north Britain, with radiocarbon dates of *c.* 1490 and *c.* 1360 in southern Scotland.[20] The second-phase burial of *B ii* AMESBURY 71 was under what appears to have been a bell-barrow, with a C14 date of as early as *c.* 2010 B.C. (see p. 316). If such an association is valid the origin of the encircled-

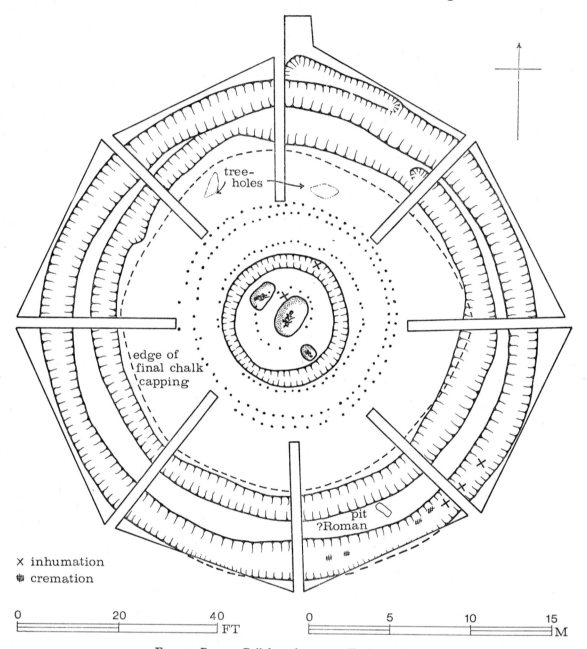

FIG. 17. Barrow *B ii* Amesbury 71, all phases plan.

barrow tradition in Wessex might be seen to be connected with the introduction of the cremation rite, and the cultural complex consisting of shaft-hole mace-heads etc., already referred to, as belonging to a Late Neolithic Phase (see p. 339).

Since virtually all the evidence comes from early barrow-digging, few details survive of funerary ritual or structures within the barrow. Lightly flexed inhumations seem normal, but it is very probable that the Bush Barrow burial was extended in a manner

[20] *Prehist. Peoples Scotland*, ed. Stuart Piggott, 95.

known sporadically in Britain in broadly contemporary graves. Cremations seem to be exceptionally in a pot but sometimes in wooden containers or boxes, as in *B iv* COLLINGBOURNE DUCIS 4, *B ii* WILSFORD (S.) 43, and *B iv* WINTERBOURNE STOKE 4. The inhumation burial in *B iv* AMESBURY 15 lay on an elm plank or bier in a shallow grave, and Hoare records that in the substance of the mound there were at least three cavities, containing the remains of oak timbers, which 'diverged in an angular direction' and 'extended from the top of the barrow to the interment'. It seems very likely that he had encountered a gable-roofed wooden mortuary house of the type of Leubingen and Helmsdorf in Saxo-Thuringia, the Helmsdorf one with a C14 date of *c.* 1660 B.C.[21] In *B ii* WEST OVERTON 1 and WINTERBOURNE STOKE 9, and *B iv* WINTERBOURNE STOKE 5 the burial was in a dug-out coffin cut from a half tree-trunk and said in the last case to be of elm. Such coffins are not infrequent but almost wholly concentrated in Wessex and Yorkshire.[22]

MATERIAL CULTURE

The Daggers

The distinctive grave-goods, on which the concept of a Wessex culture was based, were discussed and mostly illustrated in 1938, and since then several important additional studies have appeared.[23] Here it will be sufficient to comment on specific types from the viewpoint of the problems set out at the beginning of the section.

To the two types of dagger isolated by ApSimon a third group may be added. This comprises the small riveted flat knives known from nine graves of little diagnostic value except that some may represent women's tools. The large daggers show clearly by their triangular outline, the grooving parallel to the edges, and their small rivets, that they cannot typologically be derived from the flat series. That series, without grooves but with massive rivets, and tending to a rounded or tongue-shaped outline, were, as shown, an insular development characteristic of Late-Phase Beaker and contemporary graves in Britain. The type of sheath, where it can be distinguished in corrosion-replacements, is similarly of leather in the Late Beaker and Bush Barrow daggers, but characteristically with a rigid wooden cross-bar at the mouth in ApSimon's second group. The flat hilt with trough-shaped pommel is replaced, so far as the evidence goes, by one with an oval pommel related in form to continental metal prototypes, but already present on the Shrewton tanged knife with a northern Dutch-derived beaker. The gold-ornamented Bush Barrow pommel was flat, but apparently *sui generis*. The appearance of the new forms must denote renewed or intensified contacts with some area or areas of Europe where such types had appeared, either in the Saale–Oder–Elbe region or further west. The type was appearing on the Continent as early as the Singen (Lake Constance) examples, some made of copper, and with the adoption of the 'omega' hilt-plate had become the characteristic form of the Únětice culture and its congeners. In Brittany specialized forms, with a small tang or languette, evolved, probably from central European originals, in the context of the first series of barrow-graves. The Saxo-Thuringian Leubingen culture seems to have taken shape as early as *c.* 1950 B.C.;[24] the Helmsdorf grave of the same culture is *c.* 1660 B.C., and a Breton first-series grave at Lescongar-en-Plouhinec is *c.* 1620 B.C., with bone copies of daggers of fairly developed

[21] Piggott, *Anc. Europe*, 127.
[22] Paul Ashbee, *Bronze Age Round Barrow in Brit.* 86 with map.
[23] Univ. Lond. Inst. Arch. *Ann. Rep.* x. 37; Ashbee,

Bronze Age Round Barrow; *D.M. Cat. Neo. and Bronze Age Colls.* (1964); *W.A.M.* lxi. 1–8.
[24] *Antiq.* xxxix. 222.

types.[25] One Wessex culture dagger, one of two from Bush Barrow, is of specifically Breton type, with languette and a gold-studded haft, but it stands alone (fig. 21 A 10).

Metal analyses supply further information.[26] The Bush Barrow dagger in question is of copper with a high (5 per cent) arsenic content and the other daggers of the class all

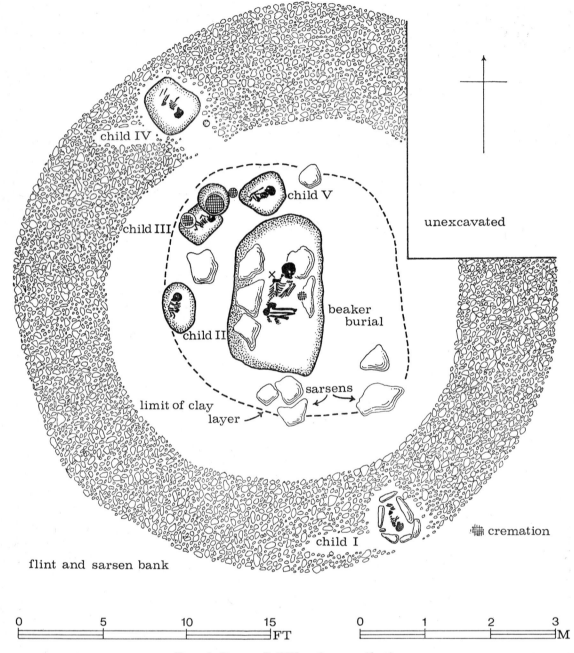

FIG. 18. Barrow *B ii* West Overton 6*b*, plan.

have a low tin (averaging 9·5 per cent) and a relatively high arsenic content, resembling the Breton first series.[27] In ApSimon's 'later' Wessex culture daggers the tin percentage averages 12·7 or more, and there are low arsenic values. In terms of the Stuttgart school the earlier daggers are in groups Eoo and Eo1, the later in F1 and F2. Conventionally Eo1 is 'Iberian' metal and F is 'Alpine', but the interpretation of the analyses is

[25] *Gallia Préhist.* xi. 247.
[26] *Archaeometry*, iv. 39.

[27] P.-R. Giot and others, *Anal. Spect. d'Objets Préhist.* 14.

still under discussion.[28] At all events the daggers of the Bush Barrow group are of a metal dissimilar from that of the Late-Phase Beaker riveted bronze daggers, which are mainly Group E11, with no arsenic, and this underlines the typological distinction already made. What has emerged is a reaffirmation of the distinction between ApSimon's two groups in typology and metal, but since it has been shown that association with cremation cannot be used to indicate a date later than inhumation, and that the insular derivation of the Camerton–Snowshill type from that of Bush Barrow is an assumption, an alternative possibility may be considered. It is possible that the two typological groups have distinct continental origins but need not be in the chronological order of 'Wessex I' and 'Wessex II'; they could be contemporary or even in reverse order. The rarity of graves with Bush Barrow daggers may mean that the period during which such daggers were used as grave-goods was brief, whereas the high tin content of the Late Beaker riveted daggers may link them with the Camerton-Snowshill series. There would then be two separate strains in the grooved daggers taken as characteristic of the Wessex culture. Both would be of central European origin, but one would be allied to or derived from variants typical of the Breton barrow graves and the other more directly linked to the schools of metallurgy in areas such as the Rhineland, where contact had been established since early Beaker times. To anticipate, other connexions with Brittany are limited to a few finds of flint arrowheads of distinctive form, but central European contacts are implied by a large number of parallels.

Other Metal Types

The cast-flange bronze axe-blade (fig. 21 A 6) from *B ii* WILSFORD (S.) 5 (Bush Barrow), as well as six stray finds from other parts of Wiltshire, are of a type long recognized as related to central European cultures such as Únĕtice, appearing in graves with riveted daggers as the second 'weapon-group' in Torbrügge's Phase A in Bavaria, and in hoards of the Leubingen aspect of Únĕtice in Saxo-Thuringia.[29] Typologically related are the very small blades, which may be chisels, from *B iv* WILSFORD (S.) 44 and 58, and a stray find from the Lake region in Wilsford. In *B ii* COLLINGBOURNE KINGSTON 4 such a blade was mounted as a chisel in an antler-tine haft. The bronze awls from some 15 Wessex culture graves are uninformative and are either of the double-pointed type also known from Beaker contexts, or with the flat tang which appears to be an insular development. The double-pointed awl with expanded centre, characteristic of Straubing–Adlerberg Early Bronze Age contexts in Germany, is represented by four Wiltshire finds, all dissociated from the graves to which they belonged. There is a metal-worker's 'tracer' from a bell-barrow grave (*B iv* WILSFORD (S.) 42) which has counterparts in the south German Langquaid hoard.[30]

Perhaps the most decisive evidence of central European contacts are the dress-pins from a number of Wessex culture contexts. The use of such pins is wholly foreign to British traditions, although universal in the European Bronze Age, and their scarcity in Britain underlines their exotic nature. In Wiltshire there are three finds of bronze crutch-headed pins (*B ii* MILSTON 7, WILSFORD (S.) 23 (fig. 22 B 4)), and an unlocated example. One other bronze pin of this type is known in the Wessex culture and comes from Snowshill (Glos.). Bone versions also occur, some, like two of the Wiltshire examples, with twisted stems.[31] Such twisted stems on the Continent are especially

[28] *Helinium*, iv. 3; v. 227.
[29] *Památky Archeologické*, xlv. 115; *Ber. R.-G. Komm.* xl. 1; W. A. von Brunn, *Bronzezeit. Hortfunde*, i, *passim*.
[30] *Ant. Jnl.* xviii. 245; R. Hachmann, *Frühe Bronzezeit*, pl. 54.
[31] *P.P.S.* xxix. 425.

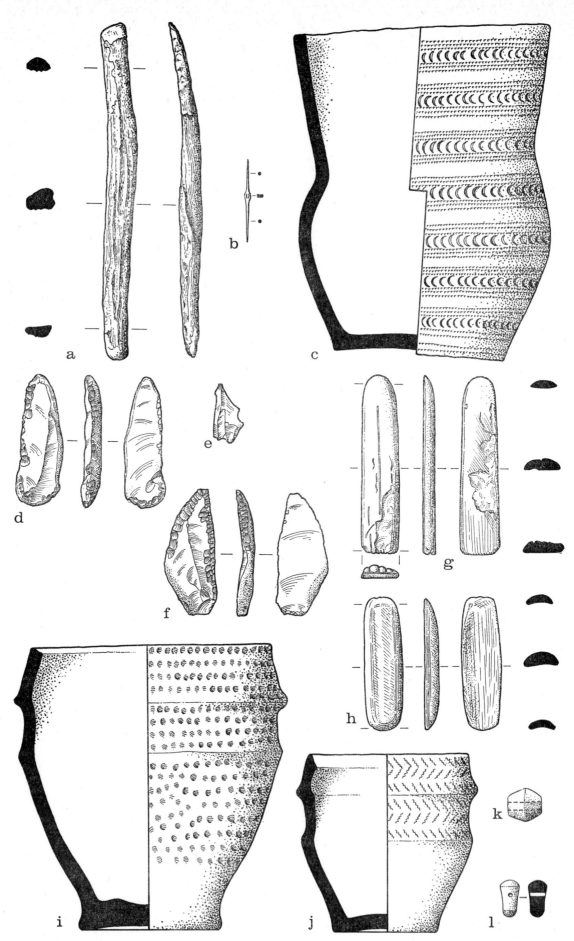

Fig. 19. Grave-goods from *B ii* West Overton 6*b*. From primary inhumation grave: a, antler tool, b, bronze awl, c, beaker, d, e, f, flint tools, g, h, slate polishers. From contemporary mound: i, j, cinerary urns, k, shale bead, l, shale pendant. (½).

characteristic of the globe-headed pin series, as at Langquaid, but the Wessex culture pin of the type from Camerton (Som.) has a plain stem. Crutch-headed pins in bronze or bone are not numerous on the Continent, but occur at Straubing and in Únětice contexts in Bohemia. An aberrant example comes from the Tréboul hoard in Finistère.[32] Ring-headed pins of various forms in Wiltshire Wessex culture graves belong to the same cultural background in Early Bronze-Age Europe. Single-ring examples are known in bronze from *B ii* AMESBURY 24 and in bone from *B ii* WILSFORD (S.) 40 and 56. That from *B iv* COLLINGBOURNE DUCIS 4 is bronze and has double rings, each with a loose ring attached (fig. 22 A 2), and from *B iv* ALDBOURNE 11 comes a bone copy of a four-ringed pin. All have counterparts in Únětice contexts, the Aldbourne pin being related in Britain to those from Brough and Loose Howe (both Yorks. N.R.).[33] In *B ii* NORTON BAVANT 1 there was a fragment of a twisted-shaft pin and another of the West Germany Tumulus Bronze (Reinecke B) type.[34]

The bronze object from *B iv* WILSFORD (S.) 58, a curved fork-shaped casting with twisted prongs, a central slot carrying three bronze rings, and a flat riveted hafting-tang is unique (fig. 22 D 5). It has been interpreted as a 'standard' but hardly convincingly.[35] A possible alternative is to regard it as the head of a horse-goad or stimulus of a type known in the Late Bronze Age from the British Isles and France and originally interpreted as flesh-forks.[36] If so interpreted, the implication of domesticated horses in the earlier 2nd millennium B.C. in Britain must be faced—a possibility supported by the presence of the horse in the Hilversum culture settlement of Vogelenzang in the Netherlands,[37] the spoked-wheel models in immediately post-Únětice contexts in Czechoslovakia, and other models such as that from Trundholm in south Scandinavia.[38]

Halberd and Ingot-Torc Pendants

Two exceptionally important ornaments in the form of miniature weapons come from two graves, *B ii* PRESHUTE 1a and *B iv* WILSFORD (S.) 8 (fig. 22 C 2). Both have bronze blades, and that from Preshute has a completely gold-sheathed shaft while the one from Wilsford has an amber shaft with gold bands. Bronze or copper halberds, hafted at right angles to the shaft, have a wide European distribution and probably originate in the Leubingen version of the Únětice culture in Saxo-Thuringia and adjacent regions, where halberds with metal-sheathed or banded shafts occur.[39] The Wiltshire miniature versions, therefore, denote explicit relations with this area, and it may be noted that a burial with a full-sized bronze shafted halberd at Łeki Małe in Poland has a C14 date of *c*. 1655 B.C. in close agreement with the date of *c*.1660 from the Helmsdorf burial of the same culture. This suggests contemporaneity between the graves with halberd-pendants and those (by inhumation and cremation) in Phase III of *B ii* AMESBURY 71, with a C14 date of *c*. 1640 B.C. (see p. 347). The Wilsford grave also contained a small bronze, gold-plated, crescent-shaped pendant, copying in miniature an 'ingot-torc' of characteristic central European Early Bronze-Age form (fig. 22 C 11). A comparable bronze pendant on a chain from Radewill near Halle reinforces the Saxo-Thuringian connexions.[40]

[32] Hundt, *Katalog Straubing*, i, pl. 11, no. 53; Hachmann, *Frühe Bronzezeit*, 88; J. Briard, *Les Dépôts Bretons et l'Âge du Bronze Atlantique*, 94.

[33] *Pamatky Arch.* xliv. 229; xlv. 115; *P.P.S.* xv. 100.

[34] *P.P.S.* viii. 41.

[35] *W.A.M.* lv. 321, 326.

[36] *Ant. Jnl.* xv. 449–51; *Bull. Mus. Roy. d'Art et d'Hist.* (Brussels, 1946), 16.

[37] *In Het Voetspoor A. E. van Giffen* (2nd edn.), ed. Glasbergen and Groenman-van Waateringe, 87, 176.

[38] *Sbornik Narod. Mus. v Praze*, A, xx. 124.

[39] Piggott, *Anc. Europe*, 162.

[40] Ashbee, *Bronze Age Round Barrow*, 146, pl. xxviii a, b.

Archery Equipment

There is some evidence for archery in Wessex culture and allied graves: a flint barbed-and-tanged arrowhead came from *B ii* ROUNDWAY 5*b*, five from *B ii* COLLINGBOURNE KINGSTON 19, and others from unaccompanied cremation graves of uncertain date. In *B ii* ALDBOURNE 13 part of a reworked four-hole stone bracer and an oval pendant almost certainly made from another were found, and in *B v* BISHOP'S CANNINGS 12 was a fragment of a six-hole bracer. These suggest contact with surviving Beaker traditions of the Wessex–Middle Rhine group rather than an assemblage of antiquities, and in the context of archery equipment possibly come the 'shaft-smoothers' found in several graves (fig. 22 D 7).[41] The arrowheads are normally of types rather larger than those from Beaker graves, and in exceptional instances, such as the five from a cremation in *B ii* COLLINGBOURNE KINGSTON 19, approximate to forms which appear to be related to those from the Breton tumulus-graves and some Late Beaker graves in Britain.[42]

Battle-Axes, Maces, and Mace-Pendants

It was seen when dealing with the Late Beaker graves that these on occasion, in Wiltshire as elsewhere, contained shaft-hole stone battle-axes of simple types classified within Stages I and II of Mrs. F. E. S. Roe's series.[43] The insular developmental series proceeds, with southern and northern variants, smoothly from the earlier forms, and representatives of the developed series appear in a number of Wessex culture graves: Stage III battle-axes in *B iv* CODFORD 4, *B ii* UPTON LOVELL 2*a*, and an unlocated barrow on Windmill Hill; Stage IV in *B ii* KILMINGTON 1 and *B iv* WILSFORD (S.) 58 (fig. 22 D 4); and Stage V in *B ii* CODFORD 5, SHREWTON 27, and 'a barrow near Stonehenge'. Mrs. Roe notes the difficulty of assigning her Stage III axes to the conventional 'Wessex I' phase where they would theoretically belong. In terms of inhumation and cremation rites, the axes are equally divided in Stages IV and V, while in Stage III there is one cremation to two inhumations, one of which is the extraordinary burial at Upton Lovell, with grave-goods including the metal-workers' stone tools already mentioned (see p. 344), flint axes, and fringes of perforated pointed bones.[44] In general the main conclusion suggested by the continuance of the battle-axe tradition of Stages III–V in the Wessex culture is that there was a strong element of affinity or continuity between the Late Beaker population and those responsible for the burials, by inhumation or cremation, in which beakers cease to be used. The source of the stones for these Wessex culture battle-axes includes several from the Hyssington (Mont.) outcrops and the Whin Sill (Teesdale), and one from a Nuneaton (Warws.) source, all pointing to northern connexions perhaps not unassociated with the exploitation of copper ores.[45]

The battle-axe as an object of prestige was replaced in the Bush Barrow grave by a mace with a head of polished stone from the region west of Teignmouth (Devon) (fig. 21 A 2). Similar maces in analogous graves are known from Clandon (Dors.) and Towthorpe (Yorks. E.R.), but the Bush Barrow mace-head is of anomalous form and does not come within the typological series studied by Mrs. Roe.[46] It nevertheless represents a 'mace tradition' which is further expressed in Wessex culture graves by amber or shale pendants in the form of miniature maces of recognizable 'pestle' form from *B iv* WILSFORD (S.) 8 (fig. 22 C 4–8) and *B vi* DURRINGTON 14. Pendants also occur outside Wiltshire at Cressingham (Norf.) and Halwill (Devon), and a shale example was contem-

[41] *W.A.M.* xlv. 432–58.
[42] *Culture and Environment*, ed. Foster and Alcock, 77.
[43] *P.P.S.* xxxii. 199–245.
[44] *W.A.M.* lviii. 93–7; lxi. 1–24.
[45] *P.P.S.* xxviii. 238.
[46] *Anc. Europe*, ed. Coles and Simpson, 145–72.

porary with a Beaker inhumation and cremations in cinerary urns in *B ii* WEST OVERTON 6*b* (fig. 19 l).[47] In Ireland there is a large series of similar pendants from passage-graves, where they must represent secondary deposits, as must the actual pestle-maces from Scottish chambered tombs.[48] The pendants can no longer be regarded as primary constituents in a 'Boyne Culture', with dates of around 2500 B.C. as at Newgrange (co. Meath),[49] but are probably related to the V-bored buttons and food vessels from Irish chambered tombs within the first half of the 2nd millennium B.C.[50] All presumably belong to the Late Neolithic phase in Wiltshire already outlined. The pestle mace-head from the Stonehenge cemetery, as well as the bead from Overton, suggest that the Wilsford, Durrington, and Cressingham graves were contemporary with the Late Phase of Wessex beakers, with cremation cemeteries, and with the northern traditions implied also by the mace-heads and probably Rinyo-Clacton pottery. It will be remembered that the Wilsford grave also contained a halberd-pendant, for which the Polish evidence suggests a date around 1650 B.C. A further overlap with late beakers is provided by the grave of this period on Charmy Down, Bath, containing a ribbed shale bead paralleled only in such Wessex culture graves as *B ii* PRESHUTE 1*a* (fig. 21 B 12), WILSFORD (S.) 7, and *B iva* WILSFORD (S.) 16, the first of which also contained a halberd-pendant.[51]

In 1938 it was wrongly assumed that the shaft of the Bush Barrow mace had been inlaid with zigzag terminal and medial bone mounts, but it was later realized that these must have belonged to a separate staff. The discovery of close counterparts of these mounts in Shaft-Grave Iota of the B Circle at Mycenae (still unpublished) seems to provide good evidence for Mycenaean–Wessex connexions. Furthermore, a firm point in chronology is provided by the Middle Helladic III pottery in the grave, which should date from a little before 1600 B.C. The situation, however, is more complicated than it appears on the surface, and is discussed at a later stage.

Amber and Space-Plate Necklaces

In 1938 it was reckoned that about 40 per cent of the graves assigned to the Wessex culture contained beads or other ornaments of amber, and the proportion would probably be higher today, in contrast to the very few finds of amber in Beaker contexts, all of which come from Yorkshire or further north. The appearance of amber in quantity is, therefore, another factor distinguishing the graves under discussion from others contemporary or earlier, and there is also a distinction in type. In Beaker contexts there are only crudely perforated lumps or simple V-bored buttons,[52] but with the Wessex culture graves are encountered a whole series of new forms of amber ornaments, gold-mounted or forming components of composite necklaces with space-beads to separate the strings.

The amber and gold halberd-pendant has already been noted, and other ornaments of these substances (chryselectrine?) which have received much discussion are the gold-mounted amber disks, perforated for suspension perhaps as ear-ornaments, from the two halberd-pendant graves of *B ii* PRESHUTE 1*a* and *B iv* WILSFORD (S.) 8 (figs. 21 B 11; 22 C 13, 14). What appears from Stukeley's record to be a similar disk came from *B iv a* AMESBURY 44. Much has been made of the resemblance between these disks and the

[47] *P.P.S.* xxxii. 122–55.
[48] Piggott, *Neo. Cultures Brit. Isles*, 207, 220; *Anc. Europe*, ed. Coles and Simpson, 145–72.
[49] *Antiq.* xliii. 140.
[50] *Jnl. R. Soc. Ant. Ireland*, xcviii. 163.
[51] *Ant. Jnl.* xxx. 34–46.
[52] Ardiffery, Cruden (Aberdeens.) provides an example of the first: Acklam Wold (Mortimer no. 124) and Kelleythorpe (Mortimer no. C 38) both in Yorks. are examples of the second: J. R. Mortimer, *Burial Mounds E. Yorks.*

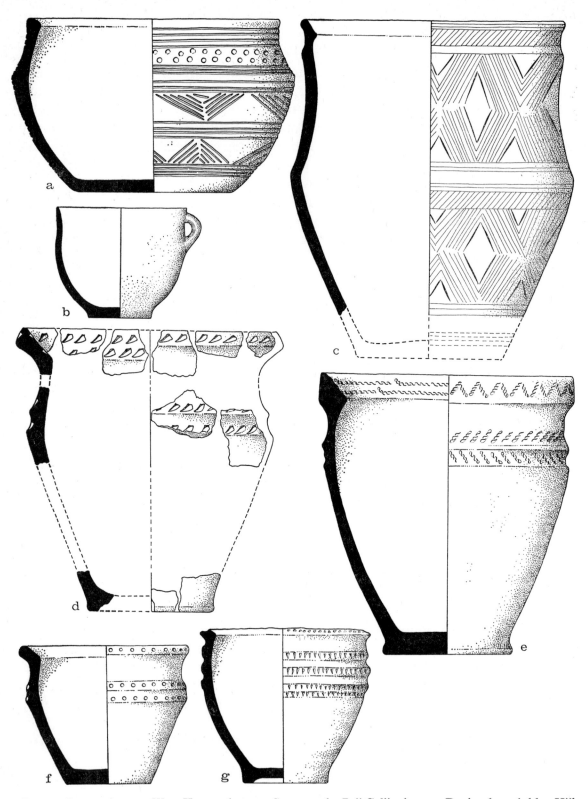

FIG. 20. Pottery from: a, West Kennet Avenue, Stone 31; b, *B ii* Collingbourne Ducis 16; c, Ashley Hill (Laverstock and Ford); d, e, f, *B ii* Amesbury 71; g, Fargo henge monument. ($\frac{1}{3}$).

364

amber disk with very narrow gold edging from the Double-Axe tomb at Knossos; J. M. de Navarro also quoted more elaborate gold-mounted stone disks from Cyprus.[53] The Knossos disk (not really a strikingly close parallel) is Late Minoan IIIa, c. 1350–1400, while the halberd-pendant associations imply a C14 date of c. 1650 B.C. The chronological problems raised by these and other factors are discussed later.

Composite necklaces of amber beads with space-plates are known from four Wiltshire graves (*B ii* UPTON LOVELL 2e (fig. 21 C 1), WILSFORD (S.) 50a, *B iv a* AMESBURY 44, and *B v* KINGSTON DEVERILL 5). Elsewhere in Britain they are known only from three finds, Oakley Down in Dorset, Beaulieu in Hampshire, and the Knowes of Trotty in Orkney. These, and a large group of continental finds, were illustrated and discussed by Hachmann in 1957[54] and since he wrote other German finds have been published,[55] as have two outlying examples from Andrup in Jutland and Lastours (Aude) in France.[56] Their great interest lies in the fact that identical amber space-plate necklaces, or fragments of them, are known from three Mycenaean contexts: in Shaft-Grave IV of Schliemann's Grave-Circle A, Grave Omicron of the B Circle at Mycenae itself, and in a chamber-tomb at Kakovatos in Elis.

A difficulty, which at first seemed to present itself, was equating an historical date of c. 1660–1550 B.C. for Grave Omicron not only with the Wessex culture graves in question, where such a date would not have seemed out of place so far as an absolute chronology could be framed at all, but equating such a date for a large group of German finds which appear to be later. Miss N. K. Sandars helped matters by isolating a 'basic pattern' of space-bead with 'complex' borings, both transverse and V-shaped (as in Upton Lovell or Oakley Down, Dorset, and in Grave Omicron at Mycenae), and by emphasizing what Hachmann had already stressed, that many late finds were of isolated beads, now no longer functional in composite necklaces and reasonably considered as heirlooms.[57] The parallels between Greece and Wessex still remain, therefore, as valid evidence of presumptive contact, the more so since the new investigations by infra-red spectroscopy of the composition of Aegean Bronze-Age amber are demonstrating without doubt its Baltic origin.[58] The problem of ultimate origins for the complex-bored, space-plate necklace remains. Ebbe Lomborg has looked to Germany, although the Wessex culture itself is as good a claimant as any, bearing in mind the use of V-boring on buttons and the large series of what must be derivative forms in jet (as in north Britain), or translated into sheet gold as lunulae. Nicholas Thomas has suggested that the nicked disk of gold-covered bone from *B iv* WILSFORD (S.) 8 may have been intended to represent a lunula (fig. 22 C 13, 14).[59] It is possible that the flat shale or jet pendant from *B ii* BISHOP'S CANNINGS 46 is reworked from a space-plate, and Thomas has pointed out that a single bone space-plate from a double-stringed necklace comes from *B ii* COLLINGBOURNE KINGSTON 4 with good parallels from Suffolk.[60]

The dates of the Mycenaean finds, obtained by historical extrapolation from Egyptian chronology, range from c. 1550 (Grave Omicron) and c. 1500 (Shaft-Grave IV) to c. 1500–1450 B.C. (Kakovatos), so that the finds could span a century or so. The Grave Omicron find was described as 'a necklace . . . made of beads of Baltic amber' which 'reached all the way to the waist'[61] and may have been complete. At Kakovatos there were only stray pieces.

[53] de Navarro, *Early Cultures in NW. Europe*, 102.

[54] *Bayerische Vorgeschichtsblätter*, xxii. 1.

[55] e.g. R. Feustel, *Bronzezeit. Hügelgräberkult. von Schwarza*, 19.

[56] *Antiq.* xli. 221–2.

[57] Ibid. xxxiii. 292–5.

[58] *Greek, Rom. and Byz. Studies*, vii. 191, ix. 5.

[59] *W.A.M.* lxi. 7.

[60] Ibid. lv. 319.

[61] *Studies in Medit. Arch.* vii. 5.

Faience Beads

Since their first recognition sixty years ago as exotic objects of probably Oriental origin, the faience beads of the British Bronze Age have alternatively induced the highest hopes and the deepest disillusionment in archaeologists seeking chronological links between the barbarian north-west and the historically documented Near East. The classic studies are those written in 1935 and 1956.[62] The promise of elucidation by spectrographic analysis of trace elements suggested in 1935 was found to be unfulfilled after the examination of 70 samples twenty years later, although it has recently been suggested that the analyses might be susceptible to a different interpretation. Pending agreement on this, however, L.C. Thomas's verdict must stand, namely that 'strict and rigorous adherence to morphological characters and archaeological evidence alone remains the only sure guide'.[63]

The 21 Wiltshire finds are uniformly of the segmented tubular type and come almost wholly from cremation graves, frequently in disk-barrows. The only certain inhumation is in *B ii* AMESBURY 54. Possible but uncertain instances are in *B ii* IDMISTON 25e and WILSFORD (S.) 54, but both records are unreliable. The Amesbury burial appears to have been secondary to a Late Beaker inhumation with a flint dagger. Significant associations are those in *B iv a* AMESBURY 44 (space-plate amber necklace and gold-mounted amber disk) and *B v* KINGSTON DEVERILL 5 (space-plate amber necklace). The WILSFORD (S.) 54 association, if acceptable, would be with another space-plate necklace. The two undoubted associations would place these faience-bead finds at least within whatever 'horizon' is denoted by the gold-mounted amber disks (and through them, the halberd-pendants) and the space-plate amber necklaces. It does not necessarily follow, however, that all other finds, even in Wiltshire, are of this date. The beads might easily become heirlooms, as has been suspected of the space-plates, and finds of single beads with cremation burials, which not infrequently occur, might be suspected to be of later date than those with comparatively large numbers, such as the sixteen found in *B iv* UPTON LOVELL 1.

The continental distribution of segmented and other faience beads is complex. There is a central European group, which should be regarded as separate from those beads found in the British Isles or the west generally, where they only occur sporadically. The unaccompanied find of a single faience segmented bead of 'Wessex' type in a north Jutland cist-grave does not help chronologically,[64] but the well known Odoorn necklace from the Netherlands has closer links with Wiltshire. In addition to amber and segmented faience beads, the Odoorn necklace is composed of crimped tube-beads of tin sheet, and a similar tin bead was recorded from a cremation-grave in *B v* SUTTON VENY 11c. The Odoorn necklace is a stray find, but a recent discovery of a segmented faience bead in a settlement of the Hilversum culture gives an indication of the chronological position of such beads in the Dutch sequence.

The ultimate origin of the Wiltshire and other British segmented beads, and of faience beads and pendants of other types, is still unknown. Stone demonstrated the high antiquity of faience manufacture in the ancient Near East, and there is no doubt that typologically the Wiltshire beads come extremely close to examples from Abydos in Egypt and Lachish in the Levant, well dated to c. 1400 B.C., and the analyses are not incompatible with such a relationship. While independent invention cannot be ruled out, the innovations in both type and material represented by the faience objects of the British Isles and west Europe generally demand something more than native genius to

---

[62] *Arch.* lxxxv. 203–52; *P.P.S.* xxii. 37–84.   [63] *P.P.S.* xxii. 77.   [64] *Acta Arch.* xxv. 241.

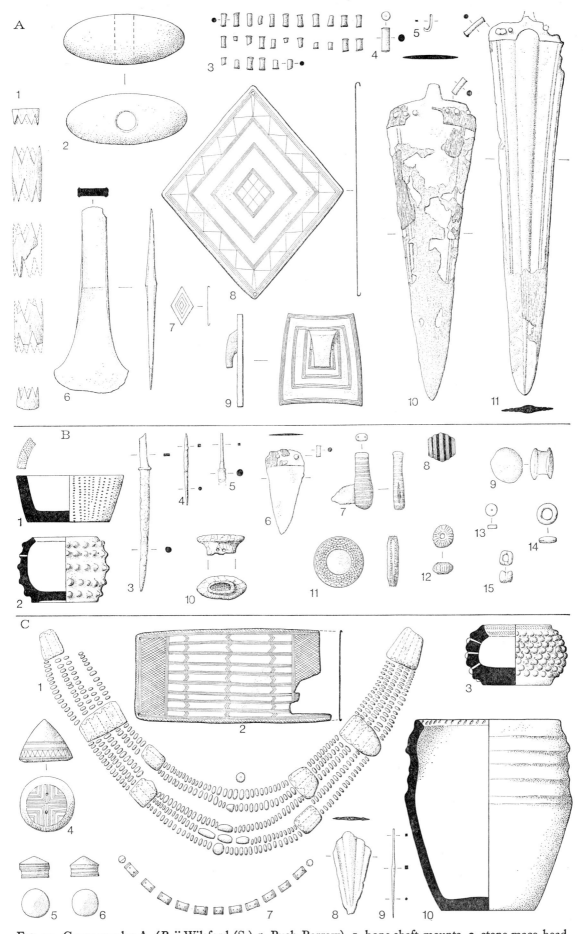

Fig. 21. Grave-goods: A, (*B ii* Wilsford (S.) 5, Bush Barrow), 1, bone shaft-mounts, 2, stone mace-head, 3, 4, bronze rivets, 5, bronze wire, 6, bronze axe, 7, 8, gold plates, 9, gold-plated belt-hook, 10, copper dagger, 11, bronze dagger; B, (*B ii* Preshute 1*a*), 1, miniature cup, 2, miniature 'grape cup', 3–5, bronze awls, 6, bronze knife, 7, bronze and gold halberd pendant, 8, shale and gold bead, 9, pottery stud, 10, bone knife-pommel, 11, amber and gold disk, 12–15, stone beads; C, (*B ii* Upton Lovell 2*e*), 1, amber necklace, 2, gold plate, 3, miniature 'grape cup', 4, gold-plated shale cone, 5, 6, gold studs, 7, gold beads, 8, bronze knife, 9, bronze awl, 10, pottery vessel. ($\frac{1}{3}$).

367

explain them. Once a type and technique have been introduced from outside, independent development and imitation can follow, and the divergences between the Wessex and the Scottish faience objects have long been the subject of comment. Pending a thorough re-examination of the whole problem the probability can surely be accepted that the Wiltshire beads at least represent imports from some distance.

Similar segmented beads were found with Mycenaean Late Helladic IIIa pottery on Salina in the Lipari Islands, implying a date of c. 1400–1300 B.C., consonant with the Abydos and Lachish dating. Beyond this piece of evidence there is nothing to associate the distribution of segmented (or other) faience beads in Europe north of the Alps to 'specifically Mycenaean activities'.[65]

Gold and Other Ornaments

Some gold objects from Wessex culture graves have already been considered, and most of the other types are *sui generis*. Miss J. J. Taylor has recently shown that 'three distinctive styles of technique are clearly apparent in the gold-sheet work of the Early Bronze Age' of the British Isles: the thin gold-foil work of the Beaker culture disks, the style exemplified by the lunulae, and the Wessex culture gold-work. The lunula group has been described as 'spanning the other two with several decorative styles within it'.[66] If the lunulae, or at least those with skeuomorphic space-plate ornament, are broadly contemporary with, or a little later than, the amber space-plate necklaces, this overlap would be substantiated, and the 'Wessex' characteristic of dots within incised lines[67] could be considered as a Beaker heritage. The small gold disks from *B ii* WILSFORD (S.) 50a, with incised and dotted ornament, are near to the Beaker type of disk itself.[68] The quadrangular gold plates from Bush Barrow have a close parallel at Clandon in Dorset, and the oblong plate from *B ii* UPTON LOVELL 2e (fig. 21 C 2) has a less close counterpart in that from Cressingham in Norfolk. The ornament on the Upton Lovell plate suggests a rolled-out version of a decorated Únětice cuff-armlet, but the gold sheet has never been bent. The resemblances between the ornament on the larger Bush Barrow plate (fig. 21 A 8) and that on gold from the Mycenae shaft-graves[69] are too unspecific and simple to be relevant.

The sheet-gold cones covering shale or jet cores as at *B iv* WILSFORD (S.) 8 and *B ii* UPTON LOVELL 2e (figs. 21 C 4; 22 C 14) are exaggerated versions of V-bored buttons, with Late Beaker antecedents, and are represented in simple smaller form from, for instance, *B ii* ALDBOURNE 6 and FIGHELDEAN 12, or *B v* SUTTON VENY 11c and WINTERBOURNE STOKE 14 and 67. The ring-and-button fastening, however, characteristic of that phase (see p. 346) is changed in the Wessex culture to a hooked attachment, the most splendid being the gold-sheathed example (originally wood?) from Bush Barrow (fig. 21 A 9). Other (bone) belt-hooks are known from several Wiltshire graves, as in *B ii* WILSFORD (S.) 18, *B iv* WEST OVERTON 4, and *B iva* WILSFORD (S.) 15. Such belt-hooks are known outside Wessex, and have been commented on by D. D. A. Simpson;[70] their appearance without earlier antecedents in Britain may be related to their equally unheralded occurrence in Early Bronze-Age cultures in east-central Europe.[71]

Among miscellaneous types not yet commented upon the perforated whetstones (fig. 22 B 3) and the so-called bone 'tweezers' may be noted, both recently discussed by

---

[65] *Sbornik Narod. Mus. v Praze*, A, xx. 120.
[66] *P.P.S.* xxxiv. 259–65.
[67] As on the Preshute disk: *D.M. Cat. Neo. and B.A. Colls.* (1964), no. 195 with enlarged photograph.

[68] Cf. E. C. R. Armstrong, *Cat. Irish Gold Ornaments*, 85, no. 336, pl. xix, 428.
[69] Univ. Lond. Inst. Arch. *Ann. Rep.* x. 44.
[70] *Anc. Europe*, ed. Coles and Simpson, 202.
[71] *Festschrift Gustav Schwantes*, ed. K. Kersten, 151–6.

Mrs. Proudfoot.[72] The whetstones have good counterparts in Early Bronze-Age contexts in central and north Europe, but the tweezers (which may not be tweezers at all)[73] have a very restricted Wessex distribution.[74] A bone pipe made from a swan's ulna from *B ii* WILSFORD (S.) 23 is a rare example of a widespread series of early musical instruments and might have originally been provided with a simple split-straw reed (fig. 22 A 5).[75]

Two remarkable objects remain to be mentioned, namely the unlocated shale-handled cups, almost certainly from burials in the Amesbury region. These, as R. S. Newall showed,[76] are related to those in Wessex culture contexts at Broad Down, Farway (Devon),[77] and the amber versions at Clandon (Dors.) and (less directly) Hove (Suss.). The gold-handled cup from Fritzdorf near Bonn is closely comparable, and is linked by details of its handle to the corrugated gold cup from Rillaton (Cornw.)[78] The dotted ornament on the Fritzdorf piece has affinities with Miss Taylor's Beaker-style gold-work, and the shape has affinities with the late beakers of southern Germany, handled and undecorated, and with the Adlerberg handled cups. The Rillaton cup is frankly a copy of a beaker, with a good prototype in the handled beaker from Balmuick, Comrie (Perths.), which copies an All-Over-Cord vessel and should not be very late in the beaker sequence.[79] The corrugated body of the Rillaton cup, which has been quoted as copying Mycenaean goldsmiths' techniques, could also originate from a pottery original, as the Balmuick vessel suggests.

Pottery

The placing of a pottery vessel within the cinerary-urn class with inhumation burials was very exceptional in a Wessex culture context. The association in *B ii* WILSFORD (S.) 7 is undoubted, but the situation in *B ii* UPTON LOVELL 2e is dubious, and in *B ii* PRESHUTE 1a the vessel was found 9 ft. from the burial. Cremation burials with grave-goods of Wessex culture type were contained in urns in the Easton Down cemetery, and one with an unaccompanied cremation was in the bell-barrow *B iv* AVEBURY 38. The Wilsford urn is a remarkable example of I. H. Longworth's primary series of collared urns, with fine whipped-cord ornament and a neatness of zonal design reminiscent of beakers of the European or Wessex–Middle Rhine series rather than of later types. In general, however, Longworth felt that the Fengate style of Neolithic pottery, from which his collared-urn series derived, suggested 'the absorption in the Late Neolithic of several ceramic traits drawn from divergent sources including both Rinyo-Clacton and the complex including Rusticated Ware and Necked Beakers, into a basic Peterborough tradition'.[80] More than 20 vessels in his primary collared-urn series come from Wiltshire barrows, and, as has been shown, the type originates in Late Neolithic times and was current in Wiltshire as a cremation container at a period contemporary with Late Beaker inhumations and Wessex culture mace-head pendants.[81] It is, therefore, impossible to assign cremation burials in such pots to a position in relation to the Wessex culture graves, but all could be contemporary.

The distinctive pottery form in Wessex culture graves comprises various forms of miniature cups, some of which are of types with very localized distributions within Wessex. The 'grape cups' (fig. 21 B 2, C 3) of older nomenclature, better renamed Manton

[72] *P.P.S.* xxix. 411–12, 422–5.
[73] *W.A.M.* lxi. 6–7.
[74] To Mrs. Proudfoot's list should be added the find made subsequently from a ploughed-out cremation on Ford Down, Laverstock: *Ant. Jnl.* xlix. 102.
[75] *Anc. Europe*, ed. Coles and Simpson, 336, 342.

[76] *W.A.M.* xliv. 111–17.
[77] *Proc. Devon Arch. Explor. Soc.* iv. 1.
[78] Piggott, *Anc. Europe*, pl. xvii.
[79] *Proc. Soc. Ant. Scot.* lxviii. 132, no. 254.
[80] *P.P.S.* xxvii. 263–306.
[81] Ibid. xxxii. 131–2.

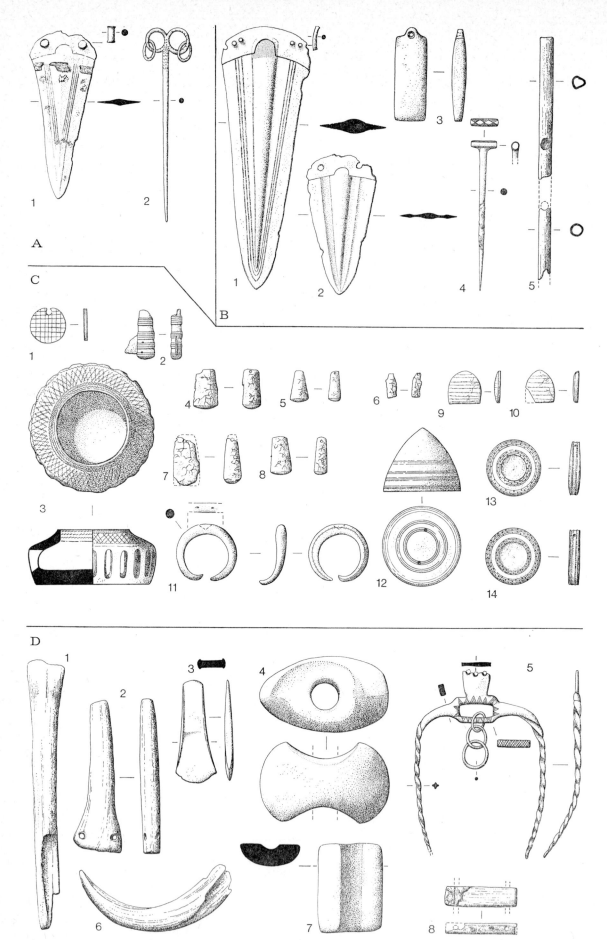

FIG. 22. Grave-goods: A, (*B iv* Collingbourne Ducis 4), 1, bronze dagger, 2, bronze pin; B, (*B ii* Wilsford (S.) 23), 1, 2, brozne daggers, 3, whetstone, 4, bronze pin, 5, bone pipe; C, (*B iv* Wilsford (S.) 8), 1, gold-plated bone disk, 2, gold amber and bronze halberd-pendant, 3, miniature cup, 4–10, amber pendants, 11, gold-plated bronze pendant, 12, gold-plated shale cone, 13–14, gold and amber disks; D, (*B iv* Wilsford (S.) 58), 1, worked bone, 2, antler handle, 3, bronze axe, 4, stone shaft-hole axe, 5, bronze pronged object, 6, boar's tusk, 7, stone rubber, 8, perforated bone plate. ($\frac{1}{3}$).

cups (from the Manton Barrow, *B ii* PRESHUTE 1*a*), and the Aldbourne cups are peculiar to this area; 6 of the Manton cups were with inhumations, but another 3, and all 7 of the Aldbourne cups, were with cremations. Both types occur with presumptively male as well as undifferentiated graves. The incised decoration with dotted filling on the Aldbourne cups recalls the bowl from the grave against Stone 31 of the Avebury Avenue and Rinyo-Clacton styles in general. The use of plastic ornament in the form of knobs on the Manton cups, moreover, might come from a similar background, while Stone and W. L. Scott independently urged a connexion between Rinyo-Clacton wares and miniature cups.[82] Another form, with a wider distribution, is the cup with oval perforations or slits in the side, as in *B iv* WILSFORD (S.) 8 (fig. 22 C 3) and three Wessex culture graves outside Wiltshire. The miniature-cup tradition is also expressed in the use of such cups as accessory vessels to cinerary-urn burials, conventionally assigned to a Middle Bronze-Age phase subsequent to the Wessex culture, but with equal plausibility largely contemporary with it. In all, the pottery of the Wessex culture graves represents a highly individual and localized selection and development of types in Wessex, derived from local indigenous tradition but used in a new funeral rite owing nothing to Beaker traditions. There may finally be noted here, only to dismiss them, the contentious sherds surviving from a five-handled jar of burnished red ware, said to have been found with an inhumation burial and two bronze daggers in *B iv* WINTER-BOURNE STOKE 5. There seems no doubt that the sherds are of the Early Iron Age, although their presence in alleged association with the primary burial in the barrow remains unexplained.[83]

INTERPRETATION

The foregoing enumeration of large numbers of individual objects has been rendered necessary by the fact that what differentiates the graves under consideration from, for instance, the Late Beaker inhumations that in part probably precede them, or the simple cremations in cinerary urns that, again in part, succeed them, is the variety, complexity, and precious nature of the grave-goods. Furthermore, these exotic objects appear suddenly in the funerary record, are current, with very few exceptions, within a remarkably restricted geographical area, and then, apparently after a period of short duration, disappear from subsequent burials. Many of the objects are, *sui generis*, known from three or four finds only of closely related type, and, indeed, are often likely to be the work of a single craftsman; others represent imports from recognizable areas of continental Europe. Is an archaeological 'culture' to be constituted out of these factors, within the terms of V. G. Childe's definition, namely 'certain types of remains —pots, implements, ornaments, burial rites, house forms—constantly recurring together'?[84] Or do these simply denote, as J. G. D. Clark thinks, 'economic and social change' in the form of the local enrichment in Wessex of communities in the Late Beaker–Late Neolithic tradition, stimulated by increased trade with the Continent?

It will be as well to take two points at this stage. First the estimation of what is indigenous and what is new or intrusive and then the question whether the phenomenon is unitary or divided into two chronological phases with the second derived from the first. The 'old' traditions are not difficult to pick out: the Single-Grave inhumation rite under a barrow (of Beaker origin), and the cremation rite in cemeteries or individually (of northern Late Neolithic derivation) are among the most important.

[82] *P.P.S.* xv. 122–7; *Proc. Soc. Ant. Scot.* lxxxii. 38.   [84] V. G. Childe, *Danube in Prehistory*, pp. v–vi.
[83] *W.A.M.* lxi. 5–6.

Persisting with such indigenous features the continuance may be noticed of archery with flint barbed-and-tanged arrowheads; the continued use of stone battle-axes or maces as weapons of prestige, though with developed battle-axe forms; **V**-bored buttons as dress fastenings; all pottery forms (cinerary urns and miniature cups) and perhaps a handled beaker element in the shale and amber cups. New or introduced features include the development of encircled barrows; both of ApSimon's types of bronze daggers; narrow cast-flange bronze axes; crutch-headed and other pins; halberds (in the form of miniature pendants); the lavish use of amber in new bead and necklace forms; an equally profuse use of gold with new, non-Beaker, techniques; and, in part at least, the appearance of faience beads. Presented thus, the evidence may be seen as indicating either an enrichment of indigenous traditions by trade and similar contacts or the incoming of persons with short-lived dynastic power. Perhaps the choice of alternative cannot be decided on the archaeological evidence available, but the matter must be pursued further.

If a short-lived phase, how short? The concept of a divided Wessex culture has been bound up with two factors, namely ApSimon's dagger classification and the assumption of the priority of the inhumation over the cremation rite. ApSimon made it clear that he was primarily concerned with classifying daggers and therefore with the presumptively male dagger-graves of the Wessex culture. His enquiry did not extend to the undifferentiated graves, i.e. the possibly female ones. His Bush Barrow type of triangular dagger, flat or with marked midrib and edge-grooving, small-riveted, and sometimes with a functionless tang or languette, was contrasted with the Camerton–Snowshill type, ogival or sub-triangular in outline, with deep grooving, thick midribs, and large thick rivets. The Bush Barrow type was shown to have early antecedents, going back, as is now known, to copper forms at Singen on Lake Constance, and to be related to Otto Uenze's Saale–Oder–Elbe type, and to Brittany. The Camerton–Snowshill type was shown to have rather later associations, with good parallels in, for instance, Switzerland. They were, therefore, placed in an early and a later Wessex phase, implying that their prototypes reached Britain successively and in that order, and the high proportion of cremation associations of the second type carried with it the implication that this rite was late too. Later, Dennis Britton's analyses of the Wessex daggers confirmed the reality of ApSimon's division from another viewpoint, showing his first group to be of bronze with a low tin content or even, as at Bush Barrow, of copper, and the second group to have very high tin values, averaging 12·7 per cent.

ApSimon convincingly demonstrated that there were two dagger types but his chronological distinction is much harder to substantiate. The Saale–Oder–Elbe and Breton prototypes for his first group had a long life. In Saxo-Thuringia they play a part in the evolution of the halberd, and as at Neuenheiligen and Kladow flat bronze hilts echo the Bush Barrow form, even on occasion with dotted ornament. The languette is a specifically Breton feature, and the Bush Barrow multiple gold wire-work is only paralleled, in coarser technique, in Breton tumulus-graves of the first series. These daggers, too, have low tin values and can even be of copper, and the relationship of the Breton and Bush Barrow types seems a fair inference: the Breton C14 dates of c. 1600 for first series tumulus-graves apply here. When the British ogival dagger series is considered, it is found that the continental counterparts need be no later than the Saale–Oder–Elbe series, but appear in geographical areas distinct from Saxo-Thuringia or Brittany. In Britain they are distinguished by their massive rivets, for which the closest counterparts are those of the insular halberds and the flat riveted knife-daggers known from Late Beaker and allied graves. It is, moreover, striking that five out of seven analyses available for these daggers show tin values of over 10 per cent, with an average of 14·86 per cent, suggesting a metallurgical tradition shared with the Camerton-Snowshill group. If it be admitted that cremation in Wessex co-existed for a time with burial by inhumation before prevailing exclusively, then its value in dating ApSimon's second dagger group is diminished. Moreover, if, as has been shown above, his second dagger group is not necessarily an insular derivation from his first, then it may be inferred that there are daggers with two separate, although ultimately related, continental origins, appearing in Wessex either simultaneously or in the reverse order of that hitherto assumed. Whatever the chronological relationship, the Bush Barrow tradition was of less account than that of Camerton-Snowshill, which was the dominant formative influence in British Bronze-Age metallurgy for centuries to come.

This concept of a single-period phenomenon may make it possible to see other factors in a new light. As Mrs. Roe has demonstrated, the typological development of the stone battle-axes as between the 'Late Beaker' (Stages I and II) and the 'Wessex' types (Stages III–V) is a smooth and continuous one, but, as she noted, none has been found in what could be called 'Bush Barrow' associations, and it was difficult to assign those that had been found in terms of 'Wessex I' and 'Wessex II'. If there is no need to do so, the series makes good sense and indeed gives a valuable indication of developmental stages within the phase.

A situation may be seen then in Late Neolithic–Late Beaker Wessex when a mixed heritage of indigenous traditions, represented archaeologically by a series of barrow-burials by inhumation or cremation, is brought to a climax by foreign contacts from at least two regions of Early Bronze-Age Europe. These contacts are reflected in the grave-goods by imports, or copies, with a distinctive and novel character in type and workmanship. The next question, impossible to answer in direct terms, is whether the material available can better be interpreted as being the result of miscellaneous exchange operations in raw materials and manufactured goods or of the influx of a new population. With the answer will also be linked the status of the Wessex phenomenon as an archaeological culture, questioned by Clark, who would prefer to see it as a final and local enrichment of the Wessex Beaker cultures.

A classic example of such an enrichment, owing nothing, so far as is known, to immigration of even a small body of persons, is the Hopewell phase of Indian culture of the North American Plains around Ohio in the early centuries of the Christian era. Archaeologically represented by earthwork ceremonial monuments and rich barrow-burials, containing among other things elaborate artefacts in copper, the parallel is almost disconcertingly similar to the Wessex phenomenon and could be thought of as a viable model for the latter. In the Old World, V. G. Childe noted among early civilized and barbarian communities a recurrent phenomenon, namely 'a single transitional phase in social evolution', characterized by 'Royal Tombs', and in these tombs he saw the new and short-lived appearance of richly furnished graves as the result of contacts with more technologically advanced societies.[85] The Wessex graves might qualify for inclusion here and with them might go the contemporary barrow-burials of what has been called the Leubingen culture in Saxo-Thuringia. Stukeley's enthusiastic comment on the Salisbury Plain barrows may not have been so far off the mark: 'they are assuredly, the single sepulchres of kings, and great personages'.[86] Childe instanced the Shang Dynasty of China, where the possible introduction from the west of advanced bronze technology seemed the only external motivating force (although perhaps chariotry should also be included), and the Late Helladic I phase of Greece as

[85] V. G. Childe, *Progress and Archaeology*, 92.   [86] William Stukeley, *Stonehenge* (1740), 43.

represented by the shaft-graves, where, on an indigenous Middle Helladic substratum, an enrichment now usually attributed to an intrusive foreign dynasty suddenly appears. In later prehistoric Europe 'Royal Tombs' appear again as the late Hallstatt and early La Tène *Fürstengräber*, resulting not from immigrant rulers but from enhanced trade relations with the Mediterranean world. An immigrant dynasty in Wessex cannot be disproved and equally cannot be proved on the archaeological evidence alone, but it need not be invoked as the only conceivable instigator of the phenomena encountered. What is encountered is surely as much a culture, in the prehistorian's technical sense, as those of Leubingen or early La Tène just quoted.

Childe's concept of 'Royal Tombs' further involved circumstances where 'barbarian societies suddenly irradiated from a much higher civilization' can be inferred, and it is in this context that the much debated question of the nature and importance of possible Mycenaean connexions with Wessex has been posed. In their more precise form, these connexions consist of the shaft-mounts in Bush Barrow and Grave Iota at Mycenae and the amber space-plate necklaces in several Wessex culture contexts and in three Mycenaean tombs. Less directly the faience beads, if accepted as of broadly Aegean or Near Eastern origin, have been taken as in some way associated with Mycenaean trade with barbarian communities; even more tenuous, links have been seen in metal-working techniques between Wessex and the Aegean, and the unique architectural sophistication of Stonehenge III has again been attributed to the introduction of advanced technological skills from similar sources. The implications of such contacts would be significant, not only in the general picture of Bronze-Age Europe but as dating-points for the Wessex culture itself.

It is, however, when turning to absolute chronology that serious difficulties present themselves. At first sight a date of *c.* 1600 B.C. for Grave Iota, of *c.* 1650 for metal-shafted halberds, and of *c.* 1620 for a contemporary Breton grave seem remarkably coincident, until it is remembered that while the first date is obtained by extrapolation from Egyptian historical records, the others come from isotopic dating based on the rate of radioactive decay of carbon. The comparison is not of like with like, and as already stated, radiocarbon 'years' need not necessarily have a one-to-one equivalence with calendrical years.

Scientific investigation, still in progress, has shown that dates given in C14 'years' may be higher when transposed into the historical annual time-scale. As a result of certain experimental checks,[87] a curve of deviation from 'true' dates has been plotted for some 6,000 years before the present day, making it possible to 'correct' approximately isotopic dates to their historical equivalent: conversely an estimate can be made of the expected radiocarbon date that a sample from a historically dated context would yield. It is too early to embark upon a wholesale revision of radiocarbon dates, but the general proposition has seemed acceptable to physicists working in the field, and indeed a number of apparent discrepancies between C14 and historical dates in Egypt and the Near East are resolved by the application of the appropriate correction-factor. The effect of this upon the correlations between Wessex and Mycenae may now be considered.

There are no direct C14 dates for the Wessex culture, but it is known that it overlaps with late beakers. British beaker dates (all types) range between *c.* 1850–1650 B.C. on the C14 scale. The earlier date would read 2180 B.C. and the latter, which is applicable to the Leubingen graves and metal-shafted halberds, is *c.* 2090 B.C. in 'historical' terms. This is the approximate historically computed date for the beginning of the

[87] *Radiocarbon*, viii. 534; *Radioactive Dating and Methods of Low-level Counting* (Internat. Atom. En. Agency, Vienna, 1967), 143–51; *Archaeometry*, x. 3; *Science*, clix. 839.

Middle Helladic II phase in Greece, and the date for its end and for the first shaft-graves (1600–1550 B.C.) would be expected to give a C14 reading of *c.* 1300 B.C. The Breton tumulus-graves of the first series (*c.* 1600–1620 B.C. in radiocarbon terms) would fall around *c.* 2070 B.C. in historical years. If, therefore, the Leubingen culture dates are used to place the Wessex graves with halberd pendants at *c.* 1650 in radiocarbon years, the date becomes *c.* 2090 B.C. when compared with the historically computed dates for the Mycenaean counterparts of the Bush Barrow shaft-mounts. The Upton Lovell and the Wilsford amber necklaces are dated by this means at *c.* 1600–1500 B.C. If the radiocarbon dating process with its dendro-chronological calibration is accepted for conversion to historical dates one of two conclusions must follow. On the assumption that it is a short phase the Wessex culture must be some four or five centuries earlier than the Mycenae shaft-graves and the apparent parallels in shaft-mounts and necklaces illusory. Alternatively it spans a period of comparable length itself, with the halberd-pendant graves being earlier by half a millennium than Bush Barrow or the Upton Lovell necklace. The second possibility seems very difficult to accept for a variety of archaeological reasons, but the first is equally difficult. There is in fact an unresolved problem, with ramifications far beyond the dating of the Wessex culture, and here it must be left in the present state of knowledge.

A comment may, however, be added on the effect of the radiocarbon corrections on the dates of the building periods of Stonehenge. Applying the appropriate factors the following chronological sequences in 'historical' years is obtained:

Stonehenge I	(antler from Ditch)	2900±105 B.C.
Stonehenge II	(antler from unfinished 'R' Hole)	2080±110 B.C.
Stonehenge IIIa/b	(antler from ramp of Stone 56)	2130±150 B.C.
Stonehenge IIIa	(antler from Hole Y 30)	1500±105 B.C.

The aberrant date is that of Stonehenge IIIa/b, which is inconsistent with that for Stonehenge III, derived from one of the Y Holes. If it is assumed that the antler from the ramp of Stone 56 is in fact a stray from Period II and that the Y Holes are quite certainly of Period III, this would place Period III in an historical context of *c.* 1600–1400 during which Mycenaean contact could chronologically be accepted. If, on the other hand, the dates are taken as evidence at their face value, Hole Y 30 at least is 500 years or so later than the erection of Stone 56.

THE FINAL PHASE OF BRONZE TECHNOLOGY

c. 1500–*c.* 500 B.C.

CULTURES AND CHRONOLOGY

IN conventional archaeological terminology it has been customary to regard the Wessex culture discussed above as a final phase within the 'Early Bronze Age'. The archaeological material demonstrably or inferentially later than this is then placed in a 'Middle Bronze Age'. The 'Middle Bronze Age' itself is followed by a 'Late Bronze Age', which continues to a point when it is terminated by the introduction or adoption of an iron-using technology, which marks the beginning of the 'Early Iron Age'. The difficulties arising from the adoption of the concept 'Early Bronze Age' for the complex assemblage of archaeological cultures and traditions within the first half of the 2nd millennium B.C. have already been noted, and those difficulties increase as the second half is entered.[1]

By *c.* 1500 B.C. cremation, normally followed by burial of the ashes under a barrow, seems to have been universally adopted in Wiltshire as elsewhere in southern Britain. A marked change, however, occurs in the type of artefact deposited with the dead. Male equipment (e.g. daggers) becomes very rare or is wholly absent; a few uninformative objects such as flint arrowheads, bone, stone or shell beads, or bone pins appear. Bronze objects are virtually confined to three types. These are small riveted knives with no distinctive typology, awls, and double-edge tanged blades or razors. The last, as will be shown, are more informative. In Wiltshire there exist records of some 250 cremation burials under simple bowl-barrows, excluding those of the Wessex culture already described, or of the Deverel–Rimbury culture discussed below. In about 24 per cent of those burials the cremation was contained in or, more rarely, was accompanied by a pottery vessel within the wide range of cinerary-urn types; 8 per cent were accompanied by the small bronze knives mentioned above, and in a dozen graves were bronze awls of types similar to those of the Wessex culture; other objects, apart from the beads, pins etc. already noted, included small pottery accessory vessels of the incense-cup class found in 15 or so Wiltshire graves. The three razor finds are discussed below.

It has been customary to spread this grave-material, side by side with various types of bronze tools and weapons known from hoards and stray finds but not from burials, over a 'Middle Bronze Age'. That 'Middle Bronze Age', it is assumed, ran from whatever date is given for the end of the Wessex culture to somewhere around 900–850 B.C., when technological and typological considerations show a moment of change in the bronze industries of Britain. It is felt, however, that such a view may need re-examination when the burials are considered. In attempting to arrange the Wiltshire burials, quite typical of most of southern Britain at least, in a chronological sequence over these postulated 'Middle Bronze Age' centuries, namely *c.* 1500–900 B.C., real difficulties are encountered.

---

[1] *Ant. Jnl.* xlix. 22–9.

376

The cinerary-urn series, as shown, begins in domestic pottery types themselves going back to the 3rd millennium B.C. and is seen beginning its funerary functions at a time contemporary with Beaker culture inhumations (e.g. *B ii* WEST OVERTON 6*b*; figs. 18, 19 i, j). Of the primary series isolated by I. H. Longworth,[2] only one is recorded from Wiltshire, in the Wessex culture grave of *B ii* WILSFORD (S.) 7, and typology is a hazardous process in assigning most of the remaining Wiltshire examples to a chronological position. One group, however, can be isolated, the Wessex biconical urns (fig. 23) to be considered later: on evidence from the Netherlands they can be given a radiocarbon date of *c.* 1500. The miniature accessory vessels have clear relationships with those of the Wessex culture and may reasonably be assigned to a similar date. Indeed, considering the peculiarly limited features used to define the Wessex culture, it is as likely that the cremation burials under discussion were 'poor relations' contemporary with the richly furnished graves, as that they constituted a later 'Middle Bronze Age' series. There is in fact no good evidence for assigning any of the burials under consideration to a position much after the middle of the 2nd millennium B.C.

When the sequence can be taken up again there are not only distinctive pottery types, but also associated bronzes, burials and settlements, earthwork enclosures and field-systems. This Deverel–Rimbury culture[3] has in its essentials been recognized for many years, but its relationship to the 'Middle' and 'Late' Bronze-Age nomenclature has caused confusion in the past which may persist in the present. A brief explanation is, therefore, demanded. From the time of its recognition as an entity the culture was referred to as the 'Late Bronze Age', and initially was seen as occupying a chronological position immediately preceding the beginnings of the 'Early Iron Age'. Later its beginnings were placed at *c.* 750 B.C. and it was usually assumed that it lasted in some form until the advent of the first iron technology, a view supported by evidence in Sussex at least.[4] It was in accordance with such assumptions that the term 'Late Bronze Age' was used throughout part one of this volume, published in 1957.

By 1961, however, a series of fundamental studies[5] had made it clear that an important part at least of the Deverel–Rimbury culture must date to the 12th century B.C., contemporary with the Montelius III phase of the northern European Bronze Age. The pottery types in the Netherlands once regarded as ancestral to those of Deverel–Rimbury were shown on the contrary to derive from British types which included the Wessex biconical urns referred to above. An indigenous, rather than, as had previously been thought, an intrusive origin for the culture in Britain then became a possibility. Such a chronological shift, with the 'Late Bronze Age' beginning around 900–850 B.C., necessitated placing the Deverel–Rimbury culture in the 'Middle Bronze Age', where, if the traditional nomenclature is used, it remains. The date around the 12th century B.C., arrived at by archaeological means, has been confirmed by radiocarbon determinations, but another date, that from the ritual shaft at Wilsford (S.), to be discussed later, implies that characteristic Deverel–Rimbury pottery types had already emerged in Wiltshire by not long after *c.* 1380 B.C. As will be seen, the 12th-century date was originally based on bronze types, occasionally found in Deverel–Rimbury contexts but not an integral part of the culture, making an initial date before and a terminal date after that point of contact likely.

[2] *P.P.S.* xxvii. 263–306.

[3] Used in the older inclusive sense which has received wide continental acceptance; see also p. 382.

[4] In 1935 Prof. C. F. C. Hawkes saw that the pottery from Plumpton Plain Site A went back to *c.* 1000 B.C.; Site B (with iron traces on the whetstones and a winged bronze axe) he dated to *c.* 750–500 B.C.: *P.P.S.* i. 39–59.

The axe is of the 'Carp's Tongue Sword Complex' of *c.* 750–650 B.C.

[5] W. Glasbergen, *Palaeohist.* ii. 1–134, iii. 1–204; J. J. Butler and Isobel Smith, Univ. Lond. Inst. Arch. *Ann. Rep.* xii. 20–52; M. A. Smith, *P.P.S.* xxv. 144–87; C. F. C. Hawkes, 'Scheme for the Brit. Bronze Age' (duplicated TS., 1960); Isobel Smith, *Helinium*, i. 97–118.

The date of the end of the Deverel–Rimbury culture in Wiltshire, as practically everywhere else, remains unknown. Beyond that point, wherever it may be, evidence for the 'Late Bronze Age' consists of the bronzes alone. In Wiltshire these are scanty enough, since the region lies outside the areas of the main developments in bronze technology in southern Britain. One or two hoards of bronze or gold objects, namely DONHEAD ST. MARY and TISBURY, belong to a phase assignable to c. 750–650 B.C., and others, with several stray finds including bronze axes imported from Brittany, belong to a century or so later. One find of such axes in their homeland has a radio-carbon date of c. 559 B.C. A broken fragment of such an axe was found on the Early Iron-Age site of All Cannings Cross, and the broadly contemporary Longbridge Deverill Cow Down settlement has its C14 dates of c. 530 B.C. and c. 630 B.C.

Rather than use the terms 'Early', 'Middle', and 'Late' Bronze Age for the ensuing treatment of the Wiltshire evidence it will perhaps be more suitable to think in terms of successive local phases. In the first, overlapping with the Wessex culture however defined, Wessex biconical urns form a pottery type which may be used to name the phase which would cover the 16th and 15th centuries B.C., and with which some bronze types without burial associations, e.g. decorated axes, could be taken (fig. 23). By c. 1400 B.C. the Wilsford (S.) evidence suggests that the Deverel–Rimbury 'barrel' and 'globular' pottery types had appeared, and here the term Deverel–Rimbury culture in the wider sense may be used to cover its manifestations up to such sites as Thorny Down, where bronze types of the 12th century occur. Thereafter metal objects alone remain, defining a Donhead–Tisbury phase around 750–650 B.C., and a Preshute–Breton Axe final phase of c. 650–550 B.C.

THE WESSEX BICONICAL URN PHASE

Definition and Pottery

This rather clumsy nomenclature seems at the moment the best available, even though a detailed study and corpus of the pottery and associated objects is still awaited. The recognition of the phase results from the close co-operation of Dutch and English archaeologists in the 1950s, following on the revolutionary ideas on the British Deverel–Rimbury culture put forward by W. Glasbergen in 1954.[6] It is enough here to say that the Dutch pottery previously thought to be ancestral to the Deverel–Rimbury series was conclusively shown to be in fact derived from British prototypes, of which the most important were vessels defined as biconical urns. The Dutch evidence, with radiocarbon determinations, demanded a date for these prototypes hardly later than 1500 B.C., although British archaeological thought at that time had placed them considerably later. A reassessment of the main burials and their associated finds, which in some instances included the small tanged bronze razors already referred to, showed that this higher chronological position was perfectly acceptable, and that the Wessex Biconical Urn phase had to be regarded as overlapping with, or as a part of, the Wessex culture. In the Netherlands the pottery, together with other features such as encircled barrows, barbed-and-tanged flint arrowheads, etc., defines a Hilversum culture, its origins lying in an immigrant settlement from southern England around 1500 B.C. Later phases are

[6] J. J. Butler and Isobel Smith, op. cit.; Isobel Smith, op. cit.; J. J. Butler, 'Bronze Connections across the N. Sea', Palaeohist. ix; P. J. R. Modderman, Ber. Rijks. Oudheid. Bodem. ix. 288–9; S. J. de Laet, Helinium, i. 121–6; W. Glasbergen, Helinium, ii. 260–5; H. Mariette, Ber. V. Internat. Kong. Vor- u. Frühgesch. Hamburg, 1958 (1961), 523; H. T. Waterbolk, Helinium, iv. 118–21; W. Glasbergen, Nogmaals HVS/DKS (Haarlemse Voor-drachten, xxviii, 1969).

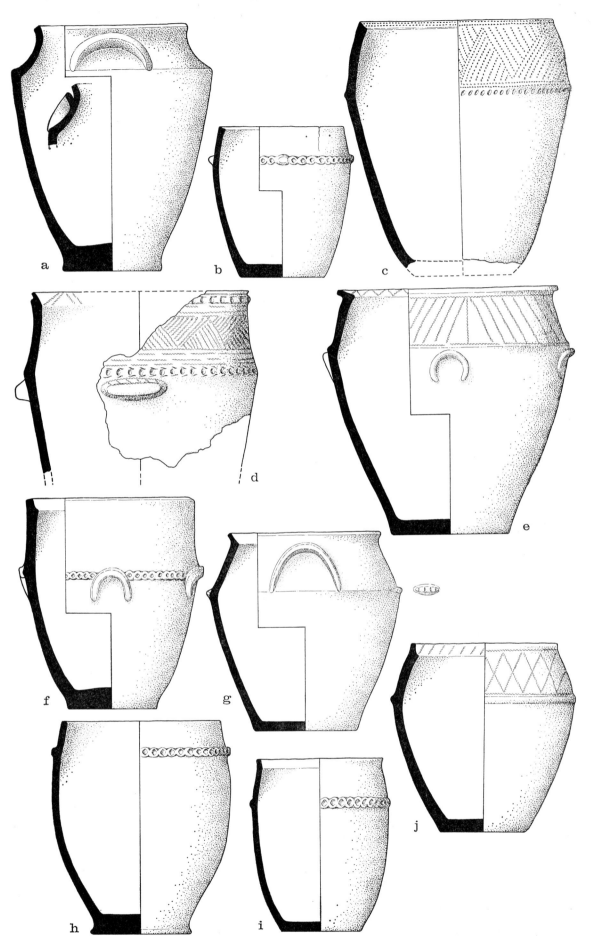

FIG. 23. Wessex biconical and allied urns: a, *B ii* Amesbury 71; b, *B ii* Collingbourne Ducis 9; c, *B ii* Cherhill 1; d, *B ii* Wilsford (S.) 5; e, *B iv* Bulford 47; f, *B vi* Bulford 40; g, *B iv* Bulford 47; h, *B ii* Shrewton 2 or 3; i, *B ii* Collingbourne Ducis 19; j, *B iv* Winterbourne Monkton 2. (⅓).

379

marked by the internal development of the Drakenstein and Laren vessels, with dates around 1100 B.C. The Hilversum phase would be that in which Wessex culture elements such as faience beads and Hiberno-British bronzes reached the Low Countries and adjacent areas.

Ten characteristic biconical urns from Wiltshire have been reviewed and 47 examples from the county are listed (fig. 23).[7] Of these, one, that from *B ii* CHERHILL 1 (fig. 23 c), appears to have covered a primary cremation in a small barrow 2·5 ft. high, and the remainder come from secondary cremation burials inserted in earlier barrows. Those from the bowl-barrows *B ii* COLLINGBOURNE DUCIS 9 and SHREWTON 2 or 3 are uninformative, but more significant are those secondary in barrows of the Wessex culture encircled types, as for instance bell-barrows (*B ii* AMESBURY 71, *B iv* BULFORD 47, WINTERBOURNE MONKTON 2, WINTERSLOW 3), a disk-barrow (*B v* IDMISTON 1 or 3), or a saucer-barrow (*B vi* BULFORD 40). Finally the biconical urn from *B ii* WILSFORD (S.) 5 was secondary to the well-known Bush Barrow burial of the Wessex culture. This stratigraphic evidence agrees with the evidence of associated finds in placing such urns overlapping with, but mainly immediately after, the Wessex culture. In *B ii* AMESBURY 71 the biconical urn burial (fig. 23 a), with a bronze razor, appears to have been secondary to cremations with a radiocarbon date of *c.* 1640 B.C. That date would fit well with the Dutch Hilversum urn evidence.[8]

In the Netherlands the Hilversum culture, with its later Drakenstein phase, is represented by both burials and settlements. Radiocarbon dates for burials range from 1470±45 B.C. (GrN-1828) at Toterfout-Halve Mijl to 1380±70 (GrN-2968) for what must be an early phase of Drakenstein at den Treek and 1140±30 (GrN-1028) for the final stage at Knegsel.[9] The settlement site at Vogelenzang[10] has produced a date of 1139±70 B.C. (GrN-2997) but this must mark the latest stage of its occupation, and the settlement at Nijnsel, late in the Drakenstein phase, is dated at 1140±75 B.C. (GrN-5716).[11] A segmented barrel-shaped bead of faience was found at Vogelenzang, as well as barbed-and-tanged flint arrowheads of types alien to the Netherlands but perfectly familiar in Britain. The identification, moreover, of circular post-built huts at the Hilversum–Drakenstein settlements of Nijnsel, Dodewaard, and Zijderveld, suggests comparisons with the British tradition of circular houses in the 2nd millennium B.C. This fact, as will be seen, has bearing on the Deverel–Rimbury culture, and since the Hilversum and Drakenstein pots, which for long passed for prototypes of Deverel–Rimbury vessels, are now seen as derivatives from the indigenous British tradition embodied in the biconical urns, the question of insular derivatives, as well as those produced by colonists *in partibus*, will naturally arise.

Bronze Types

One of the factors hampering an acceptance of a mid-2nd-millennium date for many burials accompanied by cinerary urns, some within the biconical class, was the belief that the bronze razors of Mrs. C. M. Piggott's Class I were not far removed in date from those of Class II, i.e. not 'much before the end of the 8th century B.C.',[12] for a number of these burials were associated with such Class I blades. In 1956, however, it was shown that this late dating was unwarranted, and that in southern England razors

[7] Reviewed by Isobel Smith, *Helinium*, i. 97–118; listed by J. B. Calkin, *Arch. Jnl.* cxix. 35, which also covers Dors. and SW. Hants.

[8] *P.P.S.* xxxiii. 336–66.

[9] *Helinium*, iv. 118–21; W. Glasbergen, *Nogmaals HVS/DKS*, 20.

[10] *In het Voetspoor van A. E. van Giffen* (2nd edn.), ed. Glasbergen and Groenman-van Waateringe, 81, 158, 176. The C14 dates for the Hague site of the Hilversum culture are conflicting: ibid. 87, 158.

[11] *Ber. Rijks. Oudheid. Bodem.* xxix. 117–29.

[12] *P.P.S.* xii. 125.

and pottery alike could be related to the then newly defined Hilversum culture in the manner indicated above. In Wiltshire there is a stray find of a Class I razor from IDMISTON, and two associated with burials from *B ii* AMESBURY 71 and *B iv* WINTERS-LOW 3.

The Amesbury find was recovered, before excavation of the site, when exposed only 6 in. below the turf near the top of a barrow which is now known to be of several periods of construction from *c.* 2020 B.C. The secondary burial in question was a cremation in an inverted biconical urn with applied horseshoe handles and was accompanied by a bronze razor. It must have been inserted at a time later than construction phase III, when cremation burials, some with food vessels, were associated with a hearth dated at 1640±90 B.C. (NPL–75).[13] The situation at Winterslow is more complicated because of the inadequacies of the accounts of an excavation conducted in 1814.[14] The sequence here starts unambiguously enough with the well-known inhumation burial accompanied by a Wessex–Middle Rhine beaker, tanged copper dagger and archer's bracer, and flint arrowheads (see p. 342). This on analogy is likely to have been covered by a small low barrow (cf. *B ii* MERE 6*a*, *c.* 36 ft. diameter by 6 in. high; ROUNDWAY 8, *c.* 54 ft. diameter by 6 in. high), and 'the bell-barrow of chalk', as it appeared to the excavators, should be a Wessex culture enlargement, of which the primary interment was not certainly found. Clearly secondary to that again, however, was the cremation burial under discussion, found under a cairn of flints only 18 in. below the top of the barrow. It consisted of two inverted vessels, one covering the cremation, which was accompanied by conical and pyramidal amber beads, a bronze awl, a bronze razor, and a quantity of hair, identified in recent times as human eyebrows.[15] The urn is a biconical urn of unusual type for Wiltshire, having strong affinities with the Cornish ribbon-handled urn series;[16] the accompanying vessel, also biconical, has applied horseshoe handles and fingertip decoration. The presence of amber suggests a period not too remote from the use of that substance in the Wessex culture, and the unique pyramidal beads might be compared with the similar bosses on the gold shoulder-cape from Mold (Flints.), which seems in part to be a skeuomorph of a multiple bead necklace or pectoral.[17] T. G. E. Powell's dating of the Mold piece as contemporary with the Montelius II phase of the north European Bronze Age, around the Hilversum–Drakenstein boundary, would not be inappropriate, as continental prototypes or analogies for the British Class I razors first appear in Montelius I or early in II.[18]

There remains for comment a small group of stray finds of bronze axe-blades that chronologically should be referred to around the middle of the 2nd millennium B.C. The emergence in the British Isles, after an initial typological and technological phase of flat axes cast in open moulds, of types of axes with side flanges either beaten up or cast in a bivalve mould, has been frequently commented upon but never worked out in detail.[19] The overall distribution of cast-flange axes in Britain, as Cyril Fox originally demonstrated, has a markedly eastern and southern incidence, and there has been a long-standing assumption that the type and casting technique derive from later Únětice metallurgy on the Continent. Very slightly flanged axes are, as shown, occasionally found in Wessex culture graves, as at Bush Barrow (*B ii* WILSFORD (S.) 5), or *B iv* WILSFORD (S.) 58. In *B ii* WILSFORD (S.) 64 such a little axe was found with a cremation, bone pin, and bone ring. These axes are, however, both very small and very slightly

---

[13] Ibid. xxxiii. 336–66.
[14] Summarized in *W.A.M.* xlviii. 174–82.
[15] The total bulk of surviving hair indicates the eyebrows of more than one person: *W.A.M.* lii. 126.
[16] *Arch. Jnl.* ci. 17 (class B urns); cxix. 34 (Cornish derivative urns in Wessex).

[17] *P.P.S.* xix. 161–79.
[18] The Dutch Bronze-Age sequence (with C14 dates) is set out in *Helinium*, iv. 120.
[19] Cf. J. J. Butler, 'Bronze Age Connections', *Palaeohist.* ix. 27 sqq.; *P.P.S.* xxix. 258–325; for moulds see *Sibrium*, iv. 129–37; v. 153–62; vi. 223–44.

flanged, and the main series lies within Dennis Britton's 'Arreton Tradition' of earlier Bronze-Age metallurgy.[20]

The 'Arreton Tradition' appears to overlap with the Wessex culture graves, with which it shares dagger and exceptionally (at Snowshill, Glos.) spearhead types. The daggers are those of A. M. ApSimon's second series, though the acceptance of these as necessarily defining a 'Wessex II' phase has already been questioned (see p. 359). However that may be, the hoards which characterize the 'Arreton Tradition' are all peripheral to Wiltshire, and Britton has pointed out their coastal distribution. In general they may mark a chronological phase extending into that of the biconical urns.

The half-dozen stray finds of flanged axes in Wiltshire were listed by J. F. S. Stone:[21] one, from between Stonehenge and Fargo, has a counterpart in the Plymstock (Devon) hoard of 'Arreton Tradition' bronzes, and both are of a north German type contemporary with Sögel–Montelius I, indicating contacts between Britain and north Europe at the time.[22] The Hiberno-British decorated flat or flanged axes illustrate such relationships in a distinctive manner, and two, possibly three, Wiltshire finds represent this group.[23]

Typologically the earliest is the decorated flat axe from Figheldean, with curved transverse shallow grooves on the lower part of the blade and zigzag punch-marks towards the butt.[24] This axe, of B. R. S. Megaw's and E. M. Hardy's Type I, has close parallels in axes exported and subsequently copied in south Scandinavia and north Germany, as in the Gallemose hoard from Denmark.[25] Another find, from Stonehenge Down, is a good example of Type II, with hammered flanges, herring-bone punched ornament on both faces, and diagonal ribbed decoration on the flanges.[26] The third axe is that allegedly found when digging into a long barrow near Stonehenge which Thurnam took to be Knighton Barrow (*B i* FIGHELDEAN 27). Stukeley records that it was given by a Mr. Stallard of Amesbury to Lord Burlington, who in turn gave it to Sir Hans Sloane. In the Sloane MS. catalogue, however, what appears to be this axe is attributed to an unspecified Yorkshire source. It is a small, hammer-flanged axe with herring-bone punched ornament, and although Megaw and Hardy accepted the York-shire provenance, Thurnam was more prepared to take it as a Wiltshire find, as was Stone.[27] A find in a long barrow is by no means impossible, since what are presumably votive deposits of bronze implements have been found in earlier barrows. A good example is the hoard of cast-flange axes, two with curved transverse ripple-ornament, found immediately under the turf of a round barrow on Combe Hill, Jevington (Suss.).[28] Three of the Combe Hill axes had been deliberately broken in antiquity. Similar circumstances may explain the anciently broken half of a very slightly flanged axe, found by a shepherd 'on' a barrow on Laverstock Down, probably *B ii* LAVERSTOCK AND FORD 1.[29]

THE DEVEREL–RIMBURY PHASE

Definition and Chronology

It has already been noted that the assemblage of cultural traits used to define a Deverel–Rimbury culture in Wessex and other parts of southern Britain was before

[20] *P.P.S.* xxix. 284. [21] *W.A.M.* lv. 30–3.

[22] J. J. Butler, 'Bronze Age Connections', *Palaeohist.* ix. 44; for Plymstock, see *Invent. Arch.* GB. 9, 2(2), 14.

[23] *P.P.S.* iv. 272–307; xxxii. 343–6.

[24] Unpublished: Sar. Mus.

[25] *P.P.S.* iv, pl. lvb (Gallemose); cf. also the axe from Skane (Sweden): ibid. fig. 17 and others; Butler, 'Bronze Age Connections', *Palaeohist.* ix. 30; cf. also *Ber. R.-G. Komm.* xxxi, A66, 48, 49.

[26] *W.A.M.* lv. 30–3.

[27] *P.P.S.* iv. 302 (no. 113 in register); *W.A.M.* lv. 30–3,

with refs., including *Arch.* xliii. 444 and Stukeley, *Stone-henge* (1740), 46: 'In the great long barrow farthest north from *Stonehenge*, which I call north long barrow'.

[28] *Suss. N. & Q.* viii. 108–11; E. C. Curwen, *Arch. of Suss.* (2nd edn.), 151 and pl. xiv. The hoard is not in-cluded in *P.P.S.* iv, but is no. 11 of Britton's list of 'Arreton Tradition' hoards: *P.P.S.* xxix. 317, App. A iv; for votive deposits in barrows see *Folklore*, lxxviii. 1–38.

[29] *Arch. Jnl.* civ. 20. In *V.C.H. Wilts.* i (1), p. 180, it is suggested that this mound may be a medieval or later 'pillow-mound' but the axe is not recorded.

1960 placed in a 'Late Bronze Age' context from *c.* 750 B.C., but now can be shown to be largely contemporary with Montelius III in north Europe, around 1200–1100 B.C. Two subsequent studies[30] have discussed the Wessex aspect in particular, and both authors have expressed dissatisfaction with the continued use of the term 'Deverel–Rimbury culture' as an inclusive one. There is good sense in this, and the whole conception of the culture needs to be reassessed in detail especially by re-examining the abundant pottery. In addition to other problems there is, as will be seen, a case for contrary views on intrusive or indigenous origins for the culture in whole or part. Until such a reassessment has been made it seems reasonable to agree with J. B. Calkin that the wide (and perhaps usefully vague) term Deverel–Rimbury should continue.[31] Calkin's and ApSimon's definition within this wider grouping of a Cranborne Chase culture is, however, a valuable step towards the isolation of analogous local variants elsewhere.

The position of Wiltshire within the main southern English distribution area of Deverel–Rimbury material is well shown on Calkin's map,[32] plotting the distribution of two of the three main pottery types. This area includes the northern edge of Cranborne Chase, sites between it and the Ebble Valley, a group of sites north-east of Salisbury, and a small scatter in the Amesbury region. There is also a northerly group on the Marlborough Downs. Most of the barrel and globular urns mapped lie southwards of this area, around Christchurch (Hants), and thence up the Stour Valley towards Wimborne (Dors.) and in the southern part of Cranborne Chase. Those favouring an intrusive origin for these pottery types have argued for landings and initial settlement in the Avon–Stour estuary by Hengistbury Head (Hants).

The archaeological evidence whereby the culture has been defined consists in the first place of large quantities of pottery—over 400 vessels from the area included on the map quoted above. These are divisible into the three main classes of barrel, bucket, and globular urns. They come from cremation burials, which may be primary under barrows or secondary in earlier barrows. They are also frequently found in flat cemeteries, and in Cranborne Chase and Wiltshire they come from settlements and enclosure ditches. In a few instances there are associated bronze types, which may be an integral part of the culture (tanged bifid razors and small socketed spearheads) or acquired from outside (objects from the 'Ornament Horizon' group discussed below). There is one exceptional ritual shaft attributable to the period of barrel and globular urns, and the settlements can be related to surviving areas of ancient field-systems and a pattern of boundary dykes.

Dates for the Deverel–Rimbury culture can be obtained from more than one source. The earliest comes from the 100-ft. deep ritual shaft on Normanton Gorse, Wilsford (S.), which will be described below. Here in the clean chalk silting which filled the shaft and must have accumulated very quickly, unweathered sherds of a globular urn were found at 80 ft. and of a barrel urn at 60 ft. (fig. 24). Wood at the bottom of the shaft gave a C14 date of 1380±90 B.C. (NPL–74).[33] The Deverel–Rimbury culture in Wiltshire must then have been recognizably in existence by the 14th century B.C. The initial recognition of a date in the 2nd millennium, however, was due to the identification of bronze objects in Deverel–Rimbury contexts which belonged to the south-west English 'Ornament Horizon' defined by Miss M. A. Smith,[34] which showed continental contacts in Montelius III, i.e. *c.* 1200–1100 B.C. on current archaeological dating. This identification has been confirmed by the radiocarbon date from a Deverel–Rimbury

[30] J. B. Calkin, *Arch. Jnl.* cxix. 1–65; A. M. ApSimon in Rahtz and ApSimon, *P.P.S.* xxviii. 319–28.

[31] *Arch. Jnl.* cxix. 16.

[32] Ibid. fig. 9.

[33] *Antiq.* xxxvii. 116–20.

[34] *P.P.S.* xxv. 144 ff.

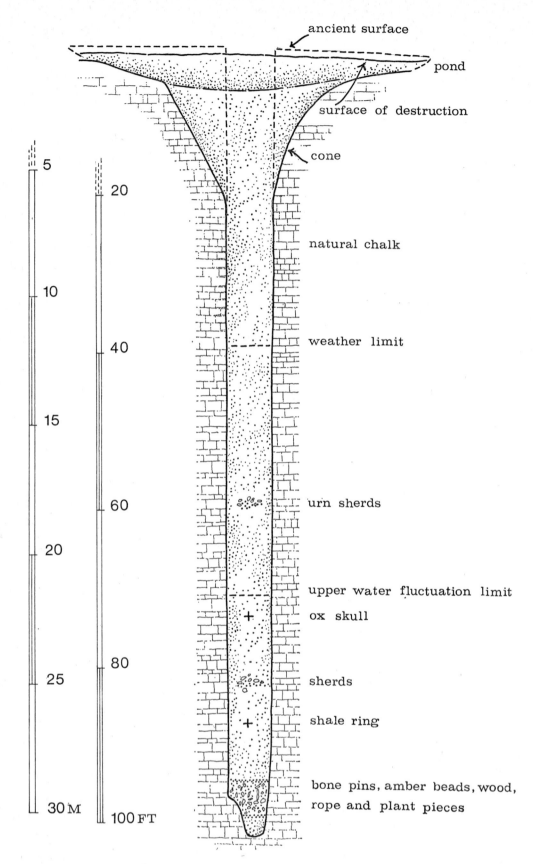

ancient surface

pond

surface of destruction

cone

natural chalk

weather limit

urn sherds

upper water fluctuation limit

ox skull

sherds

shale ring

bone pins, amber beads, wood,
rope and plant pieces

5
10
15
20
25
30 M

20
40
60
80
100 FT

WILSFORD SHAFT

FIG. 24. Section of ritual shaft, Wilsford (S.).

384

settlement on Shearplace Hill in Dorset, of 1180±180 B.C. (NPL–19),[35] contemporary with Drakenstein sites such as Nijnsel in the Netherlands (1140±75 B.C. GrN–5716). Beyond this point the survival of the culture cannot be demonstrated in Wessex, unless the Class II razor finds in primary Deverel–Rimbury contexts (e.g. the Angle Ditch in Dorset) may indicate a date later than the 'Ornament Horizon'.

Pottery

As has been seen, a full and detailed assessment is still awaited of the pottery by which the Deverel–Rimbury culture is now to be defined. All that can be attempted here is a brief discussion of the Wiltshire evidence in its more general Wessex context. As Calkin has shown, Abercromby's basic division into three main types, the barrel, bucket, and globular urns, still stands as a useful classification for the main bulk of the material, and it is clear that all three types are present both in domestic and funeral circumstances. In certain superficial respects all three types appear to show a complete break with other ceramic traditions in 2nd-millennium Britain, and this has contributed to the view long held that the culture was intrusive and introduced by immigrants of continental origin. But these distinct features are perhaps no more than the underlying continuity of tradition, at least in the barrel and bucket types (fig. 25).

In the barrel type and especially Calkin's 'South Lodge' type, large pots are found with barrel-shaped bodies and flat thickened rims in wares which certainly contrast with the normal fabric of cinerary urns of earlier date. The fabric is gritty and vesicular and often made into surprisingly thin-walled vessels (0·18 in. in a 12 in. high pot). Cord ornament is absent, as in the bucket and barrel types, but there is abundant use of fingertip impressions on applied horizontal or vertical cordons, or plastic ornament below the rim in horseshoe, arched, or zigzag motifs. Applied cruciform or star-pattern cordons sometimes occur inside the base. In Wiltshire good examples can be quoted from the South Lodge enclosure, in BERWICK ST. JOHN, *B ii* AMESBURY 3 (the 'Stonehenge Urn', probably from this barrow) or *B ii* BOWER CHALKE 2 (fig. 25 a).[36] The bucket type, with straight sides, infrequent cordons or moulded ornament, but fingertip impressions now usually on the body of the pot, and made of gritty ware, can again be quoted from *B ii* COLLINGBOURNE DUCIS 8, 9, 11. One from Shepherd's Shore (BISHOP'S CANNINGS) has applied horseshoes.[37]

The globular urns form a highly distinctive group in form, technique, and decoration (figs. 25 e, f; 26). As their name implies, they are squat vessels of rounded profile, and are either of gritty vesicular ware similar to the South Lodge barrel urns, or of finer features often with finely smoothed surfaces. The ornament on and above the shoulder and on the neck is lightly tooled or incised, in horizontal rilling or in filled triangles or zigzag motifs, and perforated lug-handles occur. Globular urns appear to be associated with barrel rather than bucket urns, and like the barrel urns occur in settlements as well as with burials. Wiltshire examples (a total of 9) come from *B ii* BOWER CHALKE 1, a barrow near Salisbury, and the South Lodge, Thorny Down (fig. 26), Boscombe Down East, Ogbourne, and Preshute enclosures.[38] The absence of local antecedents in Wessex creates a strong presumption that this pottery type does not originate in that area, and leads us to the question of the origins of all three pottery forms, with which the whole status of the Deverel–Rimbury culture is bound up.

[35] *P.P.S.* xxviii. 319–28.
[36] Pitt-Rivers, *Cranborne Chase*, iv, pl. 240; *D.M. Cat. Neo. and B. A. Colls.* (1964), nos. 576, 567.
[37] *D.M. Cat. Neo. and B.A. Colls.* (1964), nos. 555, 571, 580, 583, 565.
[38] Ibid. nos. 582, 566; Pitt-Rivers, *Cranborne Chase*, iv. pls. 241, 13; 242, 1–3; *P.P.S.* vii. 114, figs. 2, 3; *W.A.M.* xlvii. 466, pls. iii, iv; *P.P.S.* viii. 48, fig. 5.

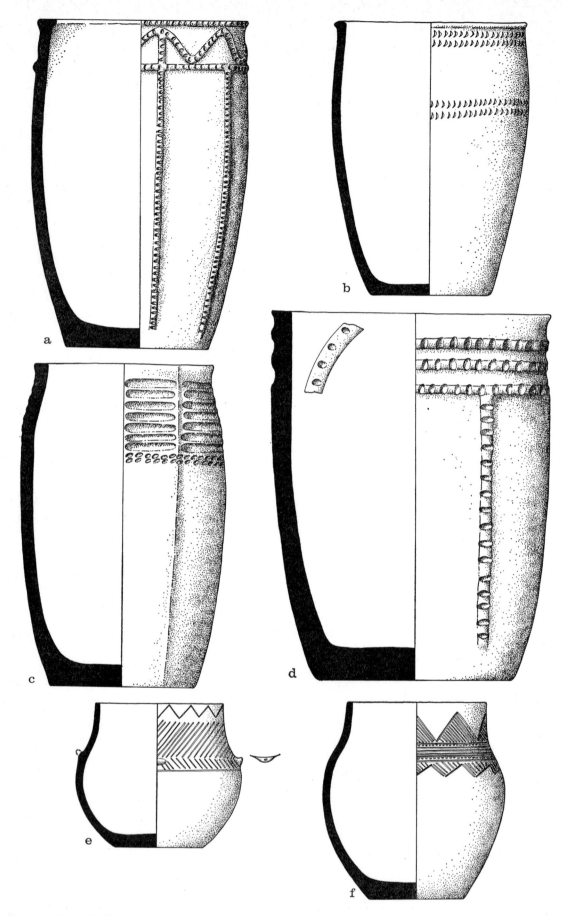

FIG. 25. Deverel–Rimbury pottery: a, *B ii* Bower Chalke 2; b, *B ii* Bower Chalke 10; c, *B ii* Ebbesborne Wake 8; d, *B ii* Amesbury 3; e, *B ii* Bower Chalke 1; f, 'near Salisbury'. (⅛).

386

In the early stages of the study of the problem, indeed since Abercromby isolated the main pottery types in 1912, it was not difficult to postulate an immigrant 'Late Bronze Age Invasion', which conflated pottery and metal types now known to be separated by

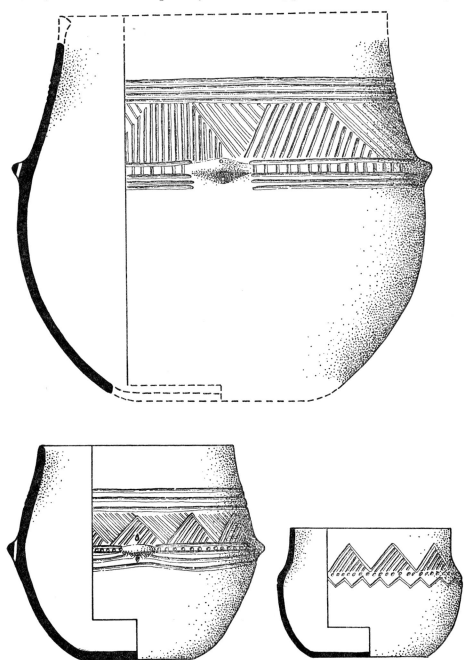

FIG. 26. Deverel–Rimbury pottery, Thorny Down. (¼).

both chronological and cultural factors. With Miss Smith's redefinition of the relevant bronzes, it became clear, as will be seen in more detail below, that the bronze objects in Wessex Deverel–Rimbury contexts were either the products of insular development or were acquisitions from adjacent groups, themselves in touch with north German metallurgy in the 12th century B.C. The pottery remains as a challenge to two schools of thought, that favourable to an immigrant origin from the Continent and that which would prefer to look to an insular development in southern Britain, if not wholly within Wessex.

When discussing the Wessex biconical urns, Dr. Isobel Smith noted how, through the Hilversum series, they had given rise in the Netherlands to the Drakenstein–Laren urns, which are clear counterparts of the British bucket urns.[39] In other words, on both sides of the North Sea parallel developments from original biconical urn stock had taken place, in a manner not dissimilar from the reverse situation in the Beaker period, when Dutch Veluwe and British late insular derivatives show common lines of development from Dutch prototypes. It does not seem too difficult, if this is allowed, to admit a comparable derivation from biconical and other mid-2nd-millennium south English sources for the barrel urns as well, where the looped and horseshoe plastic ornament on the South Lodge type of pots would directly relate to Wessex biconicals. Somewhere in this ancestry, too, would come the anomalous cinerary urn with horizontal fingertip ornamented cordons from *B ii* BROMHAM 1.[40] It does not seem necessary to look for a continental origin for cordoned and fingertip ornamented vessels, when these features are so bewilderingly common from Late Neolithic times. C. F. C. Hawkes, however, has drawn attention to vessels in Tumulus Bronze contexts in south Germany which certainly might be held to bear a resemblance to British biconical urns, if it were felt necessary to seek outside, and so far outside, Britain for the features that they display.[41] As with the insular sequence of Neolithic pottery from the Windmill Hill to the startlingly dissimilar Fengate style, it seems preferable and reasonable to regard both bucket and barrel urns as a similarly indigenous development from types current in southern England earlier in the 2nd millennium B.C.

The globular urns do at first sight present a much more exotic appearance, and the most devoted proponent of indigenous development would be hard put to it to point to Wessex prototypes for these vessels. ApSimon, however, has put forward a case for deriving the Type II globular urns of Wessex from Cornish types including those from the Knackyboy cairn, St. Martin's, in Scilly, as had been suggested by B. H. St. J. O'Neil and Lady Fox.[42] ApSimon's case is largely based on unpublished material from a settlement at Trevisker in Cornwall and it is difficult to make a critical assessment until this site and its counterpart at Gwithian in the same county have been fully published. There was clearly much contact between Wessex and Cornwall around the middle of the 2nd millennium B.C. and after, perhaps mainly motivated by the tin trade, and interchange of pottery styles is perceptible in many instances. If a Cornish origin for the Wessex globulars is accepted, those in Wiltshire could be the earlier; if an intrusive element from across the Channel to the Stour–Avon estuary has to be sought, prototypes in the French Bronze Age not later than *c.* 1400, on the Wilsford shaft evidence, would have to be sought, and none seem forthcoming; and if new pottery types, globular urns, and barrel urns as well, have to be given an intrusive origin, the absence of any of the characteristic bronze types that should have accompanied them is very remarkable. Thus, on balance, an insular seems preferable to an immigrant origin for all three types of Deverel–Rimbury pottery.

Bronze Tools, Weapons, and Ornaments

Of the bronzes assignable to the Deverel–Rimbury phase in Wiltshire, *c.* 1400–1100 B.C., some are represented by stray finds and others are in association with pottery, burials, or settlements of the Deverel–Rimbury culture itself. The narrowed axe form,

[39] *Helinium*, i. 97–118.
[40] *D.M. Cat. Neo. and B.A. Colls.* (1964), no. 526.
[41] In discussion Prof. Hawkes has instanced W. Kimmig and H. Hell, *Vorzeit an Rhein und Donau*, 45 (from Degernau, Kr. Waldshut), but further comment must be reserved pending publication.
[42] *P.P.S.* xxviii. 319; O'Neil, *Antiq. Jnl.* xxxii. 21–34; Aileen Fox, *Trans. Devon Assoc.* lxxix. 18.

which becomes technically a palstave[43] as early as the first part of Montelius II (c. 1400–1100 B.C.), must in this form overlap the Wessex Biconical Urn phase. One broken looped palstave was found in a Deverel–Rimbury context in the Angle Ditch, Handley Down (Dors.).[44] The Wiltshire finds, however, are strays, either without a side-loop (e.g. MARLBOROUGH),[45] or looped forms such as a series from BROAD HINTON, Milton Hill (PEWSEY) and WILTON, of types found as exports or close copies of exports in hoards of early Montelius II in north Europe such as those from Frøjk in Denmark and Ilsmoor in Germany. Later types, such as another find from PEWSEY,[46] are of forms occurring in the Somerset bronze hoards of the 'Ornament Horizon' described below, of around 1200–1100 B.C. Two small narrow socketed axes from Wiltshire, namely from Little Langford (STEEPLE LANGFORD) and 'Salisbury Plain', are a north German type again found in one of these hoards (Taunton) and named the Taunton–Hademarschen type by J. J. Butler.[47]

For some time it has been recognized that a characteristic type of small double-looped spearhead was a feature of Deverel–Rimbury bronze equipment, two complete specimens being found in Wiltshire on the Thorny Down and South Lodge settlements. A burnt fragment with a cremation-burial also occurred in a barrel-urn from Launceston Down (Dors.).[48] The Wiltshire example claimed by Thurnam to be with a cremation, burial in a Wilsford barrow is, however, as C. F. C. Hawkes showed, from just under the turf of B ii AMESBURY 1, 2, or 3,[49] and stray finds from the county include those from BISHOP'S CANNINGS, BECKHAMPTON, and Tan Hill (ALL CANNINGS).[50] Such spearheads occur in the Somerset and related hoards of the 12th century B.C., and stray finds are widespread in Britain.[51] A larger, basal-looped spearhead is also found in the same contexts, and that from Millbrow (WINTERBOURNE BASSETT) is a good Wiltshire example.[52] A larger weapon, that from near WILCOT, with basal loops and an angular blade, is of a type which occurs in hoards of C. B. Burgess's Wallington phase in the north of England (assigned to the 10th–early 8th centuries B.C.). But it is also found in earlier hoards in the context of his Penard-Rosnoën phase which is of the late 11th–10th centuries,[53] and so follows, or overlaps the later part of the Deverel–Rimbury phase in Wessex.

In Britain, as throughout Europe, there seems to have been a tendency in the 2nd millennium B.C., as good bronze alloys and casting techniques were developed, to make the earlier daggers into longer and narrower thrusting weapons, known conventionally in the British series as dirks and rapiers. With several variants in type, such weapons as those from TEFFONT, Fisherton Anger (SALISBURY) and WILSFORD (S.)[54] must date from about 1400–1200 B.C., and a little later, in Burgess's Penard-Rosnoën and Wallington phases, come those of the Cults-Lisburn type. This type has hafting-rivets held by notches not holes in the base of the blade, such as that from OGBOURNE ST. GEORGE.

[43] P.P.S. xxv. 144; Butler, 'Bronze Age Connections', Palaeohist. ix. 48; Proc. Soc. Ant. Scot. xcvii. 82, all other classifications differing in detail. For N. Europe, see Ber. R.-G. Komm. xxxi. 1–138.

[44] Pitt-Rivers, Cranborne Chase, iv, pl. 263, 1.

[45] D.M. Cat. Neo. and B.A. Colls. (1964), no. 594.

[46] For refs. see n. 43; D.M. Cat. Neo. and B.A. Colls. (1964), nos. 588, 593, 599, 597.

[47] Butler, 'Bronze Age Connections', Palaeohist. ix. 75; Ber. R.-G. Komm. xxxi. (2) 112.

[48] Small versions of Greenwell and Brewis class IV: Arch. lxi. 439–72. First discussed by C. F. C. Hawkes in P.P.S. vii. 128. For Launceston see Arch. xc. 60.

[49] Thurnam, Arch. xliii. 447, fig. 153; Hawkes, P.P.S. vii. 130.

[50] D.M. Cat. Neo. and B.A. Colls. (1964), nos. 629, 634, 640.

[51] Hoards, see e.g. Stump Bottom (Suss.): P.P.S. xxv. 153, fig. 4; Monkswood (Som.): Invent. Arch. GB. 42; Burgesses' Meadow (Oxford): Invent. Arch. GB. 6; N. Britain: Proc. Soc. Ant. Scot. xciii. 18–19.

[52] D.M. Cat. Neo. and B.A. Colls. (1964), no. 635; cf. Taunton workhouse hoard: Invent. Arch. GB. 43 (2), 1, 16; Sherford (Taunton) hoard: Invent. Arch. GB. 45, 1.

[53] D.M. Cat. Neo. and B.A. Colls. (1964), no. 633 (Wilcot spearhead); C. B. Burgess, Bronze Age Metalwork in N. Eng.; Arch. Jnl. cxxv. 1–45. The angular basal-looped spearhead in the Maentwrog hoard (with rapiers) is such an early example: Invent. Arch. GB. 10.

[54] For rapiers see P.P.S. xxviii. 80–102, criticized and corrected in Proc. Soc. Ant. Scot. xcvii. 111; D.M. Cat. Neo. and B.A. Colls. (1964), no. 631 (Teffont); no. 632 (Wilsford); no. 630 (Ogbourne). Comment in Burgess, Bronze Age Metalwork in N. Eng.

Small tanged double-edged blades or razors were already current, as shown, in the Wessex Biconical Urn phase (see p. 378), where they were placed in a Class I group. In the original discussion of such razors, they were followed by Class II, to which those found in Deverel–Rimbury and later contexts were assigned,[55] although intermediate forms were recognized as hybrid types. At the time when a single comparatively short 'Late Bronze Age' containing Deverel–Rimbury was assumed, no great chronological discrepancy between Class II razors occurring in, for instance, the Taunton (Som.) and Glentrool (Kirkcudbrights.) hoards on the one hand, and at Heathery Burn (co. Dur.) or the Adabrock (Lewis) hoard on the other, could be perceived. It is now known, however, that the first contexts are of the 12th, the second of the 7th and 6th centuries respectively. Re-examination of the range of type within Class II shows that the extreme chronological poles can in fact be distinguished typologically. It is suggested, therefore, that a numerical classification should be abandoned and instead there should be recognized three phases: a Wessex Biconical Urn phase; a Taunton–Glentrool phase, broadly contemporary with Deverel–Rimbury, with razors retaining the ovoid outline but with new features such as mid-ribs; and a Heathery Burn–Adabrock phase in which, probably as a result of continental contacts, the shoulders of the blade are angular and there is a marked notch at the top of the blade. The late date of the last group is reinforced by the examples from All Cannings Cross (fig. 32 c) and Ivinghoe Beacon (Bucks.) in final Bronze-Age assemblages immediately preceding iron-working and the cultural associations of the earliest southern British Iron Age.[56] The bronze assembly at All Cannings Cross is discussed below, and in the same context may be taken the Wiltshire stray razor finds from BECKHAMPTON, IDMISTON, B ii SHREWTON 4 or 5, and that from 'Oldfield', perhaps in AMESBURY parish, allegedly associated with a ribbed socketed axe and a tracer.[57] All these are of the Heathery Burn–Adabrock type and in a Deverel–Rimbury context in Wiltshire remain the two razors from South Lodge (BERWICK ST. JOHN).

At Berwick St. John the circumstances of discovery in Pitt-Rivers's classic excavation were as follows.[58] In the primary silting of the narrow 6 ft.-deep ditch were found a bronze razor usually placed in 'Class I' but with angular shoulders; a bronze tracer described below, and Deverel–Rimbury pottery, including a virtually complete barrel urn. In the slow secondary silt at 3 ft., with the mixture of finds, including Roman sherds, typical of such a location in ditch silting, was a Class II razor, with central thickening and shallow grooving, rounded shoulders and a distal notch. Other bronzes comprised a piece of a ribbed armlet of Somerset hoards type and bronze wire apparently from a twisted ornament, both described below. In the surface mould was a small bronze socketed spearhead of the type already described from, for example, Thorny Down. It seems reasonable to take all finds as broadly contemporary in view of the rapidity of silting in a narrow ditch, and so probably both razors should be taken as variants within the Taunton–Glentrool class. Outside the county the razor from the Deverel–Rimbury Angle Ditch, Handley Down, is anomalous, for it is holed and probably was originally notched. The stray find from the turf over the nearby ditch of Wor Barrow is of Heathery Burn–Adabrock type, but there is no reason to associate it with a Deverel–Rimbury context.

[55] P.P.S. xii. 125.
[56] Taunton: Invent. Arch. GB. 43 (2), 1, 18; Glentrool: Proc. Soc. Ant. Scot. xciii. 113, pl. 1, 'hardly later than 11th cent. B.C.'; Heathery Burn: Invent. Arch. GB. 55, 10 (7), 91, 'final 8th and 7th cents. B.C.'; Adabrock: Proc. Soc. Ant. Scot. xciii. 49 with Hallstatt C bronze vessel;

All Cannings Cross: Maud E. Cunnington, All Canning's Cross (Devizes, 1923), pl. 19, 2; Ivinghoe: Recs. Bucks. xviii. 204, 'late 8th to 7th cent. B.C.'.
[57] D.M. Cat. Neo. and B.A. Colls. (1964), nos. 619, 627; P.P.S. xii. 138.
[58] Pitt-Rivers, Cranborne Chase, iv. 3.

As seen above, there was with the razor in the primary silt at South Lodge an object which has been described as a massive awl, 4·35 in. long. It is preferable to regard this as a metal-worker's tracer, like that already mentioned from the 'Oldfield' find. Herbert Maryon has suggested such a use for the 'awl' from *B iv* WILSFORD (S.) 42, which is smaller.[59]

Attention may now be turned to the ornaments which from their presence in a group of hoards have given their name to the 12th-century B.C. 'Ornament Horizon'. In

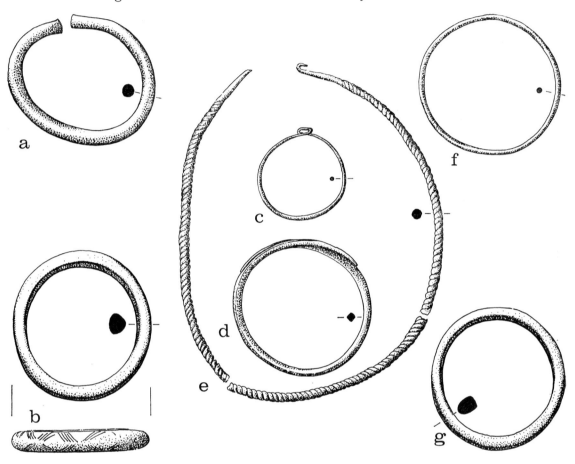

FIG. 27. Bronze hoard, Elcombe Down. a–d, armlets, e, torc, f, armlet. (½).

Wiltshire there are two such hoards, both entirely of neck-, arm-, and finger-rings. One comes from Elcombe Down (EBBESBORNE WAKE) where it had been buried in the soil of an ancient field, forming part of a system of well-known 'Celtic field' type discussed below, and the other from somewhere along the Amesbury–Salisbury road probably in WILSFORD (S.) parish.[60]

The Elcombe Down hoard (fig. 27) consists of the following bronze ornaments: 1 cast mock-twisted torc, 1 heavy decorated armlet, 4 ring-armlets, 3 penannular armlets, 6 armlets of lighter work with overlapping ends, and 2 small plain armlets with hooked terminals. The torc is typical of the Somerset and allied hoards, such as Barton Bendish (Norf.) and Glentrool, and the decorated armlet is of particular interest in view of continental counterparts as in the Villers-sur-Authie hoard of Montelius III

[59] *Ant. Jnl.* xviii. 245.
[60] Neither hoard has been adequately published. El-combe Down: *W.A.M.* liii. 104–12; Amesbury–Salisbury road: ibid. 257–8, for location and identification as hoard (or hoards) not barrow-finds. The objects are divided between Devizes, Sar., and Pitt-Rivers (Farnham) museums. See also *D.M. Cat. Neo. and B.A. Colls.* (1964), nos. 621–6. The Elcombe Down hoard in field not lynchet: H. C. Bowen, *Anc. Fields*, 18, 37.

date.[61] Lozenge-section armlets (3 in the hoard) are paralleled in the hoard from Barton Bendish, and the small hooked-terminal armlets are related to twisted-wire examples such as that found in the Monkswood (Som.) hoard, probably that from *B ii* AMESBURY 11, and the fragment from the ditch silt of *B ii* BERWICK ST. JOHN 10.[62]

The Amesbury–Salisbury road find, probably a single hoard, appears to have consisted of the following pieces: 3 cast mock-twisted torcs, 7 armlets, including lozenge-section and hooked-wire examples, 1 ribbed armlet, and 3 spiral finger-rings. The types represented by the torcs and the lozenge-section and hooked-wire armlets have been commented upon above. The ribbed armlet has parallels not only in the Somerset hoards, but in those from the settlement sites of South Lodge and Thorny Down in Wiltshire. The finger-rings are also of types characteristic of those hoards.[63]

The finds from Deverel–Rimbury settlements have already been noted. The ribbed bracelet found in the same context in the secondary silt of the ditch of South Lodge as the second razor is of the simple form characteristic of the hoards. The bracelet from Thorny Down, with bossed and plain ribs alternating, comes near to continental prototypes and to that with larger bosses from West Buckland (Som.). From burials there is only the Amesbury twisted-wire find mentioned above, found with a cremation in a 'rude urn'. Like the Berwick St. John fragment, it could as well come from the nearby settlement as from a burial. A pin from Rushall Down has a bossed disk head, and may be a local copy of a central European urnfield type of around the 12th century B.C. There are also a couple of Wiltshire stray finds of pins, which may be small relatives of the huge quoit-headed pins of the hoards, one from an unknown location and the other probably from Shepherd's Shore (BISHOP'S CANNINGS).[64]

Although the finds strictly characteristic of Miss M. A. Smith's 'Ornament Horizon' of the 12th century B.C. are comparatively few, they show that Wiltshire, and within the county the Deverel–Rimbury culture in particular, was at this time in contact with the centres where these objects were produced and traded. Her map[65] shows clearly how the central geographical position of Wiltshire, even though on the northern edge of the main area of distribution, would enable its inhabitants to share in such a trade.

Gold

There are two gold ornaments from Wiltshire which can be referred to at least late in the Deverel–Rimbury phase under consideration. The first is the fragmentary gold torc from Allington Down (ALL CANNINGS); its body is made from a twisted bar of metal chiselled into 4 leaves and one recurved bar-terminal survives. It belongs to an Irish group of 'bar torcs', developed as 'insular and elaborate versions of the bronze torcs of the "Ornament Horizon"', which is represented by the Bishopsland phase of the Irish Bronze Age. Such torcs must have been made from this time onward and may therefore date from the 12th to 10th centuries B.C.[66] The second find, from Levett's Farm (Clench Common), SAVERNAKE, can now be assigned to this same phase, though it was regarded as Early Iron Age at the time of the compilation of part one of this volume.[67] It is a gold wire armlet of two twisted strands and loop terminals, and is

[61] *P.P.S.* xxv. 161.
[62] Ibid. 159; Monkswood: *Invent. Arch.* GB. 42 (2), 10–11.
[63] *P.P.S.* xxv. 159; armlets in Monkswood hoard (see n. 62), Edington Burtle: *Invent. Arch.* GB. 44, 2 (1), 4–5; S. Lodge and Thorny Down see below, and variant with bosses from W. Buckland: Sir John Evans, *Anc. Bronze Implements*, fig. 81. Finger-rings, Edington Burtle, Barton

Bendish, Stump Bottom: *P.P.S.* xxv. 153, fig. 4; Blackrock: *Invent. Arch.* GB. 47, 2 (1), 5.
[64] *D.M. Cat. Neo. and B.A. Colls.* (1964), nos. 613, 616, 618 (Rushall); Butler, 'Bronze Age Connections', *Palaeohist.* ix. 149.
[65] *P.P.S.* xxv. 154, map 1.
[66] *Jnl. R. Soc. Ant. Ireland*, xcvii. 129–75. Allington torc is no. 54 in list, App. A. 167.   [67] p. 104.

exactly paralleled in the (lost) gold hoard from Beer Hackett (Dors.), containing a twisted torc of Allington type. It can now be recognized as not far, if at all, removed in time from the 'Ornament Horizon', with bronze analogues in the Barton Bendish hoard.[68] There is much evidence of contact between Ireland and south-western England at this time, carrying on a tradition going back to the gold lunulae, decorated bronze axes, and halberds, and underlining the essential continuity of cultures during the 2nd millennium B.C. Copper deposits were being worked in Ireland by the middle of the millennium,[69] and characteristic gold types manufactured there, even if the origins of the metal are in dispute.[70]

Burials

The Deverel–Rimbury culture is mainly known from cremation-burials in either primary or secondary positions in small round barrows, or cremation-cemeteries set either in or at the edge of barrows or by themselves. Of the eponymous sites designating the culture, Deverel was a barrow-cemetery and Rimbury a cremation-cemetery, both in Dorset. In that county and around the Stour–Avon estuary in West Hampshire large cemeteries occur, and for the latter region alone Calkin estimated a minimum total of 418 burials with a probable extra 50.[71] Northwards the distribution-pattern is markedly thinner and in Wiltshire L. V. Grinsell listed an approximate total (with many figures derived from old and vague accounts) of around 180 cremation-burials which may be considered certainly or probably Deverel–Rimbury.[72] Some of these appear to be primary to small barrows (there are 18 probable instances), but others are secondary. The latter class ranges from individual burials to cemeteries of up to 18 unaccompanied cremations or 45 in 'plain urns', as in the very badly recorded instance of *B ii* COLLINGBOURNE DUCIS 11, or the 21 well-attested burials in urns secondary to *B ii* BOWER CHALKE 1 (the Woodminton cemetery). In the Heale Hill site, Middle Woodford, there were two secondary burials in a small barrow and a further three constituting a small flat cemetery outside.[73] The distribution pattern in terms of numbers shows how for instance four barrows in Bower Chalke parish (*B ii* BOWER CHALKE 1, 2, 10, 11), together with *B ii* BERWICK ST. JOHN 10, produced a total of 38 burials, and are clearly outliers of the main Cranborne Chase concentration. *B ii* COLLINGBOURNE DUCIS 9 and 11, near the county boundary adjacent to the west Hampshire groups, yielded another 83 cremations. The two groups total 121 out of the estimated total of 180 for the whole of Wiltshire.

Two other facts emerge from a study of distributions. First there is the lack of correlation between Deverel–Rimbury cemeteries and the settlements of the Boscombe Down–Thorny Down group on the one hand and the Ogbourne Down series on the other. Secondly there is the paucity of such burials in the Salisbury Plain area so extensively explored by Hoare. Lack of discovery might be pleaded as an explanation in the first instance, and the 'central shaft' method of excavation in the second, but recent agricultural activity in all three areas seems to have brought no new burials to light, except at Heale Hill already noted, and to confirm the reality of the distribution.[74] Indeed, on the assumption that the Wessex culture burials of an earlier date indicate settlement there, the apparent lack of both Deverel–Rimbury settlements and burials

[68] *Jnl. R. Soc. Ant. Ireland*, fig. 4; Barton Bendish: *Invent. Arch.* GB. 7, 2 (2), 5.

[69] A radiocarbon date from Mount Gabriel (co. Cork) copper workings is 1500±120 B.C. (VRI–66): *Radiocarbon*, xii. 1, 136, presumably correcting the date of 1270±90 B.C. previously published under this laboratory number: *Arch. Austriaca*, xliii. 92.

[70] *Celticum*, xii. 27–44.

[71] *Arch. Jnl.* cxix. 18.

[72] List in *V.C.H. Wilts* i (1), Table *B ix, e* (p. 240).

[73] *W.A.M.* lvi. 253–61.

[74] *Arch. Jnl.* cxix. 45. Attention is drawn here to lack of evidence for settlements in Bournemouth area where over 400 Deverel–Rimbury cremation-burials are recorded.

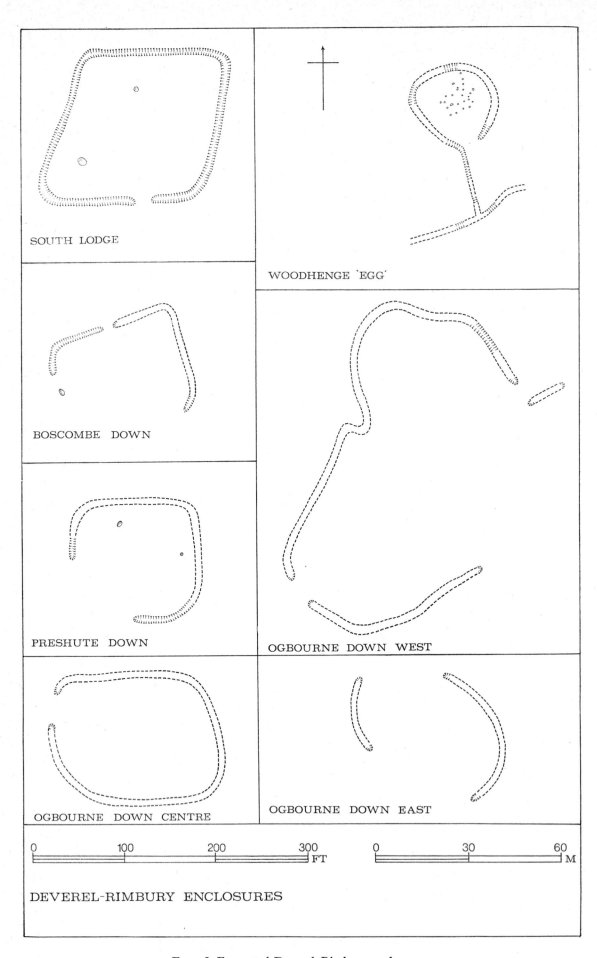

SOUTH LODGE

WOODHENGE 'EGG'

BOSCOMBE DOWN

OGBOURNE DOWN WEST

PRESHUTE DOWN

OGBOURNE DOWN CENTRE

OGBOURNE DOWN EAST

DEVEREL-RIMBURY ENCLOSURES

FIG. 28. Excavated Deverel–Rimbury enclosures.

394

in the Stonehenge area might be thought to indicate virtual desertion of the region soon after the mid 2nd millennium. Furthermore, if the concentration of such burials attests the sanctity of the monument in the earlier period, the absence of Deverel–Rimbury burials suggests that the sanctity waned or disappeared. There is, however, the evidence of the Wilsford 'ritual shaft' (with barrel and globular urns) and the indirect evidence, cited below, of agriculture in the Stonehenge area around the mid 13th century B.C., and a chronological overlap of the Wessex culture and Deverel–Rimbury may be a better assumption.

There is little to be said about Deverel–Rimbury primary barrow-burials in Wiltshire. They are ill-recorded and few in number; *B ii* AMESBURY 11 with a hook-terminal bronze armlet has been noted, and *B ii* AMESBURY 3 produced the famous 'Stonehenge Urn', a large barrel-urn 23 in. high.[75] Grinsell has compared the average size of Wessex culture bell- and bowl-barrows with that of bowl-barrows with primary Deverel–Rimbury burials in Wessex; the Deverel–Rimbury barrows, averaging about 40 ft. in diameter and 2·5 ft. high, are half the Wessex culture mean.[76]

The widespread practice of burial in cremation-cemeteries in the Deverel–Rimbury culture gave rise to complicated misunderstandings in the studies of a generation ago, when this rite, wherever found in the British Isles, was believed to owe its origin to Deverel–Rimbury, which itself owed it to its late urnfield origins on the Continent. It has already been shown in earlier sections how the cremation rite, individually or in flat cemeteries, which may or may not be enclosed within circular ditches or banks, can be seen to go back at least to the late 3rd millennium B.C. in north Britain and to the earlier 2nd in the south, including Wiltshire. There the linear cremation-cemetery with seven burials, four in cinerary urns, on Easton Down, *B ii* WINTERSLOW 21, although covered by a flint paving up to 12 in. thick, can hardly be called a 'barrow', and similar paving is indeed known in Deverel–Rimbury cremation-cemeteries. At Easton Down the pots are of 'Overhanging Rim' type, approximately dated by the segmented faience bead found, with shale, and amber bicone beads, in urn no. 1. This would imply a date after *c.* 1500 B.C., contemporary with part of the Wessex culture and the Biconical Urn phase antecedent to Deverel–Rimbury and the Dutch Hilversum culture. Thus it is also appropriate to the Deverel–Rimbury tradition of cremation-cemeteries. The cremation-cemetery idea can in fact be best seen as an insular recrudescence of a cremation rite long existing side by side with barrow burial (at first by inhumation, later by cremation) in northern Britain. After the Biconical Urn phase this custom of cremation-burial without a barrow played an increasingly important part in the developing Deverel–Rimbury culture in Wessex. The widespread adoption of the custom of cremation-burial in southern England should date from a time later than the transference to the Low Countries of what was to develop into the Hilversum culture, for in that culture barrow-burial in the earlier Wessex tradition is maintained until the appearance in the Low Countries of the cremation-cemeteries of the urnfield cultures. As the Hilversum culture is established in its primary form by *c.* 1500 B.C. that would entirely accord with the Wessex evidence for a flourishing Deverel–Rimbury culture, with frequent cremation-cemeteries, by the 12th century B.C.

The Wilsford 'Ritual Shaft'

A remarkable site not far south of Stonehenge, of which only a preliminary report has yet appeared,[77] must be considered here. Its discovery was due to the excavation of

[75] *D.M. Cat. Neo. and B.A. Colls.* (1964), no. 576.
[76] L. V. Grinsell, *Arch. Wessex*, 127.
[77] *Antiq.* xxxvii. 116–20.

what appeared to be a Wessex culture pond-barrow, a circular embanked hollow of a type already referred to (see p. 354), listed in part one of this volume as *B vii* WILSFORD (S.) 33*a* (fig. 24).[78] It was found, however, that the depression, some 40 ft. in diameter, was in fact the silted-up mouth of the weathered upper part of a circular shaft no less less than 100 ft. deep and 6 ft. in diameter, the unweathered sides of which (below 20 ft.) showed clear evidence of being trimmed by a broad-bladed axe or similar tool. At the bottom, in the water-logged filling which occupied the shaft for about half its depth, were quantities of wood and other plant remains, including such worked wooden objects as stave-built tubs, composite stitched vessels, and a turned bowl. There were also amber beads (disks and one oblate), a bone ring-headed pin, a needle and bone points, animal bones and, among the plant remains, cereal straw and pollen. From wood at this level a C14 date of 1380±90 B.C. (NPL–74) was obtained. The unweathered sides of the shaft below a depth of 20 ft. show that the lower part of the filling accumulated very rapidly. At a depth of 60 ft. the unweathered sherds of a large barrel urn were found, and at a little below 80 ft., those of a globular urn. There seems no doubt that both finds must be regarded as virtually primary and not far removed in date from *c.* 1380 B.C.

The interpretation of this site must to some degree await the full publication of the evidence. On the face of it, however, it seems less probable that it was a functional well-shaft than that it represents an early example of a type of 'ritual shaft' well known in later Celtic prehistory. Such shafts were carefully dug to depths of up to over 100 ft. and even if for a time they functioned as wells, they were eventually filled with deposits of pottery and other objects which can hardly be other than votive in some sense.[79] A contemporary counterpart to the Wilsford shaft is that at Swanwick (Hants), 24 ft. deep and containing in the upper filling a number of clay loom-weights of types known from Deverel–Rimbury settlements, including Thorny Down. At Swanwick the upright-post and traces of probable blood or flesh at the bottom link it to the parallel circumstances in a similar pit in the late La Tène sanctuary at Holzhausen in Bavaria. The continuity in ritual and practice that must be embodied in these shafts from the mid 2nd millennium B.C. to the early centuries A.D. is thus emphasized.[80]

Settlements and Ditched Enclosures

Within the Deverel–Rimbury culture may be placed a number of settlements with or without accompanying banks and ditches (fig. 28). Since the excavation by Pitt-Rivers of the ditch-enclosed sites of South Lodge, Martin Down (Hants), and the Angle Ditch near Wor Barrow (Dors.), it has been recognized that such enclosures could be earlier than the Iron Age. According to then current thought they were 'Late Bronze Age'. Their proportions clearly precluded them from being classified as forts. Pitt-Rivers non-committally called them 'camps' in the accepted terminology of the day, and thought that the Martin Down site may have been used 'chiefly for cattle' because of the fewness of the finds and the absence of storage-pits such as he had found at Woodcutts (Dors.) and Rotherley Down in Berwick St. John.[81] Hawkes was one of the first to use the phrase 'kraal', and when Stone excavated the Boscombe Down East enclosure in 1935 the term 'cattle-kraal' was used as a matter of course.[82] The 'cattle-kraal' thesis was later supported by the apparent absence of post-holes for timber

[78] p. 225.
[79] Stuart Piggott, *The Druids*, 80; K. Schwarz, *Jahresber. Bayer. Bodendenkmalpfl. 1962*, 22–77; *Anc. Europe*, ed. Coles and Simpson, 255. [80] *Ant. Jnl.* xliii. 286–7.
[81] Pitt-Rivers, *Cranborne Chase*, iv. 188.
[82] Hawkes in T. D. Kendrick and C. F. C. Hawkes, *Arch. in Eng. and Wales, 1914–31*, 146; *W.A.M.* xlvii. 466; Hawkes, *Proc. Hants. F.C. and Arch. Soc.* xiv. 136.

buildings within the three sites extensively excavated by Pitt-Rivers, in contrast with those becoming recognized in Iron-Age sites after the excavations of Little Woodbury (BRITFORD) in 1938. Stone's total stripping of the Thorny Down site, with a single embanked side, produced over 260 post- and stake-holes of timber structures (fig. 29), and in the 'Egg' enclosure near Woodhenge 25 post-holes were found in a relatively

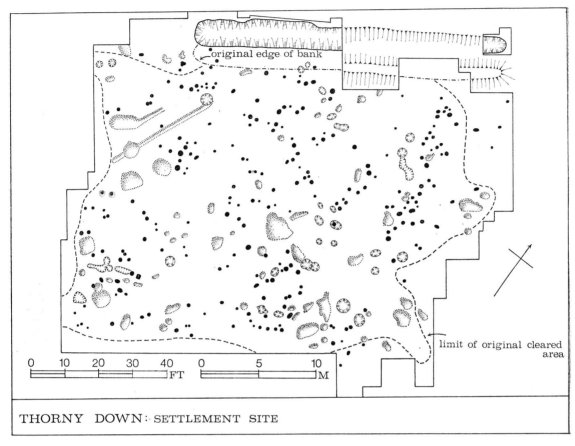

THORNY DOWN: SETTLEMENT SITE

FIG. 29. Plan of Deverel–Rimbury settlement, Thorny Down.

small area, as will be seen below (fig. 28). Before, however, necessarily accepting the two classes of site, one with and one without internal timber buildings, it must be remembered that Pitt-Rivers's methods and assumptions were such that he did not expect to find small post- or stake-holes and that he did not clear the interior of the sites in a modern manner.

Hawkes drew attention to this in the instance of the Iron-Age sites of Woodcutts and Rotherley, where the massive granary post-holes were alone recorded.[83] At South Lodge Pitt-Rivers 'determined to dig the Camp all over, down to the undisturbed chalk', and his plan, indicating areas of 'ground not trenched', shows how the digging was carried out, and that plan is confirmed by his explicit statement that at Martin Down 'the camp was trenched to the undisturbed chalk' over large areas.[84] In such conditions the post-holes of the type found at Thorny Down, and on nearly every Sussex site of the culture excavated, would never have been recognized. In the other Wiltshire enclosures of the Deverel–Rimbury culture only very small areas within the site or none at all have been stripped.

With the proviso then that it cannot be said of any site with certainty that it was

[83] *Arch. Jnl.* civ. 39, 44.   [84] Pitt-Rivers, *Cranborne Chase*, iv. 5, pls. 234, 187.

originally devoid of wooden structures, there are in Wiltshire ten excavated sites wholly or in part attributable to the Deverel–Rimbury culture, and three possible additional unexcavated sites. The unexcavated sites are listed in part one of this volume, Table *E*, nos. 100 (East Kennet, Harestone Down), 125 (Idmiston Down), and 126 (Porton Down).[85] Intensive field-work would certainly identify more. The excavated sites are briefly described below.

Boscombe Down East (*E* 11 ALLINGTON)

An enclosure *c.* 150 ft. by 120 ft. ditched on three sides and containing $\frac{1}{4}$ acre. There are two entrances, one 10 ft. wide with internal post-holes, the second 20 ft. wide. The open side is against a linear ditch, probably secondary, and the enclosure ditch is very steep-sided, 6–7 ft. wide at the top, 8–18 in. at the bottom, and 4 ft. deep. A 10 ft. by 10 ft. cutting in the interior revealed no features (fig. 28).

South Lodge Camp (*E* 29 BERWICK ST. JOHN)

The most regular enclosure of its type known, rhomboid, 165 ft. by 155 ft. internally, with one entrance 11 ft. wide and enclosing $\frac{3}{4}$ acre. The only internal features recognized were a probable post-hole (P), 2 ft. in diameter, and a pit (Q) 10·5 ft. by 3 ft. (fig. 28).

Woodhenge, The 'Egg' Enclosure (*E* 99 DURRINGTON)

A small egg-shaped ditched enclosure of only $\frac{1}{10}$ acre, 80 ft. by 75 ft. with an entrance 20 ft. wide, one side of which was subsequently linked by a ditch to a linear earthwork. The ditch was of variable section, averaging 7 ft. wide at the top, 1 ft. at the bottom, and about 3·5 ft. deep. An area of about 65 ft. by 40 ft. when stripped showed a concentration of 25 post-holes and pits towards the centre, possibly representing a circular house about 20 ft. in diameter and other structures or fences (fig. 28).

Ogbourne Down West (*E* 170 OGBOURNE ST. ANDREW)

An extremely irregular system of curvilinear ditches, some 350 ft. by 200 ft., containing 2 acres, and with two gaps, one 30 ft. and the other 200 ft. across (fig. 28).

Ogbourne Down Central (*E* 171 OGBOURNE ST. ANDREW)

A sub-rectangular enclosure 185 ft. by 145 ft., containing $\frac{1}{2}$ acre, with one entrance 30 ft. wide (fig. 28).

Ogbourne Down East (*E* 172 OGBOURNE ST. ANDREW)

Two curved segments of ditch bounding an area approximately 165 ft. by 140 ft., with gaps of 120 ft. and 90 ft., containing $\frac{2}{5}$ acre (fig. 28).

Ogbourne Maizey Down A (*E* 173 OGBOURNE ST. ANDREW)

A sub-rectangular enclosure, about 200 ft. by 200 ft., with a 10 ft.-wide entrance enclosing 1 acre. Unexcavated, but surface finds of Deverel–Rimbury pottery. The enclosure is later than the lynchet of an ancient field-system.

[85] pp. 265, 266.

Ogbourne Maizey Down B (*E* 174 OGBOURNE ST. ANDREW)

No plan has been published of this enclosure, containing ¾ acre, but a section of the ditch yielded Deverel–Rimbury pottery, burnt grain, etc.

Preshute Down (*E* 183 PRESHUTE)

A sub-rectangular enclosure 150 ft. by 135 ft., with a 90 ft.-wide opening, enclosing ¾ acre. The ditch was narrow-bottomed and some 6 ft. wide at the top. One post-hole and one pit found in two very small internal areas stripped. The enclosure is earlier than the lynchet of an ancient field-system (fig. 28).

Thorny Down (*E* 235 WINTERBOURNE)

There was no enclosure but an 87 ft.-length of ditch bounded one side of the settlement area of ½ acre, about 115 ft. by 85 ft. The ditch varied from 7·5 ft. to 8·5 ft. wide at the top, and 3 in. to 7 in. at the bottom, and averaged 3·5 ft. deep. In the occupied area 199 post-holes, 63 stake-holes, 9 small pits, and 62 shallow natural or artificial scoops defined 9 circular houses and related structures (fig. 29).[86]

The main features of these sites may here be summarized. In size they range from 2 acres to $\frac{1}{10}$ acre, but in the main tend to be between 1 acre and ¼ acre. In some, for instance South Lodge or Martin Down and to a less extent in Boscombe Down, Preshute, and Ogbourne Maizey Down A, there is a tendency to rectilinearity and sub-rectangular plans. Breaks in the bank and ditch range from entrances 10 ft. wide (at Boscombe Down with the post-holes of a gate) to gaps of up to 200 ft. At Thorny Down the ditch bounds one side of the settlement but does not enclose it. The ditches are all narrow-bottomed, and in their present weathered condition, V-shaped, but the observations of Cecil Curwen and others have shown that such a profile would result from the erosion of a virtually vertically-sided ditch over a period of about 10–15 years.[87] At Thorny Down in particular, with a ditch having an average width of between 3 and 7 in. at the bottom, the question is posed whether these ditches were in some instances at least palisade-trenches for a timber facing to the bank and not normal ditches at all.

As already shown, it cannot be certain that post-structures were wholly absent at South Lodge, or on other sites dug by Pitt-Rivers, and the total stripping of the ¾ acre Early Iron-Age enclosure on Berwick Down, Tollard Royal (see p. 426), shows how the post-structures and pits were here concentrated in one area and could easily have been missed by incomplete excavation.[88] Circumstances may well have been similar in the Deverel–Rimbury enclosures under discussion, but at Thorny Down a close-set complex of post-holes could be resolved into nine circular and related structures, the most distinctive house being about 20 ft. in diameter. At the 'Egg' enclosure the post-holes in the central area might be interpreted as in part representing a single house of comparable size. At Thorny Down again a number of small pits, associated with burnt flints, ash, pottery, and other occupation-debris, were interpreted as cooking-holes, and a couple of holes at the 'Egg' might be similarly interpreted, one with some burnt grain in it. The absence of large storage-pits of Early Iron-Age type is a noteworthy feature. It is one incidentally which contributes to the comparative scarcity of pottery in, for instance, the Pitt-Rivers enclosures, where this factor has been used to support the

---

[86] Not rectangular houses as erroneously invented by Piggott, *Anc. Europe*, fig. 87.

[87] *Experimental Earthwork on Overton Down*, ed. P. A. Jewell, 8–11, with fig. 2 from Curwen, *Antiq.* iv. 97.

[88] *P.P.S.* xxxiv. 102–47.

cattle-kraal thesis. In fact, however, Deverel–Rimbury sherds would not survive many winters on the surface and could only be expected from ditches or pits. The quantity of such sherds from the bank of South Lodge (56 per cent of the whole site, including the ditch silt) implies a settlement on the site immediately before the construction of the earthwork, which would have incorporated the pottery in its make-up. Even if all the post-structures at Thorny Down were not dwelling-houses, or not all in use concurrently, it looks as though here there may have been a larger human group than at the 'Egg', which suggests the farmstead of a single natural family.

Reserving for the moment the question of the husbandry and economy to be inferred from these sites, certain parallels in southern England may be very briefly considered. The only comparable ditch-enclosed site which could stand as an earlier prototype is that on Ram's Hill (Berks.).[89] Here both the pottery and the type of ditch, exactly comparable with that round a contemporary barrow, indicate a likely date before or around the mid 2nd millennium B.C. The interior was not excavated, so it is unknown whether there were post-structures. The main series of comparable sites are elsewhere in Wessex and in Sussex,[90] and in Sussex the anomalous Cock Hill site may be regarded as transitional, with certain features indicating an early Deverel–Rimbury date soon after c. 1500 B.C. Angular or rectilinear enclosures are not characteristic of these sites, and wherever excavation has taken place post-structures comprising circular houses and other features have been found. At Cock Hill there was a setting of four post-holes like an Iron-Age 'granary'. In several instances there were small pits or cooking-holes in the Thorny Down manner, and at Itford Hill (Suss.) a pit contained a mass of burnt barley. Pottery from the sites is broadly within the Deverel–Rimbury class, though with local variants, and it is clear that two geographical areas are represented within a single south English province.

Recent excavations in the Netherlands have shown that while ditched enclosures of the Hilversum culture have not yet been identified, open settlements can have post-structures which are closely paralleled in at least the Sussex Deverel–Rimbury sites. At Nijnsel, Zijderveld, and Dodewaard circular houses of types not normally found in the Netherlands but very similar to, for instance, those of Itford or Cock Hill appear, and at Nijnsel there are square 'granary' settings as well as three storage-pits. The parallel developments seen in the pottery on both shores of the North Sea are here reflected in the settlement-plans themselves.[91]

Economy and Agriculture

Considerable inferences about the basic economy of the Deverel–Rimbury culture can be made from the settlement evidence. While bronze tools and ornaments were in use, the only possible evidence for local metal-working is the slag fragment from a primary context in the Boscombe Down East ditch silt. In 1935 this was tentatively identified by A. F. Hallimond as 'an artificial slag, full of gas cavities'.[92] As the Deverel–Rimbury culture was at that time believed to be immediately antecedent to the Early Iron Age, the presence of iron slag would not be out of the question, and in this 'Late Bronze Age' sense it was accepted as such by R. F. Tylecote,[93] but the iron identification must now be regarded with great suspicion, although metalliferous slag from copper- or bronze-working would be acceptable.

[89] *Ant. Jnl.* xx. 465–80.
[90] Dorset, Martin Down and Angle Ditch: Pitt-Rivers, *Cranborne Chase*, iv; Shearplace Hill: *P.P.S.* xxviii. 319–28; Sussex: E. C. Curwen, *Arch. Sussex* (2nd edn.), 169–93; *Suss. Arch. Colls.* xci. 69–83; xcix. 78–101 (Cock Hill). [91] *Ber. Rijks. Oudheid. Bodem.* lx. 117–29.
[92] *W.A.M.* xlvii. 484.
[93] *Metallurgy in Antiquity*, 199.

One technological point clearly emerges, and that point is the continued importance in the Deverel–Rimbury culture of flint-working. This awaits full study by modern methods, but meanwhile several very pertinent observations on the industry have been made by Stone. He first recognized its rather massive quality and distinctive flaking techniques and suggested that mined flint might have been used. He contrasted it with the equally distinctive but dissimilar industry of the Beaker culture at, for instance, Easton Down (see p. 301), and also with the flint series associated with pottery of the overhanging-rim urn type, presumably before the mid 2nd millennium, in a pit on Stockbridge Down (Hants). Further, he noted a less marked distinction from the Mildenhall Fen (Suff.) flint industry, with biconical urn pottery, and at Thorny Down he isolated a type of scraper proper to this among the normal Deverel–Rimbury types.[94] The comparisons and contrasts made are completely in agreement with what is known of the cultural and chronological sequence within the 2nd millennium B.C., and the Deverel–Rimbury flint industry appears as the end-product of an indigenous process of development beginning in Beaker times.

A point of some interest is that no flint arrowheads have been found in Deverel–Rimbury contexts, though as seen, archery played an important part in the earlier 2nd millennium B.C. (see p. 342). In Dutch sites of the Hilversum culture, such as Vogelenzang, barbed-and-tanged flint arrowheads, alien to the Netherlands and generally considered to be 'Wessex' types, do however appear.

The basic farming economy of the Deverel–Rimbury culture comprised grain-growing and animal husbandry. The swing in the relative proportions of wheat and barley as between Neolithic times and the early 2nd millennium has been noted above (see p. 287). The essential change to a greater proportion of barley begins with the Beaker immigrations and remains constant to the Early Iron Age, and the Wiltshire evidence in the Deverel–Rimbury culture is confirmatory. Charred barley was found in a small pit (24) in the 'Egg' enclosure at Woodhenge, and again, with tubers of onion couch (*Arrhenatherum avenaceum*) in a trial cutting made across the ditch of the Ogbourne Maizey Down B enclosure. Grain impressions of hulled and naked barley were found on the Deverel–Rimbury vessels from *B ii* COLLINGBOURNE DUCIS 9 and ALL CANNINGS 22* respectively.[95] With this direct evidence of cereal cultivation go the finds of saddle-querns at South Lodge and Thorny Down and on almost every excavated site elsewhere, and the cereal pollen and straw in the Wilsford shaft.

The technique of grain preparation and storage clearly did not employ the Early Iron-Age storage-pit and square granary system, though the Cock Hill (Suss.) post-setting, and others at Nijnsel in the Netherlands, look suspiciously like prototypes of the latter. Burnt grain was associated by Hans Helbaek with the Iron-Age practice of corn-parching and induced him to include Itford Hill in his Iron-Age category, but it could of course be explicable in other terms. A question remains, however, as to the function of the quantities of burnt flint nodules on Deverel–Rimbury sites, notably in Wiltshire at Thorny Down. These, sometimes called 'pot-boilers', were originally thought of as being used to heat water, and it is known from exceptional evidence in Ireland that this technique of stone-boiling was used there in the early 2nd millennium B.C.[96] On the other hand, in Iron-Age contexts, such burnt flints have, since Gerhard Bersu's interpretations at Little Woodbury,[97] usually been taken as related to

[94] *W.A.M.* xlvii. 480–2 (Boscombe Down); 654–8; *P.P.S.* vii. 131–2 (Thorny Down); iv. 249–57 (Stockbridge Down).
[95] Cunnington, *Woodhenge*, 50; *New Phytologist*, xlviii. 253–4; *P.P.S.* xviii. 194–233.
[96] 1763±270 B.C. (C–878) and 1556±203 B.C. (C–877):

Jnl. R. Soc. Ant. Ireland, lxxxiv. 105–55. Modern ethnographic parallels in H. E. Driver and W. C. Massey, *Comp. Studies N. Amer. Indians*, 229; practical difficulties of paunch and skin boiling: *Antiq.* xl. 225–30; xliii. 218–20.
[97] *P.P.S.* vi. 62.

corn-parching processes. The question must be left open pending further evidence, but certainly constitutes a possibility. Burnt flints in Beaker sites as at Easton Down have already been noted (see p. 348).

With this evidence of cereal production may finally be taken the actual surviving systems of rectangular ancient fields cultivated with a traction-plough, and in Wiltshire these can be assigned to a date contemporary with the Deverel–Rimbury culture in two instances. The unexcavated enclosure of Ogbourne Maizey Down A (see p. 398) was partly cut into an earlier lynchet belonging to such a system, and the Elcombe Down 'Ornament Horizon' hoard of the 12th century B.C. had been buried in what must have been the plough-soil of one of a group of similar fields (see p. 391). The Marleycombe Hill barrows in Bower Chalke of Deverel–Rimbury date, once thought to be later than a lynchet, are in fact earlier.[98] Plough-agriculture in Neolithic contexts in Wiltshire has already been discussed (see p. 288) and it may be noted that a wooden plough of simple 'ard' type in Denmark has been dated to 1490±100 B.C. (K–1301).[99] What may be taken as indirect evidence of cultivated fields in the Stonehenge region is the wind-blown soil filling the Y and Z holes of the monument, with a date of 1240±105 B.C. (I–2445), a point already referred to (see p. 285). Such a date would be appropriate to a Deverel–Rimbury context. The field systems under consideration are of the 'Celtic Field' type so characteristic of Iron-Age and Romano-British agriculture in southern Britain.

The animal husbandry represented in the Deverel–Rimbury settlements has several points of interest. Sheep or goat and to a less degree pig are represented, but cattle preponderate. The cattle are almost uniformly of a distinctive small breed, unknown in Neolithic contexts and usually classed as *Bos longifrons*, the cattle which above all are typical of the British Early Iron Age. In Wiltshire such cattle have been identified at South Lodge, Thorny Down, Boscombe Down East, and Ogbourne Down West in Deverel–Rimbury contexts, and in contemporary sites outside the county such as Martin Down (Dors.), Angle Ditch (Dors.), Itford (Suss.), Cock Hill (Suss.), and Ramsgate (Kent). This is not, however, the first appearance of the type, as it occurs first in Beaker or allied contexts in Wiltshire at Easton Down, the Sanctuary at Avebury, and Snail Down, and outside the county at Giants' Hills long barrow, Skendleby (Lincs.).[1] It appears again in the Biconical-Urn site at Mildenhall Fen (Suff.) and, in post-Deverel–Rimbury times, in the Minnis Bay site in Kent and, as will be seen, consistently in the Early Iron Age. At Mildenhall Fen, Boscombe Down East, and Ogbourne Down West there was evidence for a larger breed being present, but in very small numbers.[2] The Deverel–Rimbury cattle appear in fact to have a good pedigree going back to Beaker times, and are themselves ancestral to those of the Early Iron Age.

This topic has been discussed by Robert Trow-Smith and P. A. Jewell.[3] Jewell, having pointed out that *Bos longifrons* was widespread on the Continent so that importation could well be the source for the British stock, goes on to remark that genetically the diminution of size distinguishing *Bos longifrons* from earlier breeds in Britain could be the result of selection and nutritional factors in this country, so that all British pre-historic cattle would be of insular derivation from the primary Neolithic breed. Trow-Smith compares *Bos primigenius* and its close congeners in Neolithic times to the modern beef type, and *Bos longifrons* to the milk type of cow as exemplified by the Jersey. If the possibility or likelihood is accepted of the importation of a new breed rather than its

[98] *V.C.H. Wilts.* i(1), p. 273 where they are correctly said to be earlier.

[99] From Hvorslev, Jutland: *Tools and Tillage*, i. 56.

[1] A complete skeleton.

[2] Identifications by J. W. Jackson in most relevant excav. reps. summarized by him in *P.P.S.* ix. 41–4.

[3] R. Trow-Smith, *Hist. Brit. Livestock Husbandry*, 20 sqq.; P. A. Jewell, 'Cattle from Brit. Arch. Sites', *Man and Cattle* (R. Anthrop. Inst. Occasional Paper, No. 18), ed. A. E. Mourant and F. E. Zeuner, 80–101.

insular evolution, it is clear that the most likely context is that of the Beaker immigrations early in the 2nd millennium B.C., with subsequent continuity to Roman times.

Horse bones are present in small quantities on Deverel–Rimbury sites, such as Boscombe Down and Thorny Down. They may furnish evidence of the appearance of a domesticated breed, as they do at Vogelenzang, though domestication is better attested in later Bronze-Age contexts as at Heathery Burn (co. Durham) in the late 8th–7th centuries B.C. That sheep were bred for wool as well as meat and milk is shown by the clay loom-weights from Thorny Down, comparable to those from Cock Hill (Suss.) and other contemporary sites, but spindle-whorls were not found on any of the Wiltshire sites.

Finally, connected with the question of animal husbandry are the linear earthwork systems, some at least of pre-Iron-Age or Deverel–Rimbury date, forming systems over large areas of the Wiltshire–Hampshire downland. Wiltshire examples, almost all undated, are listed in part one of this volume, Table D,[4] and the ditch systems of east Wiltshire–west Hampshire were treated by Hawkes in 1939.[5] Here Hawkes demonstrated that a ditch system was earlier than the Iron-Age hill-fort of Quarley Hill (Hants) and this system is representative of a larger series which include the ditches presumptively earlier than the Wiltshire hill-fort of Sidbury Camp (North Tidworth) or at Liddington (D 4). One of these ditches, on Snail Down (D 96), was sectioned without producing dating evidence, and the same negative result was obtained from a ditch at Bulford (D 78). Ditches which may be Deverel–Rimbury are D 11 (Allington–Idmiston–Winterslow), D 56 (Grim's Ditch, at least in part), and D 188 (Winterbourne) and 194 (Winterslow). Hawkes has suggested that the large-scale land-divisions marked by these ditches might be associated with some form of cattle-ranching, and a map of the Bourne Valley ditches suggests the possibility of parallel strip-allotments running from water-meadows to hill pasture in the manner of many Wiltshire medieval parishes. More field-work and excavation are needed before a coherent pattern can be extracted from so large a number of earthworks spread, as is now known, over six or seven hundred years before the Iron Age.

THE DONHEAD–TISBURY PHASE

In the Deverel–Rimbury phase circumstances have been dealt with which fully justify the use of the term 'culture' in archaeological phraseology, namely a consistent assemblage of settlements, burials, pottery, and bronze and flint industries. The Deverel–Rimbury culture is in fact one of the best defined in southern English pre-history, and emerges as the culmination of traditions and cultural processes beginning in Beaker times at the outset of the 2nd millennium B.C. It exists in its most characteristic form around the 11th–12th centuries B.C. but beyond that date its continuance is unknown. A period follows of five or six hundred years, the Late Bronze Age of conventional terminology, where the archaeological evidence consists almost wholly of bronze tools and weapons, and in which Wiltshire seems to be part of an area outside the main regions of development. A few hoards and stray finds alone can be assigned to this period, which is divisible into two phases.

Into the earlier phase, datable to c. 750–650 B.C., comes first the metal-worker's hoard from the Clift (DONHEAD ST. MARY). This comprises the following objects in bronze and stone: 1 bivalve bronze mould for casting faceted socketed axes, 3 socketed axes (two triple-ribbed), 8 'end-winged' axes, 1 socketed hammer, 1 narrow socketed

---

[4] p. 249.   [5] *Proc. Hants. F.C. and Arch. Soc.* xiv. 136–94.

gouge, 1 oval-sectioned armlet, 2 bronze ingot-fragments of scrap bronze, coils of wire 8 mm. and 6 mm. gauge, 1 square stone polisher. The scrap-metal, the wire, and the stone polisher (comparable with those from the 'occupational graves' of the early 2nd millennium, see p. 344) indicate a founder's or metal-worker's hoard, and the end-winged axes relate it to the 'Carp's Tongue Sword' complex of Burgess's third phase, c. 750–650 B.C.; the faceted and the slender ribbed socketed axes would also be appropriate here, as would be the gouge and hammer. As a map of the bronzes of this complex shows, the Donhead hoard is peripheral to the main south-east English concentration, which has strong links with west France.[6]

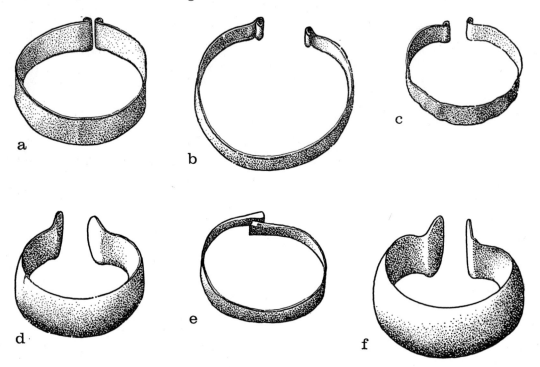

FIG. 30. Hoard of gold armlets, Tisbury. a–c, coil ended, d, f, offset-ended, hollowed bow, e, flat bow, expanded ends. (½).

It is probably to this chronological position that should be assigned the socketed bronze sickle of Fox's Group I from WINTERBOURNE MONKTON, and the fragment found with a socketed chisel at ALDERBURY.[7] A faceted axe from CHERHILL and another stray find from DONHEAD ST. MARY have been compared to north European types by Butler,[8] and some other stray finds of socketed axes from the county may belong to this phase as may the socketed gouges (as that from Oldbury in Calne) and tanged chisels (as at East Kennet).[9]

The second hoard is of gold objects found somewhere in the parish of TISBURY (fig. 30). In a recent detailed study R. R. Clarke and C. F. C. Hawkes[10] have shown it not to have contained, as has often been stated, a 'dress-fastener' of Irish type but to have comprised the following gold ornaments: 2 massive armlets forming a pair, 3 flat coiled-terminal armlets, and 1 fragment of a similar armlet. The pair of massive armlets with hollow bow and out-turned ends are of a type known in bronze on the Continent, originating in late urnfield contexts, and in west France and east England

[6] *Arch. Jnl.* cxxv. 1–45 with map, fig. 14; J. Briard, *Dépots Bretons et l'Âge du Bronze Atlantique.*

[7] *P.P.S.* v. 222–48, nos. 18, 17.

[8] Butler, 'Bronze Age Connections', *Palaeohist.* ix. 87–8.

[9] *D.M. Cat. Neo. and B.A. Colls.* (1964), nos. 645, 612.

[10] *Culture and Environment*, ed. Foster and Alcock, 193–250.

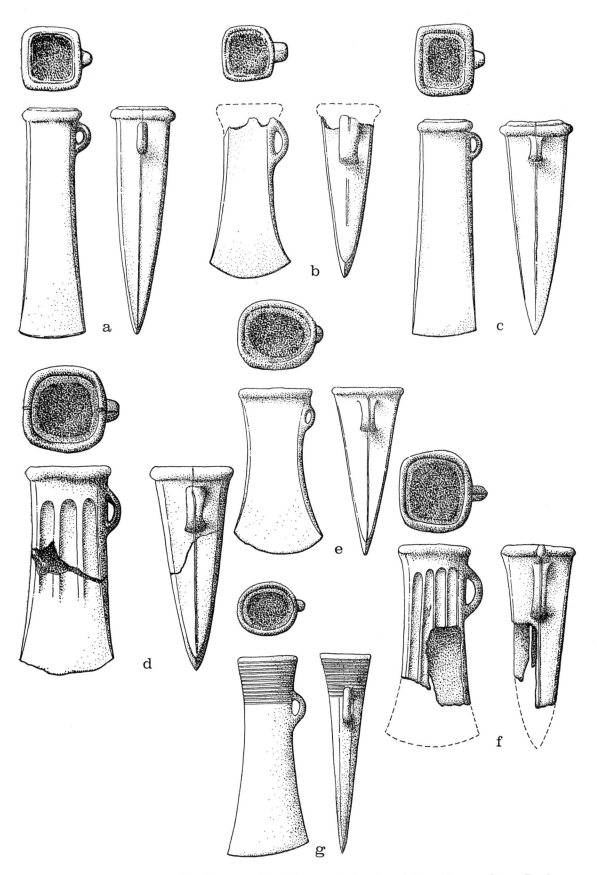

FIG. 31. Late Bronze-Age socketed axes: a, East Kennet; b, d–g, hoard from Manton Copse, Preshute; c, 'Salisbury Plain'. ($\frac{1}{2}$).

forming a component of the 'Carp's Tongue Sword' and winged-axe complex, represented in Wiltshire by the Donhead hoard just discussed. The flat coiled-terminal armlets are represented in British hoards such as Morvah (Cornw.), Bexley (Kent), and Cottingham (Yorks. E.R.), and, though like the other armlets they are presumptively of Irish gold, they are specifically British types and imply local goldsmiths copying foreign patterns or inventing their own.

An Italic bronze brooch, a stray find from Box, should be mentioned here, as it is an 8th-century type. The appearance of such brooches as stray finds in Britain (some 78 finds of the 9th–4th centuries B.C.) is still unexplained, and while some may well be strays from recent collections, the possibility of others being genuine prehistoric imports cannot be dismissed.[11]

THE PRESHUTE–BRETON AXE PHASE

The final pre-Iron-Age phase of prehistoric Wiltshire is very exiguously represented, but elsewhere in Britain is marked by the appearance of new metal types indicating contacts with the continental cultural traditions of the Hallstatt C phase and the first use of iron for weapons and tools north of the Alps. In Wiltshire the hoard of nine

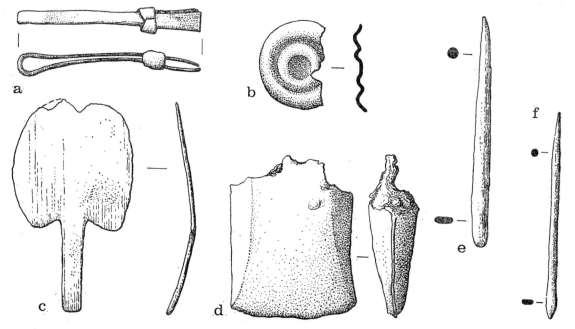

FIG. 32. Late Bronze-Age objects from All Cannings Cross: a, tweezers, b, ribbed disk, c, razor, d, socketed axe, e, f, awls. (Full size).

socketed axes from PRESHUTE (fig. 31 b, d–g) and the other stray finds of short three-ribbed axes of the same type can be assigned to this phase. To the same phase belongs the bronze leaf-shaped sword from Figsbury Rings (WINTERBOURNE) of a type generally within the Ewart Park group of north Britain or the 'Thames' group in the south, derived from Hallstatt bronze sword types.[12] At a time contemporary with these Hallstatt C contacts, however, renewed west French connexions led to the importation into Britain by trade of a peculiarly Breton type of narrow parallel-sided form of socketed axe. In Brittany such axes are found in great numbers, often in enor-

[11] D. Harden, *Atti 1º Cong. Internaz. Preist. Protost.*   [12] *Ant. Jnl.* xlix. 32; *P.P.S.* xxxiii. 377–454.
Mediterranea (1950), 315–24.

mous hoards, and their frequently unfinished condition has suggested that they were used as some form of currency. A recent study by Jacques Briard has demonstrated their wide distribution in Europe and the British Isles beyond their area of origin, and the general probability of a date around the 6th century B.C. is corroborated by a C14 date of 559 ± 130 B.C. (GSY–42) for the context of a characteristic Breton hoard.[13] In Wiltshire imported axes of Breton type are known as stray finds from CHILTON FOLIAT, EAST KENNET, OGBOURNE ST. ANDREW, Rivar Hill, SHALBOURNE, and 'Salisbury Plain' (fig. 31 a, c), and, most interesting of all, there is a fragment of a characteristically unfinished axe of this type from the Iron-Age settlement at All Cannings Cross.[14]

A brief consideration of the bronzes from that site can appropriately form the final section of this chapter. There were found, scattered over the site and so not explicable as a disturbed hoard, at least seven bronze objects of Late Bronze-Age types around the 7th–6th centuries B.C., an assemblage comparable to those of Ivinghoe Beacon (Bucks.), Staple Howe and Scarborough (Yorks. E.R., N.R.).[15] The All Cannings objects (fig. 32) comprised the fragmentary Breton axe already mentioned; a razor of the Heathery Burn–Adabrock type again referred to earlier (see p. 390) and paralleled also at Ivinghoe; a pair of tweezers of a type again known at Ivinghoe and Staple Howe, and in the contemporary Llangwyllog (Anglesey) hoard;[16] a ribbed disk or button, again as at Llangwyllog and in the Reach Fen (Cambs.) hoard,[17] and three bronze awls of general types found at Heathery Burn.[18] In addition to these clearly pre-Iron-Age pieces, a bossed strip, if not from a 'false-rivet' decoration on a bowl or cauldron of Spettisbury–Glastonbury type,[19] could perhaps be from a Late Bronze-Age vessel of analogous form, and the wire armlets and (?) ear-rings, some with hooked terminals, may have better Bronze-Age than Iron-Age counterparts. Two double-perforated bone 'toggles' have a partial parallel to one from South Lodge and to a stray from Cold Kitchen Hill in Brixton Deverill.

In sum the All Cannings Late Bronze-Age objects must be taken as indicating an occupation around the 6th century B.C. by people who were not necessarily cognizant of iron metallurgy and with whom presumably some of the pottery from the site may have been associated. At this point, however, a new chapter of Wiltshire prehistory is reached. In its early stages it looks back to and incorporates much of a tradition stretching not only to the beginning of the 1st millennium B.C., but beyond into the Deverel–Rimbury phase and perhaps as far back as the Beaker immigrants in the second.

[13] Briard, *Dépots Bretons et l'Âge du Bronze Atlantique*, cap. xiii.

[14] First recognized as such by C. B. Burgess: *Ant. Jnl.* xlix. 32; Cunnington, *All Cannings Cross*, pl. 18, 3, with other bronzes, pls. 18–19.

[15] *Recs. Bucks.* xviii. 187–260; T. C. M. Brewster, *Excav. Staple Howe; Arch.* lxxvii. 179–200.

[16] J. Evans, *Anc. Bronze Implements*, fig. 229.

[17] Ibid. 400; *Invent. Arch.* GB. 17, 3 (3), 26–7.

[18] *Invent. Arch.* GB. 55, 10 (7), 89–90.

[19] C. Fox, *Llyn Cerrig Bach*, 88.

THE EARLY PRE-ROMAN IRON AGE

c. 650–*c.* 400 B.C.

DURING the 7th century widespread regions of Britain, particularly those areas on routes of easy penetration from the sea, received cultural influences from the Continent which had at this time reached the Hallstatt C technological stage of its development. In terms of material culture the contact is manifest in certain classes of imported objects such as swords and chapes, bronze vessels, and occasionally horse trappings. Technologically, knowledge of iron smelting was introduced. What all this means in cultural terms is less certain, but the generally accepted assumption that Britain was now subjected to a small-scale incursion by a warrior caste may not be far from the truth.[1]

It is at present unwise to dogmatize on how these new influences affected the apparently stable Late Bronze-Age population of Wiltshire. As shown in the preceding chapter, the multi-period site of All Cannings Cross (ALL CANNINGS), occupied throughout most of this early period, produced, among other objects, a tanged bifid razor and socketed bronze axe (fig. 32 c, d), both of Late Bronze-Age type. These finds suggest perhaps an early beginning for the settlement, but the evidence is hardly conclusive. The unstratified collection of artefacts from Cold Kitchen Hill (BRIXTON DEVERILL) included a socketed axe made in iron (fig. 33 a), a curious combination of new technology and old-style typology, indicating perhaps an early experiment carried out by local bronze-smiths using the new material. How far back in the 'Bronze Age' primitive iron-smelting was practised is still open to debate. The slag supposed to be iron slag from Boscombe Down East (BOSCOMBE) may hint at an early introduction, but by the 7th century, the probable date of the Cold Kitchen Hill axe, it is clear that skilled iron-smiths were now operating.

The earliest ceramic component of the material culture (fig. 35) includes two forms: bipartite furrowed bowls and large jars decorated with stabbed, stamped, and incised geometric designs, both of which can be paralleled in the late urnfield assemblage of eastern France.[2] Similarities are so striking that cultural contact between the peripheral urnfield cultures of western Europe and Wiltshire must be postulated. Whether, however, this was in the form of a direct folk movement or simply the result of the local copying of containers made of bronze, and possibly leather, traded over considerable areas, cannot at present be assessed. Among other things it must wait until a detailed petrological examination of the pottery fabrics. A single radiocarbon date of *c.* 630 B.C. (NPL–105, 2580±155) for wood charcoal taken from the post-holes of an early house at Cow Down (LONGBRIDGE DEVERILL) associated with pottery of this early type suggests a broad contemporaneity between the British and continental material.

The somewhat uneven evidence summarized above provides a starting point in the 7th century for what may be classed as the early pre-Roman Iron Age in Wiltshire. Thereafter, until about 400 B.C., there appears to have been an uninterrupted local development marked by a gradual evolution of pottery styles and an increase in the diversity and complexity of settlement form.

[1] *Problems of the Iron Age in S. Brit.* ed. S. S. Frere, 9–11.

[2] N. K. Sanders, *Bronze-Age Cultures in France*, fig. 54.

Although the Iron-Age sites of Wiltshire have been more intensively investigated than those of any other county in Britain, only two sites, Cow Down[3] and Little Woodbury (BRITFORD), have been sufficiently thoroughly excavated to provide any clear indication of total settlement form. Other sites have been either sampled on a small scale or were examined before modern methods of area excavation, suitable for the discovery of timber buildings, were developed. Thus, while many fragments of evidence are available, the general picture is still incomplete.

One of the commoner forms of settlement in this early period is the farmstead or hamlet unit which may or may not be enclosed. Little Woodbury, the best known example, demonstrates the complex development of one such site (fig. 43). It appears that in the early period of its existence a single circular house, 46 ft. in diameter, stood towards the centre of a palisaded enclosure of uncertain size but probably between 3 and 6 acres in extent. The house is one of the most complex Iron-Age structures yet found in southern Britain, with its central setting of four large posts, presumably to support the roof structure, surrounded by a circular setting of the main vertical supports beyond which were shallower holes, perhaps to tie down the sloping rafters of a conical roof. A single wedge-shaped entrance-porch was provided facing towards a gate in the enclosing palisade. However the house is reconstructed, and there are several possibilities, there is little doubt that it was a sophisticated piece of construction yet unparalleled in the domestic architecture of the preceding periods. A similar house, but without the unique central feature, was found at Cow Down in Enclosure A, while three simpler circular houses of early date, 30 ft., 35 ft., and 45 ft. in diameter, were uncovered in the roughly circular 7-acre Enclosure B.

While there can be little doubt that in its early phase Little Woodbury was a single farmstead, more complex sites such as Cow Down, where traces of several houses exist, raise the general problem whether these may not also have been hamlets or even small villages. In advance of the final report on the Cow Down excavation it would be unwise to speculate, except to say that the excavator's interim reports suggest that it is unlikely that more than one house existed at one time.[4] In the absence of positive evidence to the contrary, it may be assumed that isolated farmsteads, comprising a circular house often with an enclosure, constitute one of the elements in the early Iron-Age settlement pattern of Wiltshire, always bearing in mind that there may be considerable variation in the status of different farms.

Some of the farms, such as Cow Down, continued in use for a considerable time, probably from the 7th to the 2nd or 1st century B.C. Little Woodbury, which probably began a century or two later than Cow Down, continued until much the same time. Generally, the changes which took place were not dramatic. At Little Woodbury the palisade was replaced by a ditched enclosure and the original house appears to have been replaced by a simpler and somewhat smaller building. The most noticeable innovation is the development of deep pits for storage, which will be considered again below. Continuity of occupation without an increase in size seems to have been the general rule. Some sites, including very early settlements at All Cannings Cross and Cold Kitchen Hill, were abandoned before the beginning of the middle pre-Roman Iron Age, while others such as Boscombe Down West (ALLINGTON), SWALLOWCLIFFE, Fifield Bavant Down (EBBESBORNE WAKE), and Harnham Hill (SALISBURY) originate within the early period but not at its beginning. Tentatively, therefore, the evidence, as it stands at present, suggests a gradual opening up of the countryside throughout the first three centuries or so of the Iron Age.

---

[3] *W.A.M.* lvii. 9–10; lviii. 31–2.   [4] Ibid.

Many of the farms were, by the end of the early period, enclosed by ditches varying in size but seldom exceeding about 9½ ft. in depth. While the larger ditches could clearly have afforded some protection from raiding, the smaller examples were probably intended to be no more than convenient boundaries, perhaps to prevent the unhindered movement of livestock into the occupied area, or to offer some protection from predatory animals. Ditched enclosures of a more substantial nature were, however, being constructed, usually on hill tops or spurs with good natural defences of their own. Such sites are normally classified under the rather unsatisfactory blanket term of 'hill-fort'. In Wiltshire exact evidence of their dating is not always forthcoming, but at Yarnbury (BERWICK ST. JAMES/STEEPLE LANGFORD) the discovery of early pre-Roman Iron-Age sherds low down in the filling of the ditch of the inner enclosure is reasonably conclusive (fig. 39). The other relevant sites, Oliver's Castle (fig. 41) (BROMHAM), Lidbury Camp (ENFORD),[5] Figsbury Rings (WINTERBOURNE), Chisenbury Trendle (ENFORD), and Winklebury (BERWICK ST. JOHN), have all produced early pottery either from below the ramparts or within the enclosure. This fact, combined with the absence of later material, is suggestive of a date towards the end of the early period for the construction of the defences. That the more massive banks and ditches replace earlier enclosures, perhaps of palisaded type, is a possibility which should not be overlooked, but no positive evidence for such a relationship has yet been recovered from any of the Wiltshire sites.

Three of the excavated hill-forts possess some similar characteristics. Lidbury is a small sub-rectangular enclosure with an entrance on the south side (fig. 41). The rampart appears to have been dump-constructed but the possibility of timber revetting, missed in the excavation, cannot be ruled out. The entrance shows two phases of construction. The first, with ditch-ends slightly *en échelon*, was modified in the second by squaring off the front and making the ditch-ends directly opposed. Oliver's Castle is of similar sub-rectangular form, situated on a promontory and protected by a two-phase dump-constructed rampart fronted by a flat-bottomed ditch. The single entrance was bounded by four large post-holes, two each side of the entrance passage, serving both to retain the ends of the rampart and to provide supports for the gates. As with the second phase of Lidbury, the ditch-ends were opposed. Winklebury Camp, substantially larger, is also sited on the end of a spur and is enclosed within a dump-constructed rampart fronted by a flat-bottomed ditch (fig. 41). The entrance, though unexcavated, is of the *en échelon* type.

The three forts in question may, therefore, be of a generalized type which is perhaps descended from the rectangular enclosures of Mid–Late Bronze-Age date considered above (see p. 396). They bear a striking resemblance to a class of sub-rectangular forts of a similar early date which lie along the Sussex Downs.[6]

A second class of hill-fort is typified by the first (inner) enclosure at Yarnbury, a roughly circular enclosure 12 acres in extent, defended by a ditch 13 ft. deep and 19 ft. wide, backed by a timber-revetted rampart. The entrance appears to have been a funnel-type about 35 ft. long, revetted with a flint wall. To the same general category may tentatively be assigned Figsbury, Chisenbury Trendle, Scratchbury (NORTON BAVANT), and possibly the crop-mark site of Great Woodbury (BRITFORD). There may well be others which have suffered from obliteration by ploughing, or which may have become incorporated in later enlargements.

---

[5] Lidbury is rather different from the other early 'forts'. It covers only *c*. 1 a. (not 8 a. as in *W.A.M.* xl, pl. 11 facing p. 28). Its close association with linear ditches might indicate a function linked to cattle hus-bandry, but at least 11 storage-pits were found. These might, however, predate the defences.

[6] *Suss. Arch. Coll.* civ. 109–20.

YARNBURY CASTLE, BERWICK ST. JAMES: IRON-AGE HILL-FORT

WHITE SHEET HILL, KILMINGTON
Neolithic causewayed camp in foreground with iron-age site beyond

While it is possible to recognize these two general types of hill-fort, the almost complete absence of excavation within them makes it difficult to assess their function. In general they are no larger than the enclosed farmsteads of Little Woodbury type but their siting tends to be more closely related to the defensive rather than to the agrarian potentialities of the land. A variety of explanations present themselves: they may be the farms of an aristocracy, equivalent perhaps to medieval baronial castles, or places of refuge for tribal groups, or convenient collecting depots for stock at certain times during the year. All these views have been canvassed at one time or another, and all are possible. Until several of the sites have been extensively examined by excavation, the true explanation cannot emerge.

The existence of an expanding farming community and the availability of surplus labour necessary for the construction of the hill-forts implies a stable subsistence economy based upon mixed farming.[7] Most of the developments apparent in the early part of the Iron Age are a continuation of traditions already deeply rooted in the preceding Bronze Age. The small squarish 'Celtic fields', tilled by a simple ard and already a familiar feature of the landscape, were used to grow a wide range of cereals. At Fifield Bavant a mass of charred grain found in a pit included oats, black oats, six-row barley, hulled barley, erect six-row barley, bere, emmer, club wheat, spelt, and rye. Many of these varieties are represented on other broadly contemporary sites. That spelt and hulled barley, both winter-sown crops, are not yet known from preceding Bronze-Age contexts has suggested to some observers that winter sowing, with its resulting beneficial extension of the harvest period, was an innovation introduced towards the middle of the 1st millennium.

Corn, when cut, was brought into the settlement for further treatment. After the selection of the seed corn, which was probably hung on racks to dry and then stored in small granaries supported on settings of four posts, the bulk of the crop was parched, possibly to facilitate threshing, and stored in pits, some of which were large enough to hold 60–70 bushels. Although small pits, possibly for grain storage, are not entirely unknown in the early 1st millennium, they do not become common until the 4th century B.C. Evidently other storage methods must have been prevalent throughout most of the early period.[8]

The fertility of the fields was closely bound up with the carefully controlled use of flocks and herds for manuring. It may be assumed that throughout the winter the animals roamed the fields, gleaning what they could and in return enriching the ground with their manure. When the time came for the spring sowing they would be driven to areas of open pasture and woodland to browse off the spring and summer herbage. Without an extensive livestock population Iron-Age agriculture would have been unworkable.

The statistics, such as they are, show that on the downland sites of Wiltshire sheep (and goat) and ox constituted the bulk of the livestock population with pig in the minority, reflecting no doubt lack of suitable pannage for swine away from well-watered river valleys. The bones of horses, about the size of an Exmoor pony some 12 hands high, and of various breeds of domestic dogs were found on most of the sites. The meat supply was also occasionally augmented by red and roe deer, wild duck, and chub. While the species represented on the excavated sites have usually been carefully identified, too little information is available concerning the problems of optimum killing age, the over-wintering of stock, breed and nutritional variations, and butchering

---

[7] For a discussion of Iron-Age farming see H. C. Bowen in *Roman Villa in Brit.* ed. A. L. F. Rivet, pp. 1–48.

[8] H. C. Bowen has suggested that the introduction of the extensive system of below-ground storage might be linked to the more warlike nature of late Iron-Age society.

techniques. On the evidence of faunal material from sites outside Wiltshire, however, it is clear that a substantial percentage of the herds was over-wintered for at least one or two years. It is unlikely that systematic selective breeding had begun at this early date. The importance of stock-rearing is reflected in the systems of linear ditches which straddle the countryside.[9] Some clearly originate before the 7th century (see p. 403), but, whatever their date of construction, many of them must have remained a noticeable, and presumably functional, feature of the landscape in the Iron Age. Two groups, those in the region of the hill-fort at Sidbury (NORTH TIDWORTH) and those on the Ebble–Nadder ridge, serve to illustrate the main features of the type (fig. 46).

Sidbury lies on a hilltop, 700 ft. O.D., overlooking undulating chalkland dissected on the east by the river Bourne. Converging upon the summit are no fewer than seven linear ditches, some of which run across country for more than 5 miles, dividing the surrounding countryside into a series of wedge-shaped territories pendent upon the fort. On analogy with the Hampshire site of Ladle Hill, it is reasonable to suppose that the ditches originally led to an enclosure, later obliterated by the construction of the fort.[10] If this is indeed the case at Sidbury, it might reasonably be suggested that at an early stage the site formed the focus, perhaps a collecting kraal, for several pastoral units, the ditches, therefore, serving as 'ranch boundaries'.[11]

A recent survey of the Ebble–Nadder ridge[12] has shown that the land was divided into blocks by means of bivallate cross-dykes, running across the ridge from scarp to scarp with occasional univallate ditches cutting across the spurs. Although dykes of this kind have given rise to a considerable archaeological literature, they may be nothing more than pastoral boundaries designed to divide a ridge conveniently in the same way as the linear ditches divide the plain. Several of the 'territories' between the Ebble and Nadder are conveniently served with trackways leading from the lowland, some of them passing through areas of cultivated land, to reach the ridge-top. It is, therefore, tempting to see them as cattle-ways, joining meadows to the hill pasture. Centuries of use and modification have, however, added confusion to the pattern.

A third type of boundary is represented by a single length of shallow ditch flanked on either side by posts, found at Winterbourne Dauntsey (WINTERBOURNE) in association with early Iron-Age pottery. Its discovery is a firm reminder that not all boundary works can be expected to survive as visible monuments. It is probably for this reason that the category of structures is not well known, but a second example was found recently in Hampshire, on Portsdown, associated with a rectangular enclosure of pastoral type.[13]

While individual settlements were probably largely self-supporting so far as the basic food requirements of the community were concerned, specialist production and a well developed trading system were necessary to provide many of the material needs. The place of iron is of particular interest, for it almost totally replaced bronze as the material from which tools, weapons, and to some extent even ornaments, were made (fig. 33). Whereas the production and distribution of bronze artefacts had required a well developed system of itinerant craftsmen-traders, iron-smelting could become virtually a cottage industry, particularly in the north of the county where iron deposits were reasonably near at hand. That iron was in fact worked on settlement sites is shown by slag found at All Cannings Cross and Cow Down. Further south, well away

[9] For list see part one, pp. 249–60.
[10] *Antiq.* v. 474–84.
[11] Unpublished fieldwork by R.C.H.M. (Eng.) shows that at some points the ditches post-date field systems and one at least joins the outworks of the fort. This implies that the ditches are relatively late and may have been constructed after the fort was erected. Excavations at Danebury (Hants) in 1969 suggest a similarly late date for the linear ditches there. [12] *W.A.M.* lix. 46–57.
[13] *Hants Field Club*, xxiv. 42–58.

from naturally occurring iron ore, either the crude metal, or more probably the finished products, were carried by traders, but even here, once a sufficient bulk of metal objects had been accumulated, broken implements could be melted down and re-worked by the local population. The general effect of the change-over to the use of iron would, therefore, have been a breakdown, or at least a lessening, in the intensity of itinerant trading with a consequent regionalization and decrease in the innovating qualities of the communities. This is not to say, however, that there was no widespread trade at all. Salt from the coast would have reached the interior; Kimmeridge shale from Dorset, in the form of bracelets and pendants, penetrated as far north as All Cannings Cross; glass beads were imported, eventually arriving at Swallowcliffe and All Cannings Cross; and a gold-plated ring reached Swallowcliffe. In addition a wide range of bronze trinkets and fittings changed hands (figs. 33, 34), including bracelets, pins, tweezers, belt-hooks, button-ornaments, belt plates, and awls. It may also be that some of the Italian-derived fibulae from the county arrived during this period but direct association in archaeological contexts is lacking. Evidently the trading network was functioning to serve the luxury market which seems to have been gradually developing as the stability and efficiency of the local subsistence economy increased.

Pottery, the most copiously surviving element of the material culture, provides one of the few media available for calibrating, albeit relatively, time divisions within the early period (figs. 35, 36). Since associated metal objects are rare, and until many more radiocarbon dates are produced, pottery will offer the only basis for constructing chronologies.

In broad general terms it is possible to distinguish three overlapping stages in the early Iron-Age ceramic development of Wiltshire. In the first, well represented at All Cannings Cross, Cow Down, and Cold Kitchen Hill, and sporadically elsewhere, finely made bipartite bowls with angular shoulders predominate, often decorated with furrowing, stamping, or incisions above the shoulder. Many of them have been coated with haematite and fired deliberately in an oxidizing atmosphere to give a reddish-brown bronze-like surface. There can be little doubt that these bowls, particularly those with furrowed decoration, were made in imitation of bronze vessels similar to the cup found with an assortment of 7th-century bronze objects in the Welby hoard in Leicestershire.[14] Besides the bowls a range of coarser jars was produced: some, with S-shaped profiles, were usually stamped or incised with geometric decorations, while others, with more angular shoulders, were left plain or simply decorated with finger-tip impressions. The assemblage of this first stage gradually developed into the second. The copious decoration tended to decrease, furrowed bowls were provided with upstanding or flared rims, and the coarse jars became plainer. During the second stage a distinctive bowl-type was introduced with a flaring rim and a body composed of a series of facets, the junction of which was often marked by cordons. Usually the body was scratched after firing with simple geometric designs inlaid with white paste, contrasting with red haematite of the surface finish. While the scratch-cordoned bowls continued in use into the third stage, there was a general decline in the quality of both haematite-coating and of the bowl form, and a replacement with high shouldered bowls with foot-rings or even squat pedestal bases invariably fired to a black surface-colour and burnished. The coarse jars by the third stage had become much simpler in profile, with less well defined shoulder angles.

The impression given by the early Iron-Age ceramic development in Wiltshire is of a general continuity in tradition, gradually modified by local changes in fashion. Most of

[14] *Arch. Jnl.* cv. 27–40.

the types mentioned above are restricted to the Wiltshire–Hampshire area and some, particularly the bowls, are quite clearly of highly specialized forms, embodying certain well defined technological and aesthetic concepts. Presumably they are the output of commercial production centres geared to an essentially local market. The scratched-cordoned bowls for example were all found within a 25-mile radius of Salisbury, a convenient maximum distance for the efficient distribution of ceramics. The only indication at present known of pottery manufacture from within the county is a waster from the collection of material at Cold Kitchen Hill, which implies the local production of pottery of the earliest group. Eventually with the wider application of techniques for the petrological and spectrographical examination of pottery fabrics, the nature of the ceramic industry will become much clearer.

While it may reasonably be assumed that the finer pots were commercially produced and distributed, the coarse wares in everyday use were most likely made at the homesteads. Several Wiltshire sites have produced oven-daub which may well have derived from the small kilns and furnaces used in the day-to-day production of such household utilities as coarse-ware vessels for cooking and storage.

Many other aspects of home production are reflected in the remains of the material culture surviving on the Wiltshire settlement sites. Spinning and weaving, for example, were widespread. The wool would first have been spun, using spindles weighted with whorls of baked clay or chalk (fig. 33 f). Weaving took place on an upright loom, one of which may be represented by a small fragment of charred timber found at Swallowcliffe, the warp being kept taut by heavy loom-weights of baked clay, chalk, or stone. Threading the weft may have been carried out with a bobbin incorporating a bone point, usually a sharpened sheep's tibia of a type found frequently on occupation sites of this date (fig. 33 p). Admittedly some doubt attaches to the use of these bone objects: all that can safely be said is that their blunted and polished points would have admirably suited them to this function and might have resulted from it. The weave could have been consolidated in two ways: either by the use of a wooden sword for tamping down the weft, or with the small bone combs which occur on most sites (fig. 33 o). In practical terms a sword would have been more useful on a broad loom producing coarse cloth, while the combs were better suited to the production of braids or finer fabrics. Dyeing, either of the finished cloth or, in the case of multicoloured fabrics, of the yarn before it was woven has left no archaeological trace.

Leather-working would have been of equal importance with weaving, but it tends to leave little evidence. Nevertheless the general production processes are evident. Skins would first need to be stretched out on the ground for de-hairing and for the removal of fat. It may be that the commonly occurring spatula-shaped knives made from rib bones were used to remove the fatty substance from the exposed undersurface of the skin (fig. 33 e). After curing it is likely that some form of tanning was undertaken but the details are generally obscure. Pliny mentions a considerable trade in oak galls, a convenient source of tannin, but the only evidence for this in southern Britain is a small collection of oak galls found in an Iron-Age pit at Chalton (Hants).[15] It may be, however, that some of the pits found on settlement sites were used as vats in the tanning process.

The conversion of cloth and leather into clothing of various kinds required the use of iron knives, bronze and bone awls for perforating the leather, and bone needles for sewing: examples of these artefacts are known from most Wiltshire sites (fig. 33 d, q). Clothing may well have been decorated with plaques of bone and perforated animals' teeth which occur from time to time.

[15] Pliny, *Nat. Hist.* ed. H. Rackham, iv. 404–7. Chalton excavations unpublished.

Iron tools and implements are not particularly well represented on the early sites, probably because broken objects were melted down for re-use, but among those which survive are socketed gouges, simple tanged knives, small sickles or reaping knives riveted to their handles, awls, and miscellaneous fittings (figs. 33, 34). Iron was also used for ornaments such as ring-headed pins which became popular towards the end of the early period (fig. 33 i).

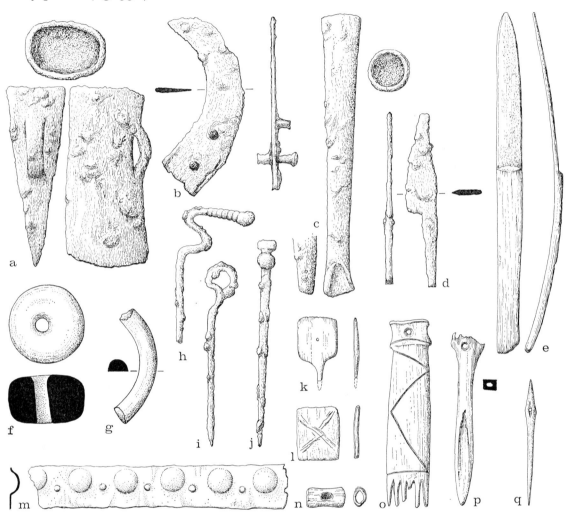

FIG. 33. Early Pre-Roman Iron-Age tools and weapons: a, iron axe, from Cold Kitchen Hill ($\frac{1}{3}$); b, curved iron blade, c, socketed iron gouge, d, iron knife blade, e, bone rib-knife, f, baked clay whorl, g, shale fragment, h, swan-neck iron pin, i, ring-headed iron pin, j, flat-headed iron pin, k, bone spatula-like object, l, bone? counter, m, bronze band, n, bone object, o, bone comb, p, bone implement, q, bone needle, all from All Cannings Cross (a, e $\frac{1}{3}$, all others $\frac{1}{2}$).

The nature of the archaeological evidence allows the economy and the crafts of the early Iron-Age communities to be described in some detail, but it is less satisfactory when considering matters of social structure and religious beliefs. In rather surprising contrast to the late stages of the Bronze Age, practically nothing is known of the burial customs of the earliest iron-using communities. Since, however, there is no evidence of a change in burial-rite away from cremation, it must be assumed that the dead continued to be cremated and were buried in urnfields unaccompanied by vessels or offerings. Whether this implies a decrease in interest in the dead and afterlife it is impossible to tell. Several of the occupation sites have, however, produced fragments of uncremated human bones mixed up with the general rubbish. At All Cannings Cross

32 fragments of human skulls were found scattered about the excavated area. Of these, four had been deliberately cut, one into a perforated roundel, another into a rough oblong polished on both sides, and a third was polished smooth all over. At Lidbury a fragment of a human temporal bone had been shaped and perforated, and several skull fragments were also recovered from Swallowcliffe. While skull fragments are reasonably common, other human bones tend to occur much less frequently, suggesting the hoarding of skulls perhaps as reminders of the dead or as trophies of enemies. The selection of the human skull, either whole or fragmentary, for careful treatment was a practice widespread among primitive peoples.

No religious sites of the early period can be identified with certainty, but the remarkable collections of artefacts from Cold Kitchen Hill, stretching from the 7th century B.C. until well into the Roman period, hint at the possible use of the site as a temple or shrine. No adequate excavation has ever been undertaken, so the problem must be left open.

Several generalizations concerning the social structure of the period begin to emerge. There is as yet little evidence of a marked disparity in the size of settlements, unless the small hill-forts are thought of as the castles of an aristocratic class. Variations no doubt existed in the size and productivity of the individual farms, but there is little to suggest that surplus was used to purchase articles of display other than trinkets such as beads, rings, and brooches. Indeed the general impression given is of small farming units of extended-family size, essentially self-supporting and undergoing little change over several centuries. If the present knowledge of settlement distribution is a fair reflection of the total picture, it must be assumed that new settlements were constantly springing up, presumably colonizing unbroken land. A general regularity and alignment in the layout of large areas of field systems is highly suggestive of a certain order and control. The increase in population which this implies may well have led to conflict, giving rise to the development of the warlike overtones which become more evident in the following period.

THE MIDDLE PRE-ROMAN IRON AGE

c. 400–*c.* 100 B.C.

DURING the 4th century B.C. Wiltshire, along with much of the rest of Britain, received new influences from the Continent which by this time had reached the La Tène stage of its development. Contact seems to have been particularly strong across the North Sea leading to significant alterations in the settlement pattern and material culture of parts of eastern Britain, but in Wiltshire there was very little change. Indeed continuity is a characteristic of the area. The La Tène I brooch introduced into Britain was copied in Wiltshire, giving rise to distinctive local developments, while at settlement sites such as Swallowcliffe, Fifield Bavant, and Boscombe Down West the gradual changeover to black burnished pottery tends to reflect changes parallel with continental developments. There is nothing to suggest an influx of new people, nor is there any form of observable disruption in the established way of life.

Almost every known settlement site occupied in the preceding early period continued in use. At Little Woodbury the enclosing ditch was added to provide additional protection, while the original house appears to have been abandoned and replaced with a simpler building (fig. 43). At Cow Down the nucleus of the occupied area shifted slightly,[1] as was also the case with the Boscombe Down West settlement, where a distance of 1,500 ft. separates the early and middle period settlements. That a shift of centre could take place is a warning against placing too much weight on absence of evidence for occupation. For example, while on present showing the All Cannings Cross settlement does not appear to have lasted long into the middle period, it should be remembered that only a relatively small area has been excavated and later occupation may lie close by in unexplored areas.

It was during the middle period of the pre-Roman Iron Age that most of the great hill-forts of Wiltshire were erected. In form they contrast with the 'forts' of the early period: they enclose a much larger area, usually between 15 and 30 acres in extent, they are defended by more substantial ramparts and ditches, and they are almost invariably contour works placed in prominent positions on hill-tops. Apart from scraps of evidence, however, recovered sporadically, sometimes as the result of very limited trial excavation early in the 20th century, practically nothing is known of their detailed structure, development, or internal arrangements. Two forts, Yarnbury and Bury Wood Camp (COLERNE), have, however, been sufficiently extensively examined to provide a fair indication of the main characteristics of the type.

At Yarnbury the first fortified 12-acre enclosure has already been described (see p. 410 and fig. 39). If indeed it belongs to the early period, as the finds stratified in the ditch suggest, its univallate contour construction, size, and short in-turned entrance provide a good prototype for the larger hill-forts of the middle period. Some time after its construction the inner defences were abandoned and a much larger fort constructed around it, enclosing an area of 28½ acres and defended by a massive bank and ditch with a smaller ring of possibly later date outside. The single entrance passage, still an imposing feature of the site, was flanked by the in-turned ends of the inner rampart for

---

[1] *W.A.M.* lvii. 9–10; lviii. 31–2.

a distance of almost 90 ft., while the approach to the entrance is protected by out-works of some complexity. Although this outer defensive circuit has not been excavated, the excavation of the early fort produced a quantity of pottery of 'saucepan pot' type (see below), which was probably current in the 2nd and 1st centuries B.C. Some of it came

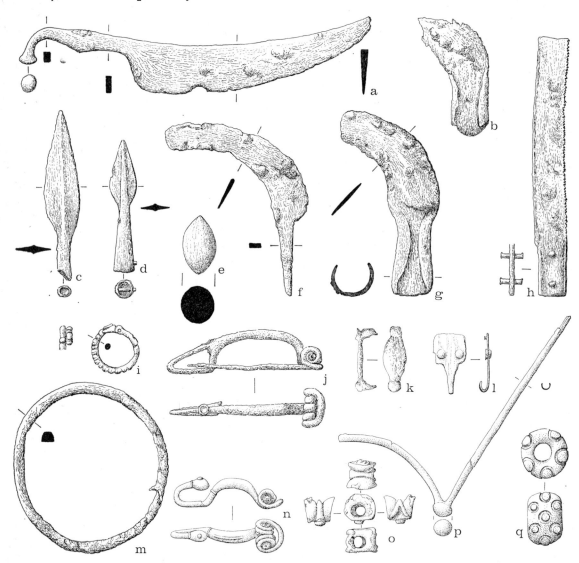

FIG. 34. Middle Pre-Roman Iron-Age tools and weapons: a, knife, c, d, spearheads, f, g, sickles, i, m, rings, all iron, from Barbury Castle ($\frac{1}{3}$); e, baked clay bullet, from Yarnbury Castle ($\frac{1}{3}$); h, iron saw, from Battlesbury Camp ($\frac{1}{3}$); b, iron bill-hook, j, iron fibula, k, iron cleat, l, bronze belt-hook, q, glass bead, all from Swallowcliffe Down (b $\frac{1}{3}$, others $\frac{1}{2}$); n, bronze fibula, from Cold Kitchen Hill ($\frac{1}{2}$); o, bronze ring-casting, from Bilbury Rings ($\frac{1}{2}$); p, bronze scabbard binding, from Wilsford (N.) ($\frac{1}{3}$).

from storage-pits dug in the interior, indicating a period of occupation of undefined intensity and duration.

The second fort, Bury Wood Camp,[2] lies on a promontory of the Great Oolite towards the north-west corner of the county (fig. 39). It is an impressive amalgam of several periods of building activity, as the excavations of the 1960s showed, but at the time of writing only a tentative assessment can be offered. The south side of the promontory was crossed by a multiple-period defence, which in the first phase was provided with a central entrance passage, flanked on one side by the out-turned end of

[2] *W.A.M.* lviii. 40–7; lxii. 1–15.

one rampart, revetted by dry-stone walling: the other rampart end was aligned with the outer end of the out-turn. Superficially this rather unusual arrangement might be thought of as a logical development from the simple *en échelon* entrance of the earlier period. At a later date the entrance passage was blocked and the ditch was continued across the front by the removal of the causeway. Later still work appears to have begun on an outer defence, but the surviving surface configurations of the land suggest that the new line was never completed. The fort was provided with two other entrances, on the north-west and north-east sides, both of which are of inturned type. Of these, the north-east entrance has been thoroughly excavated. Its entrance passage, as little as 12 ft. wide at its narrowest, was flanked for a distance of more than 60 ft. with vertical dry-stone walls. At the inner end of these were four large post-holes to take a timber gate-tower of considerable proportions which had evidently been destroyed by fire. From occupation areas within the fort quantities of 'saucepan pots' of the 2nd or 1st century were recovered, some in association with alterations to the defences.

The above brief summary emphasizes the main characteristics of the hill-forts: they were massively constructed with an eye to defence, enclosed a large area, underwent frequent modifications, and show signs of having been occupied, if only sporadically. Most of these characteristics are probably true of most of the other large forts of Wiltshire. The Wiltshire forts must be seen against the distribution pattern of similar contemporary structures which spread across Britain in a broad arc from east Sussex into south Wales and the Welsh borderland. Such a widespread parallel development must be the result of a convergent evolution influenced by the same social, economic, or military factors. What exactly the forts represent in terms of social structure is not easy to determine, but certain generalizations can be made. In Sussex, and to a lesser extent in Hampshire and Wiltshire, each large fort lies in the centre of a block of downland usually between 35 and 45 square miles in extent. They, therefore, seem to be the largest physical structure upon which the population of a geographical unit of this size was dependent, and thus might be considered as a physical manifestation of the society's labour surplus for both construction and maintenance. This much is not unreasonable, but to understand the motive force is more difficult. Simply stated there are two possible explanations: the forts may be seen as places of refuge in time of war, constructed by the community for the common good, or they may be thought of as the strongholds of the upper ranks of a class society, made possible by forced labour or tribute extracted from the peasant classes. These explanations are essentially extremes: in reality the forts were more likely to have been the result of communal labour, under coercion from the society's leaders, providing a strong focus suitable for a wide range of functions.

The only forts in southern Britain to have been extensively excavated, Hod Hill and Maiden Castle (both in Dorset) and South Cadbury (Som.), prove to have contained large numbers of houses at the time of the Roman conquest. At Hod Hill one differed from the rest because it was provided with a hexagonal enclosure and was perhaps suitable for the habitation of a prominent person.[3] Although it has been argued that the individual houses need not have been in continuous use, the evidence suggests a nucleated settlement and indeed nucleation is one possible consequence of the very existence of hill-forts. This point will be considered in more detail below (see p. 429).

Enclosed settlements of 3–6 acres and hill-forts of more than 15 acres are the two extremes of the settlement spectrum. Between those two is a variety of smallish

[3] I. A. Richmond, *Hod Hill*, ii; R. E. M. Wheeler, *Maiden Castle* (Rep. Res. Cttee. Soc. Antiq. 1943); for S. Cadbury, see *Antiq.* xxxix. 184–95; *Ant. Jnl.* xlviii. 6–17, xlix. 30–40, l. 14–25.

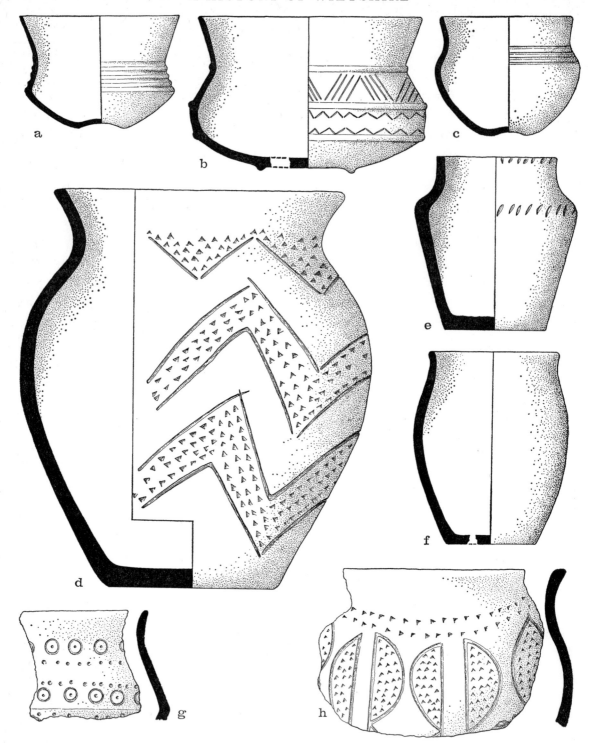

FIG. 35. Early Pre-Roman Iron-Age pottery from All Cannings Cross: a, small bowl red-coated ware; b, c, bowls of grey red-coated ware; d, chevron-ornamented vessel; e, small urn-shaped pot; f, barrel-shaped pot; g, rim piece of fine grey ware; h, rim fragment of large vessel of grey ware. ($\frac{1}{3}$).

enclosures such as Great Woodbury, Chiselbury (FOVANT), Bilbury (WYLYE), and others, about which very little is known. The same is true of the even smaller enclosures of about an acre, like Mancombe Down, near Battlesbury, Warminster (fig. 40),[4] of which many have presumably been ploughed out. Whether they were the homesteads of small farmers or stock-enclosures is at present unknown.

[4] *W.A.M.* lx. 52–6.

The growing complexity of the settlement pattern tends to underline the stability of the basic subsistence economy, of which some account has already been given (see p. 411). Little change is distinguishable from the 7th to the 1st century, except for the great increase in the number of storage-pits in the later period, implying perhaps more a change in storage methods than an increase in productivity. Cattle-rearing continued to play an important and increasing part in the farming economy, and while the earlier arrangements for controlling stock probably continued to function, a new type of stock-collecting enclosure seems to have been introduced. This consisted of a small ditched area, $\frac{1}{2}$–$1\frac{1}{2}$ acre in size, entered by means of a long causeway, defined by continuous ditches, which splay outwards at the end, sometimes becoming linear ditches extending for considerable distances. Although the two Wiltshire examples, Hamshill Ditches (BARFORD ST. MARTIN) and Church End Ring (STEEPLE LANGFORD), have not been satisfactorily dated (figs. 40, 45), the similar structures at Blagdon Copse and Bramdean (both Hants), can be shown to belong to the 2nd or 1st century B.C.[5] The funnel-shaped causeway has obvious advantages for the selection and treatment necessary at certain times during the year in animal husbandry. The idea is not entirely new, but is a modification of the antennae ditches, which funnel towards the entrance gaps in the enclosures surrounding some of the larger farms, including Little Woodbury. Other small enclosures, without funnel ditches, like the $\frac{1}{2}$-acre sub-rectangular site on Down Barn West, in Winterbourne Gunner (fig. 40),[6] may also have served as kraals for stock.

A general survey of the changing composition of flocks and herds from 3000 B.C. to 1 B.C., carried out in the 1940s,[7] pointed to a gradual decrease in oxen and a corresponding increase in the number of sheep. This, it was suggested, reflected the destruction of woodland and its conversion to arable and pasture, creating open conditions more suitable for sheep, the ox being essentially a woodland browsing animal. Although detailed statistics are not available for Wiltshire, the figures from Bury Wood Camp show that more than 60 per cent of the animal population was sheep, with oxen accounting for about a quarter of the stock.[8] At Highfield (SALISBURY) there were more than 30 sheep and only some 5 or 6 oxen. By the 1st century B.C. therefore, it appears that numerically sheep predominated, but that in terms of meat yield mutton and beef were eaten in about equal quantities. Highfield has produced evidence of a somewhat atypical animal population with pigs equal in number to sheep (each about $\frac{1}{3}$ of the total). This may be because the settlement was close to several river valleys where suitable pannage for pigs might have biased the balance of the stock rearing. Another peculiarity of the Highfield figures is the exceptionally large number of dogs, 22 per cent of the total, of at least three different breeds. While it is possible that there was some special reason for this, it seems very likely that dogs played an essential part in swine-herding activities, so clearly in evidence here.

Pottery, which as a plastic medium is sometimes susceptible to social or economic changes, develops gradually throughout the period (fig. 36). At first the high-shouldered, dark-surfaced bowls and the weak-shouldered jars of the third stage of the early pre-Roman Iron-Age, continue in use, probably into the 3rd century if not later, the haematite-coated vessels having by then completely died out. Some ceramic elements penetrated the north of the county from the vigorous communities living in the Thames Valley, but generally it may be said that the main development proceeded unhindered by external influences. By the 1st century B.C. a distinctive local style had arisen, in which

[5] *Hants Field Club*, xxiii. 81–9; for Bramdean, unpublished inf. from excavator.

[6] *W.A.M.* lx. 56–61.
[7] *Antiq.* xxi. 122–36.

[8] *W.A.M.* lxii. 13.

four major pot-types commonly occurred (fig. 37): a straight sided 'saucepan'; a bowl with a gently curving shoulder and thickened beaded rim, sometimes with a foot-ring base; a large jar with a higher neck and out-curved rim; and a simple barrel-shaped coarse-ware jar, sometimes provided with perforated lugs. The first three types, the fine table wares, were usually decorated with a variety of curvilinear motifs, drawn on

Fig. 36. Middle Pre-Roman Iron-Age pottery: a, b, Swallowcliffe; c, Boscombe Down West; d, All Cannings Cross. (⅓).

the surface of the pots with a blunt point before firing. Commonly recurring motifs included arcs springing from indentations and zones infilled with oblique lines, cross-hatching, or dots. The stylistic similarities of this group are so close that the vessels are likely to have come from a single production centre. The fact that pottery in this style is unknown beyond a 15-mile radius from Salisbury supports the suggestion, but proof must await scientific analysis of the individual fabrics.

Beyond the Salisbury region very little pottery of the period under review has yet been recorded. 'Saucepan pots' occur widely but apart from a vessel from All Cannings Cross, which has close similarities to types in the Cotswolds, it is as yet impossible to characterize distinctive groups.

The 'saucepan pot' assemblages of Wiltshire are only part of a much wider continuum which spreads across the whole of southern England from Sussex to the Welsh borderland, in fact much the same area as that occupied by the large hill-forts. While a series of distinctive regional styles can be defined, reflecting local production centres and folk culture, the broad similarities result from a parallel, and even convergent, development, demonstrating widespread cultural contact throughout most of the region.

Iron came more widely into use at this time, particularly for the manufacture of tools and weapons. In addition to knives, sickles, and billhooks, new types including saws, hammers, and latch-lifters occur while iron cleats, presumably for the soles of boots, become more common. Iron weapons also make an appearance. The small bivallate hill-fort of Barbury Castle in Ogbourne St. Andrew[9] has yielded a collection of iron-work (fig. 34 a–d), including three spears of various sizes and a ferrule from a spear-butt, while a specialized form of flamboyant spear, probably of this date, was found on Bidcombe Down (LONGBRIDGE DEVERILL). Other more warlike artefacts include sling bullets of clay found on a number of sites, fragments of a chape and sword-scabbard from Cold Kitchen Hill, and bronze scabbard bindings (fig. 34 p), possibly of late date, from WILSFORD, N. While these finds can all be explained as weapons for hunting or display, the general impression gained is that warrior equipment was becoming more widespread, which taken in conjunction with the growth in the numbers and defensive strength of hill-forts might imply more warlike trends emerging among certain levels of the community.

The presence of small horses is well attested on Iron-Age sites of various dates in Wiltshire. Normally horses as well as oxen would have been used to pull carts, but from Caesar's accounts of the tribes he encountered in eastern Britain in the mid 1st century B.C., horses were also used to pull the war chariots handled so skilfully by those who opposed his advance. It is, therefore, a possibility that war chariots were used in Wiltshire in the 2nd or 1st century. Indeed two iron nave rings, thought to be fittings for chariots rather than carts, have been recovered from the hill-forts of Barbury Castle and Battlesbury. Barbury Castle also produced a series of decorated iron rings suitable as harness fittings.[10]

Other aspects of the material culture seem to have changed very little. Bone objects of earlier type continued in use much as before, and traded trinkets, such as glass beads from the Continent and Kimmeridge shale bracelets from Dorset, were still imported. Brooches of various local types made in bronze and iron (fig. 34 j, n) suggest that the basic nature of clothing remained much the same. Other personal and clothing ornaments include pins, bracelets, and spiral finger- and toe-rings. The only major innovation noticeable by the end of the 2nd century B.C., or a little later, is the introduction of the rotary hand-quern, which replaced the old saddle quern for grinding corn. Querns of the new type have been found in late contexts at Little Woodbury and on Boscombe Down West in levels predating the beginnings of wheel-made pottery which characterized the late pre-Roman Iron Age.

Burial practices appear to remain of little interest to the population. On occupation sites like Highfield 14 broken human bones, half of them skull fragments, were found lying around the site in much the same manner as in the early period. On other sites some attempt had been made at rather unceremonial inhumation. At Boscombe Down West, for example, a body lying on its back with knees drawn up had been disposed of in a rubbish pit. Bodies were also found in two rubbish pits, probably of the same

---

[9] *W.A.M.* lviii. 394–402. [10] Ibid. 399.

period, at Yarnbury, and a similar burial of slightly earlier date was discovered in a pit at Cow Down.[11] Numerous burials, thought to be the result of a massacre, were disposed of in pits just outside the north-west entrance of Battlesbury Camp. The impression gained from these discoveries is that burial was governed more by expediency than by ritual: bodies were simply flung into convenient pits or ditches along

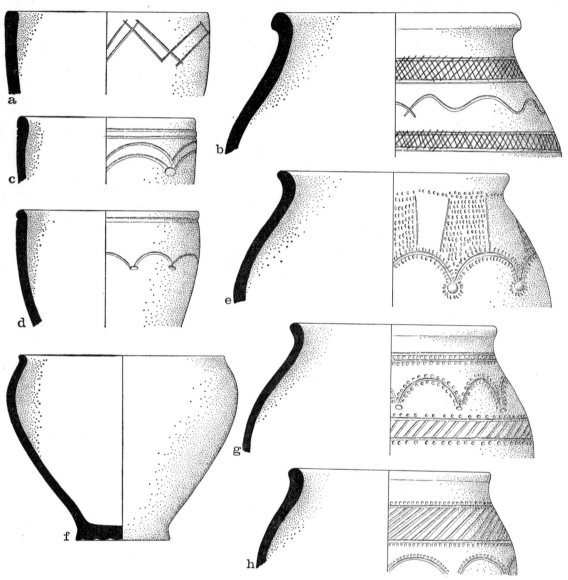

FIG. 37. Middle Pre-Roman Iron-Age pottery: a, b, c, e, h, Yarnbury Castle; d, g, Highfield (Salisbury); f, Fifield Bavant. (⅓).

with other household rubbish, although it could always be argued that burials placed in pits had some religious significance. The isolated fragments found on occupation sites could as well result accidentally from disturbance as from the deliberate retention of mementoes. The nature of the evidence may of course distort the picture. It may be that it was the lower ranks of society whose bodies were thus treated, and those of status and wealth may have been more carefully buried. Nevertheless, the inescapable impression remains that the dead body was neither revered nor feared by the community, implying a radical change in religious beliefs compared with those of the 3rd and 2nd millennia.

[11] *W.A.M.* lviii. 32.

The above summary of the middle period of the pre-Roman Iron Age shows that while there was a large measure of continuity, both culturally and economically, social changes were beginning to take place. Elsewhere, particularly in Hampshire, it can be shown that the middle period was a time of rapid increase in the size of the population, leading to the colonization of new land. The same may well be true of Wiltshire, where, however, the evidence is less clear. Population expansion on chalkland areas would inevitably lead to conflict over the rights to grazing and arable land, and it might be in the conditions of growing insecurity, consequent upon this, that the more warlike elements in the material culture, and the growth of the hill-forts, have their origin. In primitive societies subjected to such pressures it is not unusual for the principal men to be endowed with coercive powers of military leadership, giving rise, should the pressures continue, to a well defined warrior aristocracy. The well documented changes in Germanic society from the 1st century B.C. to the 1st century A.D. provide an excellent example of these processes.[12] How far the communities of Wiltshire had developed along these lines by the 1st century B.C. cannot yet be assessed, but the strongly defended hill-forts, providing a focus for regional nucleation, the weapons, and the objects of display are all consistent with the view that insecurity was beginning to alter the structure of society.

[12] E. A. Thompson, *The Early Germans.*

THE LATE PRE-ROMAN IRON AGE

c. 100 B.C.–43 A.D.

IT may fairly be said that throughout the first century B.C. much of Britain came into a far closer contact with the Continent than it had been for centuries. The reasons are clear. From the end of the 2nd century B.C. western Europe was subjected to the massive folk movements caused, initially, by the migration of the Cimbri and Teutones from the Rhine to the Mediterranean, where they were eventually halted by the Roman army. The ripples which followed in the wake of this invasion were intensified towards the middle of the 1st century by Caesar's campaigns through Gaul to the Rhine and into southern Britain, and by the ultimate Roman annexation of Europe south of the Rhine–Danube axis. Upheavals of this magnitude necessarily impinged upon the British Isles. Probably about the time of the movements of the Cimbri and Teutones a community from the territory of the Belgae in northern Gaul settled in eastern Britain, whether as a pioneer thrust to be followed by subsequent arrivals, or as a follow-up to earlier colonization is still not clear. Much of the south coast of Britain was also subject to influences from adjacent parts of Gaul at about this time, but there is nothing to suggest that this constituted a colonization. Indeed it seems more likely that the contacts which can be observed are the result of vigorous trading activities across the English Channel which served to link Britain to neighbouring parts of the Continent. The 1st century B.C. is, therefore, a time of innovation, of cultural and political regrouping, and, in some parts of the country, of turmoil. It is also a time when historical personalities begin to emerge.

Without prejudice to the discussion which follows, it should be stated here that in Wiltshire there is no evidence at all of social upheaval or of any sudden cultural change; everything points to continuity and gradual development. Admittedly the introduction of the potters' wheel improved the technical quality of the pottery and a few imported types trickled into the area along with new La Tène III brooches which at last bring to an end local variations of the earlier La Tène types, but these are quite minor changes. The introduction of money economy probably had a more far-reaching effect. These matters will, however, be considered in more detail below.

The basic unit of settlement throughout the later period remained the small enclosed farmstead of which a typical example is situated on Berwick Down (Tollard Royal)[1] in the southern part of the county (fig. 44). Since the site has been totally excavated under modern conditions, it is of considerable value as a type site, a value enhanced by the fact that the farm seems to have been in use for a relatively short time and is, therefore, devoid of later alterations. The farm-house itself was a circular hut, 14 ft. in diameter, set within a kite-shaped enclosure, less than an acre in extent, delineated by a shallow ditch, barely 3 ft. deep and 4 ft. wide, provided with a single ungated entrance. Within the enclosure were four above-ground granaries and 33 pits of varying proportions and size, some of them suitable for grain-storage. One impressive feature of the ground plan is the large amount of open space within the enclosure, suitable for the temporary penning of animals. Outside the main enclosure, on the downhill side, an arc-shaped ditch was provided, offering cover to the south side in which the entrance lay.

---

[1] *P.P.S.* xxxiv. 102–47.

Presumably it was in some way connected with the movement or control of animals, but exactly how it functioned is not immediately apparent.

Tollard Royal provides an excellent example of a small late Iron-Age farm unencumbered by later Roman additions, but this does not mean that the site was abandoned at the beginning of the Roman period, for less than 500 ft. away is a 2-acre complex of earthworks providing surface finds of Roman pottery.[2] Presumably the nucleus of the farm simply shifted, either just before or just after the invasion of A.D. 43, and the new site continued in use for a further several centuries. The probability of an early Iron-Age settlement beneath the Roman earthworks emphasizes the continuity of occupation over a considerable period. At the neighbouring farm at Rotherley Down (BERWICK ST. JOHN), on the other hand, occupation, which began at the beginning of the 1st century A.D., continued on the same spot for 300 years before the site was finally abandoned (fig. 44). The resulting complex, which covers an area approaching 5 acres, is impossible to untangle in any detail, but several of the principal elements are clearly distinguishable. The nucleus of the site appears to be a circular ditched enclosure, some ¾ acre in size (the 'main circle'), containing storage-pits, a granary, and probably a timber house, though this was not recognized by the excavator. Other enclosed areas may have been broadly contemporary with the main circle but some can definitely be shown to be of later Roman date. It is, therefore, not possible to guess the size of the community at any one time, except to say that it was never likely to have exceeded three or four houses and in all probability remained a single farm throughout.

A third farmstead, at Woodcutts in Dorset, is close to the other two and deserves a brief mention.[3] It, too, began in the late pre-Roman Iron Age and continued in use until the end of the 4th century A.D. In its original 1st-century style it consisted simply of a partially ditched enclosure of about 2 acres, through which passed a trackway. Inside the enclosure were large numbers of pits, a working hollow, and space suitable for a hut. Subsequent additions and alterations in the Roman period do not seem to reflect any increase in the size of the community which probably remained as a single farm. Thus the three excavated farms in the Cranborne Chase area provide a clear idea of the standard farming unit which survives virtually unchanged from the late pre-Roman Iron Age into the Roman period.

A second type of settlement site is typified by the complex of earthworks known as Casterley Camp (UPAVON), partly excavated early in the 20th century (fig. 44). The central part of the site is superficially similar to the Cranborne Chase farms, consisting of a series of ditched enclosures opening out of each other, the only difference being that the enclosure in which the principal habitation site lay was sub-rectangular rather than of irregular form,[4] an arrangement not unlike that at Bilbury Rings. Although all the ditches are not necessarily of one date a logical plan seems to have been followed and it is not difficult to share the excavator's views that all but the easternmost ditches were planned as part of a single concept. This was to provide two basic enclosure units, one composed of three separate but interconnecting enclosures, the other of equivalent size, linked directly to the habitation site, with one small part of its area divided off. Although the total area of this central complex, about 9 acres, exceeds that of even the most complicated farmstead, the general arrangement is not unlike that of Rotherley

[2] *Rural Settlement in Roman Brit.* ed. Charles Thomas (C.B.A. Res. Rep. vii), 46.
[3] The most convenient source for the Pitt-Rivers Cranborne Chase excavations, whic hinclude Woodcutts, is the reconsideration by C. F. C. Hawkes in *Arch. Jnl.*

civ. 27–81.
[4] Stuart Piggott, *The Druids*, 76–7, suggests that the rectangular enclosure may have been a ritual site. Re-excavation is needed for proof either way.

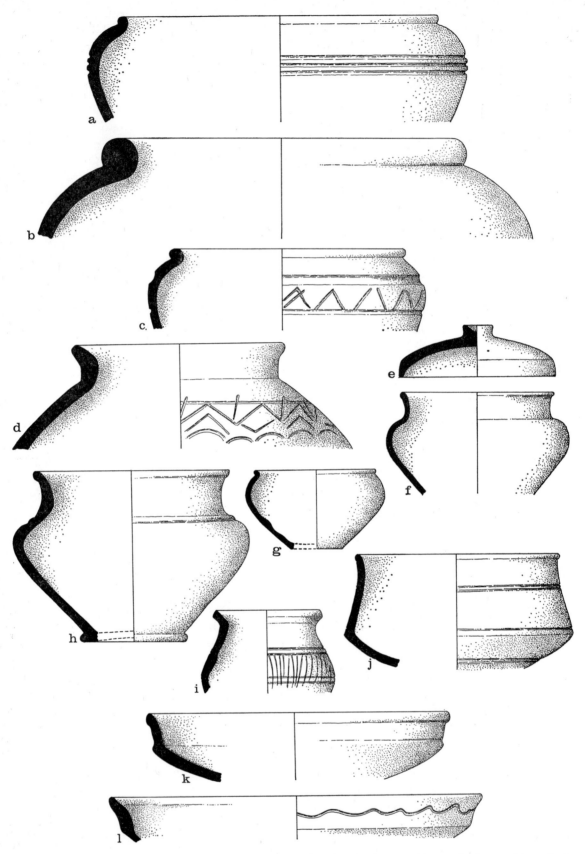

FIG. 38. Late Pre-Roman Iron-Age pottery: a, b, d, e, f, g, i, j, k, Oare; c, Boscombe Down West; h, l, Worthy Down (Hants). (⅓).

428

Down. What distinguishes the two sites is that the Casterley settlement is completely surrounded by a bank and ditch, enclosing about 62 acres, which was shown by the excavator to be of late pre-Roman Iron-Age date and broadly contemporary with the main internal features.

Before discussing the significance of the Casterley site, something must be said of some of the others which probably belong to the same class. Four of the best examples: Hamshill Ditches (BARFORD ST. MARTIN), Hanging Langford Camp (STEEPLE LANGFORD), Ebsbury (GREAT WISHFORD), and Stockton Earthworks (STOCKTON) are all sited along the Grovely ridge, between the rivers Wylye and Nadder, within 7 miles of each other. All share certain common features: a complex of interconnecting ditched enclosures; enclosing banks and ditches, which in the case of Hamshill Ditches and Ebsbury are multiple; considerable size (Hamshill 40 a., Ebsbury 60 a., Stockton Earthworks 100 a., and Hanging Langford 20 a.); and continuous occupation from the late pre-Roman Iron Age into the Roman period, often with traces of earlier occupation appearing on the same sites. The total lack of large-scale archaeological excavation makes any assessment of the function and development of these remarkable sites somewhat difficult because, as the casually collected finds show, most of them were subjected to at least four centuries of almost continuous development (see p. 445). Nevertheless, elements of the surviving ground-plans leave little doubt that the principal concern of the builders was to provide a series of interlocked enclosures, suitable for sorting or kraaling stock close to the homestead or village. In a society where subsistence economy was substantially based on animal husbandry such an arrangement offered evident advantages, but why it was necessary to construct massive encircling banks and ditches is less clear. Admittedly certain defensive factors might have been involved but other possibilities, such as the need to kraal entire flocks or herds close to the settlement during the winter, may well have been decisive. In support of such a possibility it should be noted that there is no trace of arable land within the enclosures. If the suggestion is accepted, it would imply some shift in the nature of the over-wintering arrangements compared with earlier periods, the stock now being kept within easy reach rather than being left to wander at will over the stubble throughout the entire winter period. Growing insecurity or improving farming methods could each account for the change.

One further question must be raised about the enclosures of the Casterley Camp type. What size of social unit do they represent? When they are compared with the one-family farms such as that at Tollard Royal it is difficult to argue that they are not of hamlet or village size, for the enormity of the enclosing earthwork alone must represent the surplus labour of many people. They are surely communal constructions. If, as suggested above, the hill-forts of the 2nd century begin to create a focus upon which sectors of the population depended, it may be that these 1st-century settlements are simply the next stage in the development towards regular nucleated villages. That a few centuries later some of them have become indisputably villages provides added support for the argument (see p. 445).

To what extent the hill-forts of the preceding period continued to be occupied is difficult to say with so little evidence available. The only extensively examined fort, at Yarnbury, certainly continued in use into the later period as the large quantity of material bears witness. It is even possible that the outer bank and ditch and the small kite-shaped enclosure attached to the west side of the fort were added at this date, but without excavation the problem remains unsolved. Of the fate of the other hill-forts there is little yet to be said, but outside the county at Hod Hill and Maiden

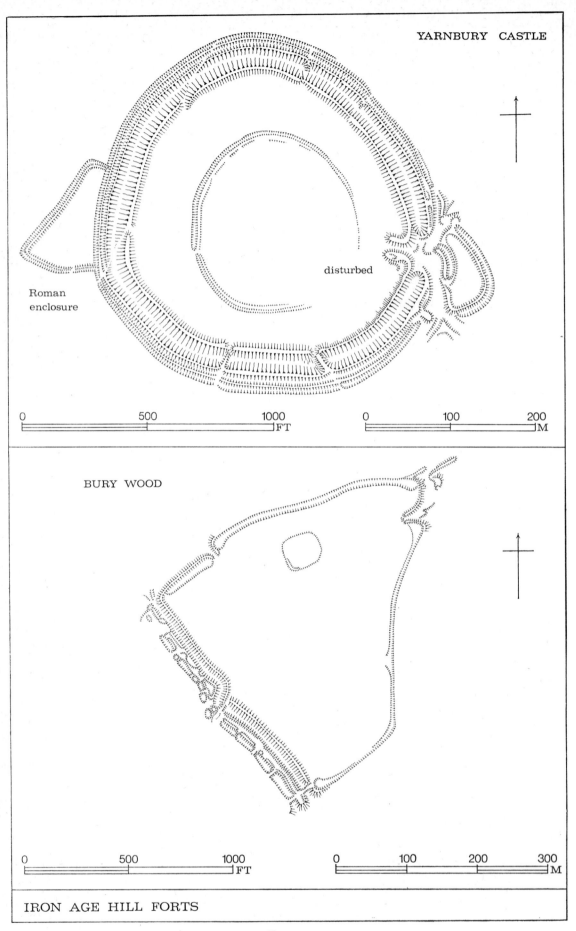

YARNBURY CASTLE

Roman
enclosure

disturbed

0   500   1000
⊨ FT

0   100   200
⊨ M

BURY WOOD

0   500   1000
⊨ FT

0   100   200   300
⊨ M

IRON AGE HILL FORTS

FIG. 39

430

Castle, in Dorset, and Danebury in Hampshire, there is clear evidence of continuous occupation.[5]

The third type of late pre-Roman Iron-Age enclosure is typified by the site designated 'area P' on Boscombe Down West (fig. 42). The type may be defined as enclosures of 10–15 acres extent delimited by at least two concentric banks and ditches. The ditches are generally V-shaped: at Boscombe Down West the inner ditch is about 10 ft. deep and the outer 7 ft. The dating evidence leaves little doubt that the enclosure was constructed some time towards the middle of the 1st century A.D., for a sherd of Neronian samian pottery was found low down in the silt of the outer ditch. It is best, however, to consider the bulk of the pottery from within the enclosure as slightly earlier than the Roman invasion. Several other Wiltshire 'forts' seem to belong to the same category. Bilbury Rings,[6] a 15-acre camp overlooking the Wylye Valley (fig. 42), produced some evidence to suggest that its concentric double ditches were open in the middle of the 1st century, and an irregular ditched enclosure inside appears to be of the same date. Less certainty attaches to the date of Chisbury Camp (LITTLE BEDWYN) but its general form, and the virtual absence of earlier material from extensive trenching within, might point to a similar date. The second phase of Bury Hill Camp (Hants) provides another good example of the same general type.[7]

Unlike the settlements previously mentioned the double-ditch systems imply the need for defence rather than the provision of boundaries to prevent animals from ranging freely. Similarly the choice of site is usually made with defensive possibilities in mind. It appears, therefore, that towards the middle of the 1st century A.D. a group of strongly defended forts was constructed in Wiltshire, possibly against the threat of Roman attack. This problem will be examined in more detail below.

While it is true to say that a greater variety of settlement form had developed by the end of the late pre-Roman Iron Age, the general subsistence economy continued much as before. The same fields continued to be ploughed, although heavier land was by now being taken into cultivation; grain was still dried in the old manner and stored in pits with the seed-corn kept in above-ground granaries, and the rotary hand-quern had completely replaced the saddle-quern. Figures relating to the animal populations of Woodcuts (Dors.) and Rotherley show that sheep and ox remained of equal numerical importance, each amounting to about a third of the animals represented by the excavated animal bones, with horses representing between 10 and 20 per cent.[8] Day-to-day life had changed little for about 700 years.

It is more difficult to say much of the material culture of sites such as Casterley, Oare (WILCOT), Rotherley, and Woodcutts which began in the 1st century. All continued in use well into the Roman period, and excavation has tended not to distinguish between artefacts in use in the pre- and post-invasion periods. The general impression gained, however, is that there was remarkably little change. Iron was now commonly used for the basic tools, weapons, and fittings, few of which show any typological development. A number of new types such as ox-goads and horseshoes appear, the latter probably as a response to the introduction of metalled roads by the new Roman government. Personal ornaments remain much the same as before, except that the La Tène III types of fibula and penannular brooch eventually oust earlier types.

It is during the late pre-Roman Iron Age that a marked cultural difference appears

[5] For Hod Hill and Maiden Castle see p. 419, n. 3. Danebury excavations 1969 unpublished.

[6] Unpublished in detail but notes on excavation in *W.A.M.* lviii. 32–4, 243–4; lix. 186–7; lx. 135.

[7] *Hants Field Club*, xiv. 3, 291–337.

[8] Pitt-Rivers, *Cranborne Chase*, ii. 217–28.

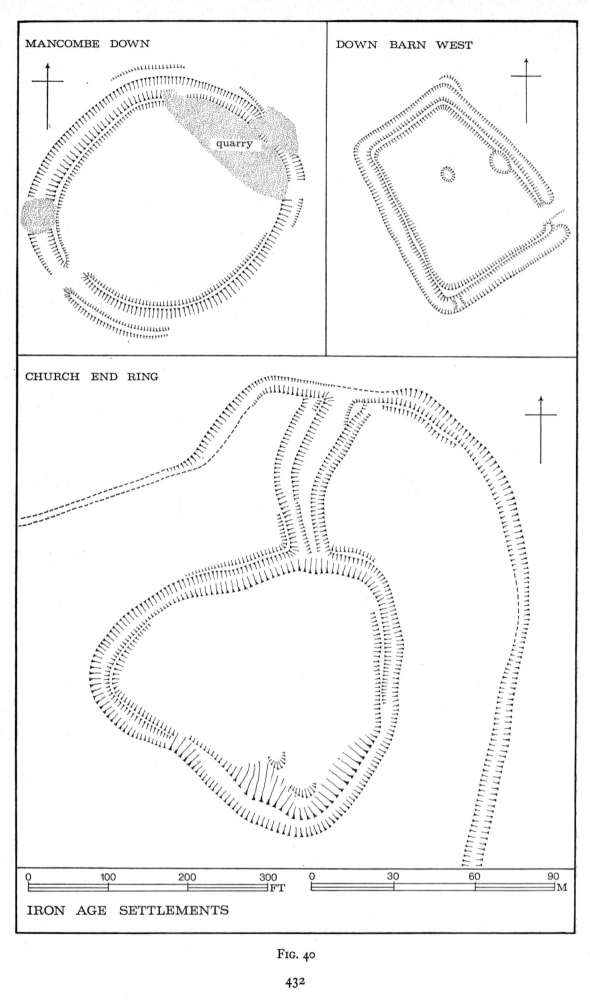

MANCOMBE DOWN

quarry

DOWN BARN WEST

CHURCH END RING

0   100   200   300 FT
0   30   60   90 M

IRON AGE SETTLEMENTS

FIG. 40

432

in the pottery of Wiltshire which, as will be suggested below, is probably a direct reflection of a major political division using the Wylye–Avon line as a frontier. South of the line the pottery is of Durotrigian type, while to the north it can be described as Atrebatic. The Durotrigian assemblage, typified by the extensive collection from the Tollard Royal farm,[9] is composed of bead-rim jars, some of which have countersunk handles, jars with everted rims, bowls with sharply carinated shoulders defined by cordons, and open bowls with simple beaded rims sometimes with pedestal bases.

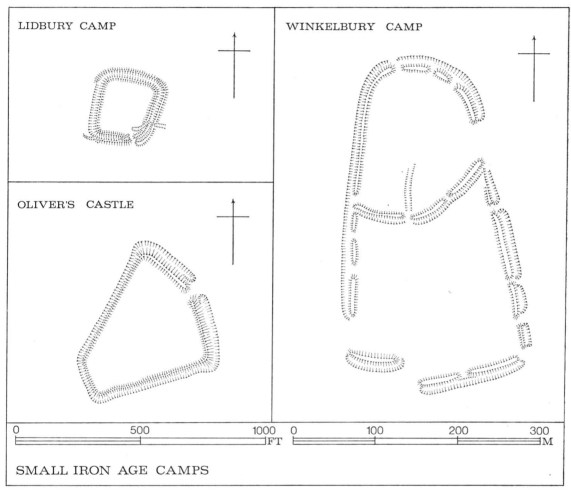

LIDBURY CAMP

WINKELBURY CAMP

OLIVER'S CASTLE

0   500   1000   0   100   200   300
FT   M

SMALL IRON AGE CAMPS

FIG. 41

Decoration, when it occurs, is usually restricted to simple curvilinear grooving, groups of circular impressions, or simple cross-hatching and wavy lines drawn with a blunt point. With the exception of the cordoned bowl, all the basic types were in existence in the preceding stage of the Iron Age, the only difference being that the introduction of wheel-turning tended to tighten and standardize the profiles. The cordoned bowl, on the other hand, appears to be a new local form, based on types imported into coastal regions, especially the trading port at Hengistbury Head (Hants), from the adjacent Normandy coast in the earlier 1st century B.C. Assemblages of this kind are found in Wiltshire at Hanging Langford, Stockton Earthworks, Tollard Royal, and Rotherley.

The Atrebatic pottery from sites to the north of the Wylye is distinctly different (fig. 38). The principal types include the high shouldered **jar** with a wide mouth and

[9] *P.P.S.* xxxiv. 119–34.

bead rim, globular jars with everted rims, smaller shouldered jars with simple up-standing rims, sometimes with a cordon at the junction of the neck and shoulder, plain straight-sided dishes, possibly copied from Gallo-Belgic imports, lids, and bowls of tazza form. Decoration is not common and when it occurs it is usually restricted to deep horizontal grooving, cross-hatched zones, or a zigzag line between horizontal lines. Pottery of these varieties is fairly common in the county, occurring in quantity at Boscombe Down West, Highfield, Yarnbury, Casterley, Chisbury, Knap Hill (ALTON), and Oare, and in smaller amounts at several other sites.

Widespread trading contacts, beginning before the Roman invasion, and influenced by the luxury demands of Catuvellaunian society in the Thames Valley and to the north on the one hand, and the growing importance of the port of Hengistbury Head on the other, introduced Gallo-Belgic pottery into the area of Wiltshire in the earlier 1st century A.D. Butt beakers have been recovered from Boscombe Down West, Casterley, Bilbury, Oare, and Rotherley; Gallo-Belgic platters from Casterley and Oare, and early forms of samian from Oare. It is tempting to see the appearance of these exotic forms as the opening up of new trade routes between the Channel coast and the sophisticated Belgic societies of the Thames Valley, using the Avon as a point of entry, linked perhaps to the Kennet. It is probably along such routes as these that Kimmeridge shale from Dorset was passing in large quantities for the manufacture of the shale vessels so popular in the east, and it may be that the tazza, a type of pottery bowl current in the Belgic areas, was being exported, perhaps as a container for some exotic foodstuff, back into Wiltshire and Dorset. Nevertheless, in spite of increased trading contacts the local ceramic development does not seem to have been materially affected.

That the two ceramic assemblages which can be defined in Wiltshire have been called Durotrigian and Atrebatic tends to beg the question of tribal identity. Previously, when distinct ceramic groups have been defined, they have been explained in terms of commercial production and local marketing. Might not the late Iron-Age material be best considered in the same terms? While this is certainly one explanation, there is a marked difference in the size of the territory covered by styles of the early and middle periods; the later Durotrigian style pottery, for example, is spread across an area 50–60 miles wide, while Atrebatic material is known over at least a 50-mile stretch. Even allowing for improved trading contacts, it seems more reasonable to explain these facts partly at least in terms of tribal differences than to assume them to be the result of distribution from individual production centres.

An innovation of some political and economic significance was the introduction of coinage some time before the beginning of the 1st century B.C. The earliest groups of coins to arrive in this country, the imported Gallo-Belgic issues, did not noticeably impinge upon the communities of Wiltshire. During the earlier 1st century B.C., however, a local development, the British B coins, sprang up in the territory of the Durotriges, and coins of that type appear sporadically in Wiltshire.[10] Subsequent influxes of Gallo-Belgic coins, on either side of Caesar's invasion, gave rise to another distinctive type, known as British Q coins, easily recognizable because of a disarticulated horse with a three-strand tail shown on the reverse. The British Q coins are densely scattered in the middle and upper Thames Valley and along the Sussex coastal plain, spreading into north Wiltshire and the Cotswolds, a distribution to some extent complementary to the British B and its developments in the Durotrigian area. The British Q coinage forms the starting-point of the dynastic coins of the Dobunni in the Cotswold region and the Atrebates of north-east Wiltshire, Hampshire, Berkshire, and Sussex.

[10] See D. F. Allen, 'Origins of Coinage in Brit.' in *Problems of the Iron Age in S. Brit.* ed. S. S. Frere, 97 sqq.

Shortly after the invasions of 55 and 54 B.C., the Atrebates issued coins based on the British Q model, inscribed with the name of their tribal leaders, of whom the first recorded is Commius. While by no means common, the inscribed coins of Commius tentatively suggest a two-centred kingdom perhaps based on *oppida* at Silchester (*Calleva*, Berks.) and Selsey (Suss.). Coins are too sparsely distributed in Wiltshire in the later 1st century B.C. to provide a firm basis for assessing tribal boundaries, but the southern part of the county, particularly the area south of the Wylye, lies firmly within the territory over which uninscribed Durotrigian silver coinage was commonly in circulation, while to the north the Bristol Avon might tentatively be assumed to form the approximate boundary between Dobunni to the west and the Atrebates to the east. It will be apparent, therefore, that in the late 1st century B.C. the distinction made on typological grounds between the pottery assemblages lying on either side of the Wylye is mirrored tolerably accurately in the coin distribution. It is not unfair, therefore, to refer Durotriges to the south and Atrebates to the north. At present, however, it is not possible to recognize much difference in the material culture of the Atrebates and Dobunni. The pottery of both tribes has close similarities, which, taken in conjunction with the wide distribution of the British Q coins, tends to suggest a certain degree of cultural unity between the two at this stage. Distinguishing between them in Wiltshire is impossible at present because of the virtual absence of archaeological material from anywhere near to the supposed Bristol Avon 'frontier'. It may, however, be relevant that a few sherds of middle Iron-Age pottery from All Cannings Cross have decorative similarities to that from the Gloucestershire area.

The subsequent political history of the area is reasonably easy to reconstruct, largely on the basis of the coin evidence. Commius was succeeded about 25 B.C. by his son Tincommius, who is thought to have pursued his father's anti-Roman policy for about ten years. About 16 B.C. a change is recognizable: the coins depicting the triple-tailed horse are abandoned and replaced by a totally new issue, modelled on the Roman *denarius* and engraved by an immigrant die-cutter. Such a development is likely to reflect a change of policy among the leaders of the Atrebates, switching from a position of hostility or indifference to Rome to one of imitation and possibly of allegiance. Horace may well have been referring to the Atrebates when he mentioned kings of Britain among the supporters of Augustus in an ode published in 13 B.C.[11] It has been suggested that such a change was unpalatable to the Dobunni, who broke off diplomatic relations with the Atrebates and struck up a new allegiance with the Catuvellauni.[12]

The next stage in the leadership is somewhat obscure. The northern part of the Atrebatic kingdom, based on Silchester, seems to have passed to Eppillus, another son of Commius, who was soon ousted and went to Kent. Thereupon leadership of the tribe passed to a third son, Verica, who may already have been in control of the southern area centred on Selsey. For how long, if at all, Verica retained command of the northern Atrebates of Wiltshire and Berkshire it is impossible to say.

The distribution of Catuvellaunian coins, particularly those of Cunobelinus, who ruled throughout most of the first half of the 1st century A.D., strongly suggests that the political leaders of the tribe were extending their influence into the northern Atrebatic area of Berkshire and northern Wiltshire. Indeed it is generally supposed that the northern Atrebatic capital of Silchester passed under Catuvellaunian sway. To what extent this reflects a political take-over is less certain; the coin evidence could equally well imply little more than Catuvellaunian control of the trade routes, through Dobunnic

[11] Horace, *Odes*, iv. 14, lines 41–52.
[12] C. F. C. Hawkes, 'The Western Third C Culture and the Belgic Dobunni' in E. M. Clifford, *Bagendon: A Belgic Oppidum*, 43–74.

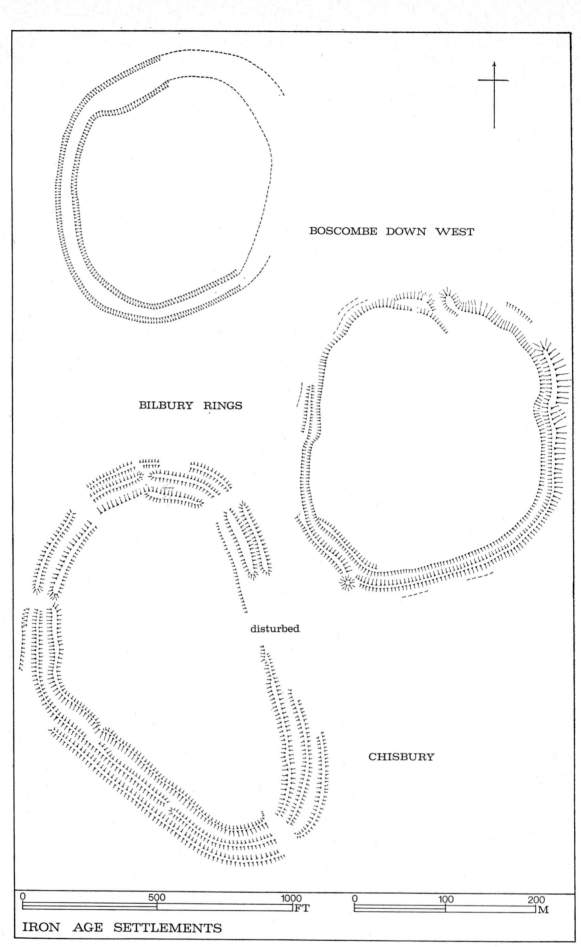

BOSCOMBE DOWN WEST

BILBURY RINGS

disturbed

CHISBURY

IRON AGE SETTLEMENTS

FIG. 42

436

territory to the Severn on the one hand, and by means of the Kennet–Avon axis to the Channel ports on the other. There is nothing in the coin distribution to suggest the colonization of Atrebatic Wiltshire at this time. With the centres of Atrebatic and Catuvellaunian culture firmly based, one on the Sussex coastal plain, the other on the river valleys of eastern England, the communities of the Wiltshire chalklands are not likely to have been much affected by changes in the ruling households. It was surely of no great consequence to the farmer of, say, Casterley, whether the few coins he may have used were minted at Silchester, Selsey, or Colchester (*Camulodunum*). The general impression given by the archaeological evidence is of continuity and relative peace, but roving war-bands may have been a nuisance.

Though it is likely that cultural influences emanating from the Catuvellaunian area had little effect on the bulk of the late Iron-Age population of Wiltshire, a burial of an important person in Catuvellaunian style was found at St. Margaret's Mead (MARL-BOROUGH) in 1807. In what appears to have been a flat grave lay a cremation, contained in a bucket of fir-wood, bound with three iron hoops (see pl., facing p. 479). The wood between the hoops was covered with three bands of bronze, bearing human heads and horses in repoussé decoration, and the bucket was provided with two side handles of iron and iron top-bar. Stylistically and functionally it belongs firmly to the Belgic cultures of an eastern England. The person it contained must have been a man of some standing, able to obtain imported Gaulish products in the middle of the 1st century B.C., and someone wishing to be buried in Belgic style. With the slightly later barrow cremation at Hurstbourne Tarrant (Hants), barely 14 miles away,[13] it is a reminder that the aristocracy of the northern Atrebatic area were adopting fashionable means of burial, unless of course the burials were of chieftains from the Catuvellaunian areas.

In Wiltshire cremation does not seem to have been generally adopted, the rite of casual inhumation continuing much as before. Several burials, probably of the late 1st century B.C., have been recorded. At Tollard Royal, for example, a single crouched inhumation of a body wearing a shale bracelet was buried in a shallow grave outside the main enclosure ditch. The arms and head were rather awkwardly arranged while the knees were drawn up to the chest.[14] There is, however, no absolute certainty that the burial was pre-Roman, nor can the isolated inhumations from Rotherley be definitely assigned to the Iron Age; but one of the burials in the pits at Yarnbury was said to have been found with bead-rimmed pottery of late pre-Roman type. Finally at MILDEN-HALL remains of a cemetery, possibly pre-Roman, was found containing eight inhumations buried haphazard in various ways without sign of order. One of them was provided with an iron La Tène III brooch and another was apparently buried with part of a pre-Roman pot. The available evidence, therefore, tends to suggest that the now-ancient tradition of careless inhumation remained dominant at least among the peasant classes.

There is little else to be said about the religious susceptibilities of the population, although it cannot be doubted that ritual sites remain to be discovered. Small finds from Cold Kitchen Hill hint at the possibility that the site was a temple, as already suggested (see p. 416), beginning perhaps as early as the 7th century and continuing well into the Roman period, when a masonry structure was erected conveniently close to the Roman road from Salisbury to the Mendips to serve as a wayside shrine. Stonehenge, as might be expected, continued to attract the attention of the Iron-Age community, who were responsible for scattering potsherds, which eventually found their way into the already partly silted Y and Z holes (see p. 285). It is no surprise that the ancient religious structure continued to be revered and probably used into the Roman period.

[13] *Arch. Jnl.* lxxxvii. 304–9.   [14] *P.P.S.* xxxiv. 117–18.

It remains to sum up the main lines of the social and political development that had emerged by the eve of the Roman invasion. While it is true that the bulk of the population continued to farm in small single-family units, there is some evidence that the trend towards nucleation hinted at in the middle period continued, creating settlements of considerable size which might reasonably be referred to as hamlets or even villages. These developments were intensified in the following centuries of the Roman era. There is as yet nothing to suggest a great disparity in hoarded or displayed wealth, except the rich Marlborough cremation burial and a hoard of 65 gold coins hidden in a hollow fossil flint found at Chute (CHUTE FOREST), but surplus wealth may well have been consolidated in commodities not recognizable in the archaeological record. Trade in luxury pottery brought Gallo-Belgic ceramics into Wiltshire by the mid 1st century A.D., but the small farmer, such as the owner of Tollard Royal, was unable to obtain or afford them, or, if he did own an import or two, looked after them with such care that none was broken.

Above these basic developments tribal differences were beginning to crystallize, influenced perhaps by the activities of the Belgic war-lords carving out kingdoms for themselves. One dividing line is clear enough: the Wylye Valley, which seems to have been the northern boundary of the powerful, if somewhat culturally isolated, Durotriges. The exact tribal affiliations of the rest of Wiltshire are more obscure and, indeed, may well have been imprecise at the time. Culturally they were Atrebatic, but by the time of the Roman invasion there appears to have been an overlay of Catuvellaunian and possibly Dobunnic characteristics, which may have caused a political alignment independent of Verica's southern Atrebates in 43 A.D. The appearance of the bivallate fortified enclosures about the middle of the century prompts the suggestion that the inhabitants of the chalklands of Wessex, west of the Test, joined the Durotriges in their stand against the advancing Roman army. It is surely significant that in the pro-Roman areas of east Hampshire and west Sussex the old hill-forts stood abandoned and no multivallate forts are known.

THE PERIOD OF ROMANIZATION

43–*c*. 250 A.D.

UNLIKE Caesar's exploratory expeditions of 55 and 54 B.C., the campaign begun in A.D. 43 under the generalship of Aulus Plautius was an invasion of conquest, resulting in the eventual annexation of much of Britain and the replacement of the native kingdoms by cantonal areas administered as the regions of a unified province. The first stage of the conquest was fought in the Belgic areas of eastern Britain. The initial landing at Richborough and the advance along the Kentish coast resulted in a two-day battle at the Medway at which Catuvellaunian power was seriously weakened by a decisive defeat. The Thames was forded and Colchester fell to the victorious army, led for the occasion by Claudius himself. It is most unlikely that an experienced commander would have chanced his entire army on one thrust without some knowledge of the political affiliations of the tribes beyond his exposed flank, and Plautius would have known that between Kent and the potentially hostile south-west lay Verica's old kingdom of the southern Atrebates. Verica had, in fact, fled to Rome a little before the invasion, presumably as a result of pressure from anti-Roman elements. His action provided Rome not only with first-hand information of the current political situation, but also with a face-saving formula beneath which to hide an act of imperialist aggression: they were invading Britain to offer support to an old ally driven out by the enemies of the state. The Atrebatic kingdom, based on Selsey, therefore provided an invaluable temporary buffer in the first weeks of the occupation, but Verica, by now very old, was replaced by the pro-Roman client king Tiberius Claudius Cogidubnus who promptly set about organizing his enlarged kingdom in a Roman fashion. The results of the arrangement were evidently satisfactory, for Tacitus writing of the 60s or 70s felt it relevant to refer to Cogidubnus' continued faithfulness to Rome.

It was probably from the Atrebatic kingdom that the second stage of the invasion was launched, namely the conquest of the hostile south-west by the *Legio II Augusta* commanded by the young Vespasian. Suetonius records that Vespasian took the Isle of Wight, overcame two powerful tribes, and destroyed more than twenty fortified native settlements.[1] Excavation has shown beyond doubt that one of the tribes referred to must have been the Durotriges, for the Dorset hill-forts of Maiden Castle, Hod Hill, and possibly Spetisbury, and the Somerset fort of South Cadbury were the subjects of a violent Roman assault. Presumably they were four of Vespasian's twenty. Thereafter, to keep the area in a submissive state, garrisons were placed at strategic intervals in Dorset at Waddon Hill, Hod Hill, Lake, and probably Dorchester; and in Somerset at South Cadbury, and there may be others to be found. That such a complex network of police posts was necessary, reflects the potential danger which the Roman authorities considered to have existed among the recalcitrant Durotriges for almost a generation after the initial advance. The second tribe which Vespasian conquered was probably that part of the Dobunni which had not surrendered earlier while the army was still in Kent. What exactly this means in geographical terms is not clear, but it may tentatively be taken to include most of the territory west of the Test which,

---

[1] *C. Suetoni Tranquilli Divus Vespasianus*, ed. A. W. Braithwaite, 4.

as shown above (see p. 431), shows some evidence of having been refortified in the middle of the 1st century A.D. If this is so, the whole of Wiltshire can be regarded as initially anti-Roman.

Evidence of direct Roman assault is at present negligble. A few military ballista bolts from Rotherley, together with part of a scabbard-binding, hint at passing contact, as do the supposed military fittings from Bilbury Rings,[2] but no Wiltshire site provides the same dramatic evidence of attack and slaughter as the Dorset forts. Mere absence of evidence does not, of course, imply that there were no military campaigns conducted in the region. Indeed it is most improbable that so large an area capitulated without resistance, but resistance may have been insubstantial and shortlived.

Immediately an area was subdued, the military engineers laid out service roads for the easier and speedier movement of supplies and troops. Of these one of the most important was the Fosse Way, running from Lyme Bay (Dors.) to Lincoln and cutting diagonally across the north-west corner of the county. It has long been recognized to be of military inspiration and is now generally considered to be the rearward communication of a frontier system, nearly 20 miles in depth, which marked the first boundary of the province in the Claudian and early Neronian period. For it to function efficiently, forts would have been provided at intervals. One might be expected at White Walls (EASTON GREY) where early coins and pottery have been recovered, but there is as yet no positive evidence of military remains there. The frontier line required good supply roads leading from collection bases in the occupied hinterland to key points along its line. It is a distinct possibility that much of the road grid of Wiltshire arose at this time. The main western road, leading from London through Silchester (*Calleva*) and Old Sarum (*Sorviodunum*) to Dorchester and beyond, would have been of crucial importance in linking the south end of the frontier line to London, while the other direct routes, from Winchester through Mildenhall (*Cunetio*) and Wanborough (*Durocornovium*) to Cirencester, and from Winchester through Old Sarum to the Mendips, would also have provided significant lines of communication at an early date. The other roads, Old Sarum via Mildenhall to Wanborough, Silchester via Mildenhall to Bath, and Badbury (Chiseldon) to Bath, all possessed value in shortening the lines of communication between the principal stations.

As the map shows,[3] Wiltshire contained two important road junctions: Old Sarum to which four or possibly five roads led, and Mildenhall, the point of convergence for three, possibly five roads. Points of such strategic significance might well have been guarded by forts at an early date, but, apart from a crop-mark showing ditches resembling those of a fort at Mildenhall (see p. 461) and several bronze fittings of military type, further evidence is lacking.

The Fosse frontier, established by *c.* A.D. 47, was soon abandoned as the theatre of war moved west and north, leaving Wiltshire to develop peacefully. Any attempt to assess rural development, however, is hindered by an almost total lack of excavated evidence, particularly of the less spectacular peasant sites, and even the villas, usually more attractive to previous generations of archaeologists, have been left virtually untouched. Reliance must, therefore, be placed on the few extensive excavations and upon casually discovered scraps.

Theoretically, the imposition of the *pax Romana* with its accompanying economic and social repercussions would have created a totally new framework within which society would have developed. Two new factors deserve particular attention. The creation of civil administrative regions based on *civitas* capitals demanded, in order

[2] *Arch. Jnl.* civ. 41; *W.A.M.* lviii. 33.   [3] *V.C.H. Wilts.* i (1), Map VIII.

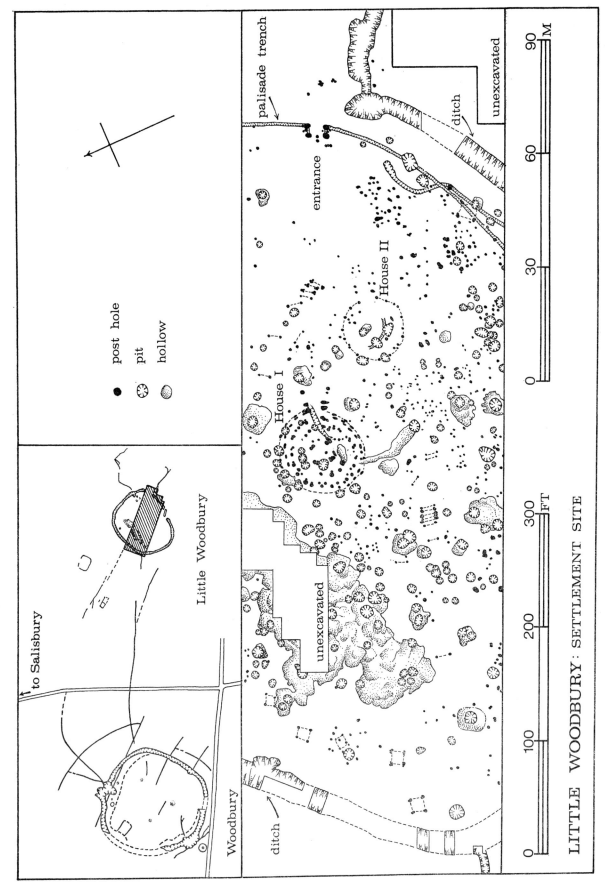

post hole
pit
hollow

palisade trench

entrance

House I

House II

unexcavated

ditch

Woodbury

ditch

unexcavated

to Salisbury

Little Woodbury

M

90

60

30

0

FT

300

200

100

0

LITTLE WOODBURY: SETTLEMENT SITE

Fig. 43

to function efficiently, a local governing class known as decurions, one hundred of whom constituted the regional council or *ordo*. To be eligible for this task it was necessary, among other things, to possess certain property qualifications. The new system, therefore, created a governing class of wealthy individuals. It is becoming increasingly apparent that not all decurions lived in the urban centres. Indeed the evidence from Silchester and Bath suggests that between two-thirds and three-quarters lived in the surrounding countryside, maintaining their wealth by farming. Thus a considerable percentage of the rural rich must have been closely bound up with local administration and government.

The second factor to influence class structure was the imposition of the Roman system of trade and marketing. Improved communications, the establishment of market centres, and the complete acceptance of a money economy meant that surplus products could now be converted into material wealth either in the form of coinage or as other possessions. More important, coinage could be accumulated to purchase luxuries, such as wine and silver plate. The new order, therefore, offered the example of material progress while providing the mechanism by which the productive population could accumulate material wealth. A new impetus was given to productivity. It must, however, be stressed that the trends outlined above were not entirely alien to Wiltshire communities of the 1st century, for the systems involved were already well rooted in late Iron-Age society; government on the Roman pattern merely intensified them. In simple practical terms the new administration meant that farmers working land capable of greater output would have been encouraged partly by the factors outlined above and partly by taxation to extract the maximum and may well have used their wealth for the improvement of their homesteads. Some farmers, on the thinner soils, would soon have reached the point of maximum productivity, while others on the richer land might have acquired sufficient surplus to construct masonry houses and eventually to adorn them with central heating, mosaic pavements, and bath suites.

The above discussion is, of course, a simplification taking scant notice of existing social conventions and hierarchies, taxation, and the added complications which may have been imposed by state ownership. Nevertheless, it is essential in an area like Wiltshire with its great variation in food producing potential that the underlying economic mechanisms should be clearly understood in terms of the new Roman marketing system.

Certain generalizations can be made about the archaeological problems of rural settlement. Continuity of settlement on existing farms is the general rule, broken only, so far as is known, by Tollard Royal (see p. 427). Tendencies towards rural nucleation continue, and a marked disparity in wealth begins to appear, particularly from the 2nd century onwards when recognizable 'Roman villas' were constructed. Pitt-Rivers's excavation of Rotherley in Berwick St. John[4] provides an excellent example of the continued occupation of a farmstead, originating at the beginning of the first century B.C. and remaining in use until the end of the 3rd century. Little seems to have changed during the period apart from the recutting and realignment of ditches. Corn-drying, however, was now carried out in a well-constructed oven, built so that the grain would not come into direct contact with the heated surface, a device designed to cut down the dangers of overheating. Towards the end of the occupation the farmer, who now lived in a substantial rectangular timber building, was able to afford a finely engraved table top or tray of Kimmeridge shale. The nearby settlement of Woodcutts (Dors.) demonstrates a similar continuity, lasting well into the 4th century (see p. 427). Here

---

[4] Pitt-Rivers, *Cranborne Chase*, ii. 51–232, and see above p. 440, n. 3.

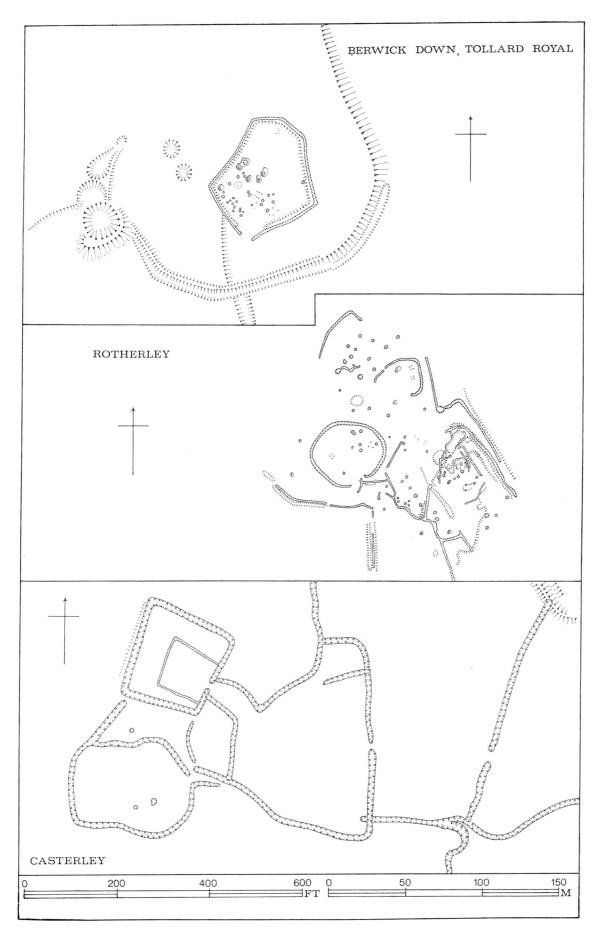

BERWICK DOWN, TOLLARD ROYAL

ROTHERLEY

CASTERLEY

| 0 | 200 | 400 | 600 | 0 | 50 | 100 | 150 |

FT   M

FIG. 44. IRON AGE FARMS.

443

the modifications to the original ground-plan take the form of additional ditched enclosures of polygonal type, corn-drying ovens, and two wells, one 188 ft. deep. Although masonry buildings are not known, quantities of painted wall plaster suggest moderate prosperity. Rotherley and Woodcutts provide, therefore, clear evidence of farming activity, continuing unbroken for 400 years with very little sign of the social aggrandizement of the owning families. Although it is possible that an apparent decrease in the numbers of storage-pits after A.D. 43 implies the heavy hand of Roman taxation, even to the extent of a virtual imperial takeover, the same facts could equally well be explained by different storage methods or even by the sale of surplus grain in the new markets. Some taxation there must have been, but it is perhaps simpler to see the two settlements as farms, the productive capacity of which was insufficient to allow much material wealth to accumulate; farms, in other words, which remained only a little above subsistence level.

The general state of Rotherley and Woodcutts in the Roman period suggests a slight increase in the size of the population, but the nature of the excavated evidence prevents certainty. It is possible, however, that the demands of intensive farming, the restrictions of Celtic land tenure, and the lack of readily available land for colonization together encouraged the growth of larger farming units, approximating to hamlets and peopled perhaps by the extended family. Settlement sites of about 4 acres in extent, similar in size to Rotherley and Woodcutts, are fairly common on the chalklands of Wessex and may well represent the gradual appearance throughout the Roman period of a rash of hamlets, many of which may have originated as small farms in the pre-invasion period. At Tollard Royal the Roman settlement seems to have grown up a few hundred feet away from the original farm (fig. 47). If one settlement replaced the other, the Roman nucleus might provide a very important sequence uncluttered by earlier remains and well worthy of extensive excavation. The three Cranborne Chase sites seem to be typical of a widespread class, of which many hundred examples must exist in Wiltshire.

Smaller homesteads are also likely to have occurred. A recent examination of West Overton Down produced surface traces of a series of hut-platforms set within an earlier field system (site XII).[5] Two of these were excavated in 1966 and have been proved to have supported the foundations of rectangular cottages of Roman date, the larger a little over 30 ft. by 20 ft., the smaller barely 12 ft. square.[6] Their walls, constructed on sills of sarsen blocks partly set in trenches, were presumably of timber. Fragments of painted plaster and tiles of various kinds might hint at fittings in the Roman manner. One important result of the excavation is that a quantity of occupation material was recovered, implying intensive occupation, beginning at the end of the 3rd century or the beginning of the 4th, by which time the fields were no longer in use. There is nothing to suggest that the cottages were intermittently used or that they served any purpose other than to provide living accommodation.

If, as the surface features indicate, the Overton Down (site XII) settlement was of restricted size, it raises the problem of the status and size of the social group it supported. Was it occupied by a family dependent on a village or an estate, or by a breakaway farmer setting up on his own? Alternatively was the settlement in some way connected with the shepherding of livestock on the open downs? While no firm answers can be provided, the questions alone demonstrate the potential importance of the site. Only after many sites of similar size have been excavated and analysed will further advances be possible in our knowledge of the lower end of the scale of the rural settlement.

[5] *W.A.M.* lxii. 26–33.   [6] Ibid. 26–9.

A significant development in the study of the rural population of Wiltshire has been the re-acceptance of the view that villages existed in the countryside.[7] Of these one of the best examples is to be found at Chisenbury Warren (ENFORD) where surface features show the existence of a long village street flanked by a cluster of more than 80 rectangular hut-platforms, averaging 40 ft. long (fig. 47). The entire complex covers almost 15 acres. To the west of the settlement is an area of 'Celtic fields', up to 200 acres in extent, laid out regularly in relation to a boundary lynchet in a manner suggestive of a Roman date. Several other villages of comparable form and size are known. On Knook Down (UPTON LOVELL), for example, Hoare planned two settlements a short distance apart, one of 8 acres the other about 20 acres; both were arranged along streets and both consisted of a number of rectangular house-platforms. Another elongated settlement of comparable proportions has been recognized on Overton Down South in West Overton where a series of hut-platforms appear to be contained within rectangular enclosures.[8] None of the above-mentioned sites has been excavated but surface finds are suggestive of a Roman date for the main occupation, while the general regularity of the lay-out might be thought to imply an occupation restricted to the Roman period. Until the foundation date and development sequence is known it is impossible to offer any reasoned assessment of the significance of these sites, but the possibility that some of them may be villages for *coloni* attached to large estates has something to commend it.

A second form of village, differing from street villages of the Chisenbury Warren type, is represented by the continued occupation of the large nucleated settlements on the Grovely ridge which originate in the 1st century B.C. or even earlier. The best example at present available is the settlement which grew up within the 40-acre enclosure of Hamshill Ditches.[9] A surface survey has shown that the interior possessed, in addition to two stock-enclosures referred to earlier (see p. 421), large numbers of hut-platforms of rectangular and circular type, the rectangular platforms predominating in the western area (fig. 45). Material found in excavations and as casual discoveries shows beyond doubt that the site was inhabited throughout the Roman period, but the only structure to be recorded was a single corn-drying oven. At the neighbouring site of Ebsbury again there is evidence of continuous occupation but a substantial part of the Roman settlement lay outside the old enclosure; how much of the interior was also built up at this time remains uncertain. The other nucleated settlements on the Grovely ridge, Stockton Earthworks and Hanging Langford Camp, have both provided evidence of continuous occupation, particularly Stockton from which a large quantity of material is known. In both cases, however, the size of the Roman settlement areas is difficult to define. It may be said, therefore, that all the old nucleated settlements along the line of the road from Salisbury to the Mendips remained in occupation in the Roman period and, if Hamshill is typical, they must have been villages of considerable extent.

While the peasant communities continued to develop along traditional lines, a few villas were built by the more wealthy. As, however, the map shows,[10] their distribution was uneven; villas are concentrated in the northern part of the county but not generally found on most of the chalk plain of the south. Assuming that the known villa-distribution is a fair reflection of those actually built, some explanation is required. Three factors may be relevant. First, it may be that the chalkland of Salisbury Plain was too poor to enable its farmers to grow prosperous enough to build villas. Significantly the three villas

[7] *Rural Settlement in Roman Brit.* ed. Charles Thomas (C.B.A. Res. Rep. vii), 43–67. [8] Ibid. 56–7. [9] *W.A.M.* lxii. 118–21. [10] *V.C.H. Wilts.* i (1), Map VIII.

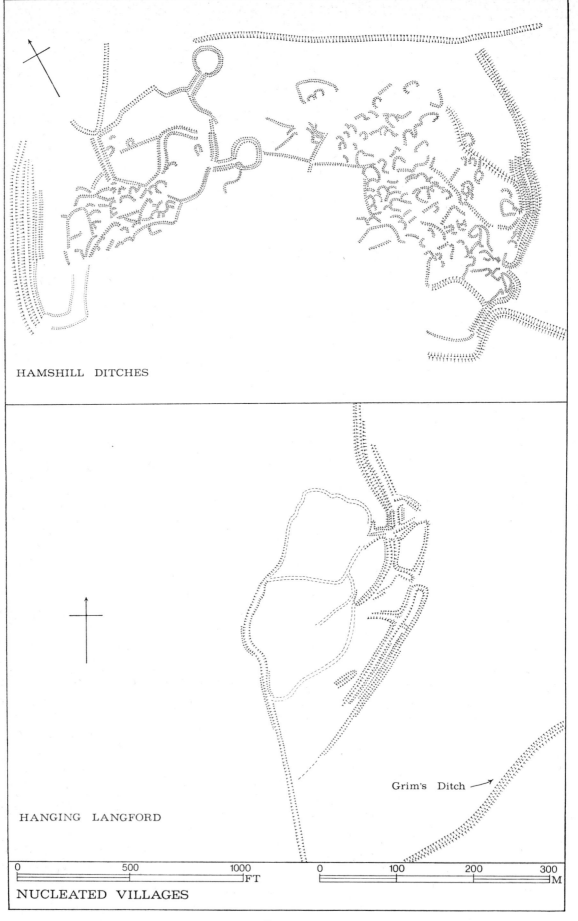

HAMSHILL DITCHES

HANGING LANGFORD

Grim's Ditch

NUCLEATED VILLAGES

0   500   1000 FT

0   100   200   300 M

FIG. 45

446

that there are in the southern half of the county are all sited in river valleys on richer lands, Pit Meads (SUTTON VENY) in the Wylye Valley (fig. 48), NETHERAVON in the upper Avon Valley, and Downton[11] in the lower valley of the Avon (fig. 48). A second factor may have been ease of marketing. Farms further than about 15 miles from a market would have been at a distinct disadvantage when it came to transporting produce to the nearest centre. If Old Sarum and Badbury Rings in Dorset were excluded, parts of southern Wiltshire would have been as much as 30 miles from the nearest markets. If it is argued, on the other hand, that surplus creates markets and not *vice versa*, the view becomes untenable. A third possibility, which has remained fashionable for many years, is that southern Wiltshire and Cranborne Chase were taken over by the government and turned into a vast imperial estate.[12] The peasants working the land would, it has been suggested, have been kept at subsistence level, all surplus being removed by state agents. Two reasons are put forward for such confiscation: that it was a punishment for opposition to the conquest, and that it was a means of providing the grain needed by the army, which by the end of the 1st century was firmly established in Wales. The theory neatly fits the few known facts and has much to commend it, but it must be stressed that there is no positive evidence to support it. It is now equally possible to explain the facts in terms of productivity and marketing outlined above. A comparison with the South Downs emphasizes the point; there, while peasant communities on the chalkland continued the Iron-Age way of life without apparent interference, the farmers on the fertile Greensand ridge to the north and those on the fringes of the rich soils along the south, were able to build masonry buildings, which throughout the 3rd and 4th centuries show signs of gradual aggrandizement, reflecting increased wealth. If there is no need to suggest the existence of an imperial estate on the poor chalk soils of the South Downs, there is no compelling reason to suppose that the similar soils of Wiltshire were selected for government ownership.

Supporters of the imperial-estate theory point to the apparent lack of urban development at the important road-junctions at Old Sarum and Badbury Rings (Dors.) as evidence of deliberate repression on the part of the government.[13] While it is certainly true that Rome did in some provinces restrict the growth of towns, it is not known to have done so in Britain. It is simpler to regard the two sites in question as potential town sites which failed. In the later 1st century there would have been two main influences affecting urban growth: deliberate encouragement by the central authorities of those settlements in which regional government was based, such as Dorchester, Winchester, Silchester, and Cirencester; and local economic factors, which encouraged the growth of markets, usually at convenient road-junctions or river-crossings. The reason for the failure of Old Sarum to develop may simply be that it was not selected as a *civitas* capital, and local production was at such a level in southern Wiltshire that no elaborate marketing facilities were required. Admittedly protagonists of the imperial-estate theory would argue that lack of surplus was the result of procuratorial confiscations and not of low yield. MILDENHALL (*Cunetio*), on the other hand, in the centre of a rather more productive countryside, had developed by the 4th century into a small urban community. It is probable that WANBOROUGH (*Durocornovium*) and Sandy Lane (*Verlucio*) (CALNE) also became trading centres of some significance, but archaeological evidence is at present somewhat sparse.

The villa distribution of northern Wiltshire tends to cluster on three centres. Ten

[11] *W.A.M.* lviii. 303–41.
[12] First suggested by R. G. Collingwood in Collingwood and Myres, *Roman Brit. and Eng. Settlements*, 323–4, 239–40, and developed by C. F. C. Hawkes, *Arch. Jnl.* civ. 27–81. Since then it has been generally accepted.
[13] *Arch. Jnl.* civ. 32.

or a dozen villas are known on mixed soils and in the river valleys around Mildenhall, at least eight villas lie, mainly on the Oolite and Greensand, within easy reach of Sandy Lane, and about a dozen of the large group of villas dependent upon Bath are scattered on the oolitic limestone within the boundary of Wiltshire. Wanborough is surrounded by a less cohesive group. The pattern leaves little doubt of the close relationship between villas, good farming land, and their market centres. Finally, one group in the south-east of the county requires comment. The Dean Brook, a tributary of the Test, has eroded deep into the Chalk, exposing a band of Reading Beds and London Clay and creating conditions of unusual fertility where the valley gravels, Chalk, and Clay occur in a strip $\frac{1}{2}$ mile wide. Along this strip three villas are known: East Grimstead (GRIMSTEAD), West Dean (Hants), and Holbury (Hants), barely $1\frac{1}{2}$ mile apart. Each villa must be the centre of an estate farming a small sector of the valley with its adjacent thick Clay and open Chalk. Clearly where conditions were favourable farms could exist in close proximity.

While it is possible to discuss in some detail the pattern of settlement reflected in villa distribution, practically nothing is known of the development of the individual buildings, most of which were dug into before the techniques and dating methods now current were adopted. Finds of coins and pottery, however, show that several of the sites originated in the 1st or early 2nd century, but not necessarily as masonry buildings, which may have been added at some subsequent date. By the late 3rd century, however, most of the Wiltshire villas were in existence in their masonry form. One of the best known and most completely excavated of the villas, the building at Downton, provides a good example of a relatively simple late 3rd- or early 4th-century house (fig. 48).[14] It comprises a single range of seven rooms, 146 ft. long, fronted by a continuous corridor, with a bath suite attached to the back by a separate corridor. The principal room, which lay in the centre of the range, was floored with an intricate geometric mosaic of some quality, while the approach to the room was given added emphasis by a slightly projecting porch. The other rooms of the wing and the corridor were floored with plain red or white tessellated pavements. The room at the south end was fitted with a channelled hypocaust to provide warmth during the winter. Although not all of the bath suite could be excavated, its general plan shows it to have been of a simple character with two *caldaria* (hot rooms), provided with apsidal recessed baths in their west walls, linked to a *tepidarium* (warm room). Next came a general concourse or undressing room which provided access from the linking corridor to both the heated range and to a cold plunge bath which lay on its east side. The arrangement was, therefore, both simple and effective; a bather entering the changing room from the house could choose between taking a cold plunge first or beginning the session in the heated rooms.

The plan of the villa is typical of a class of comfortable 'yeoman' farms provided with the modest luxury of partial central heating and well fitted bathing facilities, together with the elegance of painted walls and a polychrome mosaic. Buildings of this type must have been a common feature of the late Roman landscape. The villas at Pit Meads in Sutton Veny in the Wylye valley and at ATWORTH in its original form are of the same general type (fig. 48), and it seems probable that NORTH WRAXALL and BOX began as simple winged corridor-houses of this class (fig. 48).

The excavation of Downton is important because much of the immediate environment of the building was examined. It produced evidence of a double corn-drying oven, smaller ovens, a probable well, and a complex of metalled farm-roads, in fact all

[14] *W.A.M.* lviii. 303–41.

the details with which the average Roman farm estate would have been provided. The outbuildings such as barns and servants' quarters have not been traced in any detail, but evidence of flint walling found several hundred feet to the west, close to the roads, might indicate their siting.

The villa at North Wraxall, which remained as a single-range building, comparable in size and elaboration to Downton, through most of its life, is of interest since the residential part of the house can be seen in its surroundings. The house with its attached baths stands across the north side of a walled enclosure, 220 ft. by 155 ft., entered by a gateway in the southern side. Beyond this is an outer courtyard, containing two ranges of out-buildings, one of which seems to have originated as an aisled barn. About 60 yds. to the west a small cemetery was discovered, presumably belonging to the household. Here at North Wraxall all the principal buildings of a villa estate are known, albeit incompletely. Together with Downton it provides the type example of the average villa establishment.

Downton was built late in the 3rd century and continued to be occupied with little change into the mid 4th century. Its status, therefore, seems to have remained unaltered. But this was not so with many of the buildings further north in the county, particularly those towards Bath. Atworth, for example, began as a simple winged corridor-villa in the earlier 3rd century. A second corridor was added within the next 50 years, and by about 300 a new north range had been built and a bath suite added to the south end of the original east range. It was not until the later 4th century that a decline in comfort becomes apparent. The larger establishment at Box, although until recently less well excavated,[15] suggests a similar growth from a modest structure into an elaborate house arranged around a courtyard. More than 40 rooms, several with tessellated floors and hypocausts, a bath suite, and a collection of sculpture, indicate the wealth of the owner.

While some villas, such as Box, were evidently the homes of wealthy estate-owners, others, like the modest buildings at East Grimstead and COLERNE, were the property of less affluent farmers, belonging to a class of land-holders, either bailiffs or tenants farming parts of larger estates. East Grimstead was a simple aisled building, 50 ft. by 140 ft., which began as a single roofed space, the roof being supported on pairs of piers. Subsequently a series of rooms were partitioned off, providing a living unit at the west end, with a channelled hypocaust heating one room, and a simple bath suite at the other. The complex is made more notable by two additional bathing units detached from the main building. A somewhat similar arrangement occurs at Colerne, where again what appears to have begun as an aisled structure was eventually modified into a house with attached baths. The basic problem raised by the Colerne or East Grimstead type is whether the known parts constitute the entire establishment. Two of the better known Hampshire sites, Brading in the Isle of Wight, and Sparsholt near Winchester, both incorporate modified aisled structures as part of a complex which includes a main house of winged corridor-type.[16] There is a distinct possibility, therefore, that many of the apparently isolated 'basilican villas' are parts of much larger establishments. The problem cannot be solved without the extensive excavation of the area around each example.

It may be said that by the middle or end of the 3rd century most of the Wiltshire villas were in existence, a substantial proportion being comfortable houses but with no exceptional show of luxury. In the 4th century, however, there were important and

[15] Recent excavs. for M.O.P.B.W. by H. Hurst (unpublished).

[16] R. G. Collingwood and I. A. Richmond, *Archaeology of Roman Brit.* 135–40.

far-reaching economic changes which tended to increase the disparity in the outward signs of material wealth, as will be discussed below.

The basic economy of Wiltshire in the first three centuries of the Roman occupation was dependent almost entirely upon mixed farming of the type practised for centuries before but now on a most intensive scale. New areas of downland seem to have been broken at this time and laid out with a certain regularity in oblong-shaped fields of the kind seen to the west of the settlement on Chisenbury Warren and at Totterdown (FYFIELD), while in other areas the earlier less regular 'Celtic fields' of the Iron Age continued to be used. Expansion of agriculture on to the heavier soils[17] went hand in hand with the development of the more massive plough of the type represented at Box by a heavy iron-tanged share, thought to belong to a bow ard. Other iron shares found at Woodcuts (Dors.) point to the widespread use of the iron-shod plough among rural communities of all levels. About the crops grown there is little to be said. Wheat of various kinds and barley continued to form a substantial part of the output, but a hint of greater diversification is provided by the find of carbonized grains in the corn-drying oven at Downton.[18] Here in addition to small quantities of wheat and barley (T. *spelta*, T. *aestivum*, T. *compactum*, and *Hordeum vulgare*) about 15 per cent of the deposit was a vetch (*Vicia angustifolia*), indicating that a pulse crop was deliberately grown and dried in the usual way.

The increase in areas of arable land must imply a corresponding increase in livestock, since otherwise the fertility of the land could not have been maintained. Little is yet known of the composition of the flocks and herds of the early Roman period, nor is there much that can be said of the structures required to kraal them. By the 4th century, however, the problem takes on a new significance and is discussed below.

The increase in the number of masonry buildings throughout the Roman period created a corresponding increase in demand for building materials, including both stone and ceramic fittings. Several areas of the county were exploited on a commercial basis to meet these needs.[19] In the north the Portland and Purbeck limestones of the Swindon area were probably quarried throughout most of the Roman period for the neighbouring urban and rural buildings. Bath stone, the best outcrops of which lie outside the county boundary, found its way into the surrounding villas for use as architectural fittings and sculptures. In the south of the county the malmstone (Upper Greensand) of the Chilmark region may well have been exploited for building purposes together with flint, while the Purbeck limestone from the Isle of Purbeck was being imported in some quantity for roofing slabs. The same areas were also providing, in a ready-made form, Purbeck marble mortars and pestles and the Kimmeridge shale furniture which turns up sporadically even on peasant sites, particularly in the south of the county.

Pottery production on a commercial scale was based on the clayey soils of Savernake Forest[20] two or three miles south of Mildenhall and conveniently linked to the market by the roads leading from Old Sarum and Winchester. Even as early as the later 1st century some of the kilns were in production, turning out a range of types deriving much from the style of the local pre-Roman forms. These included dishes, bead-rimmed jars, ovoid jars, and shouldered bowls, often ornamented with horizontal groovings and shallow tooled zones, a style common amongst the late Atrebatic pottery of the region. In addition to these native types, dishes and flagons based on imported models were being produced. How long the Savernake kilns remained in production

[17] *W.A.M.* lxiii. 27–38.
[18] Ibid. lviii. 328.
[19] *V.C.H. Wilts.* iv. 247.
[20] *W.A.M.* lviii. 143–55.

has not yet been precisely determined, but the complexities and superimposition of kilns indicate extensive use. Typological considerations suggest the distinct possibility that the Roman industry grew directly out of a preceding late Iron-Age production, but until a detailed study of the ceramic fabrics has been made the question is best left open.

Commercial production in the Roman period in Wiltshire was, therefore, very limited. Stone, pottery, and probably the iron extraction south of Sandy Lane could never have involved a large proportion of the population, nor is it likely to have contributed noticeably to the prosperity of the area. Wiltshire remained basically a farming region throughout.

Religious monuments of the Roman era are hardly more plentiful than in the preceding period. The general impression gained, however, from the large number of burials scattered evenly over the county is that the native rite of inhumation persisted, as it did in the Durotrigian area, throughout the Roman period, in spite of the fact that during the first two centuries A.D. cremation was fashionable. It may be significant that the few cremations that have been unearthed all lie in the north of the county, where there is some evidence of Catuvellaunian influence just before the invasion. Although acceptance of the rite may have derived from this period, a contributing factor is likely to have been the Romanizing influences which emanated from the market centres at Mildenhall and possibly at Sandy Lane. One of the cremations, apparently in some form of vaulted tomb, was found on the outskirts of Mildenhall, while two others, from West Park Field (BROMHAM), were only 1½ mile south of Sandy Lane.

A third group of cremation burials of some considerable interest was found close to the junction of the Roman road from Mildenhall to Bath and the Ridgeway, about a mile north of the Sanctuary on Overton Down.[21] Three burials were excavated, each consisting of a pit originally containing a cremation, below a shallow mound surrounded by a circular setting of upright timbers bedded in a continuous ditch, 17 ft., 19 ft., and 24 ft. in diameter. Although the burials had been robbed, scattered cremated bones and fragments of bronze vessels with elaborate enamel decoration suggest that the cremations had originally been buried in style. No further examples are known of such an arrangement in Britain and indeed the rite appears to have been rare even on the Continent.

Few temple sites and other sacred locations are known and, apart from the magnificent and extremely large religious complex at Nettleton Shrub (NETTLETON) on the Fosse Way in the extreme north-west corner of the county, few have been extensively examined. Cold Kitchen Hill, alongside the road from Old Sarum to the Mendips, probably continued to serve as a wayside shrine and seems to have been provided with a masonry temple at some time in the Roman period; but apart from a collection of what may be considered to be votive offerings there is still no indisputable evidence that the site was religious. More certainty, however, attaches to a curious crescent-shaped earthwork at Winterslow, ¼ mile south of the Roman road from Winchester to Old Sarum built on the downhill side of what is presumably an arena.[22] Superficially the appearance of the structure might suggest that it functioned as a rural theatre in connexion with religious ceremonies. The close relationship between theatre and temple is well known on the Continent, not only in the towns but also in isolation in the countryside, and there is reason to believe that this kind of religious combination is not uncommon in Britain. Its position, close to a road, also supports the possibility of religious associations. The earthwork was directly associated with a circular well, more

[21] Ibid. lix. 68–85.   [22] *Ant. Jnl.* xliii. 197–213.

than 60 ft. deep, constructed at the same time as the mound. Here again a ritual significance is possible, but unproved.

One further discovery of some relevance, from the Roman road at Winterslow, consists of a female head carved in Celtic style from a block of local greensand.[23] The way the head is displayed on a long columnar neck suggests that it was never attached to a torso and is more likely to represent a local deity. It may well, therefore, have been related to the shrine.

The Winterslow site suggests the possibility that there may be other rural shrines yet undiscovered. A second example possessing many similarities to Winterslow was examined by Pitt-Rivers at Church Barrow on the borders of the Woodcutts settlement in Dorset in 1884–5.[24] Here again an arc-shaped earthwork of Roman date was found to flank a slightly sunken arena area 40 ft. by 50 ft. Other earthworks of this general category have been identified elsewhere in the country.

Rural shrines and temples, particularly alongside roads, would have played an important part in the life of peasant communities, serving as places for travellers to rest and perhaps make an offering to the local deity for their safe passage through his territory. On certain occasions throughout the year the local community would foregather to take part in extended ceremonies in which worship, the watching of religious performances, and fairground trading would have been closely interwoven in much the same way as these elements formed an essential part of the fair in the Middle Ages. For many peasants this might have provided the only occasions for meeting together and perhaps for buying mass-produced trinkets from the itinerant traders. Strictly speaking, Winterslow with its theatre, sacred well, and possibly temple, presided over by a Celtic deity, was only a less sophisticated version of Bath or Nettleton, which would have been accessible to those living in the more prosperous north.

[23] First published in *Ann. Rep.* Sar. Mus. 1961, 15, pl. 11B. See also J. M. C. Toynbee, *Art in Brit. under the Romans,* 105, pl. xvii.   [24] Pitt-Rivers, *Cranborne Chase,* i. 24.

THE LATER ROMAN PERIOD

c. 250–367 A.D.

THE economic development of the province in the first three-quarters of the 3rd century is a problem open to much debate, and the evidence from Wiltshire can as yet shed little light on it. Too often the lack of early-3rd-century coins and general uncertainty about the dating of 3rd-century pottery has led to the assumption that the county was in a state of economic decline. Such a view is more a product of the interpretation of the evidence than of the evidence itself and is best regarded with extreme caution. In the last quarter of the century Britain and much of the rest of Europe were in political turmoil, and for twelve years Britain was ruled by a breakaway government controlled first by Carausius and later by Allectus. It was not until 296 that the province was finally reunited with Rome, following a successful invasion by Constantius Chlorus, and the long peace of the Constantinian period began.

Apart from coastal regions, where a new system of shore forts, several destroyed buildings, and a number of coin-hoards point to unrest and possibly pirate attack in the last quarter of the century, inland areas were disturbed little in the short period of political freedom which Britain enjoyed. Indeed improved coinage and the undertaking of road repairs are two of the more obvious improvements which the Carausian government introduced. In the countryside and markets of Wiltshire the evidence, such as it is, indicates a simple continuity in the everyday life of the community largely unaffected by the barbarian raids and political controversies of the time.

The relative tranquillity of the early 4th century saw the intensification of a process which had begun much earlier, namely, the accumulation of wealth in the hands of the already wealthy. This is particularly clearly demonstrated by the outbursts of luxurious display in which some of the villa-owners were now able to indulge. The rich land-owners, particularly those near Bath, were in a position to expand their property and to act as patrons for the schools of mosaicists which sprang up in many urban centres. At Littlecote Park (RAMSBURY), for example, a superb figured mosaic was found, depicting in the centre Orpheus playing a lyre, surrounded by four panels containing female figures representing the four seasons and riding a hind, a leopard, a bull, and an antelope respectively; adjacent to it was another mosaic composed of a more geometrical design, incorporating *cantharae*, dolphins, and sea-leopards. At Pit Meads a fragment of surviving floor depicted a goat and a standing female. Human figures appeared on a mosaic at Rudge Farm villa (FROXFIELD), while fish and sea monsters adorned floors at Bromham. Other villa-owners were able to purchase sculpture of considerable artistic merit. At Box part of a relief-carved panel of Neptune was found together with a brilliant representation of what may be a hunter god dressed in a tunic and cloak and carrying an unidentified animal over one shoulder and a boar over the other. The owner of Box, together with many of his neighbours, were also able to afford painters of ability to adorn the walls of their principal rooms.

Even peasant communities were not without the means of purchasing a wide range of luxury goods, including brooches and bracelets as well as fine pottery from the large production centres in the New Forest and the Oxford region. The phenomenon was widespread in Britain, resulting more from a nation-wide revival than from any particular quality of the Wiltshire region. But inevitably the gulf between rich and poor would have widened, with those peasants who reached the lower limits of subsistence giving up the land and moving away, either to become labourers on the big estates or joining the ranks of the urban poor.

R. G. Collingwood first put forward the now well-known view that the 4th century saw a change-over from a predominantly agriculture-based farming to sheep rearing, possibly as a result of the heavy taxation on grain.[1] The evidence then stated was impressive: a large number of pastoral enclosures could be recognized, apparently later in date than field systems; Britain by the time of the Edict of Diocletian was famous for its woollen garments; there was an imperial weaving mill at *Venta* (thought to be Winchester); and evidence could be amassed to suggest an abandonment of downland settlements at this time. To that list might also have been added the occurrence of 'ranch boundaries' for preventing stock-raiding, and even the 4th-century prosperity could be explained in terms of the availability of more money resulting from the less heavily taxed wool production. Altogether the evidence seemed unshakable, but recent extensive fieldwork has shown that of the seventeen stock enclosures quoted as certainly or probably late Roman only three might reasonably be dated to that period: Brown's Barn enclosure at BISHOP'S CANNINGS, Rockbourne Down (Hants), and probably also Soldiers Rings (Hants).[2] When it is also shown that the *Venta* at which the weaving mill was sited need not be Winchester,[3] the main props of this attractive theory are removed. Nevertheless, certain observations still require explanation in terms of some kind of economic change.

The evidence from the trial excavation of the large late-Roman enclosure on Rockbourne Down[4] is of some relevance. Here it was shown that a polygonal area of 96 acres was defined by a double ditch and fence in use from the late 3rd to the late 4th century. Limited excavation within produced no less than three corn-drying ovens which served to emphasize the continued importance of corn-growing to the economy. The animal bones, though not plentiful, were almost entirely of ox with a small percentage of horse, pig, and dog. Sheep were represented by very few bones indeed. Even if the sample is regarded as sufficiently large to allow conclusions, the evidence can be argued two ways: it could be said that sheep were no longer important, their place being taken by oxen; alternatively, if sheep were no longer bred for meat but for their wool, large flocks of wool-producing sheep need not be represented in animal-bone assemblage from domestic sites. Yet however the facts are interpreted it is reasonable to suggest that the economy practised at Rockbourne was different from that practised earlier at Rotherley and Woodcutts (Dors.).[5] The other polygonal enclosure of comparable form, the 28-acre Soldiers Rings, has not been excavated, nor have any other relevant sites in Wiltshire.

A second class of evidence, the abandonment of some of the peasant settlements in the 4th century, is not particularly impressive. Admittedly, if the coin evidence is accepted, Rotherley does not seem to have lasted long into the 4th century while Woodcutts was probably abandoned soon after the decade 360–370. There is, however, no equivalent information from other sites. A superficial examination of the pottery scatters recovered from the sites of peasant settlements might suggest a lack of typical 4th-century wares from some of the sites previously occupied, but too much reliance cannot be placed on such an insubstantial basis. The excavation of a small site on

[1] Collingwood and Myres, *Rom. Brit. and Eng. Settlements*, 239–40.
[2] *Antiq.* xli. 304–6.
[3] Ibid. xl. 60–2.
[4] H. Sumner, *Excavs. Rockbourne Down, Hants*.
[5] See pp. 442–3.

Overton Down (site XII) has shown, contrary to the picture of abandonment, that here a new settlement was founded probably about A.D. 300 and lasted well into the 4th century.[6] Moreover, most of the larger settlement sites have produced quantities of 4th-century pottery. It is safer, therefore, to conclude that while some old established sites were being abandoned during the 4th century others flourished and new settlements were founded. Finally there is a factual basis to the view that areas of field-systems were no longer being used for arable production. One example is provided by the Overton Down settlement just mentioned which is tucked into the corner of an earlier field-system. There are others.

The above paragraphs summarize the basic material upon which an assessment of the late-Roman farming economy of the county has to be based. It is, to say the least, insubstantial, but when considered against the background of the earlier history of the region in particular, and economic development in the empire in general, certain broad trends are suggested.

Of crucial importance to the well-being of the empire was the maintenance of a steady population. When, throughout the 3rd and 4th centuries, the birth-rate began to fall, serious consequences followed. In Gaul and other parts of Europe south of the Rhine-Danube frontier good farming land left vacant was assigned to fresh settlers brought across the frontier for the purpose. Imperial policy in the face of such a threat was to settle barbarians on the abandoned land, expecting in return that the new inhabitants would protect their farms from further incursions. The Franks and the *laetae* of northern Gaul were such people and indeed the policy was moderately successful. But as the situation deteriorated edicts were issued forbidding movements of people away from their homes and their inherited occupations. Clearly social mobility, particularly movement from the land into the towns, was considered to be potentially disastrous. At the same time it became much easier for the large landowners to acquire neighbouring derelict estates at favourable rates, should they be prepared to take on the added responsibilities. These generalizations, well documented for most of the empire, are likely to have applied to Britain as well. It is known, for example, that settlers of Germanic origin were placed in parts of eastern Britain from the late 3rd century onwards, and the argument that the province was exceptional in not suffering from the empire-wide tragedy of a rapidly decreasing birth-rate would be difficult to sustain. If, then, it can be assumed that the population of Wiltshire was suffering a decline, might not the observed facts be explicable in these terms?

It has been suggested above that the first two centuries A.D. saw an extension of arable farming over areas of hitherto unbroken downland (see p. 450), giving rise to distinctive and regularly laid out field-systems, sometimes associated with villages. For such an extension to be possible it would have been essential correspondingly to increase the size of the flocks and herds to provide manure for the new fields, which would otherwise have soon become exhausted. Thus, even if grain production was the driving force, the animal population would of necessity have been increased. The choice presented between cattle and sheep as potential livestock was more apparent than real, for one of the crucial problems to be faced by those farming chalk downland was how to water the stock. Dew ponds could be used to some extent, but there were decided advantages in choosing sheep, since sheep could last for much longer periods on open pasture without the need of watering. Moreover, as has been seen, sheep were already increasing in relation to cattle in the latter part of the 1st millennium B.C., partly for this reason, and partly because they were in other ways better adapted to a treeless

[6] *W.A.M.* lxii. 26–30.

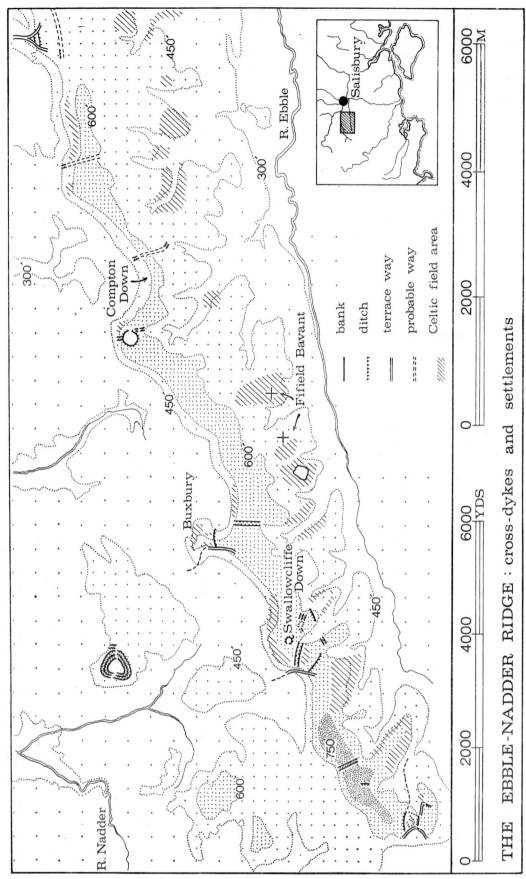

THE EBBLE-NADDER RIDGE : cross-dykes and settlements

FIG. 46

vegetation than cattle and pigs. It would be natural, then, for increase in chalkland arable and increase in numbers of sheep to go hand in hand. The pre-eminence of British-made woollen products by the late 3rd century might therefore represent a by-product of greater grain production rather than a reorientation of the subsistence economy. A carding comb found at Baydon is a reminder of the woollen industry.[7] It would be of particular interest to know whether, during the Roman period, there is any evidence of selective breeding favouring wool-producing sheep at the expense of meat yield. A detailed study of the animal bones may provide some of the answers but the work has hardly yet begun.

It can be tentatively argued that by the beginning of the 4th century Wiltshire supported a mixed economy based on grain and wool production. If it is correct to assume that the population decline began to affect the area in the 4th century if not earlier, how if at all was the economy modified? The most dramatic effect would, of course, have been a decrease in the man-power available to carry out the work, followed by a steady regression from the less conveniently situated arable which would be left to revert to waste. Gradually settlements would be abandoned, Rotherley soon after 300, Woodcutts (Dors.) by c. 370.[8] Some of the villages may also have been deserted by the end of the century or at least may have shrunk in size.

Labour was mostly engaged in grain production. Fields had to be ploughed, sown, and reaped; the grain had to be dried and threshed, and the weighty corn transported to the market centre. Moreover, grain was heavily taxed. With the labour-pool decreasing the situation would naturally have encouraged a transference of effort from grain to sheep. The large flocks were probably already in existence and could still easily be maintained with the much reduced labour force. A reorientation of labour and production along these lines might have affected the size and situation of settlements. The large agglomeration of man-power in villages would no longer be possible or necessary and fragmentation might result. Indeed it is tempting to see the small Overton Down (site XII) cottages of late-Roman date as the home of a shepherd tending his flocks over now largely abandoned fields.[9] The site, as it is at present known, can hardly be thought of as a farm in the conventional meaning of the term.

Although the reconstruction and ideas set out above are consistent with what little evidence there is and with the general trends discernible in the empire at large, it is at best a pale and inaccurate reflection of the true picture. There must have been very considerable variations between one environment and another, leading to a wide range of different land-use. Cattle would have continued to be kept in large numbers for their meat, and corn would still have been an important product, supplies were after all shipped to the continent during the reign of Julian. Archaeology can at present only generalize about the main trends while leaving the subtleties of local variations for future study.

The discussion so far has been based on the peasant communities which were the hardest hit by the economic conditions of the 4th century. The villa-owners were for the most part in a protected position. Their estates could be increased in size without much additional cost and, in the early part of the century at least, there would probably have been a plentiful supply of labour provided by the small farmers who could no longer survive on their own. The result would have meant the growing affluence of a few estates, which would have gradually become the centres depended upon by large bands of labourers or *coloni*, many of whom may have been reduced to the status of serfs. Not all the villa-owners prospered. Some may have been ruined by their

[7] *D.M. Cat.* ii, pl. lxii.   [8] *Arch. Jnl.* civ. 42, 48.   [9] *W.A.M.* lxii. 26–30.

appointment to administrative offices in the towns, which were more a financial burden than a reward. Several villas which show a marked change of status may have been affected in this way. At Atworth, after 350, there is clear evidence to show that the bath suite was dismantled and much of the building converted to farm uses. The basilican building at East Grimstead suffered in much the same way with several corn-drying ovens inserted into the living quarters, while nearby at Downton the complete absence of alterations and the lack of coins after 330–5 may well point to abandonment by the middle of the century. The number of coins recovered, however, can hardly be regarded as a statistically acceptable sample. The same limitation applies to the coin series for most of the other villa sites, several of which, including Lucknam Lodge (COLERNE), Nuthills CALNE), Plough Inn (CHISELDON), and the site on the boundary between Latton and CRICKLADE produce no evidence of occupation after the middle of the 4th century.

A consideration of the roadside settlements, which may well have served as a combination of posting stations, collecting centres for the corn tax (*annona*), and minor markets, provides some indication of the economic situation in the 4th century. Structurally there is very little to be said of them. Old Sarum (*Sorviodunum*), on an important road junction, is still practically unexplored, although excavation has shown that occupation in the old hill-fort, and on the Bishops Down to the south-east, continued from the late Iron Age until well into the 4th century A.D., if not later.[10] Woodyates (Dors.), alongside the road from Old Sarum to Badbury Rings (Dors.), developed as a settlement of some considerable size, particularly in the 3rd and 4th centuries, but apart from ditched enclosures, a few burials, and corn-drying ovens, nothing is known of its structures or even of its true extent.[11] Stockton Earthworks, on the Grovely ridge, close to the road from Winchester to the Mendips, is even less well known, except from a mass of occupation material collected from time to time. Nevertheless all the sites have produced collections of coins which provide some indication of their relative growth.[12] The period represented by coins minted between 306 and 361 produced the largest collections: 73 per cent from Woodyates, 63 per cent from Stockton Earthworks, and 49 per cent from Old Sarum. Even allowing for the greater number of coins in circulation in this period, this is an exceptionally large quantity compared with those minted in the following years, 364–5 (7·4 per cent Woodyates, 8·8 per cent Stockton Earthworks, and 9·5 per cent Old Sarum). There can be very little doubt that after the decade 360–70 the use of these stations declined rapidly. One possibility is that they may no longer have been used by the government as collecting bases for grain tax following the restoration of the province by Count Theodosius in 369. Lack of official interest could have contributed to the disuse of the sites as markets, but the theory is unsupported by facts. It is difficult to see what alternative arrangements could have been made for tax collection, always supposing that corn production still warranted it after 370.

The development of the problematical site of Woodyates is bound up with the structural history of the substantial multi-period earthwork known as Bokerly Dyke which runs, just outside the modern Wiltshire county boundary, across the chalk ridge in what can only be described as a defensive manner facing north. The earthwork has been studied in some detail on three occasions[13] and its details need not be repeated. Its first phase is currently dated to the period 325–30, after which the ditch was left

[10] *W.A.M.* lvi. 102–26; lvii. 353–70.
[11] *Arch. Jnl.* civ. 66.
[12] *W.A.M.* lvi. 109.

[13] Pitt-Rivers, *Excavs. Bokerly Dyke and Wansdyke* (vol. iii of *Cranborne Chase*); *Arch. Jnl.* civ. 62–78; cxviii. 65–99.

to silt up and pits from the habitation area were dug into the bank and ditch. The purpose for which the earthwork was constructed remains uncertain. That it was an estate boundary or a defensive work against cattle-raiders are two of the more plausible suggestions that have been put forward, but further than this it is difficult to go except to add one other possibility: that it may have served at this date as a boundary between the cantonal areas of the Durotriges to the south and the Belgae to the north.

Much of the preceding section has been concerned with the predominantly chalk areas of the southern part of the county which are much better known than the rest. Whether or not the limestone regions in the north-west, between Bath and Cirencester, were subjected to the same economic forces it is difficult to tell since practically no peasant settlements are yet recorded in the area. Some of the better known villa sites from beyond the county boundary, however, tend to support the generalizations concerning the villa system outlined above. The areas of limestone and chalk are divided by a wide strip of clay lowlands which, apart from the lighter gravelly soils along the Thames Valley and the road junction at Wanborough, are almost entirely without trace of settlement. In the Roman period this area may have remained a heavily wooded and virtually impenetrable tract dividing the two highly populous regions but the possibility remains that sites are yet to be found. Somewhat surprisingly, with the exception of a brick and tile kiln at Oaksey Common in MINETY (6 miles south of Cirencester) there is no evidence that the clays were widely utilized, although kiln sites may yet be discovered.

Much of the fine pottery commonly used in Wiltshire from the late 3rd century until the end of the Roman period was derived from two massive industrial centres outside the county: one in the New Forest, the other in the Oxford region.[14] Although the distribution of pottery from the centres still remains to be worked out in detail, it appears that Winchester, possibly together with Old Sarum, acted as the main market for the distribution of New Forest wares into south Wiltshire, while Mildenhall may have served to disseminate the products of the Oxford region throughout the north of the county. The known bulk of these wares shows that the trade must have been organized on a very large scale indeed. The degree to which the large factories had captured even the peasant markets is an indication of the extent to which mass produced consumer goods were now an essential part of the Romano-British way of life.

[14] R. G. Collingwood and I. A. Richmond, *Archaeology of Roman Brit.* 257.

THE END OF THE ROMAN ERA

367–*c*. 500 A.D.

THE year 367 marked a turning point in the history of the province, for it was then that the great 'barbarian conspiracy' was launched, a concerted attack by Picts, Scots, and Attacotti, which swept across the fully manned frontiers of Britain, throwing the countryside north of the Thames into a state of turmoil. For two years plundering bands of barbarians, runaway slaves and *coloni*, and defected troops ravaged the countryside, creating anarchy and shattering the already weakened economic structure of society. Eventually in 369 the situation was restored by Count Theodosius who, after landing in peace at Richborough in Kent, marched on London with his field army to begin the consolidation of the civil zone and the complete reorganization of the land and shore frontiers.

A disaster of this magnitude and its aftermath must have had a resounding effect on the well-being of the province, even in relatively secluded areas such as Wiltshire, but traces are not easy to find. It was the large villa estates that would have suffered most. The flight of labourers to swell the ranks of the *bagaudae*, outcasts living by robbery in the remoter parts of the country, might have left them without the man-power to maintain production. How widespread this was is impossible to assess on present evidence. East Grimstead, Atworth, North Wraxall, and probably Box continued to be occupied in some form after 370, but of the other villas there is nothing to be said.

The fate of the countryside is a little clearer. At Woodyates (Dors.) Bokerly Dyke was refurbished and extended so as to block completely the main road from London to the south-west and only later was the road opened up again.[1] These events are now assigned to the troubles of 367 and may reflect local or official response to the movement of marauding bands. The settlement itself continued to be occupied but, if the coin evidence is sufficient, on a much reduced scale. The nearby farm at Woodcutts did not outlive the troubles. The settlements at Stockton Earthworks and Old Sarum continued in use, but as at Woodyates the coin evidence suggests that the intensity of the occupation had considerably diminished.

In general terms the events of 367–9 would have tended to intensify the processes already at work in the countryside. The continued population decline, combined with the drift of workers from the land to the remaining big estates, must have continued, encouraged by the plight of the estate-owner whose need for labour would have led to the offering of reasonable terms to those prepared to stay and work. Moreover, the security offered by an estate would have been preferable to working small undefended farms in the open countryside. A further factor, which may have been of increasing relevance, was brigandage, already a serious problem in Gaul. In conditions of rigid state control verging on oppression, where the pressures of life, the exorbitant taxation, and the atmosphere of uncontrollable decline, seemed unbearable, there was nothing for it for many in the community but to join the rootless plundering *bagaudae*. To what extent the problem existed in Britain is debatable but there is little reason to suppose that the situation here was much better than it was in most other parts of the empire. The bagaudic menace must have been a force to be reckoned with.

---

[1] For Bokerly Dyke see p. 458, n. 13.

In spite of all these problems the restoration of Theodosius was thorough both from a military and civil point of view, but it was the last time that the central government intervened in British affairs. One of the new policies seems to have been the conversion of the towns into strongly defended positions. Many of those possessing town walls

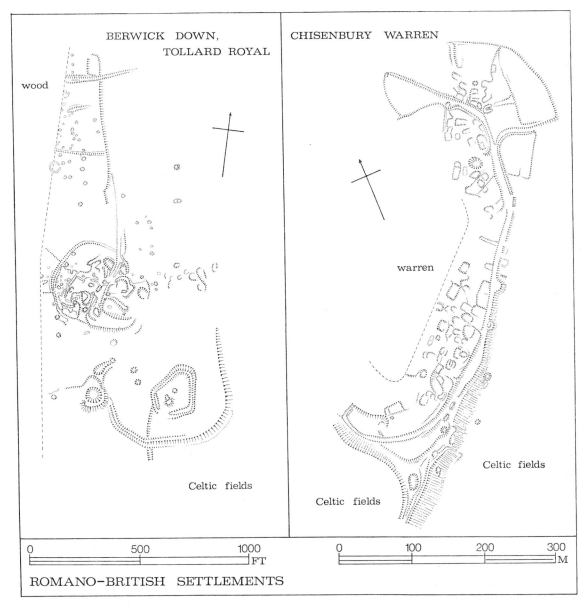

FIG. 47

dating from the 3rd century were now provided with forward-projecting bastions, fronted by wide flat-bottomed ditches, the bastions to serve as a basis for catapaults and *ballistae*, while the ditches kept any would-be attackers within the optimum killing range. In the case of those small towns or settlements without existing defences, but sited in positions considered to be of strategic importance, walls with attached bastions were built. Mildenhall belongs to this category.[2] Recent trial excavation has shown that a massive stone wall, some 16 ft. wide at the base and enclosing the town was constructed with a dry-stone core between mortared faces in a style very similar to the contemporary wall which surrounds the settlement at Gatcombe, near Bristol. The

[2] *W.A.M.* lvii. 233, 397; lviii. 35; lx. 137.

excavation of one of the forward-projecting bastions, close to the south-east corner of the town, demonstrated conclusively that bastions and wall were built at the same time. The dating of the defences depends on the discovery of a coin of *c.* 360 in the primary silting of a small ditch which predated the wall footings. Excavation has also brought to light the west gate, a simple opening reduced in width at some later date by a grill of iron bars, and one internal masonry building with an apsidal-ended room constructed after the wall had been built. The similarity of construction between Mildenhall and Gatcombe, and the considerable expenditure of money and energy which the defences must have involved, too much surely for the local inhabitants to have afforded, strongly suggests that these defences were part of an official policy financed, perhaps, by the state. The dating evidence quoted indicates that the walls may have been built *c.* 369 as part of the Theodosian programme of reorganization.

Evidence has recently been amassed to show that at about this time a wide range of imported military fittings of north European type appeared in the country, most of them in forts and towns. A second series, thought to be local copies of the first, have also been defined in much the same locations.[3] It seems reasonable to assume, therefore, that some of the troops brought over by Theodosius were stationed in Britain at selected fortified sites to serve as a local militia and that they remained in occupation for some time. The new troops and the refortification of strongpoints are evidently part of a single scheme for keeping the countryside under strict control. The selection of Mildenhall as one of the militia posts is a reflection of its important position on a major road-crossing and in the centre of a richly inhabited area. No comparable evidence has been recovered from the vicinity of Old Sarum.

The existence of the new fortifications raises the interesting question of the identity of the enemy against whom these defences were organized. While it is obvious that the garrison could have functioned against marauding bands of barbarian raiders, the possibility remains that the growing unrest in the countryside was becoming a threat to be reckoned with. A disaffected peasantry stirred up by *bagaudae* might by now have become a menace as serious as the barbarians, as indeed they were in western Gaul at this time. There is, however, little likelihood of archaeological methods throwing much further light on the problem.

Not all of the Germanic belt-fittings were found in towns and forts; some have come from villas. One was found at Upper Upham (ALDBOURNE), and at the North Wraxall villa a discovery of even more relevance was made in the well excavated in the mid 19th century. Here a military bronze fitting and a boar's tusk ornament were found, implying the presence of at least one soldier. The well also produced three human skeletons thrown in with a mass of masonry, including column shafts, bases, and capitals. The coins show that the occupation lasted until the 380s but appears to have ceased soon afterwards. It is tempting, therefore, to see the slaughter and destruction as the result of a raid made on the villa in the troubled years at the end of the century, but whether by Irish penetrating the river Severn or by local dissidents must remain undecided. These villa discoveries pose certain problems. Regular troops would not have owned villas to retire to, but the presence of their military equipment could be explained in terms of the hiring of veterans by frightened villa-owners.

The history of Roman Britain from 370 to 410, a period during which the province was attempting to maintain its internal security without the direct military intervention of the central authorities, is marked by the repetition of a single destructive process: the amassing of local armies to fight on the Continent, ostensibly to protect the island from

[3] *Medieval Arch.* v. 1–70.

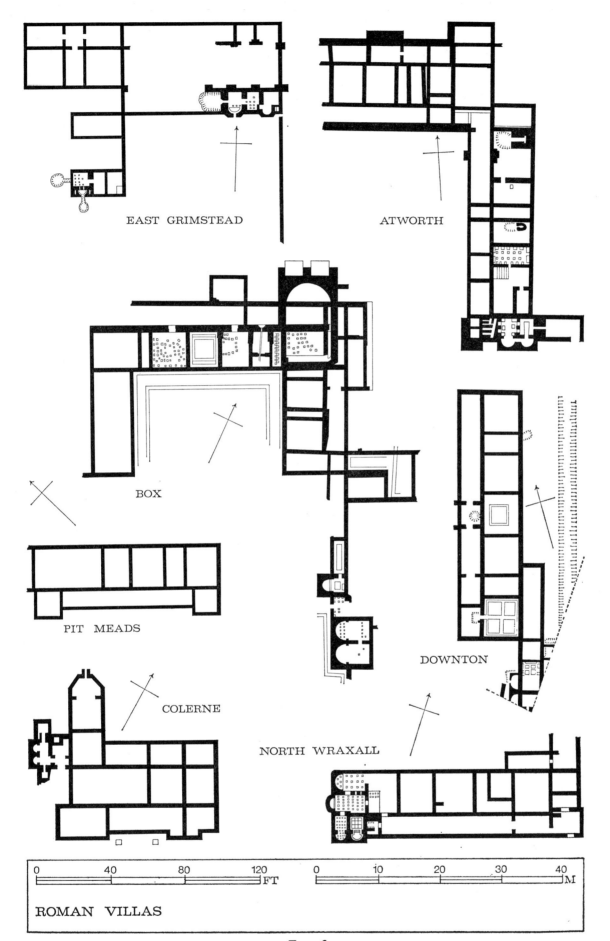

EAST GRIMSTEAD

ATWORTH

BOX

PIT MEADS

COLERNE

DOWNTON

NORTH WRAXALL

0   40   80   120
FT

0   10   20   30   40
M

ROMAN VILLAS

FIG. 48

463

barbarian attack, but in practice to support their successive leaders in a bid for the throne. This happened three times. First Magnus Maximus, a local commander, took a massive army abroad only to be soundly beaten in 388. In 401 Stilicho withdrew another army. Finally, in 409 the remnants of the British fighting force were transported to the Continent to support the cause of Constantine III, a soldier rapidly elevated by the army to the rank of commander. In a space of little more than 20 years three large forces of able-bodied men were removed from the island, most of whom were never to return. In conditions of already acute labour-shortage the action can have been little short of disastrous for the province.

While Wiltshire may have suffered from sporadic Irish raids penetrating inland from the river Severn, most of the county was well buffered from barbarian raids, unlike the coastal areas which were by now under attack. There is little to show how the end came, but Bokerly Dyke was again refurbished, cutting once more through the line of the Roman road; the villa at North Wraxall seems to have met a violent end, while the villa at Box shows traces of having been burnt. The source of the destructive power, however, remains undefined.

The historian Zosimus records that in 409 a rebellion broke out in Britain, the rebels wishing 'to live by themselves no longer obeying Roman laws'. Armorica and other Gaulish provinces followed the British example and 'liberated themselves in the same way casting out the Roman officials and establishing a state of their own by force'.[4] The implications are clear enough: the last remnants of military control having departed, the Roman-based administration, by now presumably top-heavy and out of touch with the rapidly changing situation, was overthrown. It has, however, been argued that since the situation in Armorica is known to have been a workers' revolt against both officials and landed gentry, Zosimus, by saying that Armorica followed Britain's example, implies that the events of 409 were a peasant rebellion aimed at the towns.[5] The fact that the towns wrote to the emperor Honorius to ask for help and received his famous reply of 410 telling them to look after their own defence, can be quoted as possible evidence in favour of the countryside-versus-town conflict. The theory has much to commend it, particularly if it is accepted that the refortified towns of the 370s and their military garrisons were a response to the general troubles following the 367 conspiracy, not specifically the threat of sea-borne barbarian attack. The destruction of Box and North Wraxall may then be thought to be the result of local disturbances.

However these matters are interpreted, certain indisputable facts emerge. By 410 Britain was virtually without a trained fighting force, its administrative system was undergoing rapid fragmentation, and the large-scale mass-production industries, which had depended upon efficient marketing in a relatively stable situation, could no longer continue to function. Moreover, the fact that Roman coinage ceased to be imported hastened the inevitable economic breakdown. Add to this the strong probability that the population had declined drastically as a result of a decreased birth-rate and the demands of military service, and something of the turmoil and desolation of the period can begin to be visualized. A man born in the relative peace and stability of the 350s would in middle age have been faced with a totally new situation, to which very few would have found it easy to adjust themselves.

There were three separate factors at work in the disintegration which came to a head in the early 5th century: the fragmentation of centralized government, the decline and dispersal of population, and the complete breakdown of the economic structure. In terms of the predominantly rural population of Wiltshire, it may be argued that the

[4] *Zosimi . . . Historia Nova*, ed. L. Mendelssohn, vi. 5   [5] *Antiq.* xxx. 163–7.

decreasing population was a problem to which people were already accustomed, while the vagaries of the government are unlikely by this date to have had much direct effect upon the everyday life of the populace. The economic breakdown, however, would have been far more serious and deserves further consideration. The basis of economy for 400 years had been the use of coinage as a medium for exchange. Goods could be bought and sold in the markets and money could be accumulated to enable larger purchases to be made. The vast numbers of coins found on sites of all classes is a fair indication that by the 3rd century at least a money economy was firmly entrenched throughout the province. Copper was employed for everyday purposes, with silver and gold used by the central government to pay the army and officials and recovered again by taxation. There was plenty of copper for general use and little seems to have been minted after 402. Gold continued to be imported up to 406 and silver up to 407, but soon after this the virtual loss of army and officials halted the flow with the inevitable result that silver was hoarded. At Colerne at least 118 *siliquae* were found in a hoard about a mile from the villa, at Manton (PRESHUTE) 26 *siliquae* were found with 12 pewter vessels, at New Covert (AMESBURY) a pot containing both silver and bronze coins and 3 silver finger-rings was dug up, and finally at GREAT WISHFORD two hoards were found. One contained about 1,000 late-bronze coins, the other 300 silver coins, some bronze, and 6 silver rings. All four hoards contain the latest silver coins to reach Britain in 407–8 and must, therefore, represent collections deposited early in the 5th century. That the Colerne hoard produced at least one coin of Arcadius, which shows signs of considerable use, implies that not all of the deposition was made as an immediate response to the troubles of 409–10. In any event money soon became worthless and it has been estimated that by 430 coin economy was past.[6]

The mass production of consumer goods flourished in the Roman period as a response to the increased spending power of all classes of society, better distribution being made possible by roads and well organized marketing. Consequent upon this certain skills and crafts of the peasant communities tended to die out. Bronze and pottery production, for example, which had already begun to be the preserve of specialists in the Iron Age, soon became thoroughly commercialized, while other more basic skills, such as iron-smithying, remained firmly entrenched in rural society. It is fair to assume, however, that in 400 years the population had come to rely heavily on specialist mass production. Furthermore in the pottery industry at least the trend was for the larger concerns to capture the markets, putting many small producers out of business. When the money economy collapsed, and at the same time marketing and communications became more difficult, it was inevitable that the factories should cease to exist, and since specialization was so far advanced, large sectors of the population would be without material commodities. Of these pottery is the most conspicuous in the archaeological record. It has already been pointed out that Wiltshire was supplied to a large extent from the Oxford and the New Forest kilns (see p. 459). These kilns were still producing enormous quantities of pottery of various classes late into the 4th century, and from what little evidence there is production continued into the early 5th century. It is, however, inconceivable that the large centres could have survived the eventual collapse of the monetary system. Barter over large distances, particularly to a society largely unversed in its intricacies, would have been no substitute.

It is clear, therefore, that in the first 40 years of the 5th century centralization in defence, administration, economy, and production completely broke down and the province once more reverted to the fragmented state in which it had been 500 years or

---

[6] *Dark-Age Brit. Studies Presented to E. T. Leeds*, ed. D. B. Harden, 3–9.

more before. The survival of the individual institutions of the Roman era into the sub-Roman period poses some important questions, which are now beginning to receive the attention they deserve, but at this stage only generalizations are possible. Some of the neighbouring towns such as Bath, Gloucester, and Cirencester, continued to function, for the Saxons thought them worth taking after the battle of Dyrham (Glos.) in 577. It may be presumed but cannot be proved that the major centres in Wiltshire, such as Mildenhall and Old Sarum, continued in use as small local market centres into the period of Saxon penetration. Of the fate of other large settlements, such as Woodyates (Dors.) and Stockton Earthworks, little is known. Coins later than 395 are very few compared with the numbers at Old Sarum (0·3 per cent at Woodyates, 0·6 per cent at Stockton Earthworks, 7·6 per cent at Old Sarum), a fact which might indicate a serious decline in the significance of Woodyates and Stockton before 410, but the evidence is by no means conclusive.[7] The problem of the survival of the country estates presents insuperable difficulties at present and all that can be said is that there is no reason why viable farming units should have ceased during the 5th century. The continued existence of Bath might, indeed, suggest that the surrounding countryside continued to be productive for some time; nor is it likely that the surviving peasant farms of Salisbury Plain were completely abandoned. The problem, however, is how to recognize archaeologically the continued existence of those that remained.

One artefact, which may lead to the recognition of sub-Roman communities, is a characteristic type of hand-made pottery tempered with chopped grass and straw. The technique of grass-tempering is known to have been in use in southern Britain throughout most of the Dark Ages and until the 9th century, by which time grit- and shell-tempered fabrics were beginning to replace it. The question still to be answered is when did the technique begin to be used? At Portchester Castle (Hants) the earliest grass-tempered fabrics occur in a Germanic style *grubenhaus* together with imported pottery and a gilded bronze disc of the early 5th century.[8] Pottery made in the same fabrics, but showing a gradual typological development, can be traced in contexts dating from the 5th to the 8th century. A further significant fact brought out by the 5th-century pottery from Portchester is that the basic forms closely copy the standard Roman shapes, representing, therefore, a continuation of 'Roman' traditions but using a new medium. The earliest group of grass-tempered wares can thus be seen to be the response of sub-Roman communities to the lack of mass produced ceramics.

In Wiltshire grass-tempered fabrics have been found on three occupation sites: Downton, Round Hill Down (Ogbourne St. George), and Wellhead (Westbury).[9] At Round Hill Down and Wellhead the types occur on sites that have already been occupied in the Roman period, and at Wellhead in particular the sherds appear to be mixed up with the late Roman material. At Downton the grass-tempered fabrics were recovered from the upper filling of a disused gravel-pit close to the site of the Roman villa.[10] Typologically the pottery from these contexts is somewhat indistinctive, but certain of the jars from Round Hill Down and Wellhead are close in form to late Roman everted-rim jars. While too much weight cannot be placed on the Wiltshire evidence in isolation, it may be said that since there is good reason, from Portchester, to believe that grass-tempering was a native technique arising in the early 5th century, and since some of the Wiltshire material occurs on late Roman sites made in Roman forms, it is a distinct possibility that these sites continued to be occupied from the 4th century well into the 5th, if not later. The Round Hill Down settlement and several of the Hampshire

[7] *W.A.M.* lvi. 109.
[8] *Ant. Jnl.* i. 67–85.
[9] *W.A.M.* lxi. 31–7.
[10] Ibid. lix. 124–9.

sites, where pottery of this type has been discovered, are on hilltops or hillsides, in positions commonly chosen for settlement in the Iron Age and Roman periods. This, too, might hint at a continuity among the remnants of the native population.

The burials of this 5th-century population have not been identified with certainty, although it is possible that many of the secondary inhumations in barrows may be of this period. Grass-tempered sherds were found with the inhumation buried on the edge of a Roman tomb on West Overton Down,[11] but it is extremely unlikely that the precise dating of these unaccompanied inhumations will ever be possible. Of the rest of the sub-Roman material culture there is little to be said. The penannular brooch from Oldbury Hill (CALNE) may well belong to this period, as indeed does the famous WILTON hanging-bowl, with its four riveted escutcheons ornamented with open-work pelta designs, carried out in late Roman rather than Saxon style. The remainder of the artefacts, possibly belonging to this period, are indistinguishable from late Roman or Saxon types.

The social and economic fragmentation of the sub-Roman period does not imply complete anarchy. From the *Anglo-Saxon Chronicle* and the works of Gildas and others it is possible to piece together something of the administrative structure of the period. In the place of centralized government tyrants appeared, men such as those represented by Vortigern, Ambrosius, and Arthur, who were the natural successors to the stream of local leaders of the late 4th and early 5th centuries, appointed from the ranks of the army or the urban aristocracy, while the country was still part of the empire. Two opposed defence policies soon seem to emerge: that attributed to Vortigern which was to invite north Germanic (Saxon) mercenaries and settle them on the coast to protect the country from further invasions, and that, sometimes attributed to Ambrosius, which appears to have aimed at Roman reoccupation. After conflict between the two opposing views in 442 the Saxon settlers rebelled and overran much of the east of the country. With that rebellion the leadership of the sub-Roman west, which included most of Wiltshire, passed to war leaders such as Ambrosius and Arthur. About 446 an unsuccessful appeal for help was made to the Roman leader Aetius campaigning in Gaul, and then followed a period of local resistance to Saxon advance. After many successful cavalry battles, often fought at fords, culminating in the great British victory at Mount Badon just before 500, Gildas, writing about 540, could speak of 'our present security'.[12] Within a year or two, however, the second Saxon revolt was under way and Wiltshire passed rapidly into Saxon control.

[11] Ibid. lxii. 30.
[12] Gildas, *De Excidio et Conquestu Britanniae*, ed. T. Mommsen (Mon. Hist. Germ. *Chronica Minora*, iii), 41.

THE PAGAN SAXON PERIOD

c. 500–c. 700

The British Element in Wiltshire, p. 480.

THE pagan Saxon period has no clearly marked beginning or end in Wiltshire, a feature it shares with the remainder of Wessex and most of the other parts of England concerned. The date of the arrival of the earliest Germanic settlers within the county is no more than approximately known but it is unlikely to have been much before the end of the 5th century. The conversion of the West Saxons to Christianity began with the arrival of the missionary Birinus among them in 634, but the process was clearly a lengthy one and in Wiltshire pagan practices, notably the burial of grave-goods with the dead, continued into the earlier 8th century. The sources available for the study of this period fall into three main categories: those of documentary history, of archaeology, and of place-names. The information obtainable from documentary sources is relatively scanty and in general relates to Wessex and only rarely to any specific locality or place in Wiltshire. It is unlikely that much, if any, new written evidence will come to light in the future but the analysis and interpretation of that known to exist are by no means exhausted. The study of the material remains of the period is at an altogether earlier stage and as yet archaeologists have no means of dating accurately most of the sites and objects which have so far been brought to light. Moreover the number of known pagan Saxon sites in Wiltshire is almost certainly only a fraction of what once existed, or even of what remain to be found. Their number has in recent years been augmented steadily and any conclusions based on such evidence must of necessity be regarded as tentative and provisional. The same is true of any conclusions based on the study of place-names, but as the work of toponymists continues, particularly that carried out under the aegis of the English Place-Name Society, it is seen to be of increasing relevance to the study of the early historic period. In addition to the problems inherent in the separate aspects of the study of the period there is as yet no satisfactory way in which they may be integrated to produce a convincing picture or narrative.

Two topics, closely interrelated, are of primary interest in the study of the period, namely the circumstances of the arrival and settlement of people of continental origin; and the impact of those people, especially in the areas where they settled thickly, on the indigenous Romano-British inhabitants.

As shown in the preceding chapter,[1] the employment in the earlier 5th century of Germanic ('Saxon') troops to help to protect Britain from invasion created an increasingly unstable situation. Internal dissensions among the British led to the hiring of more and more troops, who in turn invited yet more of their own kind to join them. Ultimately the mercenaries rebelled against their employers and at first met with success. Native resistance, however, marshalled under Ambrosius, was victorious at Mount Badon at the end of the 5th century, and a period of relative peace, with the British dominant, followed. By *c.* 570, however, the Saxons were in revolt again, this time with far greater success, and by the end of the century the outcome of the lengthy struggle was no longer in doubt. Effective British resistance in lowland England was at an end.[2]

[1] See pp. 465–7.
[2] For a fuller treatment of these events see *Essays Presented to Eric Birley*, ed. M. G. Jarrett and B. Dobson, 145 sqq.; *Christianity in Brit. 300–700*, ed. M. W. Barley and R. P. C. Hanson, 55–9.

This very general account of events in the 5th and 6th centuries comes largely from contemporary or near contemporary sources, in particular from the British writer Gildas.[3] For Wessex, and incidentally for the region later to become Wiltshire, a somewhat more detailed although by no means entirely reliable sequence of events is provided by the early West Saxon entries in the *Anglo-Saxon Chronicle*.[4] The nature and undoubted imperfections of that source are familiar.[5] The account given of the origins of the West Saxon kingdom raises many problems. The highly selective nature of the entries, due to the restricted information available to the compiler rather than to deliberate selection on his part, is an obvious and serious limitation. The conquest of Wessex is portrayed in terms of Saxon invaders who, late in the 5th and early in the 6th centuries, landed in the neighbourhood of Southampton Water and who, or whose immediate descendants, fought a series of successful battles against the Britons and thus established their authority over the region. No mention is made of the Germanic settlers whose presence, from the early 5th century onwards, is well attested archaeologically along the middle and upper Thames in north Wessex.[6] The Britons, as the vanquished faction, scarcely appear, and then only in defeat. There is no hint of their victory at Mount Badon, nor any evidence of the apparently lengthy period of peace which followed it.

Despite its limitations, however, the *Chronicle* provides a picture of the invasion and conquest of Wessex by Saxons who extended their control northwards from the south coast of Hampshire to embrace the whole region. It is, however, unwise to assume, as some writers have done, that the battles, which tend to occur in a northward progression, were necessarily fought at a frontier or that they represent the rate of advance from southern Hampshire into Wiltshire and beyond. The ill-fated expedition of the men of Gododdin from Edinburgh to Catterick (Yorks. N.R.) *c.* 600 serves as a reminder, even if a rather forceful one, of the troop mobility that was possible at the time and the depth to which enemy territory might be penetrated.[7] The first two events which are recorded as having taken place in Wiltshire, the battles at Salisbury (*Searoburh* 552) and Barbury (556),[8] are of interest in this respect. Both occur at major Iron-Age hill-forts, suggesting, perhaps, temporary re-use of their defences, though whether by Britons or Saxons remains unknown. *Searoburh* with little doubt denotes the large hill-fort at Old Sarum which in the Roman period had become the focal point of a number of roads and which was responsible in part for the name, and probably siting, of the Roman settlement of *Sorviodunum*.[9] Barbury Castle (Ogbourne St. Andrew) lies on the north crest of the Marlborough Downs and, though not associated with any Roman roads, occupies a commanding position in relation to the ancient and important Ridgeway which leads south-westwards from the Berkshire Downs to Salisbury Plain. That these two battles took place at strongpoints related to and, perhaps, temporarily used to control major routes is surely significant and invites comparison with the fighting which occurred in 592 and 715[10] at *Wodnesbeorg* further south on the Ridgeway at the point where it crosses the Wansdyke.

The battles recorded in the annals for 568 and 571 indicate that fighting was taking place well beyond the borders of Wiltshire and that conflict not only continued with the Britons, but that it had begun with other Anglo-Saxon kingdoms, namely Kent.[11]

[3] Gildas, *De Excidio et Conquestu Britanniae*, ed. T. Mommsen (Mon. Hist. Germ. *Chronica Minora*, iii).
[4] *A.-S. Chron.* ed. Dorothy Whitelock (1961).
[5] See e.g. F. M. Stenton, *Anglo-Saxon Eng.* 15–27.
[6] J. N. L. Myres, *A.-S. Pottery and Settlement of Eng.* 114.

[7] K. H. Jackson, *The Gododdin*, 84.
[8] *A.-S. Chron.* ed. Whitelock, 12.
[9] *Britannia*, i. 79.
[10] *A.-S. Chron.* ed. Whitelock, 14, 26.
[11] Ibid. 13.

The north-western part of Wiltshire, however, was probably only finally secured from British hold or interference by the battle of Dyrham (Glos.), assigned by the *Chronicle* to 577, in which two of the three towns that were captured, Bath and Cirencester,[12] lie just outside the county. During the following century fighting continued against the Britons, notably on the western borders of Wessex, and there is evidence of increasing warfare with the neighbouring English kingdoms, in particular the rising kingdom of Mercia.

There is also some sign of internal conflict among the West Saxons towards the end of the 6th century but its nature is difficult to determine and depends to a large extent on how the ambiguous entries in the *Chronicle* concerning the later part of Ceawlin's reign are interpreted, particularly the events of 584 and 592.[13] It seems likely that there were two rival groups of Saxons, possibly but not certainly under related rulers, one centred on Wiltshire, the other on the Thames Valley, and it has been suggested that by *c.* 630 the latter group had achieved an ascendancy.[14] Certainly the missionary activities of Birinus among the West Saxons, or the *Gewisse* as, according to Bede,[15] they were anciently known, appear to be based on the Thames Valley. Birinus was granted the *civitas* of Dorchester (Oxon.) for the seat of his bishopric and it was there that he baptized the West Saxon kings between 635 and 639, events which mark the beginning of the end of paganism in Wessex, although it is clear from archaeological evidence, as said above, that paganism was eradicated only slowly.

The archaeological record provides the clearest evidence for the presence of the pagan Saxons in Wiltshire and unlike the historical sources it may at least be restricted to the county. But it, too, is limited by its very incompleteness. Only a small proportion of the total number of sites that once existed is known and since it consists almost entirely of burials it is scarcely a representative sample. So far no settlement sites of the period have been discovered. Over 400 pagan, or probably pagan, burials are known of which more than three-quarters occur in cemeteries and the remainder as occasional flat burials or as primary and intrusive burials in barrows. All the burials are inhumations; no cremations have been recorded despite the existence of such burials in cemeteries just beyond the north and north-east limits of the county along the upper Thames.[16]

At least 13 cemeteries may be assigned with fair certainty to the pagan period, many of them ostensibly small, although it is fairly certain that several have not been fully explored. Most have been revealed by accident rather than design, and, as a result, satisfactory archaeological examination has often not been possible. The full number of burials in the cemeteries at PURTON, West Chisenbury (ENFORD), and Foxhill (WAN-BOROUGH), revealed by quarrying and similar activities, remains unknown. At Winterbourne Gunner[17] modern housing precluded total exploration of the site. Other cemeteries, such as those brought to light a century and more ago near St. Edmund's Church (SALISBURY) and at Basset Down (LYDIARD TREGOZE), were poorly recorded and the number of burials found is uncertain. At only two sites have more than 32 burials been recorded, although the cemetery at Black Patch, Pewsey, under excavation in 1971, promised to exceed that figure. At Petersfinger (CLARENDON PARK), where the whole of the cemetery appears to have been examined, some 70 burials were found. A similar number is recorded from the cemetery at Harnham Hill (SALISBURY), excavated in 1852, but there is little doubt that it originally contained more burials.

[12] *A.-S. Chron.* ed. Whitelock, 14.
[13] Ibid.
[14] *E.H.R.* lxxx. 10–29.
[15] *Bede's Eccl. Hist.* ed. Colgrave (1969), 232.

[16] *Dark-Age Brit. Studies Presented to E. T. Leeds*, ed. D. B. Harden, 123–31.
[17] *W.A.M.* lix. 86–109.

Most of the burials in the cemeteries were extended inhumations in shallow graves which appear to have been unmarked by any durable surface features. Where the evidence is forthcoming they comprised members of both sexes and of all age-groups, but on the whole adult male burials are most common and were the only burials at

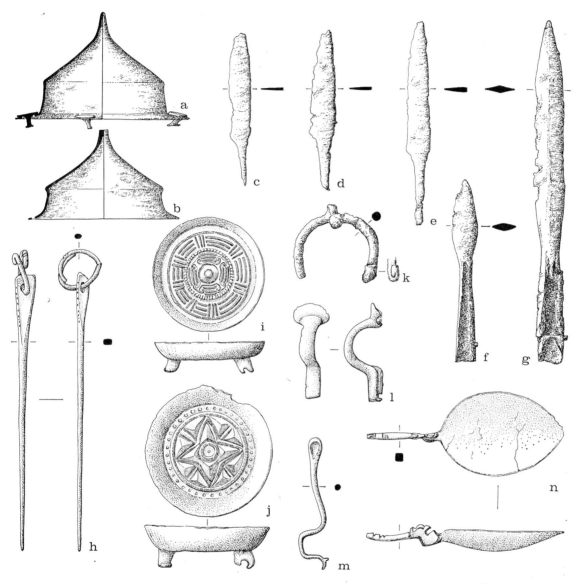

Fig. 49. Objects from pagan Saxon cemetery on Basset Down. Iron objects: a, b, shield bosses, c, d, e, knives, f, g, spearheads, k, part of penannular brooch (a–g $\frac{1}{4}$, k $\frac{2}{3}$); i, j, gilt bronze saucer brooches ($\frac{2}{3}$); bronze objects: h, pin, l, bow brooch of late Roman type, m, ear-pick ($\frac{2}{3}$); n, bowl of a spoon of late type ($\frac{2}{3}$).

Foxhill and at Purton. The majority of burials were accompanied by grave-goods, usually the imperishable items which the persons buried would have worn or had about them when they were alive. These vary both in quality and quantity, not only between graves in different cemeteries, but between graves in the same cemetery, and presumably reflect differences in the status of those buried as well as differences in burial custom. In the few cemeteries that have been carefully examined and recorded some graves contained only the simplest objects such as a knife or a few beads; others were completely unfurnished. In general, however, male burials were accompanied by weapons, especially spears and shields but only rarely swords, by knives, and less frequently by brooches, buckles, and other belt-fittings. Knives, buckles, beads, brooches, and other items of jewellery were the commonest objects placed in female graves.

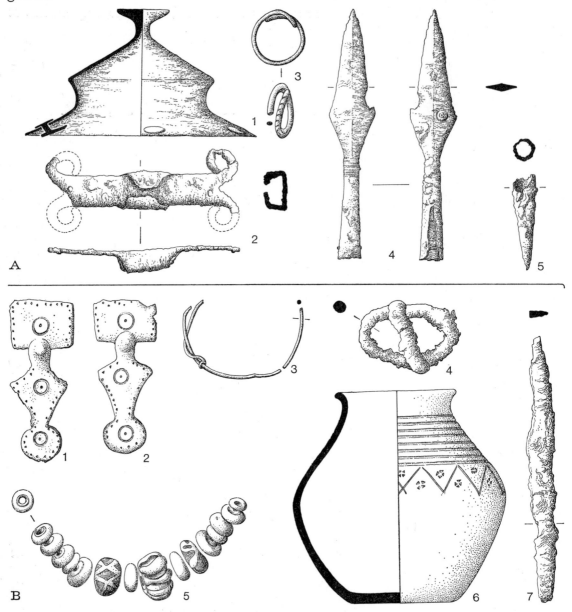

FIG. 50. Two grave-groups from pagan Saxon cemetery at Black Patch. A, Grave 8, iron objects: 1, shield boss, 2, shield grip, 4, spearhead, 5, spear ferrule ($\frac{1}{3}$); 3, bronze toe-ring ($\frac{2}{3}$). B, Grave 15, bronze objects: 1, 2, small long brooches, 3, wire fragments ($\frac{2}{3}$); iron objects: 4, buckle, 7, knife ($\frac{2}{3}$); 5, glass beads ($\frac{2}{3}$), 6, decorated urn ($\frac{1}{3}$).

The cemeteries contain nearly all of the earliest Saxon burials at present known within the county, and in most of the cemeteries such burials occur with datable objects. At Basset Down (fig. 49), Harnham Hill, Petersfinger, and Winterbourne Gunner items claimed to be of Frankish origin,[18] probably manufactured in the 5th century or the early years of the 6th, have been found in conjunction with objects traditionally regarded as Saxon. The presence of ogival spearheads and low flat shield-bosses with concave sides and broad flanges serves to emphasize an early date as does the occasional appearance of Roman objects among the grave-goods from the first three of those

[18] Vera I. Evison, *Fifth-Cent. Invasions S. of Thames*, 37 sqq.

cemeteries. Comparable early spearheads and shield-bosses have been found at Fox-hill, St. Edmund's Church, and Black Patch (fig. 50). There seems little doubt, how-ever, that some of the early cemeteries continued in use, at least well into the 6th century. Probably of the later 6th century onward are the cemeteries at Winkelbury Hill (BERWICK ST. JOHN) and BROAD CHALKE; the latest of those with datable goods is that at Purton, where the presence of seaxes indicates a date not earlier than the 7th century.

The orientation of the graves in the cemeteries, where recorded at all, appears to conform to no particular pattern. A west–east orientation has been noted at Harnham Hill, Winterbourne Gunner, and in the earlier graves at Petersfinger, but also in the later cemetery at Winkelbury Hill, and in the undated cemetery at Roche Court Down (WINTERSLOW). In the second cemetery, the so-called 'execution cemetery', at Roche Court Down at least 15 adult males, with heads to the south, were found buried in an earlier ditch. Nine had been clumsily decapitated and the wrists of a number bound before death suggesting that they were malefactors. The numerous unaccompanied burials found near the Roman road at Crofton (GREAT BEDWYN), and generally re-garded as pagan Saxon, included a series of graves which radiated from a common centre like the spokes of a wheel.

In addition to cemeteries over 20 unmarked graves certainly or probably pagan Saxon have been found, usually singly but occasionally in pairs. All have been located by chance and it is possible that in some instances they belong to incompletely explored cemeteries as for example those from Woodbridge (NORTH NEWNTON) and from the windmill site at SHREWTON.[19] The burials, nearly all of males where determinable, were mostly in simple graves but in at least one instance, i.e. Netheravon Aerodrome (FIGHELDEAN), the interment was enclosed in an iron-bound wooden coffin. The paucity of grave-goods renders dating impossible in most cases but a few burials may be assigned an approximate date. That found below Witherington Ring (ALDERBURY) was associated with a low carinated shield-boss unlikely to be much later than the mid 6th century.[20] Of somewhat later date is the burial with a shield-boss of low curved cone type (fig. 51A) from Perham Down (NORTH TIDWORTH). The interment from Barrow Hill (EBBESBORNE WAKE) with its tall conical sugar-loaf boss is fairly certainly of the later 7th century. One unusual burial, that of a female, was found shattered by a sarsen block in the filling of a Roman well on Poulton Down (MILDENHALL).

Ten barrows containing primary pagan Saxon burials are known, most of which appear to be of relatively late date. Nearly all those for which adequate descriptions survive appear to have been small bowl-barrows mostly under 30 ft. in diameter and rarely more than 1 ft. high. Exceptions are the small saucer-barrow on Rodmead Hill (*B vi* MAIDEN BRADLEY 6) and the anomalous 'barrow' at Ford, Laverstock,[21] which consisted of a penannular ditch with traces of an external bank. All the mounds covered graves mostly of modest dimensions but which were described as 'large' at King's Play Hill (*B ii* HEDDINGTON 1a), and *B ii* WEST KNOYLE 16, and as a 'room' 11 ft. deep at Ashton Valley (*B ii* CODFORD 1b). The graves contained extended male inhuma-tions, variously orientated and in two instances in wooden coffins, accompanied by grave-goods often of fairly high quality. At Race Down (*B ii* COOMBE BISSETT 2c) no burial was found, only a rich collection of grave-goods. The latter probably belong to the mid 7th century or shortly afterwards and appear to be the earliest of the deposits which occur in a primary context in a barrow. In the remaining barrows, or those to which a date may be assigned at all, the presence of shield-bosses of sugar-loaf form,

---

[19] *W.A.M.* lxiv. 128.   [20] *Ant. Jnl.* xliii. 38 sqq. for shield-bosses generally.   [21] Ibid. xlix. 98–117.

both of the straight and curved cone variety, suggests a date in the later 7th century and possibly even later (fig. 51B). The association of spearheads generally of slender form with such deposits also supports a fairly late date. The burial goods at Ford included a richly ornamented seax and sheath, a small bronze hanging bowl, a garnet-studded buckle, and a finely decorated bone comb (fig. 52).

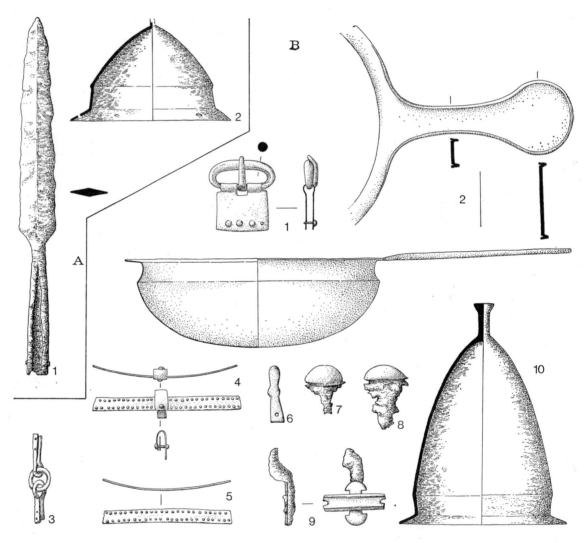

FIG. 51. A, grave-goods accompanying pagan Saxon burial on Perham Down. 1, iron spearhead, 2, iron shield boss (⅔). B, grave-goods accompanying primary Saxon burial in a barrow on Rodmead Hill. 1, bronze buckle, 2, bronze skillet, 3, ring and loops (lost) ? bronze, 4, 5, bronze strips, 6, silver strap end, 7, 8, silver-plated studs (lost), 9, bronze and iron fitting, 10, iron shield boss (2, 10, ⅓, all others ⅔).

Some 50 burials intrusive in earlier barrows have been regarded as pagan Saxon but more than half are poorly recorded or unaccompanied by grave-goods, thus making identification uncertain. Long and bowl-barrows were used most frequently but other forms of round barrow also served. The majority of the burials occur singly but in some round barrows, and in nearly all the long barrows, two or more burials have been found. Eight inhumations were recovered from the long barrow *B i* SHERRINGTON 1 and four headless skeletons, probably pagan Saxon, from the long barrow *B i* KNOOK 2. Use of long barrows for such purposes appears to have been restricted to that part of Salisbury Plain lying between the Avon and the Wylye. Most of the intrusive burials were in shallow graves but those at Winkelbury Hill (*B vi* BERWICK ST. JOHN 4),

B ii OGBOURNE ST. ANDREW 11, and ROUNDWAY 1 were in wooden coffins bound with iron clamps and set in large graves.

Few of the intrusive burials were accompanied by datable grave-goods. Those found in an unusual group of Roman 'barrows' or tombs in West Overton appear to belong

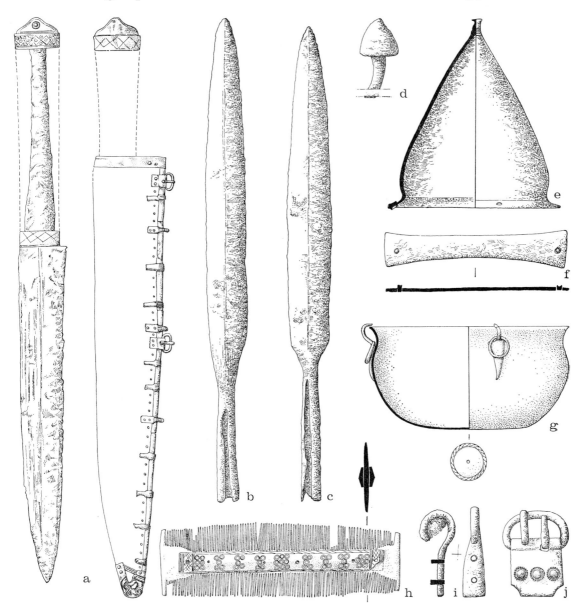

FIG. 52. Grave-goods accompanying primary Saxon burial in a barrow at Ford. Iron objects: a, seax and sheath, b, c, spearheads, d, stud, e, shield boss, f, shield grip, i, hook-ended strip, j, buckle (i, j, ⅔, all others ⅓); g, bronze hanging bowl, h, bone comb (both ⅓).

to the 6th century but one might be as early as the 5th.[22] The burial recovered from the huge bell-barrow (*B iv* IDMISTON 23) appears from the broad low carinated form of the shield-boss unlikely to be later than the mid 6th century. A similar shield-boss, now lost, was apparently associated with the interment found in a barrow of the Lake Group (*B ii* WILSFORD (S.) 50*b*). Of altogether later date are two of the most spectacular burials from the county. That found in the coffin at Roundway was of a female with a bronze-bound wooden bucket at the feet and an impressive set of gold

[22] Evison, op. cit. 40.

A HISTORY OF WILTSHIRE

jewellery near the neck (pl. facing p. 479). The jewellery consisted of a necklace of gold wire beads and pendants with settings of garnets and lignite, and of a set of linked pins with a gold-mounted blue glass stud at the centre. The stud, which has a cross moulded on it, has Irish affinities and is most probably a Christian object. It has been suggested that such studs were distributed as gifts to Saxon converts and in this instance emanated from the monastery at Malmesbury less than 20 miles away, which was founded *c.* 650 by Irish monks under Mailduib.[23] The second burial was found in 1966 in a small bowl-barrow with a causewayed ditch and outer bank (*B iii* ANSTY 3) which lies on the boundary with Swallowcliffe.[24] It contained a large, apparently intrusive, grave in which lay an inhumation accompanied by a variety of objects including a diadem, two palm cups, an incense-burner, enamelled ironwork, and the remains of bed-furniture. A date in the 7th century is indicated. On present evidence, therefore, it seems that Saxon settlers did not build barrows although the idea of barrow burial was, apparently, not unknown to them. The presence of large numbers of prehistoric barrows in Wessex presumably stimulated them to inter some of their dead in such monuments and ultimately to build barrows to receive some of their more important members, a situation paralleled in the Peak District of Derbyshire.

The distribution of these various burial sites, of which over 70 are known all told, is by no means uniform within the county. Almost all of them lie within the chalklands of the south and east, an area traditionally associated with early settlement, and one thickly occupied throughout the Roman period. Most of the burials, and certainly all of the early ones, which have a markedly easterly distribution, suggest that the pagan Saxons sought out and settled lands already occupied and cultivated. There is a marked concentration of cemeteries, many of them containing early burials, in the south, particularly in the immediate neighbourhood of Salisbury, perhaps in part due to the presence of the Roman station of *Sorviodunum* near Old Sarum and the convergence of a number of Roman roads there. That part of the county is, however, very close to Southampton Water and early settlement there is to be expected if the description of events in the *Anglo-Saxon Chronicle* has any validity. The later burials, notably those in barrows, have a decidedly more westerly distribution which accords with the idea implied in the *Chronicle* that the Saxons first occupied the eastern part of the county and gradually extended their control westwards across it. The total absence of pagan burials from the north-west probably reflects in some measure the British domination of that area until the battle at Dyrham in 577. It seems likely that the Saxons entered the county from the middle and upper Thames area in the north-east as well as from the south-east, but there is at present no means of distinguishing clearly, or of assessing the respective strengths of, those two movements. The presence of 5th-century objects of Frankish manufacture or type found not only in Wiltshire but over much of England south of the Thames has led to the suggestion that the whole of the area was invaded simultaneously in the mid 5th century by people from northern France and Belgium under the leadership of Romanized Frankish soldiers.[25] The scatter of objects seems too thin to support such a contention, and it has been pointed out that such objects, even if of Frankish origin, were not necessarily all brought to England by Franks, nor necessarily all deposited in graves here before 500.[26]

The relationship of the burials to the sites actually occupied by the pagan Saxons can only be inferred, but the cemeteries, most of which are of a civilian character, do indicate the presence of settled communities in their neighbourhood. A number of them

[23] A. L. Meaney and S. C. Hawkes, *Two A.-S. Cemeteries at Winnall* (Soc. Medieval Arch. Monograph Ser. iv), 47.
[24] *W.A.M.* lxiii. 115.
[25] Evison, op. cit. 40.
[26] *E.H.R.* lxxxi. 341–5.

lie within or on the slopes of the river valleys close to and sometimes under modern settlements. This strongly suggests that they are the burial grounds of the early inhabitants of those settlements, which thus appear to have been continuously occupied since pagan times. In fact the failure to find occupation sites of the period may be due not so much to a lack of searching as to the fact that many such sites lie under modern settlements and are therefore masked or badly disturbed. Certainly by the later Saxon period, as the land charters and more especially Domesday Book show, settlement on the Wiltshire chalklands was, as today, confined almost entirely to the river valleys. Many of the burials, especially those found in barrows and single graves, lie scattered on the downland in remote parts of parishes well away from the river valleys and the settlements there, and at first sight appear to be part of no detectable pattern. A considerable proportion, however, lie on or close to estate or parish boundaries and if they were deliberately so placed, the boundaries were in being at least as early as the pagan period.[27] These burial sites thus suggest that the landscape was in process of settlement and division among communities at a time for which no documentary evidence of such activity survives.

One boundary merits special consideration, namely the impressive but enigmatic frontier earthwork known as the Wansdyke. For long it was thought to be a single construction, extending with relatively few gaps from Maes Knoll on the Mendips, well within Somerset, eastwards through Wiltshire as far as the Berkshire boundary. Between Bath and Morgan's Hill north-east of Devizes, a distance of some 14 miles, it was assumed that it followed the line of the Roman road to Mildenhall (*Cunetio*) and that its rampart was built at a much reduced scale on top of that road. A recent study of the dyke based on a detailed field survey has shown, however, that it is in two main parts: one in Somerset, the West Wansdyke, extending from Maes Knoll to just south of Bath, the other in Wiltshire, the East Wansdyke, crossing the high chalk downland north of the Vale of Pewsey.[28] Only the East Wansdyke is of concern here. Between the two sections is the Roman road unencumbered by later additions, an observation confirmed by independent excavation.[29] The study has also shown that a number of linear earthworks east of Savernake Forest, including the cross-valley dyke in Little Bedwyn,[30] which have been held to be part of Wansdyke since the early 19th century, do not bear that name in later Saxon documents and are by no means certainly contemporary or related constructions.

The East Wansdyke (pl. facing p. 478) extends for over 12 miles across east-central Wiltshire, from the edge of the chalk escarpment on Morgan's Hill eastwards as far as New Buildings on the edge of Savernake Forest, 2 miles south of Marlborough. The western half of its course lies across high, open chalk plateau, the eastern across lower, drift-covered land, wooded and enclosed. It consists essentially of a bank with a ditch along its north side. On the open downland it is of massive proportions, as much as 90 ft. across the rampart and ditch and reinforced in this section by a counterscarp bank. These features together with its general alignment characterize it as a military work, designed to bar movement across open country from the north. In the more wooded terrain further east, however, the dyke is on a much reduced scale, especially in its final 5 miles, measuring about 50 ft. across overall. Here, in country unsuited to early warfare, it appears to have been conceived as a territorial boundary.

Wansdyke is breached by a succession of gaps most of which allow access from the villages in the Pewsey Vale to the upland grazings at the extremities of their parish

---

[27] *W.A.M.* lxi. 25–30.
[28] *Arch. Jnl.* cxv. 1–48.
[29] *Antiq.* xxxii. 89–96.
[30] *V.C.H. Wilts.* i (1), 257.

A HISTORY OF WILTSHIRE

boundaries. Most of the gaps are probably old, such as those mentioned in 9th- and 10th-century charters relating to Alton Priors, North Newnton, and Overton,[31] but so far only one opening has been suggested as original, that at Red Shore in Alton Priors.[32] That opening is on the line of the ancient Ridgeway leading southwards from the Berkshire Downs, by way of the Marlborough Downs, to Pewsey Vale and Salisbury Plain beyond, and there can be little doubt that it was to bar incursions along such a route from the north, rather than along the Roman road system, that the Wansdyke was built.

Such a conclusion raises the problem of the date of Wansdyke and the circumstances that led to its construction. At present all that can be said with certainty is that the dyke cannot be earlier than late Roman, a fact established by excavations at Brown's Barn (BISHOP'S CANNINGS) as long ago as 1890, and it cannot be later than 892, the date of its first named appearance in a written record, namely the charter relating to North Newnton.[33] The later date might be amended to 825 if the *ealdan dic* of the Alton Priors charter of that date[34] is indeed Wansdyke, as seems most likely. A more precise date for the construction of the dyke is at present impossible to give. In a period in which our knowledge of events is fragmentary it is a hazardous exercise to link an archaeological monument with a supposed general situation, let alone a specific historical event. Two possibilities, however, demand serious attention. There is the traditional view that East Wansdyke is a work of the sub-Roman period built to protect the Romano-Britons of the southern half of Wiltshire from the unwelcome attentions of the early Saxon settlers in the upper Thames Valley. Such a view inclines to a date in the late 5th century partly on the assumption that by then the Roman roads in the area had fallen out of use and probably become overgrown, especially beyond the east end of the dyke of Savernake Forest. Certainly on Morgan's Hill the Roman road from Mildenhall to Bath was blocked by the western end of East Wansdyke, and beyond that point the road alone may have served to delineate a continuation of the frontier or boundary westwards across low-lying, generally wooded terrain unsuited to early warfare. But there is no other evidence that the Roman road system in the area was obsolete when the dyke was built.

A second and rather more plausible possibility for the origin of East Wansdyke is that it was built by the Wiltshire Saxons against those of the Thames Valley, perhaps during the unsettled conditions at the end of Ceawlin's reign in the late 6th century. The battle at *Wodnesbeorg* in 592[35] strongly suggests that the dyke was in existence and that it was functioning as some form of barrier or frontier. *Wodnesbeorg* is the neolithic long barrow, now known as Adam's Grave (*B i* ALTON 14), which is prominently sited on the escarpment overlooking the Pewsey Vale, and which lies beside the Ridgeway just south of the point where it passes through the Wansdyke at Red Shore. The *Chronicle*, it may be noted, records that a second major battle took place at that strategic point in 715 when Ine king of Wessex fought with Ceolred king of Mercia.[36]

The name Wansdyke (Woden's dyke) is of some interest here and has been invoked in support of both possibilities. It has been explained as a name given by pagan Anglo-Saxons, possibly in the mid 6th century, to an earthwork whose origin and purpose was unknown to them and which was, therefore, attributed by them to supernatural agency.[37] It seems unlikely, however, that the building of a major frontier work, and the reasons for it, could have been so completely forgotten a century or so later.

[31] *Arch. Jnl.* lxxvi. 159–64, 187–91, 240–4.
[32] *W.A.M.* lxii. 127.
[33] *Arch. Jnl.* lxxvi. 190.
[34] Ibid. 161.
[35] *A.-S. Chron.* ed. Whitelock, 14.
[36] Ibid. 26.
[37] *Essays in Brit. Hist.* ed. H. R. Trevor-Roper, 1–27.

478

The East Wansdyke crossing Morgan's Hill, Bishop's Cannings

GOLD JEWELLERY FROM INTRUSIVE BURIAL IN BARROW ON ROUNDWAY HILL
(Devizes Museum)

'THE MARLBOROUGH BUCKET': IRON-AGE VAT OR BUCKET
(Devizes Museum, approx. $\frac{1}{5}$ actual size)

A second, and perhaps more plausible view, is that the dyke is indeed an early Saxon construction and therefore named after the dominant god of the pagan period.[38] No other dyke in Britain has that name attached to it, the name of the god from whom the Anglo-Saxon royal houses, including that of Wessex, traced their descent and it has been suggested as improbable that such a sacred name would be given by the Saxons to an obsolete pre-Saxon work. Furthermore, the concentration of Woden names in the vicinity of *Wodnesbeorg*, the important position of which has been noted above, has been attributed to the existence of a pagan sanctuary sacred to the god and perhaps intimately connected with the building of the dyke. A further possibility is that such a sanctuary did exist, that the district became a centre of Woden's cult, and that the dyke simply acquired its name by association.[39]

A dyke in Little Bedwyn has since the early 19th century been associated with the Wansdyke and, indeed, been regarded as part of it. It is a substantial defensive earthwork, comprising a bank and ditch facing north-east, which extends south-eastwards from Chisbury hill-fort for nearly 1½ mile to form an effective barrier across the Bedwyn valley north and east of Great Bedwyn. There is, however, no evidence that it was ever called Wansdyke; it is mentioned but is unnamed in Saxon charters relating to Great and Little Bedwyn,[40] and it is now generally known as the Bedwyn Dyke. That together with the fact that it is separated from the east end of Wansdyke by a gap of over 5 miles has led to the suggestion that it is an independent work of Saxon date, possibly built to defend an early settlement or estate at Bedwyn in the late 7th or early 8th century.[41] Such evidence does not, however, entirely rule out a connexion. Between the two dykes lies the thickly wooded area of Savernake Forest which may have rendered such earthwork defences unnecessary. Certainly dykes elsewhere are intermittent in areas of heavy woodland. On present evidence no firm conclusion is possible about the Bedwyn Dyke; all that can be said with certainty is that it is mentioned in a charter of 778.[42] It cannot be demonstrated that it is not Roman or prehistoric, but the weight of opinion appears to favour a post-Roman date.

The contribution of English place-names to the study of the pagan Saxon period in Wiltshire, as in other areas, is inevitably limited, since no reliable relative chronology, and certainly no absolute chronology, is at present attainable for such names. Early names are difficult to recognize and many probably go undetected. Many place-name elements and forms were in use over a long period of time in the name-giving process and in consequence they are of scant value from a purely chronological standpoint. The earliest comprehensive picture of English nomenclature is provided by Domesday Book, compiled some six centuries after the coming of the English to Britain. In that long period, as one authority has remarked, 'there were many far-reaching linguistic developments; ancient words and archaic place-name structures disappear and are replaced by others more appropriate to new functions in name-giving demanded by a developing countryside'.[43]

A few Old English place-names do, however, appear to belong to the earlier, if not earliest, stages of the Anglo-Saxon settlement, in particular folk-names incorporating the element *-ingas* and *-inga-* derived from personal names.[44] Such names are few in Wiltshire but the *-ingas* element is found in Cannings ('the people of Cana'), and the *-inga-* element in Manningford ('the ford of the people of Manna'), in Collingbourne ('the stream of the people of Cola'), and in Coldridge ('the ridge of the

[38] *Arch. Jnl.* cxv. 40 sqq.
[39] *Univ. Birm. Hist. Jnl.* viii. 11–13.
[40] *Arch. Jnl.* lxxvi. 151–3; lxxvii. 75–80.
[41] Ibid. cxv. 18–20.

[42] Ibid. lxxvi. 151.
[43] *Proc. Brit. Acad.* xlii. 72.
[44] Ibid. 73 sqq.; A. H. Smith, *Eng. Place-Name Elements,* i. 298–303.

people of Cola') near the eastern extremity of the two Collingbourne parishes.[45] It is noticeable that those names are all associated with relatively large areas of land, probably ancient units or holdings, each of which appears to have been divided into two or more estates by the late Saxon period.[46] They are, moreover, to be found on or adjacent to the Chalk in the eastern half of the county where most of the evidence for pagan Saxon occupation is concentrated. Other -ingas, -inga- names formed upon a topographical term, or an older place-name, were in use over a much longer period for giving names to places and in consequence are an unreliable indicator of an early date. Names incorporating the suffix -hām ('a village, manor, or household') are also likely to be early,[47] but in Wiltshire they are very difficult to distinguish from those ending in -hamm ('an enclosure or a (water-)meadow').[48] Those so far recognized are Upham in Aldbourne, where the now deserted village overlies a substantial Romano-British settlement, Cadenham in Bremhill, and Boreham (Wood) in West Overton. Numerous Old English personal names are found compounded in place-names in the county, but, as has been noted elsewhere, they include few of the obvious survivals from the personal nomenclature of the pre-migration age to be found in the eastern counties and in Sussex.[49] Recent work, however, has suggested the likelihood that place-names formed from the personal names and folk-names of the inhabitants of an area, or incorporating habitative terms such as -hām or -tūn, are secondary and that ordinary nature-names were the first to be used by settlers in a new land.[50] Certainly an analysis of the place-names in the Wiltshire section of Domesday Book shows that almost exactly half are nature-names, or contain nature-names as the essential element.

A few place-names make direct reference to Anglo-Saxon paganism and must, therefore, have been in existence before or very soon after all the settlers in the area were converted to Christianity. Such names are not necessarily indicative of very early settlement, however, and it is possible that they were formed only when heathen sites had become exceptional rather than normal features of social life.[51] The element weoh ('an idol or temple') is present in the lost Weolond in Tockenham and possibly also in Waden (Hill) near Avebury, the latter the site of several round barrows now destroyed. Haradon Hill in Amesbury probably contains the element hearg ('a heathen temple') but no early form of the name is recorded. The pagan god Thunor is commemorated in the lost Thunresfeld, which occurs as a boundary mark in a late Saxon charter for Hardenhuish,[52] and Woden appears in Wansdyke and the associated group of names noted above. It is noticeable that these pagan place-names are compounded with nature-names and not with habitative names.

THE BRITISH ELEMENT IN WILTSHIRE

The fate of the Romano-British inhabitants of Wiltshire and their descendants during the 5th century and later is difficult to determine. The limited historical sources are of a general nature and at best relate to Wessex. According to Gildas those Britons who did not flee overseas were either put to death or enslaved,[53] but there is no suggestion that the British population was totally exterminated. What is clear is that the British were subordinated to the Anglo-Saxons and that eventually they were politically subject

[45] P.N. Wilts. (E.P.N.S.) for all names in this and subsequent paragraphs.

[46] V.C.H. Wilts. ii, pp. 118, 121, 127, 131, 159, 162.

[47] Proc. Brit. Acad. xlii. 83 sqq.

[48] P.N. Wilts. (E.P.N.S.), 416.

[49] Ibid. p. xv.

[50] Medieval Arch. x. 5.

[51] Univ. Birm. Hist. Jnl. viii. 19 sqq.

[52] Arch. Jnl. lxxvi. 170–1.

[53] Gildas, De Excidio (Mon. Hist. Germ. Chronica Minora, iii), 40.

to them throughout England. It seems fairly certain that a substantial number of the wealthier and more influential Britons, both in the towns and in the countryside, joined in the attempt to repel the Anglo-Saxon invaders. Many of them perished in the struggle and others gave up or were forced to flee to the Celtic fastnesses of the West, to Wales and Dumnonia, whence some migrated to Brittany. For the less affluent and independent, especially the numerous rural labourers, flight was scarcely possible. Their livelihood, and indeed survival, was rooted in the land. Whatever part they played in the fighting, there can be little doubt that once British resistance crumbled in the later 6th century they were left largely leaderless and helpless, an impoverished and probably disorganized stratum of society readily dominated and absorbed by the victorious Anglo-Saxons.

Nowhere is this more evident than in the failure of the British or Celtic tongue to survive and in its relatively rapid replacement by English throughout most of the country. The very word used by the Anglo-Saxons to describe the British or Welsh, w(e)alas, also meant serfs or slaves in Old English.[54] Yet despite the failure to survive there is evidence in much of England, and certainly in Wiltshire, that the British language did not disappear at once and that it continued for a time to exist alongside Old English. Place-names of British origin, which are relatively prominent in the county, bear witness to this and 'their survival points clearly to a period of peaceful co-existence between the Britons, who survived the first impact of the Saxon invasion, and their conquerors'.[55] The manner in which such names were transmitted, however, is not fully understood. It is often assumed that the Anglo-Saxons learned them from the Britons and that by this means they were brought into Old English, but there is some evidence that transmission took place during a phase in which the Britons were in process of adopting English and were, in fact, bilingual.[56]

Almost all the British place-names at present recognized within the county are, in so far as they are interpretable, topographical names drawn from natural features such as streams, hills, and woods.[57] The majority are in use today but a few, mostly the names of minor streams, have been superseded by English names and are known only from documentary sources. Altogether some 22 river and stream names are known, among them those of nearly all the larger rivers. The marked concentration of such names in the north, west, and south-west of the county accords well with the general observation that British river-names increase in frequency from east to west across England, a progression plausibly held to bear some relationship to the stages of the Anglo-Saxon occupation and settlement.[58] Certainly in Wiltshire there is no conflict between the distribution of British river-names and what little may be inferred from both archaeological and historical sources of the progress of the Saxon occupation of the county. To some extent, however, that distribution is the product of geology. The Chalk in the south and east of the county gives rise to very few streams, whereas on the greensands, limestones, and especially clays in the north and west there is an abundance of surface water. In south Wiltshire the Avon, the Wylye, formerly known in its upper reaches as the Deverill, the Nadder, with its tributaries the Sem and the Fonthill, all bear British names, but the river-name Stour, once considered to be of similar origin, is now thought more likely to be of Germanic derivation.[59] In the north-west of the county British river-names are represented by the (Bristol) Avon and by its tributaries the Biss, the Gauze Brook, the Pew, and the Semington Brook. Three further tributaries, the Brinkworth

[54] A. H. Smith, *Eng. P.N. Elements*, ii. 242–4.
[55] *P.N. Wilts.* (E.P.N.S.), p. xv.
[56] K. H. Jackson, *Language and Hist. in Early Brit.* 241–6.

[57] *P.N. Wilts.* (E.P.N.S.) for all names in this and subsequent paragraphs.
[58] Jackson, op. cit. 220–3.
[59] Ibid. 195, n. 1.

Brook, the upper Marden, and the By Brook were formerly known by the British names Idover, Calne, and Marden respectively. The name Idover, which incorporates the British element *dubro, *dubrā ('water'), occurs at least a dozen times in this part of the county, mostly as the name of fields lying at or near the headwaters of minor tributaries of the (Bristol) Avon and of the Thames. Only one major tributary of the Thames in Wiltshire, the Kennet, still retains a British name. From it the Roman town of *Cunetio* took its name, as did the villages of East and West Kennet, the first of which lies at the point where the ancient Ridgeway from the Berkshire and Marlborough Downs crosses the river on its way southward towards Salisbury Plain. Other tributaries of the Thames once having British names are the Cole, the Ray, and the Key, formerly known as the *Lent*, the *Worf*, and the *Worvinchel* respectively. A minor tributary of the Cole, which rises at Chiseldon, was known variously in late Saxon charters as the *Dorcyn, Dorcan, Dorternebrok*, a name probably derived from a British form *Dorce.[60] The stream flows past the site of the Roman town of *Durocornovium* and may well have been responsible for that enigmatic name.[61] A further small group of names associated with water is that incorporating the loan element *funta* which appears to have been derived through Late British from the Latin *fontana*, 'a spring' or 'stream'. The element occurs in the names of the following villages: Urchfont, Teffont, Fovant, and Fonthill, all of which lie at or near the heads of small streams. Two further British names, now those of neighbouring villages, are probably to be associated with minor tributaries of the Avon: Cherhill appears originally to have been the name of the stream on which that village stands and Quemerford, which lies at a meeting of two streams, probably incorporates a British element meaning confluence.

In addition to river- and stream-names a number of other place-names, wholly or partly of British origin, are recognizable in the county. They, too, have a generally northerly and westerly distribution and are relatively rare on the Chalk. Hill names are commonest and mostly incorporate the elements *cunāco, *crouco, and *penno, all of which carry the general meaning 'hill, mound, or height'. From *cunaco come Conock, Knook, and probably the first element in Conkwell (Winsley), and from *crouco Crouch Hill (Highworth), the first element in Cricklade, Crookwood Farm (Urchfont), and probably Crook Hill (Alvediston). The element *penno appears in Pen Pits (Stourton), Penridge Farm near Penselwood (Som.), Pen Hill (Monkton Deverill), Penhill Farm (Stratton St. Margaret), Penn Farms (Calne and Hilmarton), and probably Penn's Lodge (Brinkworth). Other names incorporating British elements are Corsley, Lydiard, Membury (Ramsbury), and possibly Cheverell.

Apart from names of British origin there are a few place-names which possibly refer to the former presence of Britons. Cumberwell, just north of Bradford-on-Avon, appears to incorporate the element *cumbre and therefore means 'the spring of the Cymry or the Welsh'.[62] The element *wealh* meaning either 'Briton, Welshman', or 'serf', terms which were probably often synonymous in the Anglo-Saxon period, occurs in combination with habitative elements, thus indicating settlement, in Walcot (Swindon), Walton (Downton), and Walecote (near Malmesbury), the last two now lost. The same element is also present in Wallen Lane (Potterne) and Wallmead Farm (Tisbury). It is perhaps worth noting here that the place-names incorporating the above two elements all lie in the vicinity of major manorial centres and that, together with the small size and apparently lowly status of the three settlements designated by habitative names, suggests that they were probably tributary to those major

[60] E. Ekwall, *Eng. River Names*, 128–9.
[61] *Britannia*, i. 73.

[62] A. H. Smith, *Eng. P.N. Elements*, i. 119, which supersedes *P.N. Wilts*. (E.P.N.S.), 117.

PAGAN SAXON

centres, as is thought to be the case with the Charlton place-names.[63] The association of the place-name Britford, on the Avon just south of Salisbury, with the Britons (*Brettas*) though once accepted is now considered unlikely.[64]

The Romano-Britons and their descendants thus continued to live on in Wiltshire, and on the evidence of the place-names they remained a recognizable constituent of the population of the area for some time after it had been invaded and occupied by Anglo-Saxon settlers. They are, however, altogether more difficult to detect in the archaeological record. The general breakdown of the relatively sophisticated economic structure of Roman Britain and the collapse of the monetary system in the early decades of the 5th century brought about a fairly sudden decline in the manufacture and distribution of consumer goods, especially those mass-produced such as pottery. As a result the coins, pottery, metal goods, and so forth, which are usually found in quantity on Romano-British occupation sites, and which make possible or facilitate their recognition by the archaeologist, ceased to be distributed. A type of pottery, the so-called grass- or chaff-tempered ware, was made, as mentioned above,[65] during the centuries after 400, apparently as a response to the failure of the late Roman industries. Such pottery occurs in an undisputed British context in Somerset and Gloucestershire. In Wiltshire besides appearing at certain sites producing evidence of Romano-British occupation,[66] it occurs at Petersfinger in a pagan Saxon context[67] and also in the barrow at Ford, Laverstock.[68] Objects other than pottery are equally scarce. The large penannular brooch from Old-bury Castle, Calne, and the well known hanging-bowl from Wilton probably belong to the 5th century and have already been mentioned.[69] The escutcheon of a hanging-bowl, again not closely datable but also of native manufacture, was found near Liddington Castle[70] not far from the large Roman villa discovered in the late 1960s at Badbury in Chiseldon and close to the Berkshire–Marlborough Downs Ridgeway. A further item apparently of sub-Roman date and manufacture is the small bronze ornament in the form of a fish from KINGSTON DEVERILL. These objects comprise almost the entire archaeological evidence, at present recognizable, for the existence of Britons in Wiltshire in the post-Roman period.

A single historical source, sometimes held to be of relevance to the problem of the survival of Britons in Wessex, should be mentioned here. The laws of Ine king of Wessex, promulgated *c.* 690, incorporate the term '*wealh*', almost certainly in the sense of 'Briton' rather than 'serf', and indicate that some of those so designated were able to hold substantial amounts of land, although their status generally was inferior to that of the king's English subjects.[71] It would be unwise to assume, however, that many of them were living in Wiltshire. By the late 7th century the kingdom of Wessex extended as far as Devon and must have included numerous Britons in its recently acquired western territories.

There remains the question of continuity: what survived, if anything, from Romano-British times to be incorporated into the fabric of pagan Saxon and later Wiltshire. Certainly some Roman roads continued in use—pagan Saxon burials alongside them are perhaps an indication of that—and parts of the road system are still used today. The known Roman towns failed, as did many of the villas and native settlements. Nevertheless one-eighth of the known Romano-British settlements actually lie under later settlements, most of which have had a continuous existence from at least Saxon

---

[63] H. P. R. Finberg, 'Charltons and Carltons', *Lucerna*, 144–60.
[64] Smith, *Eng. P.N. Elements*, i. 55, which supersedes *P.N. Wilts.* (E.P.N.S.), 221.
[65] See p. 466.
[66] Ibid.
[67] *W.A.M.* lxiii. 103–5.
[68] *Ant. Jnl.* xlix. 110–13.
[69] See p. 467.
[70] The claim of this hill-fort to be considered as Mount Badon is strong.
[71] *Eng. Hist. Docs.* i, ed. Dorothy Whitelock, 364–72.

483

times to the present day. The figure seems too high to be explained by mere coincidence and though conclusive proof is at present lacking, the possibility that these settlement sites have been continuously occupied since Roman times cannot be ruled out. At CHERHILL, an undisputed British name, a tesselated pavement, probably part of a villa, was discovered near the church. Nearby at Calstone Wellington (CALNE), a name incorporating British elements, traces of Romano-British occupation have been found within the village. Roman villas underlie the villages of WEST DEAN, NETHERAVON, and BOX, and in Box parish remains of what appear to have been two further villas were found at Hazelbury and Cheney Court, Ditteridge, both centres of late Saxon estates. Romano-British burials, usually indicative of nearby settlement, have been found within the village of FOVANT, a place-name which incorporates a pre-Saxon element as noted above. At Upper Upham (ALDBOURNE) a substantial Romano-British settlement underlies the later hamlet whose name incorporates the element -*hām*, normally associated with an early stage of Saxon settlement and name-giving. In general the Romano-British settlement pattern, as at present understood, bears a closer resemblance to that of the early medieval period and later than is apparent at first sight. The upland nature of Romano-British occupation, particularly on the Chalk, has been over-emphasized, largely because of the remarkable state of survival, until recently at least, of the remains. Nearly a quarter of the known settlements occupy sites similar to those of Saxon and later date.

INDEX TO PARTS 1 AND 2

NOTE. Although the index covers both parts of Volume One it has been impossible within the space available to index any of the persons, or indeed all of the sites, named in part 1. Nor has it been possible to index more than a very few of the large number of objects mentioned in both parts. Individual sites named in part 1 have been indexed only when the need seemed obvious and when a further discussion of the site is given in part 2. In particular, the locality given under that heading in the lists of barrows, ditches, enclosures, and field systems in part 1 has seldom been indexed, and named groups of barrows have been indexed in two cases only. Part 2 has been selectively subject-indexed, but not part 1.

The following abbreviations have been used: Brit., British; chart., charter; Fm., Farm; I.A., Iron Age; *n*, note; Neolith., Neolithic; Mesolith., Mesolithic; P.-S. Pagan-Saxon; riv., river; s., son. An italic page-number denotes an illustration on that page or facing it.

Abercromby, John, 286, 385, 387
Aberdeenshire, *see* Ardiffery
Abingdon (Berks.), 293
Abydos (Egypt), 366, 368
Acheulian 'industry', 281
Acklam Wold (Yorks. E.R.), 363 *n*
Adabrock (Lewis, Isle of), hoard, 389
Adam's Grave, *see* Alton, barrows, long
Adena culture in Ohio region, 318
Adlerberg (Worms, Germany), 369
Aegean, the, 353, 365, 374; *and see* Mycenae
Aetius, Roman leader, 467
agriculture:
  Beaker, 348, 350
  Deverel-Rimbury, 400–3
  I.A., 411–12, 421
  Neolith., 285, 287–8
  Romano-Brit., 450, 454–8
Aldbourne, 8, **21–3**
  barrows, bell-, 206
    (*Biv* 11) Giant's Grave, 206, 361
  barrows, bowl-, 147–8
    (*Bii* 6), 147, 368
    (*Bii* 13), 148, 362
  barrows, disk-, 216
  cremations, 231, 234, 245
  cup, 147, 148, 172, 216, 371
  ditch, 249
  enclosures, 261
  field systems, 272
  inhumations, 227, 244, 245
  Lewisham Castle, 261
  Romano-Brit. brooch, 133
  Snap, 23
  Upham, Upper, 22, 23, 272, 462, 484; place-name, 480
Alderbury, **23**, 404
  Whaddon, 23
  Witherington Ring, P.-S. interments, 23, 473
All Cannings, *see* Cannings, All
All Cannings Cross, in All Cannings, 23–4, 409, 413, 415–16
  Bronze-Age objects from, 378, 390, *406*, 407, 408
  I.A. objects from, 412, *415*
  pottery from, *420*, 422, *422*, 435
Allectus, usurper, 453
Allen, riv. (Dors.), 305
Allington, **25–6**
  barrows, bowl-, 148–9
  Boscombe Down, East, 25, 261, 385, 396, **398**, 399, 400, 402, 403, 408; plan, *394*
  Boscombe Down, West, 25, 26, 261, 409, 417, 423, 431, 434; plan, *436*; pottery from, *422*, *428*
  cremation, 234
  ditches, 249, 250, 403
  enclosures, 261; *and see* Allington, Boscombe Down, East *and* Boscombe Down, West
  field systems, 272

Allington Down, *see* Cannings, All
Alton, **26–7**
  barrows, bell-, 206–7
  barrows, bowl-, 147, 149
  barrows, long, 137
    (*Bi* 14) Adam's Grave (*Wodnesbeorg*), 137, 312, 314, 478–9
  cremations, 231
  ditches, 250
  enclosures, 261; *and see* Alton, Golden Ball Hill *and* Knap Hill
  field systems, 272
  Golden Ball Hill, 26, 261, 272
  Honey Street, 26, 27
  inhumations, 227, 244, 245
  Knap Hill, 9; enclosure, 26, 27, 261, 285, 293, 294, **296**; plan, *297*; pottery from, *434*
  Red Shore, 206, 478
  Saxon chart., 478
  Walker's Hill, 9, 149, 206
Alvediston, **27**
  barrows, bowl-, 149, 246
  cremations, 231, 238, 240
  Crookhill, place-name, 482
  ditches, 250
  enclosure, 261
  field systems, 272
  inhumations, 227, 242
Ambrosius Aurelianus, 467, 468
Amerindian religion, 318
Amesbury, 12, **27–30**, 382; *and see* Fargo Plantation; Stonehenge
  'barrow near Stonehenge', 27, 302
  barrows, bell-, 207, 213, 214, 215
    (*Biv* 15), 207, 357
    (*Biv* 85), 207, 340, 345
    (*Biva* 44), 213, 363, 365, 366
  barrows, bowl-, 149–50, 205
    (*Bii* 1, 2 or 3), 149, 389
    (*Bii* 3), 149, 385, 395; pottery from, *386*
    (*Bii* 11), 150, 392, 395
    (*Bii* 24), 150, 361
    (*Bii* 51), 151, 341, 344
    (*Bii* 54), 151, 344, 346, 366; grave-group from, *343*
    (*Bii* 56), 151, 332
    (*Bii* 61), 151, 341
    (*Bii* 71), 151, 316, 325, 328, 341, 347, 354, 356, 361, 380, 381; plan, *355*, *356*; pottery from, *364*, 379
  barrows, disk-, 216, 222
  barrows, long, 137
    (*Bi* 14), 309
    (*Bi* 42), 305, 332
  barrows, pond-, 225
  barrows, saucer-, 222
  cremations, 231, 235, 238, 245
  Cursus, the, 28, 205, 320, **332**; plan, *327*
  ditches, 250, 251
  enclosure, 261–2

  field systems, 272
  Haradon Hill, 30; place-name, 480
  inhumations, 227, 242, 244
  New Covert, hoard of coins, 30, 465
  New King Barrows, 150, 151, 207
  Old King Barrows, 150, 151
  'Oldfield',? in Amesbury, 29, 152, 390, 391
  Ratfyn, 27, 29, 151, 287, 300, 346
  Totterdown, 27
  'Vespasian's Camp', 261–2
Amesbury region, 369
Ampney Brook, in Latton, 80
Andrup (Jutland), 365
Angle Ditch, Handley Down (Dors.), 385, 389, 390, 396, 402
Anglesey, *see* Llangwyllog
Anglo-Saxon Chronicle, 469, 476
animal husbandry, 287, 350, 402–3, 411–12, 421, 450, 454, 455–7; *and see* agriculture; dogs; horses
Anlo (Drenthe, Holland), 350
Ansty, **30**
  barrows, bowl-, 152, 205
    (*Biii* 3), 205, 478
  barrows, long, 137
  cremation, 238
  ditches, 250
  Whitesheet Hill (White Sheet Hill), 13, 20, 137, 152, 250
ApSimon, A. M., 345, 352–3, 354, 357–9, 382, 383, 388
Arbour Low, in Middleton and Smerrill (Derb.), 318
Ardiffery, in Cruden (Aberdeens.), 363 *n*
Arkell, W. J., 17 *n*
Arminghall (Norf.), 295, 318
Arn Hill, *see* Warminster
'Arreton Tradition', 382
Arthur, 'king', 467
Ascott-under-Wychwood (Oxon.), 306, 307
Ashbee, Paul, 303, 307, 308, 315
Ashley (Glos., formerly Wilts.), 152
Ashley Hill, *see* Laverstock and Ford
Ashton, Steeple, 17, **107**
Ashton Keynes, **30**
  barrows, bowl-, 152
  enclosures, 262
  'Hell's Claws', 262
astronomy, *see* mathematics and astronomy applied to henge monuments
Athens, 354
Atkinson, R. J. C., 286, 308, 315
Atlantic, the, 292
Atrebates, the, 435, 437, 438, 439
  coinage of, *434*, 435
Atworth, **30**
  villa, 448–9, 458, 460; plan, *462*
Aubrey, John, 311, 312, 332
Aughton Down, *see* Collingbourne Kingston